D0840249

THE REMARKABLE EXISTENTIALISTS

THE REMARKABLE EXISTENTIALISTS

MICHAEL ALLEN FOX

HB

Humanity Books

an imprint of Prometheus Books
59 John Glenn Drive, Amherst, New York 14228-2119

Published 2009 by Humanity Books, an imprint of Prometheus Books

Inquiries should be addressed to
Humanity Books
59 John Glenn Drive
Amherst, New York 14228–2119
VOICE: 716–691–0133, ext. 210
FAX: 716–691–0137

13 12 11 10 09   5 4 3 2 1

Library of Congress Cataloging-in-Publication Data on file at the Library of Congress

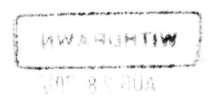

Printed in the United States of America on acid-free paper

*To future generations, and to all those everywhere
who are struggling for personal or political freedom*

Whatever situation is created, it is, in its turn, a given to be surpassed. A successful man is said to have "arrived." Where has he arrived? One never arrives anywhere. There are only points of departure.

—Simone de Beauvoir

CONTENTS

Acknowledgments   9

Preface   11

Chapter 1   What Is Existentialism?   13

Chapter 2   Historical Background   30

Chapter 3   Kierkegaard: In Search of the Individual   45

Chapter 4   Nietzsche: Reinventing Culture   83

Chapter 5   A Brief Look at Phenomenology   123

Chapter 6   Heidegger: The Quest for Being   147

Chapter 7   Sartre: Freedom without Excuses   187

Chapter 8   De Beauvoir: Freedom Maturing   233

Chapter 9   Evaluation of Existentialism and Its Legacy   256

Appendices

A. Nothingness   277
B. Meaning   280
C. Alienation   283
D. The Absurd   286
E. Angst/Anxiety/Anguish   289
F. Nihilism   291
G. A Problem about Consciousness   293
H. Self-Deception   295

Bibliography   299

Index   311

ACKNOWLEDGMENTS

I would like to thank the many students at Queen's University in Kingston, Canada, who have taken courses in existentialism and nineteenth-century European philosophy with me over the years. Their insights and challenging questions have been greatly helpful to me.

Several individuals kindly agreed to read drafts of chapters, and their advice and criticism is gratefully acknowledged: Albert Fell, Frances Gray, William McDonald, Adèle Mercier, Louise Noble, and Fiona Utley.

My appreciation extends to the School of Humanities at the University of New England, Armidale, New South Wales, Australia, for providing me with office space, and to UNE for other amenities and assistance with research expenses.

The cartoon in chapter 1 is by Sidney Harris and was discovered in the October 1983 issue of *Psychology Today* magazine. Cartoons in chapters 3 and 7 are reprinted from James Taylor, *A Porcine History of Philosophy and Religion* (Nashville, TN: Abingdon Press, 1972). The cartoon in chapter 9, by Delainey and Rasmussen, is part of the syndicated "Betty" series. It first appeared on April 6, 2002. The cartoon by Andrew Lehman in chapter 9 appeared in the January/February 1991 issue of *UpRiver/ DownRiver* magazine.

Finally, I wish to thank Zoé Noble Fox and David Greenhalgh for drawing wonderful new cartoons for chapters 4 and 6, respectively.

All illustrations, diagrams, and tables not mentioned above are by the author.

PREFACE

hy are so may people still drawn to existentialism even though its heyday is well past? Because it addresses everyone's vital concerns like no other philosophy: relationships, love, sex, honesty and role-playing, bigotry, anxiety, aloneness, absurdity and meaning, doubt and uncertainty, God and faith, the limits of language, emotions and moods, freedom, courage, self-realization, suicide and death. General readers find it challenging, inspiring, and helpful in gaining a fuller perspective on their lives. High school and university students encounter existentialism as a refreshing change from other courses that come across as dry, overly intellectualized, and focused on academic minutiae, facts, and fixed opinions. Thus, while all of the principal existentialists and many of their first-generation disciples and interpreters are dead and gone, the spirit of existentialism unquestionably survives. American philosopher Hazel Barnes, an existentialist author and translator of Sartre's *Being and Nothingness* into English, once remarked: "It used to be that people regarded Sartre, Camus, and so forth as the latest thing: obviously they don't now. But you know the old Quaker expression, 'it speaks to my condition'? Well, the students still feel that; and I find that both when I speak around the country and in my own classroom."[1] An even stronger statement comes from The Teaching Company (producers of audiovisual materials for self-education) in the *New York Times*: "Existentialism is one of the most exciting and enduring philosophies of the 20th century. It is philosophy at work in the trenches of life, calling us to immediate awareness, commitment, and passion. If these ideas are new for you, so is life."[2]

We will seek to understand together, in the pages that follow, what the sources of this intense interest and enthusiasm are, and to develop an appreciation of the lasting contribution to philosophical inquiry made by the remarkable group of thinkers known as existentialists. This book is a tribute to their creative imagination, talent, and ability to stimulate and empower us. The focus of our investigation will be on Kierkegaard, Nietzsche, Heidegger, Sartre, and de Beauvoir, who collectively brought existentialism from its beginnings to its maturity, and whose work constitutes its fullest expression. A range of concepts characteristic of existential discourse will be explored, and special attention will be devoted to the existentialists' distinctive style of argument.

People come to the study of existentialism from all walks of life, all viewpoints, and a wide variety of backgrounds. (As a teacher, I have always found that this synergy enhances the classroom experience for everyone, and it has benefited me immeasurably as an educator.) Existentialism has also enriched numerous other areas of inquiry: literature, film, theater, education, theology, psychology, and psychiatry, to name a few. So even apart from the intrinsic interest of the subject, it is worthwhile knowing more about this fascinating philosophy because of its assimilation into the cultural mainstream of our time and its function within society as an important catalyst to the development of new ideas and forms of creative expression.

NOTES

1. Hazel Barnes, quoted in Alfie Kohn, "Existentialism Here and Now," *Georgia Review* 38 (1984): 391.
2. The Teaching Company, advertisement in the *New York Times*, July 27, 1997, p. 23.

WHAT IS EXISTENTIALISM?

Existentialism is a diverse movement of thought and therefore must be defined, if at all, in a multidimensional way. We will use this approach as we take a careful look at the existential view of the human condition.

A PHILOSOPHY THAT RESISTS DEFINITION

Heidegger once wrote that philosophy "can and must be . . . the knowledge that kindles and necessitates all inquiries and thereby threatens all values."[1] Because of this subversive aspect, a hallmark of philosophy is that not only is the nature of its subject matter controversial but also, to a greater or lesser extent, so too are the various kinds of philosophy (such as materialism, idealism, realism, and so on) and the character of the sub-fields of philosophy (such as ethics, metaphysics, and the rest). The definition of philosophy, then, is never settled and always remains contentious. Every definition or attempted definition of philosophy entails commitments to a certain way of doing philosophy and of looking at the world. These commitments are not necessarily shared by all who call themselves philosophers (or materialists, ethicists, and so forth).

Existentialism is no less subject to this phenomenon of disputed definition than is any other "ism" of philosophers. The danger we encounter here is that existentialism, if not defined carefully, may become confused with something it is not.

None of the commonly recognized existentialists—other than Sartre and de Beauvoir—ever deliberately appropriated the label "existentialism" to describe their work, opting instead to disavow it or to put forward an alternative. This was partly because they wanted to distance themselves from Sartre's very distinctive brand of thought and partly because existentialism, above all, stands for independent-mindedness and iconoclasm. Hence, even to use the expression "school of thought" in reference to existentialism is something of a misnomer, so that "movement," "approach," or "tendency" might be a better term to describe it. Any philosophy that expresses its basic tenets equally well through the voices of Protestant and Catholic Christians (Kierkegaard and Marcel respectively), Jews (Buber), non-denominational religious adherents (Jaspers), atheists (Nietzsche, Sartre, de Beauvoir, Camus), and those who are unclassifiable as either theists or atheists (Heidegger) has to be seen as a maverick among belief systems. While Sartre freely identifies existentialism with atheism, other leading figures rebelled against this claim, and of course Kierkegaard, a deeply religious individual whom many revere as the founder of existentialism, died half a century before Sartre was born, leaving behind a body of writing that constitutes a not-so-silent rebuttal of Sartre's opinion. The matter is further complicated, however, by the nonetheless resonant choices that certain thinkers made in relation to their outlooks: Marcel

"Cosmology? You want Swami Katra, two mountains over. I only discuss existentialism and business management."

called his outlook the "philosophy of existence" and Jaspers fastened onto *Existenzphilosophie* ("existence philosophy"), to give two examples where the line of demarcation is not outstandingly apparent. Then again, not even Sartre can be credited with having invented the term "existentialism." De Beauvoir maintains that Marcel coined it as a label for Sartre's and her own philosophies, which they then reluctantly adopted.[2] Meanwhile, Sartre complains, as early as 1945, that "the word [existentialist] has been so stretched and has taken on so broad a meaning, that it no longer means anything at all."[3] And to compound the issue still further, Sartre himself repudiated existentialism or at any rate put it "on ice," as it were, during his later, Marxist phase (see chapter 7).[4]

Part of the problem in defining existentialism, then, stems from rivalries and disagreements among individual thinkers, the development of their philosophies, and, one must also say, their intellectual vanity. Popular misconceptions cloud the issue as well. But there is a more fundamental dilemma of definiton, flagged by Alfie Kohn, who writes: "Existentialism is difficult to define primarily because its essence, so to speak, is to oppose the kind of analytic reduction that definition entails. It is not a system of philosophy to be learned or subscribed to. . . ."[5] Here we see that resistance to definition comes from several directions. First, there is the fear that a likely response to definition will be: "Oh, is *that* all there is to it?" Second, any definition tends to lock practitioners into a particular pattern or mold, inhibiting their inventiveness. Third, and absolutely central to existential thought, this group of philosophers makes it their aim to discourage discipleship, to make people react and think for themselves.

A final point is that existentialism takes a decidedly interdisciplinary or eclectic approach to the investigation of human existence, drawing upon the techniques of philosophy, literature, drama, psychology, sociology, religious studies, and other fields. Existential philosophers deliberately violate the barriers between disciplines to become active participants in inquiry as they see fit. This explains why one encounters the (in my view, entirely fruitless) question, "Is existentialism really philosophy?" Yes it is, but of a markedly different sort, as we'll come to learn.

In spite of all this chaos and disagreement—which actually signifies creative ferment—there is, as we shall see shortly, a valid argument for using "existentialism" as a meaningful and convenient umbrella term for an important and living philosophy of recent times. Definitions—even if only provisional—are important and help us to locate ourselves within the mental geography by which we sort out our lives and experience and navigate our way through the world. Furthermore, we can adopt definitions while keeping a certain distance and skeptical reserve in relation to them, being prepared to revise them when and as necessary.

A WORKING DEFINITION OF EXISTENTIALISM

Some of the problems with definition and especially with defining existentialism have been noted above. But now it's time to get on with the job of setting out our subject matter. In my view, existentialism is best comprehended by appreciating what it is *against* and what it is *for*, in other words, by its attitudes of *revolt* and *affirmation*. Let's examine these two attitudes.

*   *   *

EXISTENTIALISM IS A REVOLT AGAINST:

ENLIGHTENMENT FAITH IN REASON.

"The Enlightenment" is a loose term used to designate the dominant ideas of eighteenth-century Europe, England, and America, a major component of which was a strong belief in the power of human rationality. Existentialism holds that reason, while an important human attribute, has serious limits, especially when it comes to knowing ourselves and our place in the world.

DEPERSONALIZING FORCES IN MODERN SOCIETY.

Existentialism is stereotypically identified with nonconformism, with bearded, beret-wearing, chain-smoking beatniks and denizens of dark cafés who talk endlessly about *angst* and life. (This caricature, again, comes from Sartre's public persona and circle of immediate influence.) But in a deeper sense, existentialism helped give birth to now-common concerns about the forces unleashed by mass society—capitalism, the media, consumerism, rapid technological change, bureaucracy, and totalitarianism—and how they tend to stifle individuality.

APATHY AND DETACHMENT.

Modern life and the complexity of world problems have led many to become alienated to some degree from the world around them, desensitized to their own inner feelings and inner selves, and overwhelmed by a feeling of powerlessness to change things. Existentialism sounds a call of alarm designed to break through this protective but defective shell.

IRRESPONSIBLITY.

Wherever people refuse to face up to their freedom and effective agency, existentialists can't be far behind with caustic criticism of this denial of our humanity. With freedom comes responsibility, and even doing nothing (omission) rather than doing something (commission) is an act that requires justification.

SELF-DECEIVING MODES OF EXISTENCE; ESSENTIALISM IN ALL ITS FORMS.

Individuals who are escaping from the difficult task of being fully human often embrace various kinds of self-deception (for example, role-playing, conformism). "Essentialism" refers to the adoption of any sort of fixity or rigidity, whereby people take on the mode of being of a thing (which is what "essence" signifies here). Having an essence represents permanence and lack of potential for meaningful change, whereas human beings are "existential" or "in existence." To "thingify" oneself is to engage in self-deception in one way or another because doing so negates our ability to change, become, or "emerge."

ABSTRACT INTELLECTUALISM AND THE IDEALS OF OBJECTIVITY AND FINALITY IN KNOWLEDGE-PURSUITS.

Knowledge has become highly specialized over the past couple of centuries to the point where it often seems esoteric in the extreme, trivial, and completely uncoupled from the vital affairs of human existence. In addition, "objectivity" (the independence of knowledge from feeling or opinion; the remote grounding of truth solely in the world) is a myth. And the search for complete systems of knowledge is a will-o'-the-wisp. Decision making (by bureaucrats, "experts," and others) often seems infected by these problems of knowledge gathering as well.

WORSHIP OF SCIENCE AND CLAIMS AS TO ITS VALUE-NEUTRALITY.

Science is not the paradigm for all knowledge and it is not free from perspectives and biases. Looking to science (and technology) for the answers to all our problems (such as global warming and world hunger) obscures other avenues to knowledge and self-understanding that are crucial to our destiny. (It also, to some extent, masks from view our own hand in producing the problems in the first place.)

ORGANIZED RELIGION.

As has already been indicated, existentialism is far from being one-dimensionally antireligious. But it is opposed to submission of the individual to authoritative pronouncements or immersion in any organization or congregation that prevents thinking for oneself.

POLITICAL COLLECTIVISM AND UTOPIANISM.

When the individual is lost in the crowd, or takes second place to the collective, what matters most is forfeited. Utopianism presents a kind of fantasy world in which the real demands of living in the moment are negated, deflected, and postponed.

As will be obvious, the positive side of existentialism expresses the opposite of the points listed above. Thus, we have the following profile.

*   *   *

EXISTENTIALISM IS AN AFFIRMATION OF:

INNER EXPERIENCE (THE NONRATIONAL—THE WORLD OF IMAGINATION, EMOTIONS, AND MOODS IN PARTICULAR).

In addition to reason, imagination and the affective modes of consciousness tell us who and what we are as human beings. Significant aspects of the world and of human relationships are revealed by feeling-states. In existentialist philosophy, we examine what William Barrett aptly calls "the shadow side of human life."[6] The Spanish existentialist Unamuno (1864–1936) amusingly reflects on the reason/feeling dichotomy:

> Man, they say, is a reasoning animal. I do not know why he has not been defined as an affective or feeling animal. And yet what differentiates him from other animals is perhaps feeling rather than reason. I have seen a cat reason more often than laugh or weep. Perhaps it laughs or weeps within itself—but then perhaps within itself a crab solves equations of the second degree.[7]

In this passage, Unamuno anticipates early in the twentieth century that reasoning ability will become viewed as a trait shared by humans and non-humans and that recognition will be given to feeling as a crucial human response to the world. It is important to remember, however, that existentialism generally celebrates the *nonrational*, not the *irrational*, as is often alleged by its critics.[8]

PERSONAL DIGNITY AND INDIVIDUALITY.

Frederick Olafson has observed that individuality is a relatively recent historical development: "It would not, I think, be an exaggeration to say that for the first time in human history, large numbers of human beings have come to think of themselves as autonomous moral agents, capable of raising and resolving for themselves all questions about what they are to do."[9] In earlier centuries, the struggle for existence, as well as social restrictions, had prevented this degree of selfhood and freedom from emerging on a large scale. Even today, there are many forces acting to undermine individuality and its expression in the public sphere. The self-chosen destiny of the individual in the modern world is the primary concern of existentialists, who, as we've seen, pride themselves on being individuals. Existentialism is, in a way, an ongoing argument for respecting personal dignity in oneself and others.

"SITUATEDNESS," ENGAGEMENT, AND THE POWER OF CHOICE, ESPECIALLY IN THE DOMAIN OF VALUES.

We are all located in a unique time, space, historical moment, and cultural context. These things, as well as our personal life circumstances, help define us and set certain limits to our lives. Yet they are all things we can choose how to react to and toward which we can take up attitudes, and in making such choices we posit the selves we wish to be. The values we hold are forged by means of our engagements with one another and the world around us.

RESPONSIBLE FREEDOM.

Freedom is the capacity to make ourselves according to our choices, to project ourselves forward into the as-yet-undetermined future. Responsibility lies in not shirking from the demands of freedom, accepting its consequences, and finding ways to enhance its scope in our lives. If a succinct formula were sought to render the existentialists' view of humans, it would be this: "Humans are free beings," or even: "Humans are freedom." Freedom, however, is not absolute, as we saw in the section on "situatedness" above. It is therefore better to think of the existential teaching on freedom as *radical* rather than *absolute* (for more on this point, see chapter 7).

SELF-DISCOVERY (HONESTY WITH ONESELF), POSSIBILITY, AND SELF-MAKING.

The task of being human is well stated by the words that the ancient Delphic oracle reportedly uttered to Socrates: "Know thyself." The quest for self-awareness and self-understanding is long and arduous, but it requires honesty and courage above all else. And because we are free, our horizons are open and possibility reigns over the present and future. Self-making occurs through the power of possibility.

HUMAN FINITUDE ("THIS-WORLDLINESS") AND APPLIED THINKING; THE SUBJECTIVE DIMENSION AND THE UNCHARTED TERRITORY OF KNOWLEDGE.

Humans are grounded in the world, in existence. Existence, for human beings, has a certain character (see chapter 3 in particular). Part of this is its inescapable "here-and-now-ness." All thinking begins from within our experience of existing and so there is a special place for thinking that can help us exist fully and realize our potential. The search for knowledge thus has a subjective, inward, self-implicating, or personal dimension (we can always ask: "What does that item of knowledge mean *for me*?"). Human knowledge can never be complete because we are not omniscient. Hence, we must learn to live with uncertainty, probability, ambiguity, and risk.

PLACING SCIENCE IN PERSPECTIVE VIS-À-VIS OTHER KINDS OF KNOWLEDGE AND CREATIVE ACTIVITIES.

Existence is not capable of being known quantitatively nor can it be subjected to analysis by formal methods. Many other types of knowledge are available, which offer more appropriate vehicles of understanding: art, religious faith, literature, insight, and intuition, for example. In addition to the unique situation each of us is in right now, there is also what we might more generally call "the human situation." This is what we refer to when we say, "What is it to be human?" When we try to address the questions "What is my situation?" or "What is the human situation?" the answers we give are part of the situation itself that we are trying to describe. We cannot step outside our situation to view it from an external, neutral, or "objective" standpoint. This fact calls for an existential approach to such matters.

THE ULTIMATE MYSTERY OF EXISTENCE; SOLITUDE AND THE NEED TO LIVE BY FAITH OF SOME KIND.

Because existence must be known qualitatively and intimately (or "subjectively"), its character cannot be fully categorized or communicated and, therefore, we can only share our perceptions and experiences of it to a degree. We are many "solitudes," who relate to one another and to the world by means of incomplete knowledge. There are delicate moments of "presence," when we may touch another person and be touched in turn, but these cannot be commanded, only awaited with a receptive, trusting openness and facilitated by sensitivity to the occasion.[10]

THE NEED FOR SOCIAL CRITICISM.

Social and psychological manipulation are to be resisted so that individuality can thrive. In aid of this resistance, critical thinking must remain sharp and focused. Existentialism and social criticism are inseparable.

These themes will weave in and out of the discussions of existential philosophers in subsequent chapters and they will be considered in greater detail as we go along.

*   *   *

Before we move on, however, it will be useful to take a closer look at what I have called the human situation. Since "situation" has a more specific meaning in existentialism, as we've seen (generally referring to the unique circumstances in which *I* must decide and act), let us substitute the term "human condition" instead.[11] ("Human predicament" would also serve just as well.) Perhaps the salient point of existential thought is that *there is no fixed human nature.* I mentioned before that existentialism is the antithesis of essentialism, and one type of essentialism is the view that there *is* an unchanging, basic human nature that is the same everywhere. This belief the existentialists reject. How are we to understand their position? First of all, as suggested earlier, existentialists do not deny that there are causal factors impinging on human existence. But they hold that these do not determine in any significant sense who we are or what we may become. Even if there is no universal human nature, however, there is a *universal human condition.* We have already become acquainted with a number of aspects of this condition; a few more points will give us a sharper picture.

THE HUMAN CONDITION: HUMANS FIRST EXIST AND THEN BECOME SOMETHING DEFINITE.

The word "exist" comes from the Latin *existere,* meaning "stand out" or "stand forth." Thus, when we say humans exist, this is taken by the existentialists to have the sense that we stand out from the past, overleap the present, and project into the future. We emerge or become; in short, we make of ourselves what we will be. This is very different from the mode of being of a thing, which is what it is, pure and simple, as set by its nature. Humans, by contrast, first find themselves existing in a certain kind of world, and then they decide what they want to do about it. We constantly choose what we will be; we exist in reference to the future as much as to the past—indeed, even more so, for the future is that in relation to which the greatest freedom flourishes. As de Beauvoir says, "In order for the past to be mine, I must make it mine again each instant by taking it toward my future."[12]

WHAT HUMANS BECOME IS A FUNCTION OF THEIR OWN CHOICES AND EFFORT.

All choices are situated; that is, they occur within a framework that includes both *facticity* and *freedom.* "Facticity" comprises whatever we can't change or control: the laws of nature, our biology, our personal heredity, the past, the behavior of others. As one author adds, facticity "includes both one's material and historical circumstances."[13] For existentialists, *my situation is the interface between the elements of facticity and freedom.* What I can do with my freedom is bounded but nonetheless vast in its possibilities. Determination overcomes determinacy.

HUMAN EXISTENCE IS FINITE.

This may sound so obvious as to be a truism, but something profound often lurks beneath the mundane, as the practice of philosophy histori- cally reveals. Existentialists make much of the fact that we are mortal and, more importantly, that death must be factored into our approach to life (see chapter 6). Human existence is "radically contingent"; that is, it is subject to many unpredictable turns, twists, and changes of fortune and circumstance.

WE ENCOUNTER "NOTHINGNESS" WITHIN EVERYDAY EXISTENCE.

Humans have key moments of awareness of the void or abyss, absence or lack, emptiness, the not-yet, the no-longer, and the possibility of personal non-being and of the non-being of everything that is. These experiences signify the paradoxical "presence of nothingness" as a backdrop to existence, so to speak. (See appendix A for some expressions of this idea.)

THE SELF IS NOT A THING; IT IS A PROCESS.

A person is a self-unfolding activity; it is what it does. The story that constitutes each person's life is only complete at her or his death, which is an ever-present horizon. Human existence always remains in the realm of incomplete, open-ended, aspiring possibility. For the existentialists, *a self or person is a process of creating a unique way of being in the world by means of conscious, ongoing choices.*

CONSCIOUSNESS IS THE SOURCE OF FREEDOM AND SELF-REALIZATION.

We may argue about what consciousness really is (see chapter 5), but for the existentialists it is the paradigm human capacity and the source of our "being-in-the-world" and of self-affirmation.

WITH FREEDOM COMES A MORAL REQUIREMENT: ULTIMATE RESPONSIBILITY.

We are responsible for who we are and what we do. Each has her or his task of self-discovery to undertake. This includes coming to terms with our time, place, and culture, and with our mortality.

THERE ARE NO ABSOLUTE GUIDELINES FOR CONDUCT.

Whether or not there is a God, we are not handed life on a platter, ready-made. There are no certainties or objective moral truths to light the way. Humans are questioning beings and none of life's "big questions" are ever settled once and for all.

WE ARE ALWAYS ENGAGED WITH THE WORLD AND WITH OTHERS AS VALUERS AND MEANING-GIVERS.

Living is positing value and meaning through our actions. To some, a mountain range looms as a barrier to travel, the end of the road; to others, it is a challenge to their climbing skills and presents a new experience; for still others, it signifies the gateway to a land or frontier beyond.[14] Furthermore, actions are public behaviors embedded in the physical and social worlds. They involve interactions with others. Human life is consequently a collective experiment in which each of us plays a part, exploring the possibilities open to all, and in which we learn from our own experience and that of others. Hence, meaning emerges from our joint projects as much as it does from our own self-focused concerns. Finally, just as everyday meaning is not discovered but invented, so too the meaning of life as a whole is not "read off" from the face of the universe but rather is made by us. (See appendix B, "Meaning.")

CRITICAL SELF-AWARENESS MUST BE OUR GUIDE.

While we may be united (to the extent that we are) by our shared desire to realize freedom (agency, autonomy), we are also in a fundamental sense ultimately alone. No one can live for or through anyone else. And in the end, each has her or his own death to face and deal with. Existentialism stands for the demand that we take charge of the human condition as we experience it and of our own unique situation at each moment. It avoids the simple recipes of New Age pop philosophy and of the self-help books that abound.

*   *   *

To summarize: *Existentialism is a philosophy that investigates and evaluates the human condition, focusing on the free, finite, self-making, responsible individual as the origin of value and meaning in the world.*

*   *   *

AFTERWORD: EXISTENTIALISM AND HUMAN NATURE

Perhaps this sounds like a very appealing credo. But might a serious problem be lurking in all this? It may strike the reader that the phrase "universal human condition" suspiciously resembles another: "universal human nature." Is there really a difference between these? Well, yes and no. There is no difference insofar as the existentialists are conceding that there are true general statements we can make about human beings' potential and how they experience their place in the scheme of things. These describe the raw material of our lives and can hardly be objected to. But there is an important distinction to be made as well. Aristotle was probably the first Western philosopher to assert that there is a universal human nature, that we all (or at least all that fit into his culturally biased sample) share the same rationality, seek happiness, and so forth. This way of thinking stems from his analysis, which maintains that what something is "by its very nature" ("in its own right," "in respect of itself," or "in virtue of itself") is its essence.[15] This is normally interpreted to mean that the irreducible and unchanging properties of a thing constitute what it is, its "whatness," so to speak, its being a thing of a certain type. In other words, the essence of X is the sine qua non (identifying characteristic) of anything's being an X. The same reasoning is then applied to being human. Whether the properties alluded to are metaphysical or physical, in the end, the result is the same: a view of things that is ahistorical, timeless, and nonsituational. The existentialists therefore regard such an outlook as limiting the possibility of change in ways that are antithetical to their understanding of the human potential.

Aristotle also prescribed (in his *Nicomachean Ethics*) the same virtue-based morality for everyone as the means to fulfilment and as the manifestation of human excellence. What we have here is a paradigm of the kind of theory that existentialism opposes. Certainly humans have many basic biological needs and nonbiological interests in common, but it does not follow that there is some single way in which they ought to use their abilities in order to either define or fulfill higher-order needs, such as meaning and self-realization. Therefore, no one has a global or transcendent perspective from which to claim the right to dictate to others specific rules on how they should live or how they should improve their lives. Beyond this, existentialists would also maintain that there is no scientific basis for circumscribing who we are or who we will become. Here, too, there is room for reservations about what the existentialists are claiming to object to. They acknowledge, as we have already seen, that we do have capacities in common that are inseparable from our humanity. They also well recognize that we can refuse to activate, cultivate, and realize these capacities and that we can remain in denial about them. But existentialists think that it is wrong ("inauthentic" or "in bad faith") to do this. Hence, they *do* have some universal prescriptions about conduct after all, a subject I shall return to later when discussing Sartre (in chapter 7) and de Beauvoir (in chapter 8).

In a sense, this whole issue we have been reviewing revolves around a misunderstanding. Very few, if any, of the great theorists of human nature would argue that there is just a single, narrow path individual development must or ought to take.[16] They may hold differing views as to the amount of freedom we have and as to the legitimacy of basing moral prescriptions on empirical data derived from mere observation of human behavior. But it's easy to see that humans can and do deviate from following their natural endowments and from what others (and even they, themselves) think would be best for them to do. On the other side of the matter, existentialists seemingly have to admit, as indicated earlier, that if there is a describable human condition—and if there isn't, existentialism has nothing to talk about—then there is some kind of human nature after all. Anthony Quinton argues that a philosopher in effect asserts that human beings have an essence if he or she believes "that for any individual who is, amongst indefinitely many other things, a human being, the fact of being human has some overriding importance."[17] I think this is correct. Therefore, on this score, there seems to remain little difference between existentialists and essentialists.

Significant differences remain elsewhere, however. For various thinkers, and especially the existentialists (since they are the ones we are most interested in), certain traits or capacities are essential to being human and others are not. And there is no single way in which these must be expressed or utilized. So, what we need to consider carefully as we go along is which features of "humanness," from among the range of possibilities, are included in the existentialists' conception of being human and which are excluded. The key issue, then, concerns how we choose ourselves, given our inborn potentials. Not so well hidden behind all this are two related and thorny questions: (1) whether we really are free rather than causally determined (unfree) and (2) whether it is up to us to craft meaning and value in our own lives as we see fit. As should be evident by now, existentialists stand out as arguing strongly in the affirmative on both counts.

NOTES

1. Martin Heidegger, *An Introduction to Metaphysics*, trans. Ralph Manheim (New Haven, CT: Yale University Press, 1959), p. 119.

2. Simone de Beauvoir, *Force of Circumstance*, trans. Richard Howard (Harmondsworth, UK: Penguin Books, 1987), pp. 45–46.

3. Jean-Paul Sartre, *Existentialism Is a Humanism*, trans. Bernard Frechtman under the title *Existentialism* and reprinted in *Existentialism and Human Emotions* (New York: Citadel Press/Kensington Publishing, 1987), p. 12.

4. Jean-Paul Sartre, *Search for a Method*, trans. Hazel E. Barnes (New York: Vintage Books/Random House, 1968).

5. Alfie Kohn, "Existentialism Here and Now," *Georgia Review* 38 (1984): 382.

6. William Barrett, *Irrational Man: A Study in Existential Philosophy* (Garden City, NY: Anchor Books/Doubleday, 1962), p. 22.

7. Miguel de Unamuno, *Selected Works of Miguel de Unamuno* (Bollingen Series LXXXV, vol. 4): *The Tragic Sense of Life in Men and Nations* (1913), trans. Anthony Kerrigan (Princeton, NJ: Princeton University Press, 1972), p. 5.

8. It is therefore unfortunate that Barrett's book (see note 6), one of the best and most influential on existentialism in English, identifies irrationality with this movement.

9. Frederick A. Olafson, *Principles and Persons: An Ethical Interpretation of Existentialism* (Baltimore, MD: Johns Hopkins University Press, 1967), p. 238.

10. See Ralph Harper, *The Existential Experience* (Baltimore, MD: Johns Hopkins University Press, 1972), ch. 5.

11. Throughout this book, the reader should take "I," "my," or "mine" as self-referring, unless it is clear that the author alone is meant by these words.

12. Simone de Beauvoir, *Pyrrhus and Cineas*, trans. Marybeth Timmerman, in *Simone de Beauvoir: Philosophical Writings*, ed. Margaret A. Simons, with Marybeth Timmerman and Mary Beth Mader (Urbana: University of Illinois Press, 2004), p. 93.

13. Kristana Arp, *The Bonds of Freedom: Simone de Beauvoir's Existentialist Ethics* (Chicago: Open Court, 2001), p. 120.

14. Sartre offers an interesting discussion of hiking and fatigue in relation to the meaning different people assign to the activity they are engaged in. See Jean-Paul Sartre, *Being and Nothingness: An Essay in Phenomenological Ontology*, trans. Hazel Barnes (New York: Philosophical Library, 1956), pp. 453–57.

15. Aristotle, *Metaphysics*, 1029b13–16.

16. See Leslie Stevenson, ed., *The Study of Human Nature: A Reader*, 2nd ed. (New York: Oxford University Press, 2000) for a generous sample of Eastern and Western views on human nature. See also Peter Loptson, *Theories of Human Nature*, 3rd ed. (Peterborough, ON: Broadview Press, 2006). For a radical challenge to the idea that humans are unique, see Felipe Fernández-Armesto, *Humankind: A Brief History* (Oxford: Oxford University Press, 2004).

17. Anthony Quinton, *Thought and Thinkers* (London: Duckworth, 1982), p. 17.

QUESTIONS FOR REFLECTION

1. What kinds of experiences have you had that (a) you would describe as "existential," or (b) aroused your interest in existentialism? In relation to (a), Why would you describe them this way? In relation to (b), Why did they have this effect?

2. What have you read, or what movies, plays, or works of art have you seen that you would describe as "existentialist"? Why?

3. Why is existentialism hard to define?

4. Is it true that all thinking begins from within our experience of existing? What does this mean? What are the implications of this perspective?

5. Is there an important difference between essentialism and existentialism?

2

HISTORICAL BACKGROUND

A vital part of understanding existentialism is being able to place it within a meaningful framework of ideas and influences. This shows that there are hints and tendencies in the past that lead up to its full flowering in the nineteenth and twentieth centuries. Historical and cultural background always enriches the ways we see things and absorb ideas.

A WEALTH OF IDEAS

A common caricature of existentialism depicts it as a transitory phenomenon that is a product of mid-twentieth-century malaise and cultural ferment. Thus, as one critic wrote in 1975: "What is Existentialism? Or, rather, what *was* Existentialism. . . . It was very much a creature of the Waste Land that was Europe during and after the last world war [World War II]."[1] Once again, this type of perspective is dictated by identifying existentialism too closely with the work of Sartre and his particular set of social and political preoccupations. More recent interpretations of existentialism—and even some older ones—move past this fixation upon Sartre (important though he is) to give a broader, more informative overview.[2] We need to move in this direction if we want to gain a proper appreciation of the value of existentialism, and some historical and cultural context will enable us to do this. My aim in this chapter is not to provide a comprehensive genealogy of existentialism but to locate it in relation to some preceding and parallel figures and events in the history of ideas that are of special interest and relevance.

A fruitful suggestion with which to begin stems from William Barrett's distinction (borrowed by him from the English poet and literary/social historian Matthew Arnold) between "Hebraism" and "Hellenism."[3] Briefly, Barrett argues that existentialism has deep roots in Western history, in both Biblical and Greek traditions. Existentialism, he suggests, is born of the tension between the Hebraic "man of faith" and the Greek "man of reason." The Hebraic man of faith is a concrete individual, thrown back on his own finite resources in a strenuous encounter with God, wherein he must make choices and justify himself and his course of action. Job of the Old Testament is the model for this kind of individual, whose faith and commitment are severely tested by God, yet who triumphs over the misfortunes of his adverse situation: "Though he slay me, yet will I trust in him."[4] While undergoing his trials, Job experiences many emotions such as anger and despair, which he must learn from and overcome, growing as a person in the process. In one such moment, Job says, "Fear came upon me, and trembling,"[5] and many will recognize this as having given birth to Kierkegaard's book title *Fear and Trembling*. The man of reason, in the Barrett-Arnold scenario, is the image that existentialism struggles to set aside in favor of the man of faith. This interpretation, I think, is somewhat facile, as I've indicated in chapter 1. For we are beings of both reason *and* passion, knowledge *and* faith, and existentialism recognizes this, steering its course between the unresolvable oppositions that characterize human existence and experience.

It is also crucial to recognize that Greek philosophy contributed concepts and insights that are central to existentialism. Socrates (c. 470–399 BCE) famously regarded the condition of humans as one of ignorance, which philosophy perpetually strives to help us conquer. He cast this outlook in the form of a personal confession of ignorance (usually understood to have a strong ironic element), and regarded his own situation as one that demands self-knowledge as a guide. The lifelong philosophical task, for Socrates, is to prepare for death so that it can be met with equanimity. Philosophy purifies the soul, enabling it to ascend to a glorious afterlife. This acute awareness of finitude and mortality, as we have seen, is crucial to existentialism.

Aristotle (384–322 BCE), too, although he held an essentialist view of human nature (see afterword to chapter 1), introduced notions that later became part of the fabric of existentialist thought. In this context can be mentioned his affirmation of humans as concrete individuals. In opposition to Plato's conception of a human being, in which each of us is a flawed and remote replica of some supersensible and perfect archetype, Aristotle revealed individual humans to be particular entities in which the universal essence of humanity is embedded and from which (collectively speaking) it is inseparable. In addition, Aristotle introduced the distinction between *potentiality* and *actuality* (or becoming and being) that is the currency of much later thought, but especially that of existentialists such as Kierkegaard, Nietzsche, and Sartre. Actuality is the end-state toward which a being moves or which it seeks, consciously or otherwise. Potentiality signifies the recognition of process, of the fact that beings are "underway" or evolving through time. Of none is this truer than members of our own species. Even though for Aristotle being was more significant than becoming, his ideas stimulated reflection on becoming and an eventual revolt (in the nineteenth century) against the philosophical accent on permanence (the enduring self, the ultimate state of reality), together with an affirmation of the world of change and process.

In the early Christian era, St. Augustine (354–430) wrote the first philosophical autobiography, his *Confessions*. In this work, Augustine sets out in a particularly poignant way his journey from youthful libertine to mature Christian man of faith. Along the way, he presents himself as an isolated individual striving to know God, the nature of time, and other equally elusive truths, observing, for instance, "What, then, is time? If no one asks of me, I know; if I wish to explain to him who asks, I know not."[6] The focus here, as is often the case in existential thought, is on intuitive, ineffable insight rather than the rational and linguistic constructions of knowledge.

We skip now over several centuries to the time of Shakespeare (1564–1616). Many of the Bard's most celebrated speeches and soliloquies concern themselves with matters of the meaning of life and the nature of existence. Hamlet's famous words are: "To be, or not to be: that is the question:/Whether 'tis nobler in the mind to suffer/The slings and arrows of outrageous fortune,/Or to take arms against a sea of troubles,/And by opposing end them?"[7] In this passage, one of Shakespeare's most memorable characters considers the value and meaning of life and whether reason enough can be found in existence to warrant its continuation. Earlier in the same play, Polonius advises his son, who is about to travel abroad: "This above all: to thine own self be true,/And it must follow, as the night the day,/Thou canst not then be false to any man."[8] This piece of timeless wisdom speaks to the issue of self-deception versus self-knowledge, one of the main topics of existential discourse. In another play, Nietzsche's view of good and evil is foreshadowed: "There is some soul of goodness in things evil,/Would men observingly distill it out."[9] Shakespeare, when translated in the early nineteenth century, powerfully shaped German philosophical tendencies that, in turn, led into existentialism.[10]

At nearly the same time as Shakespeare, the so-called "first modern philosopher," Descartes (1596–1650) was refashioning Western thought about self and world. While Descartes is usually heralded as the arch-proponent of rationality and the mathematical modelling of truth, there is actually a little-discussed existential aspect to his investigations. Anyone who studies philosophy can hardly escape reading Descartes' *Meditations* —another kind of philosophical autobiography in which the author struggles from ignorance toward knowledge of existential significance. In this work there are basically four things to notice. First, the reader looks in once more upon the loneliness of the solitary thinker plagued by doubt, and this time fearful of losing contact with the world, feeling himself to be sinking into the quicksand of solipsism. This may strike one as a somewhat disingenuous pose, but there is no question that it has proved both an effective and greatly influential device that can be (and has been) taken still more seriously by others. Second, there is the idea that self-examination is the key to truth, so far as it can be attained. Third, we may cite the claim that consciousness is the source of the highest truths and that attending to what is in consciousness (as later on the phenomenologists will teach—see chapter 5) is the proper avenue for philosophy to follow. Fourth, Descartes asserts in the fourth *Meditation* that reason may discover the truth but that it requires an (extra-rational) act of the will to affirm it.

We next come to Pascal (1623–62), another philosopher/mathematician, like Descartes, and the author of the renowned *Pensées* (*Thoughts*), a collection of sundry philosophical notes and short essays. Pascal is, to my way of thinking, the most astonishing precursor of existentialism, and for this reason I will return to him at the end of this chapter in order to examine his thought in greater detail. Suffice it to say, for the moment, that he spotlights the inadequacy of reason before the magnitude and mystery of being.

Even within the Enlightenment we find some wellsprings of existential thought. Hume (1711–76) proposed that "Reason is, and ought only to be the slave of the passions, and can never pretend to any other office than to serve and obey them."[11] He developed a brand of skepticism that has helped expose the hubris residing in the most everyday knowledge-claims.

Hume also based his ethics upon sentiment, or moral feeling that comes from within oneself and is innate. Rousseau (1712–78) brought religious feeling and feelings for nature to center stage while engaging in self-examination in his own deeply introspective *Confessions*. He revitalized the conception of what it is to be a person, freeing it from the shackles imposed by traditional interpretations of Classical and other Enlightenment thinkers. Notwithstanding his belief in a universal human nature and in a utopian form of society (presented in *The Social Contract*), Rousseau's attention to the inner life and new image of humanity enhanced the prospects for an existential revolution in thought. Kant (1724–1804), responding to Hume's challenges, carefully distinguished between the inner realm of freedom and faith in which self-awareness prevails and the outer world of sense-perception and causality presided over by reason and objective knowledge. The true moral self, though it must abide by the rational appeal of an abstract law (the "categorical imperative"), according to Kant, is nonetheless autonomous and represents an internal reality or domain that is untouchable by the methods of science. Kant's philosophy of history presented humans as emerging from nature to gain freedom and autonomy, and from barbarism to gain culture, international society, and eventually world peace.

Overlapping Kant's lifetime was the Romantic movement in philosophy and the arts (c. 1770–1850), which proved to be particularly rich and fertile in its contributions and influence. Among the orientations that came to the forefront during this period were exaltation of the creative artist as genius; focus on the individual and the inner life; emphasis on emotion and the senses (versus the intellectual and pure reason); attention to the complexities and irrationalities of human life residing below the surface; an accent on intuition, feeling, and imagination as sources of insight and truth; and a yearning for a holistic view of humans and nature. In the period circa 1770–84, the "Storm and Stress" (*Sturm und Drang*) movement in Germany featured writers like Goethe (1749–1832) and Schiller (1759–1805), whose protagonists were solitary heroes trying to stand their ground against the cruelties of destiny. For these characters, faith and sense-experience were the avenues to truth about life. All of these ideas stimulated considerably the evolution of existentialism and the concept of the existential individual.

Mary Wollstonecraft Godwin (1759–97), the celebrated feminist and author of *A Vindication of the Rights of Women*, commented, "How can a rational being be ennobled by anything that is not obtained by its own exertions?"[12] Simultaneously, she asserts here an egalitarian doctrine and

links this to a view of the self as self-constructed. She also believed that
"We reason deeply, when we forcibly feel,"[13] which suggests that inner
affective states may yield the highest form of insight, and that reason and
feelings are intertwined.

Two important figures who transformed German philosophy between
Kantian idealism and the later nineteenth century were Fichte (1762–
1814) and Schelling (1775–1854). Fichte recasts the Delphic oracle's
ancient advice in his own words: "Attend to yourself."[14] He recognizes two
types of "presentations" (or "immediate modifications of consciousness"):
those that are "accompanied by the feeling of necessity" (which he
equates with inner and outer experience) and others that are "accompanied by the feeling of freedom" (which he equates with the operations of
imagination and will).[15] The former, such as sense-perceptions and experiences of causality, we have no control over. But the latter give us experiences of our active agency and self-determination. Fichte argues for the
supremacy of moral consciousness in human life, which is characterized
by the second kind of presentations: "Consciousness of the real world pro-
ceeds from [the] need to act. . . . We do not act because we know, but we
know because we are meant to act. . . ."[16] He even asserts that knowledge
of the world is itself grounded in a decision of the will, an act of faith. Furthermore, the scope of human freedom cannot be established by argument or evidence; it is posited by an existential choice: "I am thoroughly
my own creation. . . . I did not want to be nature, but my own work; and I
have become so by willing it."[17] We choose to self-limit this freedom in
order to coexist with others. Nature is mysteriously presented to our
awareness simply in order to help fix the parameters of self-realization and
duty. Finally, philosophy is an ultimate commitment: "What sort of philosophy one chooses depends, therefore, on what sort of man one is; for a
philosophical system is not a dead piece of furniture that we can reject or
accept as we wish; it is rather a thing animated by the soul of the person
who holds it."[18] Thus, truth is a function of subjectivity—at least in those
crucial areas relating to what we ultimately stand for.

Schelling is best known today as an architect of German Romanticism,
which was both influential upon and influenced by him. His thought features antirational tendencies as well as the now-familiar stress on the individual and on aesthetic intuition as a singular source of truth. "The beginning and end of all philosophy is—freedom,"[19] Schelling urges; "the
essence of man is . . . *his own act*; necessity and freedom are mutually
immanent, as one reality which appears as one or the other only when
looked at from different sides. . . ."[20] In the last of his several periods of

intellectual development, he turned to explicitly existential themes, maintaining, as one commentator notes, that "Philosophy must deal not only with the 'what' of the world, which explains its nature, but also with the 'that' of the world—the fact of its existence, of its being there," and endeavoring, like Pascal, Kierkegaard, and Nietzsche, "to express the inexpressible pathos of existence in oracular utterances halfway between poetry and metaphysics. . . ."[21]

Nineteenth-century philosophy takes a radical turn with the metaphysics and ethics of Schopenhauer (1788–1860). Schopenhauer, too, adopts a strong antirationalist stance, positing that it is *willing* rather than *reasoning* that most distinctively characterizes human beings. This form of philosophy, known as *voluntarism,* was soon to shape the thought of Nietzsche and Freud in most profound ways. Willing includes the following: "not only all willing and deciding in the narrowest sense, but also all striving, wishing, shunning, hoping, fearing, loving, hating, in short all that directly constitutes our own weal and woe. . . ."[22] As we see here, Schopenhauer directs our attention to bodily experiences, sexuality, moods, emotions, feelings—in brief, to immediate experiences of all types. And he insists that introspection leads us inward to the basic truth about reality—that a blind, striving will drives everything and manifests itself as the "will to live" (or "will to life") of all earthly beings. In his ethics, Schopenhauer, much influenced by Hume and Buddhism, emphasizes compassion (our inborn moral emotion) as the sole motivator of all good and praiseworthy actions, thus breaking away from abstract, rationalistic conceptions of ethics, such as Kant's.

Hegel (1770–1831), the greatest systematic philosopher of modern times, perhaps of all times, might not be expected to appear in this chapter, given that he represents the last gasp of Enlightenment faith in reason and was also Kierkegaard's philosophical target of attack and foil. However, much of Hegel's legacy fed directly into existentialism. He viewed humans as self-makers, as engaged in many and varied acts of self-transcendence, in which they are fundamentally, if only semiconsciously, seeking freedom. He was acutely aware of the *dialectical* nature of the world and of existence; that is, of their being characterized by the tension between opposites—such as finite and infinite, life and death, good and bad, independence and dependence, self and other, individual and collective, peace and violence, and polarized physical and chemical forces (such as magnetism and electricity, X and Y chromosomes, and so on). Hegel was the first philosopher to talk about alienation (or estrangement), and he coined the word "phenomenology."

A rebellious follower of Hegel, Marx (1818–83) continued to develop the dialectical method, examining the theme of alienation in the industrial era, especially in his early writings. Marx saw alienation as multifaceted and pervasive. (See appendix C, "Alienation," for more details.) Like Kant, Marx depicted humans as emerging from nature, progressively casting off animal drudgery in order to earn freedom.

At about the same time, novelist George Eliot (pen name of Marian Evans Cross, 1819–80) observed that "When the commonplace 'We all must die' transforms itself suddenly into the acute consciousness 'I must die—and soon,' then death grapples us, and his fingers are cruel."[23] This foreshadows Kierkegaard's thoughts on death as a challenging aspect of the task of choosing how to live and also Heidegger's extensive consideration of death both as an everyday subject of idle chatter and as a personal issue of great magnitude that calls for the utmost honesty with oneself.

Robert Browning (1812–89), in his poetic masterwork *The Ring and the Book*, anticipated Heidegger's thoughts on being-toward-death in the following words: "Even throughout life, 'tis death that makes life live,/Gives it whatever the significance."[24]

Among other literary figures who addressed existential themes in a serious vein, the great Russian novelist Dostoevsky (1821–81) is a major example. Dostoevsky, like Schopenhauer, was a brilliant intuitive psychologist who grappled with themes like guilt, suffering, personal faith in the existence of God, and freedom and the painful cost of independence in a conformist, collectivizing, hedonistic world.

We next come to Freud (1856–1939), the founder of psychoanalysis. Freud is important to existentialism because of his focus on unconscious motivation and the dark, instinctual side of the psyche. Much of human behavior (most of it, in his view) comes from nonrational, even irrational sources. Creativity, self-deception, dreams, jokes, and many other phenomena can also be explained in this manner. Yet even though Freud, as a theorist, is often thought to be a determinist with respect to human actions, as a therapist, he left room for individual responsibility and self-overcoming. One of his most famous slogans is "Where id was, there ego shall be."[25] In other words, although the infantile, instinctual urges of the unconscious, primitive part of the self may tend to predominate, we can nevertheless free ourselves from their control by gaining insight into ourselves. By doing so, we enlarge the sphere of the ego, or the reality-adapted, autonomous part of the self, and move toward a greater degree of normality, maturity, and adulthood. Freud also argued, in a way reminiscent of Nietzsche (who anticipated many of his ideas), that "civilization" represents a compromise between the conflicting demands of basic human instincts and the higher faculties that are responsible for culture.

On a parallel track to the existentialists, the French philosopher Bergson (1859–1941) developed ideas that reinforced theirs. He claimed that we are immersed in the stream of time, which we experience as "real duration,"[26] and that this has little to do with clock time or the measurable time of physics. He also observed that intuition, by which we apprehend time and other concrete, immediate features of the world, gives us a truer sense of reality than the abstract, analytical categories of rational knowledge, which fragment what is whole and intact about the world. In some respects, Bergson's outlook resembles not only that of Romantics, existentialists, and phenomenologists, but also that of indigenous peoples in many parts of the world.

Finally, we must briefly mention Brentano (1838–1916) and Husserl (1859–1938), the sources of contemporary phenomenology. Since I will deal with phenomenology in chapter 5, the only thing necessary to record here is that they sought to create a study of the workings of consciousness in its own right. This influenced Heidegger and Sartre, in particular, but also fellow travelers such as Merleau-Ponty (1908–61), who will also be discussed in chapter 5.

PASCAL REVISITED

Pascal was a very gifted individual who not only excelled in philosophy and mathematics but also as a physicist, inventor, theologian, polemicist, and master of prose style. His *Pensées* show a skeptical mind at work, disclosing his belief that "there is a certain paradox about human nature: we possess knowledge yet recognize that this knowledge cannot be rationally justified and that rational arguments can even be directed against it."[27] This perspective is not entirely new, having surfaced earlier in the work of Montaigne (1533–92), Descartes, and Hume, but Pascal gives an original, existential twist to the problem: "What sort of freak then is man! How novel, how monstrous, how chaotic, how paradoxical, how prodigious! Judge of all things, feeble earthworm, repository of truth, sink of doubt and error, glory and refuse of the universe!"[28] Thus, Pascal rails against the precarious human condition. But there is a solution, he thinks: "We know the truth not only through our reason but also through our heart. It is through the latter that we know first principles, and reason, which has nothing to do with it, tries in vain to refute them."[29] This "evidence of the heart" includes instinct, feeling, and above all, it is underwritten by religious faith. (Characteristically, even religious belief is challenged by him in the passage that has become well-known as "Pascal's wager";[30] but there, reason, in the form of probability inference, comes to the rescue.)

A great deal of Pascal's thought revolves around human nature and expresses his sense of the human predicament, which John Macquarrie perceptively describes as "the new feeling of man's pilgrim status in the universe."[31] Since the beginning of the Renaissance, with its concentration on human concerns and artifacts, the medieval religious vision of a closed universe had been unraveling. But with this development came the unmooring of humanity from its fixed, central place in the scheme of things, its privileged position in the eyes of God. Indeed, for many, the idea of God itself could no longer go unchallenged. Pascal worked within this liberating but also troubling context, in which humans first felt the full weight of being decentered and first experienced "exile," or "metaphysical homelessness."

In a section of the *Pensées* that he revealingly titles "Transition from Knowledge of Man to Knowledge of God," Pascal expresses himself as follows: "When I see the blind and wretched state of man, when I survey the whole universe in its dumbness and man left to himself with no light, as though lost in this corner of the universe, without knowing who put him there, what he has come to do, what will become of him when he dies, incapable of knowing anything, I am moved to terror. . . ."[32] He adds that he feels like someone who has "no means of escape," and wonders how humans can ever avoid "despair." To compound the sense of our forlorn condition, Pascal continues with the observation that humans are suspended between the immenseness of the universe at large and the infinitesimally small:

> For, after all, what is man in nature? A nothing compared to the infinite, a whole compared to the nothing, a middle point between all and nothing, infinitely remote from an understanding of the extremes; the end of things and their principles are unattainably hidden from him in impenetrable secrecy.
>
> Equally incapable of seeing the nothingness from which he emerges and the infinity in which he is engulfed.[33]

Although situated in the middle of things, we find comfort in fleeing from the strange ambivalence of this very existence. And because our vision is limited in all directions, we can never be sure of knowing anything: "Such is our true state. That is what makes us incapable of certain knowledge or absolute ignorance. We are floating in a medium of vast extent, always drifting uncertainly. . . ."

These are incredibly powerful declarations, couched in a very modern idiom. We can hardly remain unmoved by them, as Pascal no doubt knew. They resonate with the temper of our times, but they also reverberate across the ages, as some of our historical precursors have shown. Consider some of the existential elements embedded in Pascal's remarks. The universe is "dumb"; it does not or cannot speak to us in order to answer our ultimate questions; we yearn for a "reply" but it does not come. This reminds one of the endless waiting in Beckett's great tragi-comedy *Waiting for Godot*.[34] It also conjures up the sense of "the absurd" that we find in *The Myth of Sisyphus* by Camus (1913–60): "The absurd is born of this confrontation between the human need and the unreasonable silence of the world."[35] (See appendix D, "The Absurd.") The "need" to which Camus refers here is the overwhelming desire to know, to be "at home" in being, to feel that there is an overriding sense to things and that our lives somehow fit into it. Pascal goes on to portray humans as "lost," ignorant of their origin, purpose, and destiny, locked in uncertainty, trapped by our condition, terrified, and driven to despair. Not a happy state to be in, but undeniably at least a partial truth about where we are at.

The metaphor of humans as "floating" uncertainly between the infinite and nothingness (see appendix A, "Nothingness") suggests that we cannot know what lies at these extremes, and that complete humility is the appropriate response. Pascal regards humans (especially philosophers) as "pretentious" in their knowledge-claims. We are so constituted as to remain unable to break out of our state of suspended cognition: "it takes no less capacity to reach nothingness [the microscopic and sub-microscopic world] than the whole [knowledge of God; final or objective truth]."

But Pascal does not leave the matter there; he advances a notion of existential courage in the face of the inevitable and tragic condition in which we find ourselves: "Let us then seek neither assurance nor stability. . . . Man is only a reed, the weakest in nature, but he is a thinking reed. . . . Thus all our dignity consists in thought. It is on thought that we must depend for our recovery." What he is telling us here is that we need to be able to tolerate and live with ambiguity, as de Beauvoir reiterates in *The Ethics of Ambiguity* (see chapter 8), even citing Pascal's "thinking reed" metaphor.[36] Pascal also judges that although humans are frail and vulnerable in the face of nature, they have a unique quality—thought—that provides them with a tool for survival and self-validation and that helps them determine where they are going as a species. The later existentialists would agree to a large extent: while our rational capacity is not the be-all and end-all, it is nevertheless important and enables us to analyze the experience of existence and view it constructively so that we can get on with the task of living.

AFTERWORD: ABIDING CONCERNS OF EXISTENCE

What this chapter shows is that both philosophers and non-philosophers have given voice to some remarkably similar existential concerns over the centuries. The character of existence, nothingness, human finitude, being and becoming, faith and knowledge, the sources of truth, the existence of God, the meaning of life, freewill and determinism, inner experience, the nature of the self, choice and action, and alienation are all themes that have manifested some sort of presence in Western culture since the beginning. One might, then, legitimately ask what is distinctive about existentialism proper. I think the short answer to this is that the existentialists are both social critics and investigators of existence in a much deeper and more exclusive sense than anyone who preceded them. That is, they take seriously the self-assigned mission of seeing all philosophical problems as starting from (a) meditations on existence and (b) our inability to surpass the limits of existence in order to obtain transcendent, extramundane, or otherworldly answers to our most fundamental questions. In short, existentialists take as their special subject the study of existence as we live it, and they treat this as a matter of the first importance. Peter Preuss points out that the notion of humans as actively self-making beings "was already anticipated by the 15th-century humanist Pico della Mirandola in his *Oration*. But with Pico it was an isolated thought without further effect. Such things occur in philosophy. Tertullian stumbled across the relation of religious faith to absurdity around 200 A.D., but it had no effect until Kierkegaard developed it."[37] These observations support what I have been saying about the difference between the existentialists and their progenitors. As we shall see, while the thinkers I cover in the following chapters disagree on the merits of being "systematic," there can be no doubt that their approach to such issues is completely dedicated to thoroughness and their results are more exhaustively laid out than ever before.

Existentialists deny that there is a universal human nature, yet they are best understood as engaging in "philosophical anthropology"—the investigation of what it is to be human within existence as they understand and describe it. In the next chapter, we will examine Kierkegaard's philosophy in some detail in order to clarify what this means and how the existentialist mind works.

NOTES

1. Max Charlesworth, *The Existentialists and Jean-Paul Sartre* (St. Lucia, AU: University of Queensland Press, in association with the Australian Broadcasting Commission, 1975), p. 1.

2. See, for example, David E. Cooper, *Existentialism*, 2nd ed. (Oxford: Blackwell, 1999); and Jack Reynolds, *Understanding Existentialism* (Chesham, UK: Acumen, 2006).

3. William Barrett, *Irrational Man* (Garden City, NY: Anchor Books/Doubleday, 1962), ch. 4.

4. Job 13:15.

5. Job 4:14.

6. St. Augustine, *Confessions* (ca. 397–400), in *Basic Writings of St. Augustine*, trans. J. G. Pilkington, ed. Whitney J. Oates (New York: Random House, 1948), vol. 1, bk. 11, ch. 14.

7. William Shakespeare, *Hamlet*, 3.1.56–59. Søren Kierkegaard refers to this passage in *Concluding Unscientific Postscript*, trans. Howard V. Hong and Edna H. Hong (Princeton, NJ: Princeton University Press, 1992), 1:193.

8. Ibid., 1.3.78–80.

9. Shakespeare, *King Henry V*, 4.1.4–5.

10. The reader may be interested in having a look at Walter Kaufmann, *From Shakespeare to Existentialism*, new ed., with additions (Freeport, NY: Books for Libraries Press, 1971), especially ch. 1.

11. David Hume, *A Treatise of Human Nature* (1739), bk. 2, pt. 3, sec. 3.

12. Mary Wollstonecraft Godwin, *A Vindication of the Rights of Women* (1792), ch. 3.

13. Mary Wollstonecraft Godwin, *Letters Written During a Short Residence in Sweden, Norway, and Denmark* (1796), no. 19.

14. Johann Gottlieb Fichte, First Introduction, *Science of Knowledge*, trans. and ed. Peter Heath and John Lachs (Cambridge: Cambridge University Press, 1982), sec. 1.

15. Ibid.

16. Johann Gottlieb Fichte, *The Vocation of Man* (1800), trans. Peter Preuss (Indianapolis, IN: Hackett, 1987), p. 79.

17. Ibid., p. 73.

18. Fichte, First Introduction, *Science of Knowledge*, sec. 5.

19. Friedrich Wilhelm Joseph von Schelling, cited by Adam Margoshes, "Schelling, Friedrich Wilhelm Joseph von," in *The Encyclopedia of Philosophy*, ed. Paul Edwards (New York: Macmillan and the Free Press, 1967), 7:306.

20. Friedrich Wilhelm Joseph von Schelling, *Werke* (*Collected Works*), ed. Manfred Schröter (Munich, 1927–28), 4:277, cited by Frederick Copleston, *A History of Philosophy*, vol. 7: *Fichte to Nietzsche* (London: Burns and Oates, 1963), p. 133 (emphasis in original).

21. Margoshes, "Schelling," p. 309.

22. Arthur Schopenhauer, *The World as Will and Representation* (first published in 1819), trans. E. F. J. Payne (New York: Dover, 1966), vol. 2, ch. 19.

23. George Eliot, *Middlemarch* (1871–72), bk. 4, ch. 42.

24. Robert Browning, *The Ring and the Book* (1868–69), 11, "Guido."

25. Sigmund Freud, *New Introductory Lectures on Psycho-Analysis* (1933), trans. James Strachey, in *Standard Edition of the Complete Psychological Works of Sigmund Freud*, ed. James Strachey (London: Hogarth Press and Institute of Psycho-Analysis, 1964), 32: 80.

26. Henri Bergson, *An Introduction to Metaphysics* (1912), trans. T. E. Hulme (New York: Liberal Arts Press, 1949; reprinted Indianapolis, IN: Hackett, 1999).

27. Daniel Fouke, "Pascal, Blaise," in Robert Audi, ed., *The Cambridge Dictionary of Philosophy*, 2nd ed. (Cambridge: Cambridge University Press, 1999), p. 648.

28. Blaise Pascal, *Pensées* (1670), rev. ed., trans. A. J. Krailsheimer (Harmondsworth, UK: Penguin Books, 1995), sec. 130.

29. Ibid., sec. 110.

30. Ibid., sec. 418.

31. John Macquarrie, *Existentialism* (Harmondsworth, UK: Penguin Books, 1973), p. 51.

32. Pascal, *Pensées*, sec. 198.

33. Ibid., sec. 199.

34. Samuel Beckett, *Waiting for Godot* (New York: Grove Press, 1954).

35. Albert Camus, *The Myth of Sisyphus and Other Essays*, trans. Justin O'Brien (New York: Vintage Books/Random House, 1959), p. 21.

36. Simone de Beauvoir, *The Ethics of Ambiguity*, trans. Bernard Frechtman (Secaucus, NJ: Citadel Press, 1948), p. 7.

37. Peter Preuss, "Translator's Introduction" in Fichte, *Vocation of Man*, p. xii.

QUESTIONS FOR REFLECTION

1. Are faith and reason equally essential for living? Can they be reconciled?

2. What does it mean to say that human existence is paradoxical or absurd? How can we come to terms with this feature of life?

3. Can we will ourselves to be free, or is this thought of our independence from external influences merely an illusion?

4. What is self-realization? How is it attained?

5. How does historical information improve our understanding of existentialism?

6. What does Pascal mean by saying that humans are a mean between infinity and nothingness and why does he think this? Does holding this view depend on one's having a religious outlook? (It will be helpful to read his *Pensées*, especially sections 193–202.)

3

KIERKEGAARD

IN SEARCH OF THE INDIVIDUAL

Søren Kierkegaard (1813–1855) is universally acknowledged to be the founding figure in the existentialist movement, for he first drew attention to the special features of human existence and argued that all worthwhile philosophizing must begin and end with existence. His enigmatic method of working through problems and provocative ideas still energize a wide variety of readers and interpreters a century and a half after his death.

AN UNQUIET DEPARTURE

It is November 18, 1855. The scene is the main Protestant cathedral of Copenhagen. Søren Kierkegaard, always a controversial figure in his native city, is about to be laid to rest. He died a week earlier from an undiagnosed illness at the age of forty-two. Kierkegaard had already refused last rites because of his conviction that all clergymen are "royal functionaries . . . not related to Christianity." Now a large group of students—self-assigned guardians—surrounds his coffin in order to prevent a scuffle between official Church of Denmark representatives and ordinary citizens. Later, at his gravesite, there is a rancorous dispute over who will speak some final words before the burial. Kierkegaard's nephew, a physician, defies the law, which permits only clerics to speak, preempting an official speaker's place and delivering a stinging attack upon the church, true to the spirit of his departed uncle.[1]

Who was this man that generated such intellectual turmoil? None less than the first existentialist—one who had declared that his epitaph should simply read: "That Individual." (This wish was not granted.) I seek only to identify Kierkegaard here, not to sketch his biography. For it was also his strong desire that we not focus on his person or his life, but look instead to his written works, with their embedded message to think for ourselves and take charge of our personal destiny in an affirmative way. He opposes the flabby complacency of ordinary modern life and calls upon our autonomy and sense of courage. One of the pseudonymous authors (pen names), whom Kierkegaard lets speak on his behalf, reports that "moved by a genuine interest in those who make everything easy, I conceived it as my task to create difficulties everywhere."[2] Kierkegaard certainly does this—in spades. And the reason is that he has chosen as his mission to prevent individuality and the essential message of Christianity from sinking into oblivion: "The greatest hazard of all, losing the self, can occur very quietly in the world, as if it were nothing at all. No other loss can occur so quietly; any other loss—an arm, a leg, five dollars, a wife, etc.—is sure to be noticed."[3] In life, as in death, Kierkegaard disturbs us and destabilizes our complacency. As with other great thinkers, we cannot go around him; instead, we must work through the challenges he throws in our path.

THE ENIGMA OF IDENTITY

The question of personal identity is one that philosophers, religious thinkers, creative writers, and psychologists have always pondered. Kierkegaard was all of these things and more, and his interest in personal identity was intense and pervasive. He explored not only the theoretical issue corresponding to the question "What is a person?" (or "What is it to be a person?") but also the problem, vital to each of us, that is expressed when we ask, "Who am I?" Kierkegaard's existentialism is concerned to a large extent with individuality and the conditions of selfhood, as we shall see. It is also about being human and the challenging—often perilous—adventure we undertake in striving to define ourselves.

Before we get into these matters, we need to address a key puzzle about Kierkegaard. I have already alluded to the fact that he uses the device of pseudonymous authorship, and many of his most celebrated books are written in this manner. But why would someone who is dedicated to the expression of individuality (his own and ours) so liberally utilize disguised authorship? To understand this is to grasp what he perceived to be his calling and opportunity as a writer. Our effort to do so is complicated by the fact that much of Kierkegaard's philosophy flows from one surrogate voice or another. Here is an incomplete list of the sub-authors he invented, with some translations to hint at the meaning of their names: Victor Eremita (The Victorious Hermit), Johannes de silentio (John the Silent), Constantin Constantius, Virgilius Haufniensis (The Watchman of Copenhagen), Nicolaus Notabene (Nicholas Take Notice), Johannes Climacus (Climactic John), Anti-Climacus, Hilarius Bookbinder, Inter et Inter (Between and Between), "A" (spokesperson for the aesthetic mode of existence), Judge William (also identified as "B," spokesperson for the ethical mode of existence), Wilhelm Afham (William by, of, or from Him), Frater Taciturnus (Uncommunicative Brother), Quidam (A Certain Person), and H. H. So how do we ever know or have the right to say that Kierkegaard is speaking for himself, that he stands behind these or those ideas? Scholars have debated this point exhaustively, and continue to do so, many insisting that we take care to cite only the assigned author of a given work, not Kierkegaard himself—and indeed, Kierkegaard was the first to make this demand.[4] Furthermore, it has been established by computerized textual analysis that the panoply of authors Kierkegaard employs in fact all have their own distinctive styles of self-expression in the original Danish![5] Clearly, we are dealing with a brilliant mind playing a sophisticated game with us. In one sense, he wants to keep us at bay but in another, he longs to draw us in, to engage us, and to cause us to react. There is always the danger that the first motive will overwhelm the second, but the ingenuity of Kierkegaard consists in keeping these purposes in a fine balance. Let's see how this works.

Several of Kierkegaard's pseudonymous works bear his name on the title page but only with the qualifier "responsible for publication" or "edited by" tacked on. This suggests that he couldn't resist making at least a cameo appearance as himself, much like Alfred Hitchcock's quick walk-through roles in his own movies. Yet Kierkegaard remains essentially in concealment. (One should not call this posture "anonymity" because his books are not written by unknown hands; on the contrary, they are authored precisely by identifiable literary personae with definite and fascinating attributes of their own, whom we come to know quite well by the time we turn the last page.) Well, then, what is the pretense all about? The answer is multileveled, and even the following account does not tell the entire story.

WILL THE REAL S. KIERKEGAARD PLEASE STEP FORWARD?

1. On the surface of things, writing under a pen name can be viewed as a narrative technique for simply telling a story and letting it speak for itself. As D. H. Lawrence once remarked, "Never trust the artist. Trust the tale."[6] In other words, find the meaning of a text within itself and the world it creates; don't look elsewhere for guidance—at the famous author's well-known theoretical, moral, or political views, for example.

2. Pseudonymous authorship permits Kierkegaard to exaggerate one aspect of humanity and to explore where this leads, both in thought and action. This is like the novelist's device of creating characters and running them through their paces, especially if she or he either has a point to make, wants to show that a certain outlook is ultimately a dead end, or just wishes to find out something about life by means of the creative process. In aid of this device, Kierkegaard frequently employs irony by portraying detachment from or skepticism toward a position he wants to promote, by having his characters hyperbolically advocate a point of view or way of life that he wishes us to reject; or by surprising you with an inversion of the truth. (For instance, in order to most effectively stimulate readers' thinking about what it means to be a Christian, Kierkegaard writes that "one does not begin . . . in this way: I am a Christian, you are not a Christian—but this way: You are a Christian, I am not Christian."[7]) He also craftily engages the reader in the project of suspending judgment about beliefs and practices that guide her or his own life so that, thus challenged, new thoughts and new directions for living might open up. These methods fit in with Kierkegaard's idea that "an illusion [for example, that one is an individual or a Christian] can never be removed directly, and basically only indirectly. . . . That is, one who is under an illusion must be approached from behind."[8]

3. Kierkegaard was a dialectical thinker, meaning that he saw the world in terms of opposing tendencies, each struggling for ascendancy. Paradox and ambiguity are features of the human condition, and we have to live in the face of uncertainty and unresolvable tensions ("contradictions") within ourselves. A spectrum of authorial personae allows Kierkegaard to advance and exemplify this view and to look at existence from diverse (sometimes even perverse and odd) angles.

4. Such a style of writing readily lends itself to dramatization. Injecting an element of theater into philosophy (or of philosophy into theater) is a time-honored way of putting across a message entertainingly and effectively. Kierkegaard's characters play out their roles, they don't just espouse ideas. As he notes, "The poetised author has his definite life-view to dance

with. . . ."[9] This should not be construed as meaning that Kierkegaard sees himself merely as a grand puppet-master, who invisibly pulls the strings that animate his characters; rather, the characters take on lives of their own and "author" their own texts ("I am merely an unknown person who is the author's author . . .").[10]

5. Creating a persona sometimes allows Kierkegaard to pose as "Everyman" (or "Everyperson"). That is, he can universalize about humanity, but in such a way as not to condescend. He can appear not to be taking the moral high ground (and can deceive the reader into believing he's not). As we shall see, his characters can themselves be "outsiders" to the position being examined (Christianity, for example). They can have their own uncertainties, anxieties, moods, obsessions, and imperfections, alongside their strengths—just like real, everyday people such as ourselves. Kierkegaard believed that psychological and philosophical insights that are universally applicable could be found within the particularity of one's individual consciousness. Much of his literary output consists of journals—thousands of manuscript pages—in which he works through the moral and spiritual quandaries of his age, and of humanity in general, searching within the depths of his own soul for answers and solutions, and encouraging us to do likewise.

6. Having a range of pseudonymous authors (sometimes within the same work), Kierkegaard can carry on a dialogue with himself. He can argue a point in an extended sense by investigating diverse perspectives on an issue or, as in (2) above, he can discover what he really thinks about the matter himself.

7. By using aliases Kierkegaard can deflect interest and attention from his own person and redirect them toward his authors. This has three distinct benefits. First, probings into his personal biography are discouraged. Many critics are wedded to the process of unearthing the connection between an author's life and her or his writing as an essential way of illuminating the author's works. Kierkegaard did not want this form of distraction to enter into the interpretation of his books. Second, he stymies those who would search for the author's intention in creating the work as a way of pinpointing its meaning. Third, he offers no inroad for the cult of personality that thrived as much in his time as it does in ours. Not wanting to be either a cult figure or a cultural superstar, he hopes to keep the focus squarely on the text itself and the problems it poses.[11] As one of his authorial voices remarks, "Here as everywhere I have no opinion of my own but, imaginatively constructing, simply present the issue."[12]

8. Being the source of many voices, often arguing among themselves,

Kierkegaard generates controversy and public debate. For him these are healthy and desirable because he is eager to evoke a response, to goad people into rethinking their fundamental assumptions about life, especially what it means to be religious. Indeed, he went to the extreme of attacking his own authors in widely read journals of the day, thereby furthering the clash of opinions on subjects of most interest to him.

INDIRECT AND DIRECT COMMUNICATION

Kierkegaard attempted, as the undisclosed author of a variety of works published between 1843 and 1846, to engage in "indirect communication." The point of this exercise was to enliven debate (which he held to be moribund) about what it is to be human, and to do this in a manner that can, in a broad sense, be described as entertaining. He did not seek merely to be titilating, humorous, bizarre, or a good storyteller, though he is all of these things by turns. What he wanted to accomplish was to plant ideas and images that might germinate in the reader's mind, and to do so without resorting to speechmaking, sermonizing, or the didactic prose of academics. A person-to-person, often confessional kind of writing seemed best: one human being addressing another human being about what it is to be human. Kierkegaard's objective in all this was to free up his readers' capacity to commit themselves, with intense concentration, to a guiding idea, a way of life. This does not mean that he aimed at facilitating our efforts to follow his line of thought or to probe our own souls. Quite the contrary: Johannes Climacus, the titular author of *Concluding Unscientific Postscript*, one of Kierkegaard's most important and philosophically deepest works, speaks of "the mortal danger of lying out on 70,000 fathoms of water, and only there finding God," observing further that "upon [these] depths the religious person is continually."[13] Living is risk taking and we must plunge into the thick of things and make our mark. Therefore, the authorial task Kierkegaard assigns to Climacus, as we saw earlier, is to create challenges and obstacles over which the reader must endeavor to triumph in order to reach a greater maturity of outlook and self-evolution.

Kierkegaard eventually abandoned his project of indirect communication, turning instead to a "direct" style. The reasons for this are complex, but his sense that the existential message was not getting through is certainly among them. (Even after this change of style, he came to feel that "it is as if my books had never been written," and, late in life, he advanced beyond direct communication to a more confrontational or "irritational" form of writing.)[14] A transitional moment occurs at the end of *Concluding Unscientific Postscript*. Shortly before this work went into printing, Kierkegaard appended "A First and Last Explanation,"[15] in which he admits to being the author of the pseudonymous works. In this much-discussed passage he nevertheless distances himself from his pseudonymous personae, and, even more interestingly, claims to have no special insight into their thoughts or any personal relationship at all to their books. Here, he steadfastly maintains the stance that individuality (even that of his authors), once communicated, is "doubly reflected"; that is, it is (1) put into words, whose meanings are then (2) translated into a private understanding by the reader or listener. This is to say that an individual's experience of existence can never be more than indirectly communicated to someone else.

What *can* be directly communicated, then? The answer to this is bound up with the difference between subjective and objective approaches to truth, as we shall see. For the moment, it will be enough to assume that direct communication is only appropriate for knowledge or information that can be absorbed in a conceptual or quantitative rather than a personal manner.

APPROACHING KIERKEGAARD

One may justifiably feel somewhat apprehensive and annoyed on first acquaintance with Kierkegaard. This is not only because he seems intent on being evasive and elusive, as already shown, but also because the need for accurate understanding and interpretation looms so large. In addition, it may feel like a betrayal to study him at all, to search for "Kierkegaard's philosophy" rather than to encounter him one on one and seek to discover secular and/or religious applications of his thought. (There is a massive industry of Kierkegaard scholarship; some texts are sandwiched between erudite introductions at the front and meticulous, extended notes and commentary at the back, so that the text itself is almost lost to view. Kierkegaard would groan in his grave if he knew.) Yet gaining entry into Kierkegaard's thought is surprisingly easy. He engages us with striking images, such as this: "The whole of existence frightens me, from the smallest fly to the mystery of the Incarnation; everything is unintelligible to me, most of all myself. . . ."[16] On reading this, we may recoil as if from the words of a madman but we are also drawn in. Finding our way thereafter is another, more difficult matter. It is therefore reasonable to seek some guidance, such as I aim to offer here.

In order to appreciate better the challenge one is up against, consider the following. An early appraisal (in the prominent philosophy journal *Mind*) of Kierkegaard's *Either/Or*, then recently translated into English, begins this way:

> Being a conscientious soul and commissioned to discuss whatever of philosophy I should find in this book, I began at the beginning and read steadily on. By the time I had finished the first enormous volume I was sadly disconsolate. Even on a wide literary interpretation of "philosophy" —and no other could be appropriate—I found very little that seemed to be worth stating in any formal way.[17]

What this shows is that the reviewer could not fathom, and was in fact put off by, Kierkegaard's style of philosophical writing, or as I should prefer to say, his style of *argument*. In order to appreciate that Kierkegaard *is* offering arguments in support of certain philosophical positions, and what these amount to, it is necessary to be tuned in to the many techniques and artifices he uses to advance our investigation of a topic. We may collectively refer to these as various patterns of "thinking existentially."

Kierkegaard moves around an issue, attacking it from all sorts of oblique angles (but in reality, more directly than may at first be apparent); his strategy calls to mind that famous slogan used by one-time champion boxer Muhammad Ali (born Cassius Marcellus Clay, 1942) to describe his own approach: "Float like a butterfly, sting like a bee." In this way, Kierkegaard keeps the issue open and slowly traps you in the vortex of his meditations. Here is a list of argumentative techniques he employs: reasoning (logical inference), dramatization, psychological sketch, humor/playfulness, parody/satire, storytelling, allegory/parable, irony, aphorism, role-playing, provocation (offending or needling the reader), autobiography (sometimes his own in veiled form, sometimes those of his literary personae), paradox (similar to the Zen koan, an unresolvable puzzle). It's easy to see how a philosopher whose training is very orthodox and whose criteria for "what counts as philosophy" are quite rigid and narrow might miss the point entirely or even fail to realize at all that a point is being made.

My suggestion is that in approaching Kierkegaard one be aware of all the above possibilities and also that Kierkegaard is, in fact, developing a new style of argument that (a) he thinks is appropriate to the study of human existence and (b) is able to forward the project of indirect communication. It is also useful to think of his method as a way of verbally painting you into a corner. Everyone is familiar with the difficulty that arises (for oneself or another, or perhaps only for a cartoon character) when, out of forgetfulness or oversight (absentmindedness), a person finds that in painting the floor no thought has been given to an exit other than walking over the fresh paint. My idea here is that Kierkegaard isolates and nudges his reader into this sort of corner except that he leaves one way out: subjectivity and Christianity. We'll examine how this works presently.

EXISTENCE

What's the big deal about existence? And why should we be frightened of it? We can hardly avoid it, after all (which is Kierkegaard's point, as we'll see in a moment). Well, for one thing, some philosophers seem to find it easy to forget that they exist, more specifically, that they are human beings—or so Kierkegaard believed: "Every speculative thinker confuses himself with humankind, whereby he becomes something infinitely great and nothing at all."[18] Metaphysicians like Hegel, who try to encompass the whole universe by their theories, tend to deal in generalized concepts or abstractions, losing touch with their roots in existence, which make them human. That is, they replace the experience of existing and the ongoing process of questioning about existence with edifices of thought, often grandiose, that signify nothing in relation to the choices and deeds by which we must live. Kierkegaard comments on this phenomenon with his usual wry, caustic wit: "A thinker erects a huge building, a system, a system embracing the whole of existence, world-history, etc., and if his personal life is considered, to our amazement the appalling and ludicrous discovery is made that he himself does not personally live in this huge, high-domed palace, but in a shed alongside it, or in a dog house, or at best in the janitor's quarters."[19]

Equally, every human being faces the same dilemma, understanding what it means to exist and dealing with it or else engaging in some form of denial and escape that is designed to soften the task of living and making the hard choices that shape one's personal destiny: "Now, all in all, there are two ways for an existing individual: *either* he can do everything to forget that he is existing and thereby manage to become comic (the comic contradiction of wanting to be what one is not . . .), because existence possesses the remarkable quality that an existing person exists whether he wants to or not; *or* he can direct all his attention to his existing."[20] In other words, if we "forget" that we exist, we turn our attention elsewhere and pretend to be something other than we are; but to do so completely is blocked by the exigencies of living (like hunger, thirst, appointments, and the demands of others), which always call us back from denials and daydreams. No one can truly transcend existence, in reality or in thought. The only choice that remains, then, is to focus one's awareness sharply on the act of existing. (Compare here the Buddhist teaching of "being in the moment."[21]) Existing, then, is all-important; it is precisely being human, and being (or becoming) you or me.

Thus, it becomes clear that Kierkegaard is not trying to promote individuality as some private fetish of his own—not individuality for its own sake. He distinguishes between "[1] being a so-called subject of sorts and [2] being a subject or becoming one and being what one is by having become that."[22] Here, he contrasts what one might call subjectivity in the bad sense, or inauthentic subjectivity ("the accidental, the angular, the selfish, the eccentric, etc., of which every human being can have plenty"), with existential, authentic, or true subjectivity. Much of what passes today for self-affirmation seems to revolve around identifying with pronouncements made by empty-headed celebrities, imbibing what's served up on "reality" TV, being absorbed by computer simulation games, finessing our own consumer lifestyles, following "new age" self-help gurus, and various other shallow and escapist activities.

But while such preoccupations miss the mark, genuine self-knowledge does not come from conventional philosophies either. This explains why Kierkegaard constantly wants to bring existence down to earth, so to speak, insisting that it cannot be comprehended by an all-embracing philosophical theory. Systematic philosophy, such as Hegel and his followers conceived and perfected, "is . . . the unity of thought and being. Existence, on the other hand, is their separation."[23] Existence is diverse, complex, and even illogical and discontinuous in certain ways. It is not a seamless whole in which everything finds a meaningful place at all times. Not only this, it must be lived in the face of uncertainty and incomplete understanding. Therefore, "a logical system can be given . . . but a system of existence cannot be given."[24] Even if an omniscient God could comprehend everything, humans cannot and must therefore be content with existence as it presents itself, in its own terms.

Given the conclusions just reached, it should be no wonder that existence is somewhat daunting or frightening. More accurately, it is *anxiety provoking*. (See appendix E, "Anxiety/Angst/Anguish.") This is because each person has to take charge of his or her life and when we apprehend existence with honesty, there are no reassuring certainties to rely upon. *We have to make ourselves what we will be.* This uncertainty is the source of anxiety, which is a feature of existing. We all know of Descartes' famous phrase, "I think, therefore I am." Contemporary American philosopher Charles

Hartshorne (1897–2000) has elaborated on this truism, stating, more profoundly, that "to be is to think is to doubt is to be anxious."[25] This represents a small but important insight; for thinking does not merely confirm that we exist, it also opens us up to uncertainty and the unsettled feelings that accompany it. Kierkegaard put it this way: "My doubt is terrible.— Nothing can withstand it—it is a cursed hunger and I can swallow up every argument, every consolation and sedative—I rush at 10,000 miles a second through every obstacle."[26] In part, this is a testimonial to his brilliant and restless mind but it also resonates with every thinking person's experience of being alive, in those private moments when we ask ourselves what it's all about and try to summon up the courage to take a stand in existence.

Kierkegaard also insists that we consider existence dialectically; that is, as a suspension of or tension between opposites: "But what is existence? It is that child who is begotten by the infinite and the finite, the eternal and the temporal, and is therefore continually striving."[27] In a number of works, he dwells in addition on other polarities: possibility (or freedom) and necessity and body and soul.[28] What we have here are fundamental dialectical dimensions of existence: we live, so to speak, with one foot in the domain of each pairing, and to be a fully developed self is to constructively meld these opposites in thought and action. Some of Kierkegaard's shrewdest psychological insights occur in *The Sickness Unto Death*; these concern character types who have swung to one extreme or another of these polarities. For example, the megalomaniac or pretender (one who has delusions of grandeur) exhibits an excess of possibility; the determinist or fatalist, on the other hand, attributes more necessity to existence than is warranted.[29] Ultimately, Kierkegaard believes that the tension between opposites, which we experience within ourselves as existing individuals, can only be turned into a harmony of opposites when understood in relationship with God. The self is a self-activated relationship of elements, but this relationship needs grounding in a superior "power" to hold it together and make it productive.[30]

Finally, we need to note two things: (1) Kierkegaard thought of his philosophical project as an "existential-corrective,"[31] meaning that he took it as his mission to redirect attention and effort away from illusory pursuits (for instance, systematic philosophy and theology, keeping up with the Joneses, and idle pleasure seeking) back to existence and how we stand in relation to it; and (2) Christianity (as we shall later discover) is "not a doctrine, but . . . an existence-communication."[32] It is a message about living from one who has lived thoughtfully, and that says something important about existence and how to be an existing individual.

OBJECTIVE AND SUBJECTIVE TRUTH

"What I really lack is to be clear in my mind *what I am to do*, not what I am to know, except in so far as a certain understanding must precede every action. The thing is to understand myself, to see what God really wishes *me* to do; the thing is to find a truth which is true *for me*, to find *the idea for which I can live and die.*"[33] What kind of truth would this be that Kierkegaard seeks to discover? Certainly not one that can be served up on a platter for easy digestion or one that appeals only to the intellect. It would have to be a truth that (to use his own term) can be "appropriated," that is, deeply felt and assimilated into one's whole being. Let us not get hung up on the source of such a truth at the moment; Kierkegaard judged that it would be found in a direct relationship with God, but his message here, as most everywhere, is much more broadly applicable for believers and nonbelievers alike.

To understand this topic better we must enter into the dialectic between objective and subjective truth. Objective truth, for Kierkegaard, is any conclusion for which evidence would be decisive or any conclusion that can be arrived at by reasoning—in short, a conclusion alleged to be true independent of the individual who maintains it. Here, it is (or at any rate, may be) proper to describe the goal of one's inquiry in terms of certainty and conclusiveness. Historical and scientific truths are of this variety, and it is something to which certain kinds of philosophers aspire. (Kierkegaard labels these as "speculative thinkers" or "system-builders.") It is important to avoid assuming that this kind of truth is denigrated here. On the contrary, it has its place in our lives, which we could scarcely lead without relying upon it, as is indicated by the quotation with which this section begins.

There is, however, an inner sort of truth by which we must also live (and die). This is subjective truth, whose properties are opposite to those of objective truth. Subjective truth is not open to proof in the usual sense, but it may sometimes be held "with the infinite passion of inwardness."[34] It is truth about existence itself, rather than about states of affairs (or facts) in the world. Unlike objective truth, it is also ineffable (or unutterable); in the language of logical discourse, it is nonpropositional. Nor is it arrived at by a discursive (or reasoning) process. Furthermore, we cannot be indifferent to subjective truth in the way we can be to objective truth. For example, I may know a given historical fact, say, that Napoléon was defeated at Waterloo in 1815. But I may say, "So what?" because the questions remain, "What (if anything) does this mean *for me*? How does it change *my life*?" Granted, one cannot reasonably be quite so blasé about more recent historical facts or about scientific facts that govern our everyday actions, but Kierkegaard wants to assert that this is still possible in a way that it is not possible for subjective truths.

His primary instance of subjective truth concerns Christianity, which we shall get to in a moment. But there are other examples as well: what it means to be an ethical person, to get married, to be an individual, or that one shall die. In each case, what one believes and how one expresses the belief will define who one is. This is why we are told that subjective truth "is essential truth, or the truth that is related essentially to existence. . . ."[35] Whereas objective truth is often the outcome of "approximation" (the incremental accumulation of established data or probabilities), subjective truth is interactive and knower-dependent. Approximation means that if certainty is the goal, it may never be reached, leaving the knower in a skeptical quandary, unable to act, decide, or form trustworthy conclusions. In Kierkegaard's view, approximation is the fate of all attempts to establish the truth of Christian belief that are undertaken by means of (objective) scientific and historical findings (such as archaeological evidence gathering).

Now, the point about subjective truth is not that thinking something is true makes it true but that there is, strictly speaking, no truth apart from the thinking that vitalizes the matter in question. For instance: Does Millie love Jared? Well, we may evaluate this from a third-party perspective, identifying telltale behaviors that are commonly taken to be signs of "loving." This satisfies us about *the fact that* Millie loves Jared. But whether Millie *actually* loves Jared is *an existential issue*, a function of their interaction and how Millie feels about it. How she feels is something about her inner life. Apart from this, there is no love to speak of in the circumstances.

This contrast goes some distance toward explaining one of the more challenging and problematic passages in Kierkegaard's *Concluding Unscientific Postscript*:

> When the question about truth is asked objectively, truth is reflected upon objectively as an object to which the knower relates himself.
>
> What is reflected upon is not the relation but that what he relates himself to is the truth, the true. If only that to which he relates himself is the truth, the true, then the subject is in the truth. When the question about truth is asked subjectively, the individual's relation is reflected upon subjectively. If only the how of this relation is in truth, the individual is in truth, even if he in this way were to relate himself to untruth.[36]

Objective truth is a static thing, and it establishes a person's *placement in the world*. Subjective truth, on the other hand, manifests a person's self-chosen *way of existing* and, in this sense, it can be said that it doesn't matter whether what he or she believes (relates to) is true or not (objectively). It appears, then, that "subjective truth" refers first and foremost to something about and internal to the person who entertains it, whereas "objective truth" is apprehended either correctly or incorrectly and is indifferent to one's inner state of mind. Once again, the claim on behalf of subjective truth isn't that thinking something is so makes it so but rather that having a certain attitude or personal orientation toward something (or someone, as in the example of love) makes all the difference in the quality of one's relationship to it and how this is to be evaluated. Therefore, if one accurately believes something about the world, one is "in the truth," objectively speaking. By contrast, if one relates honestly and with commitment to what matters most to her or him, then she or he is "in the truth," subjectively speaking. Hence, this definition of subjective truth is offered in *Concluding Unscientific Postscript*: "*An objective uncertainty, held fast through appropriation with the most passionate inwardness, is the truth*, the highest truth there is for an *existing* person."[37] Whereas objective decisiveness rests in the comfort of intersubjectively sanctioned truth norms, subjective decisiveness requires personal choice and steadfast commitment to what is chosen. Following is a summary of the different properties and end results of the two kinds of truth.

OBJECTIVE VS. SUBJECTIVE TRUTH	
Objective truth	*Subjective truth*
(concerns that which is either contingent and accidental or logically necessary)	(concerns that which is existential and essential)
knowledge	faith
states of affairs, facts	ways of life, conditions of the self
certainty of evidence, proof (conclusive results)	objective uncertainty
interpersonal verification, validity	subjective certainty
approximation	appropriation
externality, correspondence	inwardness
rationality	absurdity, paradox (as judged from the objective standpoint)
security	risk, leap, venture
abstract, theoretical, general, universal	concrete, particular, intimate, uncommunicable
detachment, contemplation	passion, action, involvement
indecisiveness, fantasy	resoluteness, commitment, decision
forgetfulness	existential self-awareness

As has already been mentioned, the dialectical relationship between the two kinds of truth is played out centrally, for Kierkegaard, in a religious context. The larger setting is, of course, his entire body of work, but we can concentrate for the present on *Philosophical Fragments* and *Concluding Unscientific Postscript*, the latter of which is intended as a sequel to the former. Before we proceed, though, let's look at the titles of these volumes. Kierkegaard deliberately chooses to characterize the first as "Fragments" (which could also be translated as "Scraps" or "Crumbs"). Now, to say that an approach is "fragmentary" means that it is disjointed or at best represents only part of a more complex treatment of the subject. And to call a book "Concluding Unscientific Postscript" is first of all oxymoronic (or self-cancelling): If a study is an unscientific (perhaps even disorganized?) afterthought, it can hardly conclude anything or be in any way conclusive. And if it is genuinely a postscript, it can scarcely be several hundred pages long. Nor does a postscript usually terminate an inquiry; instead, it adds icing to the cake: perhaps it contains some interesting but irrelevant aside, tidies up a point left unfinished, or updates information. Note too that the adjective "unscientific" also reinforces the idea that what is being presented is not intended to be either systematic or definitive and has no objective results to offer. (Indeed, at the end of *Concluding Unscientific Postscript*, in an "appendix," the fictitious author of the work, Johannes Climacus, declares that his book is "superfluous" and that he "revokes" it but adds, cryptically, that "to write a book and to revoke it is not the same as refraining from writing it. . . .")[38]

The question under review in these books is whether historical knowledge suffices to determine the truth of Christianity, specifically, what we should make of its teachings in regard to the eternal and infinite destiny of the soul. Unsurprisingly, Climacus observes in the *Postscript* that "the issue is not about the truth of Christianity but about the individual's relation to Christianity. . . ."[39] Another feature to mark is that Climacus declares himself to be an "outsider" (or onlooker), a "presenter," even a "humorist,"[40] that is, not someone to look to for a full account or even a correct account and clearly not an account that can simply be substituted for what might be acquired by one's own effort. To make a long story short, what the *Postscript* initially "establishes" (the *Fragments* having set up the problem) is that neither historical evidence nor systematic philosophy can prove the truth of Christianity, if it has any truth to offer; and this is because "all decision, all essential decision, is rooted in subjectivity" and "the truth is the subject's transformation within himself."[41] This is just the decisiveness that is lacking in one who approaches Christianity objectively because for such a person the evidence and arguments will never be complete, which means that she or he will remain a fence sitter. Kierkegaard's position on Christianity is usually thought to mark him out as a *fideist* (that is, one who views basic religious beliefs as grounded in faith, which is itself immune to independent rational assessment).

In the end, what we come back to is the idea that questions beginning within existence and centered upon problems of existence must be dealt with inside the framework of existence itself. The deepest questions philosophy has traditionally posed—such as "How should I live?" and "What is the meaning of life?"—have to be answered in terms of what we can experience and instantiate through choices and actions within our own lives. Philosophy presents ways of living; it is not just a source of theories that may or may not have practical application or that one may or may not choose indifferently to apply to one's life. For ideas are idle if they can't be put to the test of actual experience. The systematic thinker is both anchored in existence and at the same time trying to step outside existence in order to view it as a spectator would. This amounts to a part viewing the whole of which it is but a part—a curious kind of existential contradiction.[42] Here, we encounter Kierkegaard's beloved metaphor of the fork in the road: "It is at this point . . . that the road swings off for the person who knows what it means to think dialectically";[43] that is, who is able to address the uncertainties and contradictions of life via the subjective approach. We can also understand why Climacus says, "Therefore it is untruth to answer a question in a medium in which the question cannot come up. . . ."[44] The "medium" he has in mind, of course, is existence, wherein all "essential" questions have their origin, reference point, and terminus.

Interestingly, Kierkegaard, in this antimetaphysical, antitheological stance, shares an affinity with certain kinds of thinkers (common-sense, pragmatist, analytic, and positivist philosophers, in particular) who would be most likely *not* to understand him and to dismiss his work as "nonphilosophy" or a species of "postmodernism." The other connection that suggests itself here is between the above remark and the celebrated saying of Marshall McLuhan (1911–80) that "the medium is the message."[45] McLuhan's notion was that a medium such as television creates a cultural space that is of greater significance than the content of what it actually broadcasts. Similarly, existence materially configures what the existing individual feels and thinks within her or his life. Any genuine response to the problems of existence, then, is inseparable from existence itself.

A KIERKEGAARDIAN DIALOGUE

A recently discovered philosophical conversation between
Søren Kierkegaard (S.K.) and an unidentified British analytic philosopher (A.P.),
recorded by an anonymous hand.
Responsible for publication: Michael Allen Fox.

A.P. Do you believe in God?

S.K. I believe in God.

A.P. What grounds do you have for such a belief?

S.K. You mean what *rational* grounds?

A.P. Of course.

S.K. None.

A.P. Did I hear you correctly? *Why*, then, do you believe?

S.K. Because I *choose* to. There can't be any objective grounds for faith, and let me point out that what we're talking about here is more properly called "faith" than "belief."

A.P. But what could be more absurd than simply choosing to believe something, especially something so monumentally important to one's life?

S.K. I agree—that's just why I have faith. Christ is the paradox, Christianity, the offense.

A.P. (*Aside.*) These are strange utterances. Can this be the King's English?
(*To* **S.K.**) But *that* is no justification for a belief. That's the old "I believe because it's absurd" bit—as old as the hills. A dangerous doctrine (if it *has* any cognitive or truth value, that is). It could be used to endorse any kind of nonsense or insanity. Surely you don't want to accept such a consequence?

S.K. Well, of course not. I have worried, for example, about the distinction between faith and fanaticism, though I admit it's not that easy to draw clearly in practice. But really, that's another issue. What you mention is not a consequence of *my* belief, you see. A very good friend of mine, Johannes de silentio, once wrote the following in his book of genius *Fear and Trembling*: "If faith cannot make it a holy act to be willing to murder his son, then let the same judgment be passed on Abraham as on every other man. . . . It is only by faith that one achieves any resemblance to Abraham, not by murder." Silentio also stated that "the courage of faith" requires us to "plunge confidently into the absurd." I firmly believe these things.

A.P. I'm flabbergasted! But what follows from this concerning our previous discussion?

S.K. Look, I just have to maintain faith that my belief in God is true. Let me elaborate a bit by quoting from another good friend, Johannes Climacus (also a genius, by the way). "So, then, there is a man who wants to have faith; well, let the comedy begin. . . . The almost probable, the probable, the to-a-high-degree and exceedingly probable—that he can almost know, or as good as know, to a higher degree and exceedingly almost *know*—but *believe* it, that cannot be done, for the absurd is precisely the object of faith, and only that can be believed."

A.P. But then how *can* you ever know that there's a God to believe in?

S.K. That's just the point: you said "know." I'm saying one *can't* know. Let me observe (as Climacus does) that "being a Christian is defined not by the 'what' of Christianity but by the 'how' of the Christian."

A.P. Hmm, I see I'd better try a different tack. Do you accept the Bible as the Truth?

S.K. No. I rely on *personal* acceptance of revelation, which is a subjective experience. Truth, as normally understood, is an objective concept. Not even an apostle can prove to you that she or he is one. Such a person would cease to be such if she or he *tried* to prove it and would then be a mere "town crier of inwardness," as Climacus so delightfully puts it.

A.P. I'll refrain from commenting on your pernicious subjectivism for the moment. But aren't you saying nothing more than that you believe because you believe? *That*, of course, any first-year philosophy student would recognize as an empty tautology. And if you then tell me that what you *really* mean is that you believe because you can only believe what cannot be known—that is merely a trivial verbal point which follows necessarily from the meanings of the words "believe" and "know." So what have I learned that I didn't already know?

S.K. (*Aside.*) The kiss of Judas.

(*To* **A.P.**) My friend, I'm afraid that this just proves what I've been saying all along: Faith can't be made into knowledge. But you'll never find God in the Oxford common room, or in a systematic metaphysician's creative cobwebs, either. I can tell that *you'll* never even become a knight of infinite resignation, still less a knight of faith.

A.P. (*Thinking aloud to himself.*) Actually, I'd settle for being knighted by the Queen.

(*Scratches head, begins to walk away. Then, to* **S.K.**) Thanks, anyway, Mr. . . . er, I've forgotten your name.

S.K. Just call me "That Individual." (*Gets on horse, yells, "Giddyap, Regina!" and disappears into the sunset.*)

A.P. Well, I'll be . . .

Epilogue. **A.P.**, on his way home from this chance encounter, having taken the wrong fork in the road, is struck by lightning and killed instantly.

The End

Explanatory notes

"I believe because it is absurd." Terlullian, *De Carne Christi*, 5.

"If faith cannot make it a holy act . . ." Søren Kierkegaard, *Fear and Trembling*, ed. and trans. Howard V. Hong and Edna H. Hong (Princeton, NJ: Princeton University Press, 1983), pp. 30, 31.

"the courage of faith," "plunge confidently into the absurd" Kierkegaard, *Fear and Trembling*, pp. 33–34.

"So, then, there is a man who wants to have faith. . . ." Søren Kierkegaard, *Concluding Unscientific Postscript to "Philosophical Fragments,"* ed. and trans. Howard V. Hong and Edna H. Hong (Princeton, NJ: Princeton University Press, 1992), 1:211 (emphasis in original).

"Being a Christian is defined. . . ." Kierkegaard, *Concluding Unscientific Postscript*, trans. Hong and Hong, 1: 611.

"town crier of inwardness" Søren Kierkegaard, *Concluding Unscientific Postscript*, trans. David F. Swenson and Walter Lowrie (Princeton, NJ: Princeton University Press, for American-Scandinavian Foundation, 1941), p. 71.

The horse being ridden by **S.K.** is thought to have been named after Regina Olsen, to whom Kierkegaard was once engaged, but did not end up marrying.

THE PRESENT AGE

Kierkegaard's preoccupation with the two types of truth flows, as did much of his philosophy, from his perspective on the age in which he lived. In many respects, this early existential social criticism is still relevant, and his critical comments have been recycled more than once by subsequent writers, as you will readily recognize. In his short work *The Present Age* and elsewhere, Kierkegaard presents his view that modern life has become devoid of passion and is characterized by materialism, complacency, shallow religiousness, and "reflection" (meaning excessive deliberation, "procrastinating indecision,"[46] and conformist mirroring of what others think and value). People's minds increasingly yield to control by the media, advertising, and other forces that appeal to the lowest common denominator. Hypocrisy, role-playing, self-delusion, political intrigues, gossip, voyeurism, meaningless diversions—these all detract from the quest for self-knowledge and a proper "God-relationship" (or relationship to something higher that gives shape to one's life). Kierkegaard complains that "life's existential tasks have lost the interest of actuality; no illusion preserves and protects the divine growth of inwardness that matures to decisions."[47] Most significantly, the spiritual side of human existence has been allowed to atrophy. In *The Sickness Unto Death*, we encounter the bald statement that "a human being is spirit." Later in this work the claim is made that while some people are very successful in a worldly sense, "themselves they are not; spiritually speaking, they have no self. . . ."[48] Spirit, for Kierkegaard, is the self's ability to integrate itself through a relationship to the higher reality beyond itself that we call "God."

It follows that Kierkegaard's special concern, in examining his age, was the watering down of the Christian message, as he understood it. Some quotations will help get the basic idea across.

. . . the bourgeois' love of God begins when vegetable life is most active, when the hands are comfortably folded on the stomach, and the head sinks back into the cushions of the chair, while the eyes, drunk with sleep, gaze heavily for a moment towards the ceiling.[49]

*   *   *

We have what one might call a complete inventory of churches, bells, organs, benches, alms-boxes, foot-warmers, tables, hearses, etc. But when Christianity does not exist, . . . this inventory . . . is so infinitely likely to give rise to a false impression and the false inference that . . . we must of course have Christianity, too.[50]

*   *   *

The parson (collectively understood) does indeed preach about those glorious ones who sacrificed their lives for the truth. As a rule the parson is justified in assuming that there is no one present in the church who could entertain the notion of venturing upon such a thing. . . . [H]e preaches glibly, declaims vigorously, and wipes away the sweat. If on the following day one of those strong and silent men . . . were to visit the parson at his house announcing . . . that he had now resolved to sacrifice his life for the truth—what would the parson say? . . . "Why, merciful Father in heaven! How did such an idea ever occur to you? Travel, divert yourself, take a laxative. . . ."[51]

These extracts not only identify clearly what Kierkegaard thought was wrong with religion in his time (the spirit and gusto had gone out of it), but they also nicely illustrate his sense of humor and skillful use of amusing, off-the-wall commentary to make a serious point.

Kierkegaard's critique of contemporary Christian practice leads into his distinction between "Christendom" and Christianity, developed especially in later works such as *Attack Upon "Christendom."* The former term embraces everything bad he believed Christianity had become: a doctrinal creed presided over by clerics and other officials, organized and institutionalized churches that were (in the case of Denmark at least) part of the political/legal establishment, and something secondary to and "subsumed by" systematic philosophy. In this setting one counted oneself a Christian by virtue of baptism alone. Most important, contrary to what Martin Luther (1483–1546) had argued when initiating the Protestant Reformation, clergy were now inserting themselves as intermediaries between the individual believer and God. Many of these observations retain their bite in the twenty-first century.

Christianity, by contrast, is often referred to by Kierkegaard as the example Jesus set for how we should live, which a Christian must emulate or "appropriate." (His pseudonymous authors sometimes even go so far as to urge, problematically, that there is *no* doctrinal or propositional foundation to Christianity since, as we saw earlier, it is an "existence-communication.")[52] The trouble is that, humans being what they are, the Christian message was bound to be distorted, "owned" by self-appointed, self-important, self-seeking spokespersons, and turned into pious abstraction almost as soon as it was uttered. Kierkegaard is particularly harsh on academics for the role they have played in this process:

> What nonsense it is . . . that instead of following Christ or the Apostles and suffering as they suffered, one should become a professor—of what? Why, of the fact that Christ was crucified and the Apostles scourged. If only at Golgotha [Calvary hill, or "Place of the Skull," outside Jerusalem, where Jesus was crucified] there had been a professor at hand who had installed himself at once as professor . . . of theology?[53]

The implication is that crafty entrepreneurs realize there's money and power to be had in re-creating oneself as the mouthpiece of a new (or even not-so-new) religion. Like today's TV evangelists, these hustlers are what Kierkegaard described wonderfully well as "town criers of inwardness."[54]

Kierkegaard sought to illuminate what Christianity really is throughout his later writings.[55] This is not our concern because I want the focus here to remain on what he had to teach in the widest sense. In this connection, it is noteworthy that in one of his last writings Kierkegaard spoke out for honesty, stating that he could even support a *revolt against Christianity* by his contemporaries if it were undertaken in a spirit of truthfulness: "strange as it might seem, I go along with it, because I want honesty. Wherever there is honesty, I am able to go along with it; an honest rebellion against Christianity can be made only if one honestly acknowledges what Christianity is and how one relates oneself to it."[56] However, one shouldn't jump to the conclusion that it is a matter of little significance after all whether one is a Christian, for as we see here, the catch is that one must have understood Christianity and honestly examined one's relationship to it. Will there then be anyone left who can rebel against it—or who even wishes to do so?

SPHERES OF EXISTENCE

One of Kierkegaard's best known positions concerns what is usually called the "stages of existence"—the aesthetic, ethical, and religious forms of life—but which doctrine, for reasons I shall explain, is better chracterized as the "spheres of existence." This subject is covered in *Either/Or, Stages on Life's Way, Repetition,* and *Eighteen Upbuilding Discourses,* supplemented by the fuller discussions of the religious life in *Fear and Trembling, Concluding Unscientific Postscript, Sickness Unto Death,* and *Christian Discourses.*

The aesthetic sphere of existence signifies a life governed by egocentric hedonism (pleasure seeking) and generally short-term goals. It shuns commitments, not really understanding them but nonetheless viewing them as a threat to its self-defined outer limits. Its paradigm is the legendary figure of Don Juan, immortalized in poetry by Byron; in music by Mozart (as "Don Giovanni"), Liszt, and Richard Strauss; and in theater by Molière, Dumas, and Shaw. Don Juan is usually portrayed as a sexual predator, bent on conquest and self-gratification without obligation. He is an egoist; that is, one who holds the view that only one's own welfare and interests count for anything—all else is but a means to this end. (The egoist generally concedes that others also believe the same about themselves.) Egoism of this stripe can be expressed in short-term objectives but an "enlightened" egoist perceives that not all short-term projects will go her or his way and that it is therefore smarter sometimes to defer gratification *now* in exchange for a greater reward *later on.*

Given the self-restriction of the egoist's outlook, many philosophers would agree with Kierkegaard that it lacks any ethical content at all, since other people are not taken seriously (as ends in themselves) within the egoist's framework but only (if at all) within their own. Kierkegaard's prototypical egoist is Johannes the Seducer in *Either/Or* (reappearing in *Stages on Life's Way*), whose diary lays out the strategies used to forward his efforts and the results attained. Leading up to the diary is a series of writings by "A" (the aesthete, who may or may not be Johannes himself), which define the aesthetic mindset.

"A" tells us that "the art of recollecting and forgetting will also prevent a person from foundering in any particular relationship in life—and assures him complete suspension."[57] What is the nature of this "complete suspension"? Well, of course, it is the liberty or license to do exactly what one wants, to look after oneself exclusively. Notice here, too, the reference to "forgetting," which calls to mind the problem, discussed earlier, of forgetting what it means to exist. The aesthete is mired in this state of selfhood. "A" also cautions against the entanglements of friendship, marriage, and any contractual business arrangements. This is because each of these brings with it certain obligations that, from this narrow perspective, are seen merely as inhibiting the scope of one's selfish pursuits. We learn a great deal as well about "A's" dedication to music, especially to Mozart's opera *Don Giovanni*.

What is important to understand about the aesthetic mode of existence is its limitations. Kierkegaard does not mean to tell us that sensuous and sensual experience and appreciation of the arts is inferior, wrong, or bad; they have their place in the whole picture of human life and are valuable dimensions of it. But (a) they can be overemphasized at the expense of other dimensions and (b) one may indulge in them with a one-sided (egoistic) attitude. The aesthetic life, as we have seen, is amoral; it shuns any ties to others because it does not comprehend or appreciate such commitments. As Johannes writes in his diary, "The ethical is just as boring in scholarship as in life. What a difference! Under the esthetic sky, everything is buoyant, beautiful, transient; when ethics arrives on the scene, then everything becomes harsh, angular, infinitely boring."[58] Aesthetic existence is consumed with the desire to perpetuate happy moments, embellishing and renewing them as necessary in order to keep the illusion of independent selfhood alive. Thus, the aesthete tries to "make the actual possible," in other words, to transform the pleasure of the instant into something of enduring and monumental (or eternal) significance. (As "A" states, "Pleasure disappoints; possibility does not.")[59] This is the objective both of the seducer's manipulations, which seek to secure physical pleasure, and of the artist's creative works, insofar as they aim at bestowing on what is temporal a timeless significance, and/or directing consciousness away from everyday concerns.

The aesthetic life, then, is dreamlike, drifting, and self-centered, governed as it is by indulgence in the search for the immediate satisfactions provided by pleasure and beauty. In its more sophisticated, reflective form, it is motivated by the pursuit of "the interesting" and flight from boredom. This sphere of existence, however, has internal weaknesses that eventually lead to feelings of disillusionment and despair. (Despair, as we learn in *Sickness Unto Death*, is a warning sign that the self's potential is not being tended to or is corrupted by an unwillingness to be a self in the fullest sense, even to defiance of this possibility. But despair can also exist at the unconscious level, where it cannot be addressed at all. Since despair is defined as the absence of faith, aesthetic and even ethical existence is a form of despair.) The aesthete comes to the point at which happiness is elusive; even the frequent repetition of the pleasurable moment (which Kierkegaard refers to as the "rotation of crops"), embellished or deferred gratification, or the transformation of reality by thought (as in systematic philosophy) fail to achieve a stable place in the world for her or him. This is because other sides of the self—ethical and religious—are being neglected and suppressed. The aesthete falls victim to what's known as the "hedonistic fallacy": the more one seeks pleasure or happiness directly, the more one misses the target. True contentment only comes by indirect pursuits (for instance, work or study or helping others who are less fortunate bring personal rewards, which result from the main activity).

With an awareness of its own shortcomings, aesthetic existence may break down or, to put it better, yield to a larger framework: the ethical. This is the sphere in which obligation enters into one's life calculations and the welfare and interests of others take on an equal significance. It is also the sphere in which one becomes accountable to society for one's actions. Importantly, the ethical does not cancel out the aesthetic, which, as already noted, represents a valuable part of the human potential. The aesthetic is "reborn" in the ethical, in a sense—for example, in the erotic side of marriage, which is simultaneously both a binding relationship and a new opportunity for sensuous self-expression. Kierkegaard's exemplar for the ethical sphere is Judge William (or "B") in *Either/Or*. Judge William stands for the life lived according to uncompromising principles of conduct and truth. Therefore, he represents the transcendence of pure self-interest toward acceptance of community values, standards, and ideals.

The ethical individual replaces the push and pull of immediate desires and impulses by choices that have more meaning and stability within a matrix of socially-endorsed beliefs, rules, and guidelines. Ethical choice posits a new realm of decision, involving the contrast between good and bad/evil actions, where these adjectives point to something beyond mere self-interest and, hence, such choice opens up new possibilities for self-making. As Judge William maintains, "This self has not existed before, because it came into existence through the choice, and yet it has existed. . . . [T]hat which is chosen does not exist and comes into existence through the choice—and that which is chosen exists; otherwise it was not a choice. . . . [B]ut I do not create myself—I choose myself."[60] In other words, the potential to be an ethical self is present, lying dormant within the aesthetic self, but it can only become active and flourish if one wills this to happen.

The fundamental either/or choice, then, is between the aesthetic and the ethical ways of living. Judge William asserts that: "the person who lives esthetically does not choose,"[61] for it is only with entry into the ethical sphere that the tasks of life begin to be treated seriously, and the potential for self-realization is disclosed. An important threshold has been crossed. Well, if the ethical represents this robust extension of self-hood, why then do we need to look further for a still more complete account of what it is to be human? This question is especially perplexing when we consider that at least one of Kierkegaard's texts tells us: "The ethical is and remains the highest task assigned to every human being"; and "the real subject is the ethically existing subject."[62] There are several possible responses to the question just posed, but let us first examine the short quotations that followed it. If we bear in mind the either/or choice we've been discussing, then it will become clear that in order to affirm and consolidate one's status as a subject in existence, one must advance into the ethical sphere in the way suggested (that is, by positing it and choosing oneself within it). Hence, to be a "real subject" is to have matured at least to this degree. "Real" does not yet mean "fully actualized," but the ethical individual is on the right track in a way that the aesthetic person is not. Once again, a fork in the road has been reached.

But there are problems. First, Kierkegaard, like some other thinkers, sees the need for an ultimate grounding for moral principles in order to avoid relativism (the view that what a particular society approves and disapproves is all there is to morality). Often, this "absolute" ground is thought to be God's commands. Second, there are conflicts between different social obligations, and between one's present state-of-self and the ideal, with no apparent way to resolve them. Third, and closely related to the second point, interpretation (that is, a personal perspective) is arguably always needed in order to ascertain how and which general moral rules and principles (if any) apply to one's own case. Fourth, there is a serious tension between asserting one's individuality and immersing oneself in the universal demands of the ethical standpoint. Fifth, there are exceptional situations that evidently are not covered by any reasonable code of conduct. Sixth, Kierkegaard believes that Socrates' outlook (in short, pagan or secular ethics) treats wrongdoing as the result of ignorance, omitting the important category of *sin* (deliberate defiance, in the sight of God, of what one knows one ought to do). Consequently, a "higher" or more embracing view of humanity must supplant the ethical. This will amount to a further either/or choice.

The stage is now set for the religious sphere of existence, the individual's ultimate destination. As might be expected, the religious life combines elements of the aesthetic and the ethical, but it radically departs from them as well. In *Fear and Trembling*, pseudonymous author Johannes de silentio represents himself as another outsider to Christianity. *Fear and Trembling* contains a section titled "Preliminary Expectoration" (or "Preparatory Spitting"), which causes us to note once again how Kierkegaard mocks scholarly treatises. Johannes de silentio states here that "I cannot make the movement of faith, I cannot shut my eyes and plunge confidently into the absurd. . . ."[63] He then goes into the world of imagination, and, like some kind of confessional voyeur hiding behind a bush, shares with us his hope of spotting a "knight of faith," should one pass by:

> Generally, people travel around the world to see rivers and mountains, new stars, colorful birds, freakish fish, preposterous races of mankind; they indulge in the brutish stupor that gawks at life and thinks it has seen something. That does not occupy me. But if I knew where a knight of faith lived, I would travel on foot to him. . . . I would not leave him for a second, I would watch him every minute to see how he made the movements. . . . I have not found anyone like that; meanwhile, I may very well imagine him. Here he is. The acquaintance is made, I am introduced to him. The instant I first lay eyes on him, I set him apart at once; I jump back, clap my hands, and say half aloud, "Good Lord, is this the man, is this really the one—he looks just like a tax collector!"[64]

This passage is simultaneously fascinating and enormously entertaining. It opens with a satirical comment on how people (in our age no less than in Kierkegaard's) insatiably seek out new thrills in experience—"extreme" this or that—as if needing to escape from the boredom of everyday existence. Johannes, however, is really no better, in his one-dimensional obsession with spying on the religious life and remaining otherwise uninvolved. Then we learn that the knight of faith, objectively observed, appears just like anyone else (as ordinary as a tax collector); *his faith is undetectable because it is part of his inwardness or subjectivity.*

But Johannes doesn't give up easily: "I move a little closer to him, watch his slightest movement to see if it reveals a bit of heterogeneous optical telegraphy from the infinite, a glance, a facial expression, a gesture, a sadness, a smile. . . . No!" Consistent with the idea that the contents of one's inner life cannot be communicated, nothing is revealed. Faith remains elusive. Other observations Johannes makes are that the subject of his curiosity "belongs entirely to the world,"[65] walking, eating, dressing, working, going to church, chatting with people, enjoying recreation, inspiring others with his optimism—in short, living with spirit, engagement, and appreciation for the world and the people around him. There is a Zen saying, "Before enlightenment: cooking dinner, washing dishes. After enlightenment: cooking dinner, washing dishes." The point is that after the struggle for a higher state of consciousness is over, one's basic needs remain unchanged;

KIERKEGAARDIAN PIG TRYING TO UNDERSTAND ABRAHAM

and the world is the same, but experienced afresh. Now we can see that the religious individual, in Kierkegaard's idealized portrait, does not cancel out the aesthetic and ethical aspects of her- or himself but rather incorporates them almost seamlessly into this broader form of life.

So it appears that faith is what differentiates the religious individual from others. We will take a closer look at faith in the next section; for now, we'll concentrate a bit more on understanding the religious sphere. Kierkegaard evidently believes that most humans dwell in the aesthetic sphere or at most in the aesthetic and ethical spheres; and he often expressed doubts about his own ability to master the demands of faith. This suggests a second, more advanced perspective on the either/or of life: Either one remains in the aesthetic/ethical or one enters the religious sphere.

A religious person encounters the awesome task of selfhood: To choose her- or himself before God, to express her or his full human potential, venturing forth into the unknown future, trusting in the outcome. This is the art of learning to accept the burden of freedom without any guarantees, and in spite of the dread or anxiety that accompanies its acceptance. Obviously, there will always be the temptation to withdraw from the religious way or to backslide into the more comfortable aesthetic/ethical way of existing. In *Fear and Trembling*, Kierkegaard's exemplar of the religious individual, the Old Testament figure Abraham, experiences just this dynamic when God asks him to sacrifice his only son, Isaac. According to the ethical perspective, Abraham would be a murderer and would restrain himself. He'd be a "tragic hero" who could expect to receive the sympathy and understanding of the community. But according to the religious outlook, he would "infinitely resign" himself to his situation, "teleologically suspend the ethical," and take the "leap to faith." As a "knight of faith," he would do God's bidding and go about killing his son. Whether Johannes de silentio's interpretation of this tale is defensible, it expresses a symbolic truth, namely, that when one is in a personal and strenuous relationship with God: (a) it would be reassuring to flee into ethical thinking about one's duty to fellow humans, for this is capable of being shared and discussed with them; (b) the particular (one's own decision) asserts itself as higher than the universal (what is ethically obligatory, all things being equal); but (c) because of (b), no one else will actually understand what is transpiring. Are there any guidelines for determining *when* one ought to follow God's commands, or indeed, even for deciding whether it *is* really God who who issues the commands? There cannot be, for the very notion of guidelines is one that belongs to the ethical sphere of existence, not the religious. This has often been thought to be one of the most serious weaknesses in writings about religious experience, Kierkegaard's no less than those of other thinkers. But at any rate, we do know that a religious person is out on a limb and has to figure these things out for her- or himself. Simone de Beauvoir insightfully presents the issue as follows:

> Whether the voice comes from a cloud, a church, or a confessor's mouth, the transcendent must always manifest himself through an immanent presence in the world. His transcendence will always escape us. Even in my heart, this order I hear is ambiguous. There lies the source of Abraham's anguish, which Kierkegaard describes in *Fear and Trembling*. Who knows if it's not a question of a temptation of the devil or my pride? Is it really God who is speaking? Who will distinguish the saint from the heretic?[66]

It looks, then, as if we must *either* embrace this central dilemma of religion *or* reject the message it means to convey.

In defense of Kierkegaard, we should note that he makes a distinction in some of his writings between "first ethics" (customary morality) and "second ethics" (morality grounded in Christian faith and deriving its impulse from fellowship or love [*agape*]). Second ethics, unlike first ethics, cannot be teleologically suspended. From these ideas we can infer how ethics can be said to be our "highest task," and we can also better grasp how the ethical is dialectically re-expressed within the religious sphere of existence. There is no doubt that love is a potent force for good, and Kierkegaard explores this theme carefully in *Works of Love*. But whether love alone provides a sufficient basis for more mature levels of ethical decision making and behavior remains open to question.

There are two kinds of religion or "religiousness," considered in *Concluding Unscientific Postscript*. The two types are labeled "Religiousness A" and "Religiousness B." Type A is manifested in any culture and features the belief that religious goals can be accomplished through personal, temporal, mundane efforts. (Socrates is Kierkegaard's exemplar here.) Type B refers to Christianity, which involves acceptance of the concept of sin and the idea of an eternal life mediated by Jesus. Kierkegaard wishes to preserve this distinction in order to mark the departure of Christianity from pagan religion and even from other forms of revealed religion, so that the demands on the religious individual will be starkly delineated and readily identifiable as unique. Clearly, the ideal person of faith possesses the resolve of Abraham, but beyond this the ideal person of faith is also animated by Religiousness B, which is centered on *agape*.

I have maintained that Kierkegaard's three ways of being should be designated as "spheres" rather than "stages" of existence. The reason why will by now be clear: They are *dialectically related* in that they overleap each other in turn but also absorb and re-express elements of the preceding life forms with greater richness and fullness. We may represent these spheres as concentric domains, as in the diagram below.

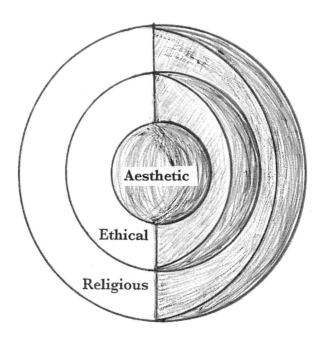

FAITH AND INWARDNESS

Existentialists, we have learned, have a keen eye for what goes on internally, within the inner life of the self. Kierkegaard's notion of inwardness includes those experiences of self that are uncommunicable, or at best indirectly communicable by "double reflection," as discussed earlier. The subjective experience of existing is a primary concern for him; another is that of faith.

In *Concluding Unscientific Postscript*, we encounter the idea of "becoming subjective." This may strike one as puzzling, for how can we become what we already are? If we aren't subjective, then we aren't human to begin with. As if tapping into our worry, Johannes Climacus says, "But now to become what one is . . .—who would waste his time on that?" He then goes on to add that this task is "the most difficult of all, because every human being has a strong natural desire and drive to become something else and more."[67] The seductions of great art, fantasy thinking, systematic philosophy, and political mass movements, for example, all have the effect of directing us away from inwardness, of making us something more than we are. Kierkegaard calls us back from this forgetfulness.

If religiousness represents the deepest dimension of selfhood, then it is to be pursued inwardly, since the self exists in the realm of subjectivity, or rather *is* subjectivity. Furthermore, if Christianity has no objective being,[68] then it must be a subjective phenomenon, if it exists and has any meaning at all. Climacus now tells us: "Behold, faith is indeed the highest passion of subjectivity";[69] that is, it represents the most difficult decision situation a person can face. It follows that one needs to validate and vitalize Christianity by an act of one's will, one's determination to believe, in the face of "objective uncertainty" (lack of proof). This is a deepening of one's subjectivity—in effect, its becoming what it has the potential to be. Objective uncertainty is the doorway to faith. As Swedish philosopher Staffan Carlshamre observes: "Kierkegaard is not a naïve Christian. He lives in an age in which atheism is a possibility. He lives in the question, 'Is there a God?' . . . You might say that Kierkegaard creates God by his own decision rather than the other way around. . . . [His imperative is] 'make God exist by your free decision,' in a way."[70] (Those who have read chapter 2 will perhaps appreciate the resonance between this thought and those of Pascal and Fichte.) The person of faith is a person of daring, who stakes a claim in uncharted lands. She or he lives in a crisis condition, for where there is no possibility of objective truth there is likewise no possibility of closure or finality. The issues that confront faith remain open, just as one's individual life remains always open to new developments.

Kierkegaard, through his subauthors, certainly dramatizes this process to an extreme and intentionally disconcerting degree. Christianity requires plunging into what is absurd: "that the eternal truth has come into existence in time" in the person of Jesus; and to make matters worse, "the absurd is precisely the object of faith and only that can be believed."[71] (See the box, "A Kierkegaardian Dialogue," earlier in this chapter.) Other vocabulary used to describe the absurd (in *Concluding Unscientific Postscript*) includes: "paradox," "contradiction," "offense," "foolishness," "the improbable." Let's focus on "paradox" for a moment. One meaning of "paradox," and the one that I think is most relevant to Kierkegaard's project of describing faith, is "a seemingly contradictory statement that may nonetheless be true."[72] From the standpoint of objectivity (reason and evidence), this is how Christian belief appears. Does faith (subjectivity) resolve the paradox? It is probably too strong a claim to say that it does—because Kierkegaard wants to portray the Christian life as a response to our existen-

KIERKEGAARDIAN PIG DEMONSTRATING
A LEAP OF FAITH

Reprinted by kind permission of James C. Taylor.

tial placement that reinforces the idea of life as a striving toward wholeness, where the process itself, not the end result, is what counts. This is why Johannes Climacus urges that "becoming subjective should give a person plenty to do as long as he lives; . . . the task of life would last as long as life lasts, that is, the task of living. . . . [T]he task is precisely that the task will be enough."[73] In other words, the task of living is never finished, since self-making is constant becoming. Neither the absurd nor one's future can be "mediated" (conceptually interpreted and thus "dealt with") by thought or knowledge, but must be met with courage and resourcefulness. The role of faith in all this is both to keep the absurd in suspension and at the same time to give the religious individual the power to believe and act accordingly; she or he lives by (and with) the absurd.

Returning to the subject of paradox, Julia Watkin makes the interesting observation that "by burdening the intellect with something impossible, Kierkegaard, like the Zen master, drives the believer away from an intellectual preoccupation with Christianity."[74] What he drives the believer *toward* is less clear, for it is the identifying feature of inwardness that it cannot be laid out in a formula or described in words but only hinted at or pointed to. "Philosophy is perfectly right," Kierkegaard maintains, "in saying that life must be understood backward. But then one forgets . . . that it must be lived forward";[75] that is, into the future and without any firm guidelines for success. Just as the student of Zen must work through the paradoxes she or he confronts, so must each of us face and deal with the paradoxes of life. If Kierkegaard is to remain consistent, however, it would seem he must allow that there is no single way to live Christianly that all are obliged to follow.

AFTERWORD: FAITH'S OWN PARADOXES

If faith does not resolve the absurd, then why should we be believers? What is the reward we can expect? Or is this the wrong question to be asking, since it seems very self-centered and materialistic? Maybe so, yet in an important sense, although Kierkegaard has successfully explained what we should and shouldn't expect from faith, perhaps he has failed to persuade us why we should have it in the first place. In addition, he has not apparently even entertained, much less adequately countered, other religions' calls to faith of different sorts. If Christianity is such that we are forced to take up a stance in regard to it, then isn't this also true of Judaism, Buddhism, and other creeds—especially Islam, which, being historically post–New Testament and recognizing Jesus as a messenger of God (but not God himself), can't be sidelined as unilluminated by Christianity in the same way as certain other faiths? Is Christianity, then, truly the only choice?

Another issue concerns faith and fanaticism. If the deliverances of faith are immune to objective scrutiny, then (as queried earlier) how do we ever know that it is God who is speaking to us? And on what basis can we rest any kind of critique of, or opposition to, those who maintain they have a mission to destroy us and our values in the name of their religion, or simply because a voice in their heads tells them so?

Finally, what about the problem of systemic conflict between religious and ethical viewpoints? It is an age-old puzzle how to give content to ethical precepts beyond their being commanded by a deity, even a loving one. What if, over time, that divine spirit changes her/his/its mind or (for example, in another religion) commands something different? Could ethical truth have an even more fundamental ground than what some people choose to call "the word of God" or "divine love"?

Kierkegaard's response to these important questions, it has to be said, is ambiguous, selective, and for the most part virtually nonexistent. It would be wrong, I think, to suppose that he wasn't aware of them or didn't think them worthy of comment. A better conclusion might be that insofar as he was arguing for Christianity, he was addressing Christians—of the nominal variety that (in his view) needed to be galvanized into taking their faith seriously—and that he chose to do so strictly on the existential level. This is why Johannes Climacus claims, both provocatively and para-doxically, that "in short: *it is easier to become a Christian if I am not a Christian than to become a Christian if I am one. . . .*"[76] Perhaps, too, Kierkegaard wanted us to take on the most difficult questions of faith for ourselves.

The argument over whether Christianity (or any other faith) should be approached objectively, subjectively, or both objectively and subjec-tively will doubtless go on forever. For many, an intellectual grasp and affirmation of what they believe is as important as any other sort. Indeed, some of the greatest minds in the Christian tradition, for example, St. Anselm (c. 1033–1109) and St. Thomas Aquinas (c. 1225–1274) wrestled with the problem of how to rationalize belief. Kierkegaard plainly had a much different agenda, and it is one that provides, for both Christians and non-Christians alike, major food for thought. But it must be said, in the end, that Kierkegaard's own philosophy is objective to an extent, inas-much as he wishes to persuade us of something—if only that we are indi-viduals and that we need to take charge of our own lives.

NOTES

1. This account is taken from Walter Lowrie, *A Short Life of Kierkegaard* (Garden City, NY: Doubleday Anchor Books, 1961), pp. 210–13.

2. Søren Kierkegaard, *Concluding Unscientific Postscript*, trans. David F. Swenson and Walter Lowrie (Princeton, NJ: Princeton University Press, for Amer-ican-Scandinavian Foundation, 1941), p. 166 (compare also p. 495).

3. Søren Kierkegaard, *The Sickness Unto Death: A Christian Psychological Exposi-tion for Upbuilding and Awakening*, ed. and trans. Howard V. Hong and Edna H. Hong (Princeton, NJ: Princeton University Press, 1980), pp. 32–33.

4. Kierkegaard, "A First and Last Explanation," in *Concluding Unscientific Post-script to "Philosophgical Fragments*," trans. Howard V. Hong and Edna H. Hong (Princeton, NJ: Princeton University Press, 1992), 1:625–30; also rendered as "A First and Last Declaration" by Swenson and Lowrie in their translation of this work and left unpaginated at the end, as Kierkegaard had stipulated.

5. See Alastair McKinnon, ed., *Kierkegaard—Resources and Results* (Waterloo, ON: Wilfrid Laurier University Press, 2000).

6. D. H. Lawrence, "The Spirit of Place," in D. H. Lawrence, *Studies in Classic American Literature* (Garden City, NY: Doubleday, 1959), chap. 1.

7. Søren Kierkegaard, *The Point of View for My Work as an Author*, ed. and trans. Howard V. Hong and Edna H. Hong (Princeton, NJ: Princeton University Press, 1998), p. 54.

8. Ibid., p. 43.

9. Søren Kierkegaard, *Concluding Unscientific Postscript*, trans. Hong and Hong, 2:110.

10. Ibid., 2:113.

11. Kierkegaard seems somewhat naïve about this prospect, it must be admitted; for the authorship of these pseudonymous works became the buzz of Danish literati, just as he might have been able to predict.

12. Kierkegaard, *Concluding Unscientific Postscript*, trans. Hong and Hong, 1:45.

13. Ibid., pp. 232, 288.

14. Kierkegaard, *Journals and Papers*, cited by Howard A. Johnson, "Kierkegaard and the Church: A Supplement to the Translator's Introduction," in Søren Kierkegaard, *Attack Upon "Christendom,"* trans. Walter Lowrie (Princeton, NJ: Princeton University Press, 1968), p. xxvi.

15. Kierkegaard, *Concluding Unscientific Postscript*, trans. Hong and Hong, vol. I, pp. 625–30.

16. Søren Kierkegaard, *Journals*, ed. and trans. Alexander Dru (London: Geoffrey Cumberlege/Oxford University Press, 1938), entry for May 12, 1839, no. 275, pp. 72–73.

17. John Laird, "Review of *Either/Or*, by S. Kierkegaard," *Mind* 55 (1946): 179.

18. Kierkegaard, *Concluding Unscientific Postscript*, trans. Hong and Hong, 1:124.

19. Kierkegaard, *Sickness Unto Death*, pp. 43–44.

20. Kierkegaard, *Concluding Unscientific Postscript*, trans. Hong and Hong, 1:120 (emphasis added). The either/or theme—choice between two mutually exclusive alternatives—frequently recurs in Kierkegaard's works.

21. See, for example, Thich Nhat Hanh, *Peace Is Every Step: The Path of Mindfulness in Everyday Life* (New York: Bantam, 1991), pt. 1; Stephen Batchelor, "Path," in *Buddhism without Beliefs: A Contemporary Guide to Awakening* (New York: Riverhead, 1997).

22. Kierkegaard, *Concluding Unscientific Postscript*, trans. Hong and Hong, 1:131.

23. Kierkegaard, *Concluding Unscientific Postscript*, trans. Swenson and Lowrie, p. 112.

24. Kierkegaard, *Concluding Unscientific Postscript*, trans. Hong and Hong, 1:109.

25. Exact source of quotation unknown.

26. Kierkegaard, *Journals*, ed. and trans. Dru, 1841, no. 354, p. 89.

27. Kierkegaard, *Concluding Unscientific Postscript*, trans. Hong and Hong, 1:92.

28. For example, *The Concept of Dread* and *The Sickness Unto Death*.

29. Kierkegaard, *Sickness Unto Death*, "Despair as Defined by Possibility/ Necessity," pt. 1, sec. C, A, b.

30. Ibid., pp. 13–14.

31. Søren Kierkegaard, *Journals and Papers*, ed. and trans. Howard V. Hong and Edna H. Hong, assisted by Gregor Malantschuk (Bloomington: Indiana University Press, 1967–78), 1:331.

32. Kierkegaard, *Concluding Unscientific Postscript*, trans. Hong and Hong, 1:379–80.

33. Kierkegaard, *Journals*, ed. and trans. Dru, August 1, 1835, no. 22, p. 15 (emphasis in original).

34. Kierkegaard, *Concluding Unscientific Postscript*, trans. Hong and Hong, 1:203ff.

35. Ibid., p. 199n.

36. Ibid., p. 199 (emphasis in original).

37. Ibid., p. 203 (emphasis in original).

38. Ibid., pp. 618, 619, 621.

39. Ibid., p. 15.

40. Ibid., pp. 16, 570, 617.

41. Ibid., pp. 33, 38.

42. According to *Concluding Unscientific Postscript*, the systematic thinker gets into this contradiction because she or he plays at being God. (See Hong and Hong trans., 1:119.)

43. Ibid., 1:200.

44. Ibid., 1:323.

45. See Marshall McLuhan, *Understanding Media: The Extensions of Man* (New York: McGraw-Hill, 1964).

46. "Historical Introduction," in Søren Kierkegaard, *Two Ages: The Age of Revolution and The Present Age, A Literary Review*, ed. and trans. Howard V. Hong and Edna H. Hong (Princeton, NJ: Princeton University Press, 1978), p. ix.

47. Ibid., p. 105.

48. Kierkegaard, *Sickness Unto Death*, pp. 13, 35.

49. Kierkegaard, *Journals*, ed. and trans. Dru, July 14, 1987, no. 150, p. 50.

50. Søren Kierkegaard, "The Religious Situation," *The Fatherland*, March 26, 1855, in Kierkegaard, *Attack Upon "Christendom,"* p. 30.

51. Søren Kierkegaard, *Has a Man the Right to Let Himself Be Put to Death for the Truth?*, trans. Walter Lowrie, cited by Walter Kaufmann, "Introduction," in Kierkegaard, *The Present Age*, p. 17.

52. See Kierkegaard, *Concluding Unscientific Postscript*, trans. Hong and Hong, 1:326.

53. Kierkegaard, Journal entry, 1852–54, cited by Lowrie, *A Short Life of Kierkegaard*, p. 189.

54. Kierkegaard, *Concluding Unscientific Postscript*, trans. Swenson and Lowrie, p. 71; Hong and Hong translate this expression as "barkers of inwardness" (vol. 1, p. 77).

55. For a good recent account, see Sylvia Walsh, *Living Christianly: Kierkegaard's Dialectic of Christian Existence* (University Park, PA: Penn State University Press, 2005).

56. Søren Kierkegaard, "What Do I Want?" in Søren Kierkegaard, *"The Moment" and Late Writings*, ed. and trans. Howard V. Hong and Edna H. Hong (Princeton, NJ: Princeton University Press, 1998), p. 48.

57. Søren Kierkegaard, *Either/Or*, ed. and trans. Howard V. Hong and Edna H. Hong (Princeton, NJ: Princeton University Press, 1987), 1:295.

58. Ibid., p. 367.

59. Ibid., p. 41.

60. Ibid., 2:215.

61. Ibid., p. 168.

62. Kierkegaard, *Concluding Unscientific Postscript*, trans. Hong and Hong, 1:151, 281.

63. Kierkegaard, *Fear and Trembling/Repetition*, ed. and trans. Howard V. Hong and Edna H. Hong (Princeton, NJ: Princeton University Press, 1983), p. 34.

64. Ibid., pp. 38–39.

65. Ibid., p. 39.

66. Simone de Beauvoir, *Pyrrhus and Cineas*, trans. Marybeth Timmerman, in *Simone de Beauvoir: Philosophical Writings*, ed. Margaret A. Simons, with Marybeth Timmerman and Mary Beth Mader (Urbana: University of Illinois Press, 2004), p. 105.

67. Kierkegaard, *Concluding Unscientific Postscript*, trans. Hong and Hong, 1:130.

68. See ibid., pp. 130, 326.

69. Ibid., p. 132.

70. Staffan Carlshamre, Stockholm University, interviewed in *What Is the Meaning of Life?* Magic Lantern Video Collection (educational materials), VHS 433–31–929 (Toronto: Magic Lantern Communications, 1998).

71. Kierkegaard, *Concluding Unscientific Postscript*, trans. Hong and Hong, 1:210, 211.

72. *American Heritage Dictionary of the English Language*, 4th ed. (Boston: Houghton Mifflin, 2000), online version at http://www.bartleby.com/61/.

73. Kierkegaard, *Concluding Unscientific Postscript*, trans. Hong and Hong, 1:163, 165.

74. Julia Watkin, *Historical Dictionary of Kierkegaard's Philosophy*, Historical Dictionaries of Religions, Philosophies, and Movements, no. 33 (Lanham, MD: Scarecrow Press, 2001), p. 189.

75. Kierkegaard, *Journals and Papers*, ed. and trans. Hong and Hong, vol. 1, no. 1030 (cited by Hong and Hong in *Concluding Unscientific Postscript*, 2:187); cf. Kierkegaard, *Journals*, ed. and trans. Dru, April 14, 1838, no. 194, p. 57.

76. Kierkegaard, *Concluding Unscientific Postscript*, trans. Hong and Hong, 1:366 (emphasis in original); cf. p. 591.

QUESTIONS FOR REFLECTION:

1. Does philosophical argument have to be equated with reasoning or does Kierkegaard successfully expand our conception of what can count as an argument?

2. Is the distinction between direct and indirect communication a useful one? What can be directly communicated? What must be indirectly communicated?

3. To say that existence is a source of anxiety is to suggest that anxiety (of a certain kind) is a permanent aspect of the human experience. Is this true?

4. Could objective truths be appropriated in such a way that they become especially meaningful to oneself? What might be some examples of this?

5. Are there subjective truths? What are some examples? Can anyone know these but oneself?

6. Does ethics need to be grounded in religious faith? Can ethics ever be suspended in exceptional circumstances? What might these be?

7. Does Kierkegaard's conception of faith demand too much from us, that is, more effort than most people are able to summon up and sustain? Could the same be said of Jesus, as in the prescriptions to "love thy enemy" or to "turn the other cheek"?

8. Johannes Climacus' idea that one can write a book (such as *Concluding Unscientific Postscript*) and then revoke it is one of several instances in philosophy where a written work is regarded by its author as a "ladder to the truth," which is then discarded when the "truth" is reached. What do you think of this metaphor and how does it apply to Kierkegaard's project?

4

NIETZSCHE

REINVENTING CULTURE

Friedrich Nietzsche (1844–1900), a stability-shattering philosopher and psychologist, changed, through the power of his insight and writing, the way we think about all sorts of things, including values, truth, culture and civilization, and language itself. He has an apocalyptic vision of the possible future for humanity if the nihilism following in the wake of "the death of God" emerges triumphant, and he sets himself the task of defeating this nihilism.

PHILOSOPHIZING WITH A HAMMER

Nietzsche is the bad boy of existentialism. He lashes out at many targets (one may think almost indiscriminately), has a love-hate relationship with famous people and idea systems, ridicules much that has been held sacred or respectfully regarded in the past and present, and generally rants and raves. He is an impassioned, often intemperate thinker: misogynistic, inegalitarian, frequently contemptuous; he has been accused of embracing nihilism, anti-Semitism, and excessive nationalism, and of promoting eugenics and praising war; he has been blamed for inspiring Hitler and he's been seen (by himself and others) as the Antichrist. To say that he is often and badly misunderstood is a gross understatement. He does seem irrational, contradictory, and out of control sometimes, and his overwhelmingly potent prose and imagery destabilize or shatter one's preconceptions—these things cannot be denied. But beneath the surface, Nietzsche serves up a relentless and devastating indictment of Western civilization and its self-destructive impulses. He sounds alarms for the future and offers a vast range of ideas and inspirations for coming to grips with the dilemmas he believes have brought modern culture to a state of imminent collapse. While realizing that serious upheavals lie ahead, he makes a broad-brushed attempt—however incomplete and imprecise—to construct an alternative to chaos.

One of Nietzsche's last works, *Twilight of the Idols,* is subtitled: *or How to Philosophize with a Hammer.* From what he says in his foreword to the work, this is usually interpreted as signalling his intention to verbally smash all that is outmoded, deficient, in a state of decline, or unhealthy— but also to detect "as with a tuning fork" what, if anything, is of lasting value.[1] Nietzsche is the paradigm of an iconoclast; that is, one who attacks cherished beliefs; but he does so, as we shall see later on, in order to clear ground for building a fresh outlook on humanity, and to advance the principles of creative self-fulfilment he believes are most relevant to our condition. In order to understand him better, we will have to examine Nietzsche's stance on many topics. But first, we need to consider how to approach Nietzsche the writer.

READING NIETZSCHE

A good place to begin orienting oneself toward Nietzsche's manner of presentation is his self-evaluations. Some of these, to be sure, must be taken with a grain of salt; it is easy to be put off, for example, by the chapter headings of *Ecce Homo,* a late work in which he reflects on his previous efforts in sections titled: "Why I Am So Wise," "Why I Am So Clever," "Why I Write Such Good Books," and "Why I Am a Destiny." It is likewise easy to be amused and dismissive in the face of his self-dramatization: "I am no man, I am dynamite."[2] There is an argument that Nietzsche wrote from behind many masks,[3] though this is not so obvious as in the case of Kierkegaard. However, if we keep a bit of distance from this kind of posturing, insight can be gained into his strategy and outlook as an author.

The convalescent. One thing to note about Nietzsche is that he was a sickly individual. He suffered from migraines, stomach cramps, vomiting, insomnia, poor vision, and he probably died from either syphilis or brain cancer. He lived and wrote in humble, sometimes freezing boarding houses, where his numerous medications and fevered creative drive kept him going. Most of us would succumb to such immobilizing ailments, but Nietzsche reacted differently: "My specialty was to endure the extremity of pain. . . . Recently my illness has done me the greatest service: it has liberated me, it has restored to me the courage to be myself."[4] Nietzsche has a motto that has become well known: "Whatever does not kill me makes me stronger."[5] He had, quite simply, the extraordinary capacity to endure hardship and transform it into self-mastery and achievement. And we learn something important about Nietzsche, just as he did about himself, from within the depths of his illness: "Looking from the perspective of the sick toward *healthier* concepts and values . . .—in this I have had the longest training, my truest experience. . . . Now I know how, have the know-how, to *reverse perspectives*: the first reason why a 'revaluation of values' is perhaps possible for me alone."[6] Again: "Freedom from resentment and the understanding of the nature of resentment—who knows how very much after all I am indebted to my long illness for these two things?" Nietzsche gives us several insights here into himself and his project: (1) Being a chronically sick person has enabled him to look upon health and well-being in a more meaningful way, from, as it were, an opposite viewpoint. (2) So too, metaphorically or by analogy, he grew able to examine social norms and values that are "sick," in order to see past them to something better, more "healthy." Nietzsche thus becomes (at least by his own reckoning) a surrogate or stand-in figure who suffers and takes up on our behalf the burdens of plumbing the dark depths of the soul and of investigating the rotten foundations of our value system that we may learn from the reports he brings back from his subterranean exploration. In short, he re-enacts within himself the cultural implosion we ourselves are living through, but with a less acute awareness than his. (3) Again referring to the liberating power of illness, he observes that it has released him from unproductive negativity directed toward himself and others, and from bottling up instinctual energy (the process of *ressentiment*, which we shall examine later in this chapter). It has also allowed him to find out what produces these damaging psychological dynamics, how they work, and how they can be overcome in order to re-energize oneself and help do the same for others.

But just because Nietzsche claims to see further than we, on our behalf, we should not think of him as talking down to us or posing as a self-appointed superior being; instead, he says, "I know both sides, for I am both sides. . . . [A]part from the fact that I am a decadent, I am also the reverse of such a creature."[7] In other words, he confesses that he contains within himself the contradiction of both the old and the new, the sick and the healthy, the values of declining civilization (decadence) and the transvalued (or revalued) ideas on which a revitalized civilization might be based. And a key to Nietzsche's appeal (in the two senses of what makes him appealing to us and what his message appeals to in us) is our *own* contradictory nature: we are members of the herd who imbibe old ("sick") values but are at the same time loaded with potential. The optimistic point in all this is that where there is decline and downfall, there is equally hope and the possibility of transcendence, redemption, and renewal.

The psychologist. Nietzsche would also have us recognize him as a psychologist—an intuitive one, of course, not an experimental psychologist such as we have today. And he was much more than just a keen observer; as we shall see, he specialized in deconstructing (taking apart for analysis) the time-honored concepts and explanations that relate to human motivation and action. To characterize Nietzsche in this manner, however, is not to exclude his being a philosopher, linguist, creative writer, and many other things, as well; it is merely to further clarify where he is coming from. He writes, for instance:

> The human soul and its limits, the range of inner human experiences reached so far, the heights, depths, and distances of these experiences, the whole history of the soul *so far* and its as yet unexhausted possibilities—that is the predestined hunting ground for a born psychologist and lover of the "great hunt." But how often he has to say to himself in despair: "One hunter! alas, only a single one! and look at this huge forest, this primeval forest!"[8]

We can see here that Nietzsche not only styles himself as a psychologist, a prober of the human soul, but he also asserts his uniqueness in this role, as well as the unlimited subject matter—the "unlimited possibilities" that human beings collectively possess that might be tapped into for the betterment of the species and the quality of our lives. Like Kierkegaard, he identifies as being of great importance the question of "how one becomes what one is"[9] (that is, how one actualizes capacities that are latent within oneself). Typically, the powerful language he uses is evident, too, as in comparing the human soul to a "huge, primeval forest," a metaphor that suggests immense richness hidden beneath dense overgrowth, waiting to reward the great exploratory toil needed to disclose it.

The philosopher. So far as Nietzsche considers himself a philosopher, he portrays this vocation as one of fearless experimentation with concepts, ideas, and theories (which he calls the "gay science").

> [Philosophy] always creates the world in its own image; it cannot do otherwise. Philosophy is this tyrannical drive itself, the most spiritual will to power, to the "creation of the world," to the *causa prima* [first cause].

*   *   *

> But the genuine philosopher . . . lives "unphilosophically" and "unwisely," above all *imprudently*, and feels the burden and the duty of a hundred attempts and temptations of life—he risks *himself* constantly, he plays the wicked game—

*   *   *

> A philosopher—is a human being who constantly experiences, sees, hears, suspects, hopes, and dreams extraordinary things. . . .[10]

*   *   *

> How much truth does a spirit *endure*, how much truth does it *dare*?
> More and more that became for me the real measure of value. . . .
> Every attainment, every step forward in knowledge, *follows* from courage, from hardness against oneself, from cleanliness in relation to oneself.[11]

This way of looking at philosophy casts it as a kind of solitary, self-disciplined meditation that almost defies description, owing to its rarity and lack of prescribed methodology and guidelines. It's more like the invention of a new subject of study than being comparable to palaeontology, archaeology, geology, or even global exploration. In common with these, it does stake out previously unknown territory, make discoveries, unearth things, and create new categories of classification. But going beyond them, philosophy not only questions what is normally unquestioned, according to Nietzsche, it also discloses truths and meanings we have sought to suppress or repress for fear of confronting them. It seeks to uncover those aspects of existence and experience that have been omitted from our organized view of the world, ignored, denied, derided, and tabooed. It is inherently *subversive*—aimed at unsettling received opinions, reversing perspectives, offending, and forcing us to re-evaluate all certainties. Each philosopher has sought to be the "unriddler of the universe."[12]

Moreover, philosophers have answered, with singular determination, the call of the "will to truth,"[13] which has been both their strength and their downfall: their strength in that this focuses energies in a way that is admirable and exemplary; their weakness in that they are beguiled by the belief that indisputable results can be discovered and posited by the human mind. They have failed to understand that "life, in spite of ourselves . . . *demands* illusion, it *lives* by illusion. . . ."[14]

Notwithstanding all of these critical efforts to position himself in sharp contrast to the traditions of Western thought, Nietzsche maintains a constant engagement with them, mining them for insights he can use.

The physiologist. Nietzsche claims to possess an "instinct for cleanliness," such that "the inmost parts, the 'entrails' of every soul are physiologically perceived by me—*smelled.*"[15] He praises the Buddha's teachings, likening them not to a religion but to "a kind of *hygiene*"[16] grounded in physiology. He declares that "all prejudices come from the intestines," and that "the German spirit is an indigestion."[17] By these various pronouncements, we may understand him to be saying that beliefs of all sorts have their origin in our instincts—still more, in our most basic bodily processes—by which we orient ourselves toward the world and toward life itself. Depicting himself as a physiologist and sometimes as a "cultural physician"[18] is a metaphorical way of pointing out that philosophy, psychology, and interpretation generally stem from how we are constituted, and that nutrition and health (both literal and figurative) are as important to the mind as they are to the body. Consequently, Nietzsche raises the disturbing question whether any given philosophical outlook or viewpoint expresses a sick or a healthy disposition and, hence, a negation or an affirmation of life. (We will return to this theme in more detail later on.)

The thinker against the grain. Under this heading, we find Nietzsche at his bombastic best. Appealing to those who would identify with him and his reformation of Western thought, he describes this group of compatriots as "free spirits"[19] who are "out of season,"[20] "born guessers of riddles who are . . . posted between today and tomorrow . . . , firstlings and premature births of the coming century,"[21] "homeless in a distinctive and honorable sense," "children of the future," and "conquerors," adding that: "we far prefer to live on mountains, apart, 'untimely'. . . ."[22] Speaking of himself, he is "a philosopher who had no contemporaries, and who did not even wish to have them,"[23] one who was "born posthumously."[24] At a certain level, the meaning of this rhetoric is plain: those who would be critics of the status quo and of conventional ideas are bound to isolate themselves as nonconformists and antiestablishment figures. But at a deeper level, Nietzsche is saying that "we" are the self-selected special ones who see beyond the horizon; "we" not only march to a different drum, but define a vision for humankind that the world is nowhere near ready to receive and enact. "We" are the ones for whom the question "How much truth can a certain mind endure; how much truth can it dare?" was intended. For "we" are the harbingers of things to come, and of how to address the quandaries that the future will bring.

The writer of aphorisms. Nietzsche is thought of by many as an unsystematic thinker, who either couldn't be bothered to organize his ideas systematically or else had such a fertile and feverish mind that he wrote on whatever inspired him at the moment. In line with these perceptions, Walter Kaufmann, one of his leading translators and commentators, described Nietzsche as "not a system-thinker but a problem-thinker."[25] There is some truth in this view, but it also appears that Nietzsche aspired to complete a systematic expression of his philosophy in the work known to us as *The Will to Power*, a collection of notes he left unfinished and unpublished when he died. Be this as it may, he had a distinctive style of writing that casts doubt on the tendency to see him as unsystematic. As Arthur Danto has remarked, Nietzsche "tried to construct a philosophy consistent with the extraordinary openness he felt was available to man, or at least a philosophy that would entail this openness as one of its consequences. In the course of his piecemeal elaborations he touched on most of the problems that have concerned philosophers, and he discussed them interestingly, even profoundly."[26] Danto cautiously concludes, then, that Nietzsche *was* a systematic thinker.

There is no doubt that Nietzsche had considered views on many subjects, even though (like many other philosophers) he sometimes changed his mind and developed his ideas in unpredictable ways, leaving the untidiness of his work for others to anguish over. His style may be classified as "aphoristic" because he frequently writes short numbered paragraphs then moves on, even to topics that aren't related at all to the preceding bit. He also frames many maxims about human behavior and other topics, which are short and pithy, and often puts his points across by means of forceful (seemingly dogmatic) statements or striking rhetorical questions. A good deal of what may be said about Nietzsche's method and style follows from his conception of philosophy as experimental, which we have already encountered above. He writes:

I approach deep problems like cold baths: quickly into them and quickly out again. That one does not get to the depths that way, not deep enough down, is the superstition of those afraid of the water. . . . [D]oes a matter necessarily remain ununderstood and unfathomed merely because it has been touched only in flight, glanced at, in a flash? . . . At least there are truths that are singularly shy and ticklish and cannot be caught except suddenly—that must be *surprised* or left alone.[27]

The idea here is that truth is elusive, possibly revealed only momentarily (as ancient mystics and the French Impressionist painters knew), or discoverable only by the mind that is in some special receptive state. (That Heidegger adopted these ideas will be apparent in chapter 6.) But also, trying to get at the truth "in a flash" keeps one from becoming bogged down by traditional concepts and ways of knowing. As Nietzsche points out elsewhere, "All that philosophers have handled for millennia has been conceptual mummies; nothing actual has escaped from their hands alive."[28] The experimental philosopher who wishes to get beyond the weight of the past must therefore not only see things more clearly and accurately but, in addition, must get to the heart of the matter before outmoded notions dull her or his sensibility. "[M]y ambition," Nietzsche announces, "is to say in ten sentences what everyone else says in a book—what everyone else *does not* say in a book."[29] How often one feels he has succeeded in doing this.

LANGUAGE, ART, AND INTERPRETATION

We can greatly enrich our understanding of Nietzsche by appreciating what he had to say about language and art as privileged ways of laying hold of the world, of transforming experience. It is not just that philosophy (at its best) represents a set of experimental interpretations of the universe—*everyone's* experience and thought is experimental. Nietzsche is thus a pragmatist in the sense that there are no absolute truths, only provisional ones, which we adopt for specific purposes or to fulfil certain needs and abandon when they are no longer productive or useful. The way things are deemed to be is a function of how we collectively come to agree they should be apprehended and appropriated, and we do this first and foremost via language. But here we confront what is quite possibly Nietzsche's most challenging idea of all:

What then is truth? A movable host of metaphors, metonymies, anthropomorphisms: in short a sum of human relations which have been poetically and rhetorically intensified, transferred, and embellished, and which, after long usage, seem to a people to be fixed, canonical, and binding. Truths are illusions which we have forgotten are illusions; they are metaphors that have become worn out and have been drained of sensuous force, coins which have lost their embossing and are now considered as metal and no longer as coins.[30]

So, what is taken for truth, according to this account, is that which has been worked over by language and imagery, and, through common usage, has taken on a life of its own. The vibrancy of the original experience that gave rise to these creations has been submerged in, and replaced by, a currency of lesser value, namely, *ideas* ("the graveyard of perceptions").[31] Ideas suck the life from vivid perceptions, abstracting content from them; language, in effect, poetizes into existence what we are pleased to call "the world," supplying the substance for what is otherwise evanescent and uncertain, namely, sense-experience.

"Here one may certainly admire man," says Nietzsche, "as a mighty genius of construction, who succeeds in piling up an infinitely complicated dome of concepts upon an unstable foundation, and, as it were, on running water."[32] "Reality"—whatever that may be—is like a snapshot of a moving object, which freezes something fluid and flowing into a structure that can be dealt with more readily. We, who are able to do this, are artists, and our act of defining "reality" and "the world" is thus an art form. This also helps explain why Nietzsche remarks elsewhere that "all life is based upon appearance, art, deception, point of view, the necessity of perspective and error," and that "the existence of the world is *justified* only as an aesthetic phenomenon."[33] Without our ability to transform the data provided by sensation and perception into a stable edifice of "knowledge" and "truth," we would be lost in the universe. Perspectives and interpretations are essential, but these are only approximations and pragmatic handles with time-limited utility; hence, they are also "errors." Finally, for one who (like Nietzsche) does not believe in God or a divinely ordained meaning for the universe and for human life within it, any account of the world that provides a rationale for the way things are can be no more than an artistic statement of some kind.

Nietzsche's *perspectivism* follows closely from the above ideas. His classic statement of this doctrine is the following: "'There are only *facts*'— I would say: No, facts is precisely what there is not, only interpretations."[34] Naturally, we have to see *this* as just a statement, not an argument. But the argument is furnished by the sorts of reflections we have been investigating in previous paragraphs, as well as by the pounding and pulverizing of innumerable "facts" and "truths" that occurs throughout Nietzsche's works. As well, there are the various fresh interpretations and perspectives that he tries out on us, and which, he argues, have at least as good a claim (if not a better one) to be taken seriously as those he wants us to reject along with him.

Nietzsche's perspectivism sounds more than a little problematic, for how can there be interpretations without there being *something* (presumably facts) for them to be interpretations *of*? That is, how can there be free-floating interpretations? Did he intend that we should think of interpretations as completely groundless? We will return to this issue in the afterword to the present chapter. But for now, let's give Nietzsche the benefit of the doubt and merely note in passing what he has achieved; for his perspectivism, although a very radical and controversial position, has nonetheless been hugely influential in bringing about postmodern and feminist standpoint theories that emerged in opposition to "objectivist," "absolutist," "detached observer," and similar theories of knowledge, truth, and value. Gone are the days when the ideas remain unchallenged that these forms of information can be established by untainted procedures of reasoning or observation; that some groups have a more privileged vantage-point than others; that truths are timeless, ahistorical, and unaffected by people's socioeconomic situation; and that the knower does not importantly influence what is known. In place of these assumptions, today's dominant proposal seems to be that what we intellectually confront are rival viewpoints (perhaps negotiable, perhaps not), each culture-bound and changeable—much as Nietzsche envisioned them.

If perspectives are all that there are, then what was Nietzsche's own perspective? To a significant extent, this question has already been answered, as everything considered so far forms part of his particular outlook. But, of course, many other aspects of his perspective still remain to be examined.

THE DEATH OF GOD

Probably Nietzsche's most famous utterance is that "God is dead." But what does he mean by this? We have to understand the slogan both literally and figuratively. Literally, Nietzsche is saying that not the person God, but the idea of God, was once a vibrant and a powerful force in ordering people's lives and the cultural institutions that guide us. For the ancient Hebrews and early Christians, for example, this was true. Over the centuries and for various reasons, however, the idea of God was drained of its creative content and transformed into a negative and inhibiting ideology. People may go through the motions of religious faith and observance; they may even claim to have experienced the reality of divine presence; but as a crucial nourishing element of culture, God's days are over, so to speak.

Figuratively, what God symbolically stands for is a cultural relic, even though it still holds sway over us to a large extent. An inherent purpose in all things, justice in the universe, reward or punishment in the afterlife, the ability to be forgiven by a higher being, a father-figure presiding over every aspect of our lives, an all-wise, all-seeing, all-good center of reference that will make things come out right—every one of these and similar notions are bogus. God and all his attributes are creations of ours, projected onto the cosmos, pretended and reified into existence by us.

What is negative about religion—especially Christianity—is the way its original impulse has been coopted by a priestly caste and distorted to suit their interests. Nietzsche, like Kierkegaard, believes that religious functionaries have corrupted and taken over Christianity; but in addition, Nietzsche thinks they have made it into a creed for the world-weary, oppressed, and weak at heart, who can then be led, kept under control, and dispossessed, but made to feel worthy even though unworthy. He writes:

> Christianity . . . turned to every kind of man who was disinherited by life, it had its allies everywhere. At the bottom of Christianity is the rancor of the sick, instinct directed *against* the healthy, *against* health itself. . . .
>
> *God on the cross*—are the horrible secret thoughts behind this symbol not understood yet? All that suffers, all that is nailed to the cross, is *divine*. All of us are nailed to the cross, consequently *we* are divine. We alone are divine. Christianity was a victory, a nobler outlook perished of it—Christianity has been the greatest misfortune of mankind so far.[35]

In short, Christianity (as it has been doctrinally developed) celebrates failure, impoverishment of spirit, pity, self-pity, and self-negation. Nietzsche construes pity as a condescending attitude, hence (unlike compassion) it falsely puffs up the giver and patronizes the receiver; and self-pity then becomes an expression of self-loathing.

For Nietzsche, then, Christianity is the Big Lie that Western civilization has lived by for so many centuries and must be freed from so that new, life-affirming values can come to the fore. It may be argued that we were already beginning to be free in this sense in an age such as Nietzsche's, when freedom of religion and of nonbelief were well established. But in his view, a crisis still had to be precipitated in order to help the demise of Christianity along to its completion, and he viewed himself as the one to do it.

The message that God is dead is delivered, in characteristic Nietzschean fashion, by a prophet who is ahead of his time, and is therefore taken by those around him to be a madman and treated with scornful laughter. But in this parable, the "madman" has the final word:

> The madman jumped into their midst and pierced them with his eyes.
> "Whither is God?" he cried; "I will tell you. *We have killed him*—you and I. But how did we do this? How could we drink up the sea?
> Who gave us the sponge to wipe away the entire horizon? . . . Is there still any up or down? Are we not straying as through an infinite nothing? . . .
> How shall we comfort ourselves, the murderers of all murderers? . . . Must we ourselves not become gods simply to appear worthy of [this deed]? . . ."
> At last he threw his lantern on the ground. . . . "I have come too early," he said then. . . . This tremendous event is still on its way, still wandering; it has not yet reached the ears of men."[36]

Here we have the theme that humans are responsible for the death of God, which is a cataclysmic event, but totally inevitable, according to Nietzsche, since religious outlooks remain fertile and inspiring only for a limited era of history.[37] But now we are cast adrift in a terrifying value vacuum; we must rise to the occasion, take charge, see this as an opportunity to free ourselves from an outmoded belief system, to re-define ourselves, and to invent new values.

In order to understand exactly why Nietzsche thought of the death of God as such a monumental event and crossroad for human culture, we need merely to reflect on the following remark: "One interpretation [of existence] has collapsed; but because it was considered *the* interpretation it now seems as if there were no meaning at all in existence, as if everything were in vain."[38] "One interpretation," of course, refers to Christianity, and Nietzsche is telling us here that those who have put all their eggs in this one basket, so to speak, now find that the basket is empty and there is nothing to replace the eggs that have vanished. But the subtext is that this was, after all, only *one* of many possible interpretations and thus, painful though it will be to discover another, the job can nevertheless be done. The death of God problem, then, can be summarized as follows:

God exists	God is dead	How did God die?	Now what?
We created him. He vitalized culture.	He ceased to exercise a unifying energizing influence on us, on culture.	We killed him (inadvertently, unconsciously).	We are set free (free *from* what? free *for* what?). We must take over, move in a new direction, create new values.

We should not leave this topic without noting once again Nietzsche's ambivalent relationship with Christianity. Although he identifies Christianity with negativism, world weariness, defeatism, hatred of life, revenge, and death symbolism ("Christianity is a metaphysics of the hangman"[39]), nevertheless, like Kierkegaard, he thinks he can somehow overleap the centuries to connect with the unadulterated message of Jesus, who then becomes an exceptional figure worthy of veneration. For example, Nietzsche comments that "in reality there has been only one Christian, and he died on the Cross"[40]; as well, when casting about for a model of the overman (the superior being that is to replace humans in the future), he envisions "the Roman Caesar with Christ's soul."[41]

Many have been offended by Nietzsche's caricature of Christianity (not to mention other religions) and have difficulty reading him for this reason. But a more constructive and personally beneficial response is to realize that he was *aiming to offend in order to goad readers into thinking for themselves.* And it is best to read him in the spirit with which one should try reading all philosophy—as a challenge to one's fundamental beliefs that has a point to make; a response to this challenge can help clarify and even strengthen one's beliefs. In any event, it may be that Nietzsche hasn't had the last word on this topic, as this piece of contemporary graffiti indicates:

> **God is dead.** —*Nietzsche*
> **Nietzsche is dead.** —*God*

NIHILISM

As I've mentioned previously, Nietzsche is sometimes taken to be a nihilist. It would be more accurate, however, to describe him as a *provisional nihilist;* that is, as one who adopts nihilism initially, using it "actively" for a specific purpose, but with the intent of passing beyond it later on. In order to understand how this works we have to look first at the meaning of "nihilism." Nihilism applies both to what we believe we know and what we value. Thus, a suitable short definition of nihilism features it as the view that no knowledge claim or value claim has any truth, objective validity, or rational justification. Still more briefly, nothing is true of the world or of reality in general and nothing has any value, nor is any activity worthwhile. A dismal doctrine, to be sure, and it is far from clear that any philosopher ever held this view, or indeed that *anyone* ever has, save for some unfortunate, deeply depressed or mentally ill individuals. (See appendix F, "Nihilism.") Yet it remains an important reference point of sorts, if only because some thinkers (like Nietzsche) have been accused of nihilism and because Nietzsche, in particular, used it as a heuristic tool (i.e., as a device to further investigation).

In the preceding section, I cited Nietzsche's speculations on the fearsome consequences of the death of God; the implication of his remarks is that without God (we suppose), there is no meaning or value in existence. Because of this belief of ours, nihilism threatens to take over and drive us to despair and to incapacitate us. But Nietzsche urges that we need not accept this outcome: we can seize the day and become creative in response to this great "event." This, in itself, shows that he is not a nihilist. But I have classified him as a provisional nihilist. This is because his "philosophising with a hammer" is a policy of smashing what he thinks is decadent in order to clear a space for a new order (of ideas, self-consciousness, social relations, etc.) to be constructed. The motto of this "hammer" is the following: "'what is falling, we should still push. Everything today falls and decays: who would check it? . . . And he whom you cannot teach to fly, teach to fall faster!'"[42] The best thing, Nietzsche contends, is to help hasten the end of the old order and its tyranny over us, to push aside those who are part of the problem, not part of the solution, and to concentrate on ushering in the new.

In order to appreciate Nietzsche's attitude toward nihilism fully we need to see that for him it's not just that the demise of Christianity ushers in a nihilistic age; in addition, Christianity *itself* is deeply nihilistic. Donald Crosby expresses this point well, as follows: "Christianity had stripped the world of immanent [or internal] meaning—thus containing in itself the seeds of the most thoroughgoing nihilism—by insisting on the necessity for a transcendent [otherworldly] ground of truths and values, and focusing most of its attention on attainment of a paradise beyond the grave where the trials and sorrows of earthly existence would be redeemed."[43] Thus, the passing of Christianity doesn't need to be lamented so much as celebrated, and any vestiges of it must be stamped out once and for all.

One further reference to nihilism clinches the argument that Nietzsche's use of it was provisional. This is a passage near the beginning of his best-known book, *Thus Spoke Zarathustra*, in which he discusses "three metamorphoses of the spirit": the camel, the lion, and the child.[44] This is an allegory delivered by "Zarathustra" (another name for the ancient spiritual leader Zoroaster), who is Nietzsche's alter ego/fictitious mentor. In it, Zarathustra enjoins readers who would help forge the future to follow a certain path. First, one should be like the camel, the beast of burden who takes up the heaviest of loads. This seems to imply that one needs to master the knowledge and values of the past and also toughen oneself by enduring various forms of hardship. Second, one should be like the lion, who is self-affirming and destructive of the old values that block the free exercise of creativity that aims to revalue values. Third, one must become like a child, who represents "'innocence and forgetting, a new beginning, a game, a self-propelled wheel, a first movement, a sacred "Yes" [to life]. . . .'" (The parallel here with Jesus' exhortation that those who would follow his way must be reborn is striking, in spite of Nietzsche's anti-Christian sentiments.)[45] Thus, the lion, who embodies nihilism, must be surpassed in order for true creativity of the spirit to flourish. As Zarathustra pronounces later in the same book, "'And he who has to be a creator in good and evil, truly, has first to be a destroyer and break values. Thus the greatest evil belongs with the greatest good: this, however, is the creative good.'"[46]

WILL TO POWER

An early and lasting influence on Nietzsche's ideas was the philosophy of Schopenhauer. Schopenhauer, as we saw in chapter 2, proposed that all phenomena of the world were animated by an underlying "will to live," and that life is what organisms strive above all to preserve. Nietzsche adopted the voluntaristic premise that the universe is more an expression of will than of reason, but he departed from Schopenhauer in two major respects: (1) asserting that the "will to power" rather than the "will to live" is most fundamental and (2) replacing Schopenhauer's unitary, amorphous, metaphysical will with a multiplicity of independent, stand-alone acts or events of will. Nietzsche was repulsed by Schopenhauer's pessimistic conclusion that every human being is an unwitting slave of a single blind metaphysical will, for he regarded this as descending into the nega-

tivism of devaluing life. In addition, Nietzsche appears to have come to his own conclusion, while serving as a battlefield medical orderly during the Franco-Prussian War (1870–71), that because people clearly do give up their lives for beliefs and causes that they cherish, it must be the case that there are many things that matter more to them than just staying alive and propagating more life.

As time went on, Nietzsche developed the concept of will to power into the central pillar of his philosophy, attempting to explain an ever-increasing number of experiential data by means of it. First of all, he found the whole range of human behavior susceptible to this approach, and his insights were expressed in many formulas. For example: "'no effecting without willing'; 'one can have an effect only on beings that will'; 'no suffering of an effect is ever pure and without consequences, but all suffering consists of an agitation of the will' (toward action, resistance, revenge, retribution)."[47] In other words, the origin of acting and being acted upon lies in a certain capacity to energize oneself into action and to be stimulated into action by others. Nietzsche goes on to state that "for will to come into being an idea of pleasure and displeasure is needed." On closer inspection, it turns out that what we call pleasure and displeasure are, for him, really functions (or by-products) of enhanced and diminished will to power, respectively. So, success in expanding one's sphere of influence, controlling a situation, or simply exerting oneself physically, for instance, are accompanied by a feeling of pleasure, but the increase of power is both the goal and the source of the pleasurable feeling. In reverse manner, failure and defeat in one's projects bring the feeling of displeasure (suffering and/or pain). (Yet, as we saw in the second section of this chapter, even illness and pain can be a gain if we learn from them how to exert ourselves more effectively.) Furthermore, and perhaps not surprisingly, that which gives pleasure is equated with the good, and the source of displeasure with the bad: "What is good? Everything that heightens the feeling of power in man, the will to power, power itself. What is bad? Everything that is born of weakness."[48]

Nietzsche's analysis of willing is complex, subtle, and ingenious, and it has influenced subsequent theory of action as well as the method by which philosophers, such as Ludwig Wittgenstein (1889–1951), have discussed issues in the philosophy of mind. Nietzsche deconstructs traditional ideas about the will, maintaining that what we call "the will" is not the name of a mental faculty, and that people are wrong to assume "that willing is something simple, a brute datum, underivable, and intelligible by itself."[49] It is characteristic of him to rail against such psychological fictions (or "phantoms") by which we have explained mental phenomena in the past. Then he offers a detailed account of how willing occurs in us, which he pointedly describes as:

> "unphilosophical": let us say that in all willing there is, first, a plurality of sensations, namely, the sensation of the state "*away from which*," the sensation of the state "*towards which*," the sensations of this "*from*" and "*towards*" themselves, and then also an accompanying muscular sensation, which, even without our putting into motion "arms and legs," begins its action by force of habit as soon as we "will" anything. . . . [S]econdly, . . . in every act of the will there is a ruling thought. . . . Third, the will is . . . above all an *affect*, and specifically the affect of the command. . . . But now let us notice what is strangest about the will—. . . in the given circumstances we are at the same time the commanding *and* the obeying parties, and as the obeying party we know the sensations of constraint, impulsion, pressure, resistance, and motion, which usually begin immediately after the act of will. . . .[50]

Nietzsche calls this analysis "unphilosophical" because it not only departs from tradition but also, in referring to sensations, deliberately violates the boundaries between philosophy, psychology, and physiology. The main things to observe, however, are these: (1) that "willing" (or "acts of will") comprise many smaller subevents, at least some of which are subjectively experienced and may be conceptually discriminated; (2) willing is a process of "commanding" and "obeying" in which we act upon ourselves reflexively; and (3) we experience the "commanding/obeying" struggle within ourselves both mentally and bodily as voluntary action unfolds.

From the above, Nietzsche immediately goes on to posit that "'freedom of the will'—that is the expression for the complex state of delight of the person exercising volition, who commands and at the same time identifies himself with the executor of the order—who, as such, enjoys also the triumph over obstacles, but thinks within himself that it was really his will itself that overcame them." This is quite a novel approach to freedom of the will, as it is grounded in the physical, derived from the analysis of willing in terms of power, and also explains the illusion of a unitary Will (like that of a solitary, indivisible "I") that exerts itself against outside resistances. As Nietzsche points out, "The 'inner world' is full of phantoms and will-o'-the-wisps: the will is one of them. . . . There are no mental causes at all."[51] Here, he is saying that the belief that stable, substantial entities, such as "the will" and "self" or "ego," are unproductive assumptions when it comes to explaining behavior and motivation, especially if they are treated as causes similar to forces and things in the physical world. He proposes to replace this apparatus with the kind of analysis—part philosophical, part psychological, and part physiological— that we have just reviewed.

Nietzsche's account of willing, then, fully explicated, would involve numerous levels of events, as shown below.

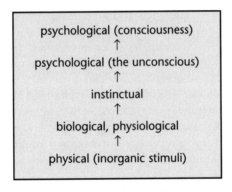

Traditional explanations of willing, by contrast, have operated only within one of these—psychological (consciousness), and it is part of his project in the analysis of the human psyche to demonstrate the inadequacy of this time-honored approach.

Now most people when they think of "power" have in mind physical force or strength, domination or control over others, political authority, raw energy, and so on. Nietzsche did embrace these things within his concept; but most importantly for understanding him and for avoiding common caricatures of his view, he focused a great deal of attention on power as *mastery over oneself*. In *Human, All Too Human*, for instance, he refers to "that *mature* freedom of spirit which is equally self-control and discipline of the heart."[52] And in *Thus Spoke Zarathustra*, we hear that "he who cannot obey himself is commanded. That is the nature of the living."[53] In other words, Nietzsche (through the words of Zarathustra) exhorts us to be in charge of our own lives, to be our own person, unique and vigorously self-affirming. Those who cannot measure up to such a standard look to others for guidance and become part of the masses. This doctrine is essential to the revaluation of values and the philosophy of the future Nietzsche is trying to construct. But it also harks back to the fundamental existentialist preoccupation with knowing oneself and the strength of independence and responsibility that flows from this.

Zarathustra (who is portrayed as a sage who has traveled far and wide and has seen many things) articulates an additional insight in the same passage just cited, noting: "'Where I found the living, there I found will to power; and even in the will of those who serve I found the will to be master.'" We have all heard of pecking orders, and the idea here is that those in the lower part of the order are still bent on pecking those below them, creating a lower target group, if necessary. Pulling rank, exploiting one's social status, being a petty bureaucrat, bullying, abusing those weaker than yourself, discriminating from within a position of being discriminated against—all of these are instances that illustrate Zarathustra's meaning. And they reinforce Nietzsche's theory that all relations are power relations, which later deeply influenced such thinkers as psychoanalyst Alfred Adler (1870–1937) and fellow philosopher Michel Foucault (1926–84).

Although Nietzsche disdained Schopenhauer's metaphysical will, the source from which everything allegedly emanates, he couldn't resist extrapolating from his own notion of will to power and drawing from it large-scale conclusions about the rest of nature. In several places (principally, in *The Will to Power*), he hypothesizes that not only living beings, but *all* things, are animated by, and even *are*, will to power. This he considers a reasonable and economical way to explain whatever occurs in the universe, whatever serves as either cause or effect of events in the world. It must be said at this point that the special usefulness and interest of will to power as a vehicle for making sense of the biological (particularly human) sphere ceases as we slide into the realization that a concept that explains everything in the end explains nothing.

REVALUATION OF VALUES

Nietzsche thought of his overall project as a "revaluation of values"—a sweeping critique and deconstruction of existing and traditional values, plus their replacement by a new value orientation that reflected his ideas about power and creative self-assertion. He believed that just as past civilizations and cultures had had their own gods, so too did they possess value clusters that defined who they were and what they stood for:

> "A table of value hangs over every people. Behold, it is the table of its overcomings; behold, it is the voice of its will to power.
>
> What it accounts hard it calls praiseworthy; what it accounts indispensable and hard it calls good; and that which relieves the greatest need, the rare, the hardest of all—it glorifies as holy.
>
> Whatever causes it to rule and conquer and glitter, to the dread and envy of its neighbour, that it accounts the sublimest, the paramount, the evaluation and the meaning of all things."[54]

Exertion, achievement, and excellence are the qualities a group of people consciously or unconsciously projects into their value system, no matter what story they tell themselves about the origin of these values. This story may feature a god (or gods), a prophet or avatar, ancient heroes, myths, or historical events and lineages. But the reality, according to Nietzsche, is that they see themselves and their higher aspirations reflected back to them from their value cluster.

Immoralism. As I explained earlier, Nietzsche believed Western, particularly Christian, cultural values had become rotten or "decadent," and that Western culture in general had gone into decline. The values in which culture are rooted therefore need to be overthrown and replaced by a new "table of values." But who will accomplish this monumental task? Who will "help fall faster" what is already "falling"? Enter the immoralist.

Nietzsche styles himself as an "immoralist" to demonstrate his rejection of traditional and institutionalized morality, and even of morality as such, as we know it. His immoralism signifies two things: (1) a deconstructive critique of Western ethics; and (2) a second-order critique or meta-critique of the concept of value itself. Not only does Nietzsche seek to undermine traditional theories of right and wrong, good and evil, he also is the first to raise the seemingly odd question, "What is the value of value?"—that is, what purpose or function do value-judgments serve, and how well (if at all) do they serve it?

The arguments Nietzsche puts forward against various moral theories are formidable, diverse, and widely scattered throughout his works. Briefly, here are a few examples. Against Kant's universalistic ethics of duty, which is alleged to appeal to reason alone, he argues that the famous categorical imperative ("Act only according to those principles that you could consistently will to be universally binding") is really a disguised expression of Kant's own egocentric will to power. Kant's subtextual message is: "'What deserves respect in me is that I can obey—and you *ought* not to be different from me.'"[55] Against utilitarianism, a universalistic ethics of consequences rather than duty, he urges that this is a value system of mediocrity, as it promotes contributions to the general happiness in society instead of individual goods that each chooses for her- or himself. Furthermore, classical utilitarianism is one of the "ways of thinking that measure the value of things in accordance with *pleasure* and *pain*, which are mere epiphenomena [by-products of something else] and wholly secondary...."[56] Recall that in the previous section it was pointed out that for Nietzsche pleasure and pain are just ways that consciousness registers power gained or lost. Therefore, hedonistic moralities (such as utilitarianism), which focus on happiness (defined in terms of pleasure) simply put the cart before the horse in their estimate of human motivation.

Beyond these specific criticisms, Nietzsche believes that all moralities that are advertized as generally applicable miss the mark and are in fact dangerous and destructive to the human spirit because "the demand of one morality for all is detrimental for the higher men; ... [for] there is an order of rank between man and man, hence also between morality and morality."[57] Odious as it may be, Nietzsche believes that the fundamental inequalities among humans should be reinforced, celebrated, and accommodated in our value systems. This would mean, presumably, that those who have talent, skill, and genius should be given the maximum opportunity to excel; to realize their singular passions; to chart their own life plan, free from interference. The rest of us—those who constitute "the herd" or "the rabble"—should step aside, make way, and also accept a lesser standard of opportunity for our own self-development.

Nietzsche's position can be classified as *meritarian*, as opposed to the *egalitarian* one we all believe we subscribe to. I would argue, however, that the society we live in (and probably every other, past or present, that claims or has claimed to be egalitarian) is a blend of meritarian and egalitarian principles; for, while we have many documents and laws setting out equal rights, obligations, privileges, rewards, and punishments, we also extend advantageous treatment to those who possess unusual gifts, abilities, influence, or wealth, even though these are often unwittingly possessed from birth rather than earned by discipline and effort. So, while Nietzsche may offend us by exalting difference in ways we are taught to disapprove of, there is undeniably some truth in his view. In any event, he would no doubt have the last word, pouring scorn on our ideas of equality as nothing more than the self-defense of the weak and inferior!

Apollonian and Dionysian energies. Although he spent most of his years as an unemployed philosopher, Nietzsche had an early, short, and abortive career as a philologist (a scholar of classical languages). During this time, he revolutionized thinking about ancient Greek culture. In his first published work, *The Birth of Tragedy*, he singled out two drives or impulses manifested in Greek tragedy, which he subsequently generalized in his account of human psychology. These are the "Dionysian" and the "Apollonian." "Dionysian" refers to a basic impetus toward disorder, union, sexuality, fertility, self-abandonment, frenzied intoxication, and ecstasy, among other things. Products of human creativity that exhibit these qualities are described as Dionysian, and these represent "an instinct for life"[58]—raw vitality and the rich sensual experience of the ever-changing world around us. "Apollonian" signifies the opposing but equally fundamental urge toward harmony, order, form, particularity, shape, calmness, transparency, rationality, stability, and similar features. Products of human creativity that exhibit these qualities are identified as Apollonian, and these represent "the beautiful illusion of the dream worlds"[59]—the creation of structure and meaning out of chaos. What was revolutionary about Nietzsche's theory is that Greek culture had previously been characterized exclusively as Apollonian, but now classical scholars were forced to contend with a powerful argument on behalf of seeing it in this two-sided fashion; beneath the surface of calm repose and order there lurked turmoil and disorder—at least according to Nietzsche.

Later on in his writing career, Nietzsche turned more toward the Dionysian. Indeed, in one of his dark autobiographical reflections toward the end of his period of authorship, he pleads: "Have I been understood?—*Dionysus versus the Crucified.*—"[60] This may be understood in light of his belief that everything Dionysian is what Christianity dedicates itself to stifling and punishing. Even before the establishment of the Church, rationalistic philosophy served to reinforce an anti-instinctual message and an otherworldly vision. Christianity then coopted philosophy as its handmaiden in the campaign to enslave and neutralize human vitality.

But for Nietzsche, the Dionysian cannot truly be suppressed and it will rise again, especially if he has anything to do with it. It may seem here as if he is simply appealing for emotional anarchy and undisciplined self-expression; however, something rather more subtle is going on. His more mature thinking on the matter of human motivation and creativity features

Dionysian drives shaped and channeled into productive outlets by Apollonian influences, in a manner rather like the process that Freud called "sublimation." Sublimated forms of behavior are avenues that are less potentially harmful to oneself and others and hence, too, they are more socially pragmatic. For example, sexual energy and desire can't always be directly vented or acted out, so substitute pathways need to be found, such as fiction writing, painting, dreaming, and so forth. Likewise, aggressive impulses may be sublimated into sports or other competitive contests.

Again, like Freud, Nietzsche saw what we call "civilization" as a compromise between unrestricted freedom (license) and over-regulation of the instincts. The essential problem of civilization is that in order to achieve a safe and sane social order, the instincts must be held in check; but to do so causes a lot of psychic tension and the festering of life energies, both of which threaten mental health and sometimes result in eruptions of violence and war. The price of civilization, therefore, can be high, and this is owing to a fundamentally inadequate compromise between opposing elements (order and disorder). Nietzsche argues that there can and must be better solutions in the world of the future. These will center on the synthesis of the Dionysian and Appolonian drives in the same individual, which he comes to think of as "Dionysian" in a new, revised sense of the term.

In a way, the Dionysian/Apollonian split tells us much about Nietzsche himself and his relationship to his readers. On the one hand, there is no doubt that he stirs us up and appeals to the rebel within us. We identify with his hammer-wielding approach. But, on the other hand, he also speaks to the more thoughtful, analytic side of our nature. At a rational level, he is a serious thinker we cannot avoid coming to terms with. Few philosophers have an impact with anything like the same scope.

The genealogy of morals, master and slave values, and "ressentiment." The project of delving into the interior of the human psyche and its cultural products stayed with Nietzsche all his life, and one prominent development stemming from it was the subproject he called "the genealogy of morals." Nietzsche had his own narrative of human development, anchored only loosely in history and anthropology, out of which he generated archetypal forms of consciousness and value perspective. His concept of a genealogy of morals refers to the path by which ethical values have evolved in relation to the situations humans have been required to respond to. The story goes like this: There was once a race of strong, self-sufficient beings, who were conquerors and authors of their own values. They defined what was "good" by reference to what made them feel more powerful, and the "bad" by reference to its opposite. Only much later did "good" and "bad" (and more especially "good" and "evil") come to be adjectives descriptive of persons and their deeds. A slow transition took place by which the weaker beings among humanity (who have their own clever deviousness) chipped away at the values of the strong and eventually subverted them altogether. Thus, what the strong had called "good" was now "bad" or "evil" (i.e., to be avoided), and vice versa. This value inversion (the first revaluation of values) enhanced the power of the weak and reduced the power of the strong, so that the weak came into the ascendant. They also had the power of superior numbers and the ability to keep still weaker ones in thrall. So, their teachings were, for example, that one should not aspire to be a conqueror but rather one should be a "loyal subject" or, later, "an equal member of the moral community." One should not be egocentric and pursue what makes one feel good but, instead, one should prepare for self-sacrificing, being a "team player," and so forth. Christianity is a fuller development of this new position, as it exalts the weak, the poor, the sick, the downtrodden, and the disadvantaged. Nietzsche commonly rails against "priestly castes" (not only within Christianity), who are experts in value subversion and gaining control over others. Those who are familiar with Dostoevsky's "Grand Inquisitor" tale in *The Brothers Karamazov* will recognize a very skilfully drawn portrait of such a priest.

A lesson from all this is that it is essential to differentiate two kinds of conflicting morality. Nietzsche writes:

> Wandering through the many subtler and coarser moralities which have so far been prevalent on earth, or are still prevalent, I found that certain features recurred regularly together and were closely associated—until I finally discovered two basic types and one basic difference.
>
> There are *master morality* and *slave morality*—and I add immediately that in all the higher and more mixed cultures there also appear attempts at mediation between these two moralities, and yet more often the interpenetration and mutual misunderstanding of both, and at times they occur directly alongside each other—even in the same human being, within a *single* soul.

Obviously, Nietzsche has studied and reflected deeply upon cultural history, from which he has drawn these conclusions. While that fact does not guarantee the truth of his observations, it does give them some force. The "mixture" of moralities to which he refers is explained by Walter Kaufmann in relation to the "manifold tensions, hypocrisies, and contradictions" present in contemporary value systems.[61] My own earlier example of our hybrid society of egalitarianism and meritocracy illustrates the point. But the contradictions within us are also clear: for instance, lavishing care on pets while turning a blind eye to the miserable condition of food animals.

Now, what is the "one basic difference" between these two moralities Nietzsche claims to have discovered? He continues:

> In the first case, when the ruling group determines what is "good," the exalted, proud states of the soul are experienced as conferring distinction and determining the order of rank. . . . The noble type of man experiences *itself* as determining values; it does not need approval; it judges "what is harmful to me is harmful in itself"; it knows itself to be that which first accords honor to things; it is *value-creating*. . . . The slave's eye is not favorable to the virtues of the powerful. . . . Conversely, those qualities are brought out and flooded with light which serve to ease existence for those who suffer: here pity, the complaisant and obliging hand, the warm heart, patience, industry, humility, and friendliness are honoured. . . .[62]

Simply put, master morality emanates from those who are strong, self-reliant, life-affirming, able to lead, and capable of creating values and of self-mastery. Slave morality springs from those who are negative-thinking, weak-willed, defeated by life's struggles, dependent, conforming, life-denigrating, and needing to be ruled.

Nietzsche also holds that slave morality is the result of what he calls (borrowing from the French) *ressentiment*. This is his word for will to power that is frustrated or blocked from expression; the concept bears some resemblance to Freud's "repression" (the blocking from consciousness of sexual energy or libido). Many emotions, motivations, and forms of behavior are considered by Nietzsche to be expressions of ressentiment, such as envy, hatred, revenge, persecution, maliciousness, self-loathing, and attempts to bring others down. Hence, slave morality is quite evidently the morality of ressentiment.

Aside from its offensiveness to most sensitive people, there are some problems in Nietzsche's account of the two moralities. First of all, it would seem that we have to acknowledge that slave thinking is also creative, since it does give rise to values; and in doing so, it is also an expression of will to power and, therefore, of power. Nietzsche actually concedes these points (recall Zarathustra's observation that "even in the will of those who serve I found the will to be master"), but he sometimes appears to have forgotten that he did so. Second, and more important, some of the values he wants to dismiss are ones we should not too hastily abandon, as they have been, and still are, of great significance in terms of preserving peace, stability, cooperation, and the bonds of mutual concern that make possible the survival of our species and the existence of society. Third, some values (such as altruism, patience, and industry) may manifest considerable strength of character, and it is therefore plainly absurd and inconsistent to suppose that they always show weakness, world weariness, etc. (Indeed, this is demonstrated by some of Nietzsche's own studies of outstanding historical persons.)

"Remain faithful to the earth." This slogan is enunciated by Zarathustra[63] and is one of his most important pronouncements. By means of it, Nietzsche drives home his point that Christianity (and Western culture) have denigrated the body and the senses; but one might even go beyond this and say also that this prescription contains an attack on the tendency to deny that we are part of nature. If my reading is accurate, then Nietzsche targets not only the denial of embodiment and physicality but also the abuse and exploitation of the environment. The latter cannot be asserted with any confidence as part of his meaning, but it does represent an intriguing possibility, or at least a tempting application of his thought.

There are two sections in *Twilight of the Idols* in which Nietzsche succinctly lays out his critique of past philosophy and, in addition, clearly expresses ideas that precipitated the slogan "remain faithful to the earth." These sections are titled "'Reason' in Philosophy" and "How the 'Real World' at Last Became a Myth (History of an Error)." In the first of these, Nietzsche maintains that philosophers of the past have been unable to deal with *becoming*: "Death, change, age, as well as procreation and growth, are for them objections—refutations even. What is, does not *become*; what becomes *is* not."[64] The point here is that the processes of life, ending in death—human mortality, in short—are apprehended as too painful in their consequences and too difficult to confront (we all are frail and will die one day), so stories have to be invented in order to rationalize them away. While this philosophical effort is itself a manifestation of will to power, Nietzsche thinks it is a poor substitute for affirming life and facing its dilemmas head-on. For what the philosophers have done, he avers, is to transform the world of the senses into a world of illusion and falsity, and in contrast they exalt a world of ideas to the status of "reality." Thus, for example, rationalist philosophers from Plato to Descartes and beyond, have thought sense-perception was (or was likely to be) deceptive and that it therefore had to be "cured"—corrected or supplanted—by thought, whose judgment would override or replace the testimony of the senses. Many of these philosophers posited the existence of an intelligible or supersensible realm where Truth resides, whose contents are eternal and unchanging, where the gods (or God) live(s), and so on. It was this that they aspired to know and immerse themselves in. In effect, Nietzsche continues, their response to the epistemological problems they created, and that have largely set the agenda for modern philosophy, was to proclaim: "'These senses, *which are so immoral as well,* it is they which deceive us about the *real* world. . . . And away, above all, with the *body,* that pitiable *idée fixe* [fixed idea] of the senses! infected with every error of logic there is, refuted, impossible even, notwithstanding it is impudent enough to behave as if it actually existed.'" According to Nietzsche's satirical caricature, these philosophers have indicted and excoriated the sense organs and the body, blaming them for our limited grasp of reality. Furthermore, they have, in effect, inverted the true order of things, making pure abstract knowledge primary and knowledge derived from sense experience secondary and inferior.

Of course, more experientially minded philosophers, from Aristotle to empiricists like Locke, Berkeley, Hume, and many later figures, have also had their say, and they have been strongly critical of rationalism in several respects. But the tendencies of rationalism that Nietzsche holds in contempt and the doctrines of early Christian thinkers dominated Western culture for many centuries. In light of this interpretation of the history of philosophy, we may see "past philosophers" as having aided in the first reversal or subversion of values—of the strong and noble—that we reviewed earlier, and Nietzsche's backlash against this then stands out as the second reversal—his celebrated *revaluation of values.*

This way of understanding Nietzsche's narrative about past philosophy is forcefully supported by examining the second passage in *Twilight of the Idols* referred to above. In "How the 'Real World' at Last Became a Myth," Nietzsche brilliantly weaves a very compressed tale of ideological inversion followed by his revaluation:

1. The real world, attainable to the wise, the pious, the virtuous man—he dwells in it, *he is it.* . . .
2. The real world, unattainable for the moment, but promised to the wise, the pious, the virtuous man ("to the sinner who repents"). . . .
3. The real world, unattainable, undemonstrable, cannot be promised, but even when merely thought of a consolation, a duty, an imperative. . . .
4. The real world—unattainable? Unattained, at any rate. And if unattained also *unknown.* Consequently also no consolation, no

redemption, no duty: how could we have a duty toward something unknown? . . .

5. The "real world"—an idea no longer of any use, not even a duty any longer—an idea grown useless, superfluous, *consequently* a refuted idea: let us abolish it! . . .

6. We have abolished the real world: what world is left? The apparent world perhaps? But no! *with the real world we have also abolished the apparent world!* . . . (INCIPIT ZARATHUSTRA)[65]

The concept of the "real world" has gone through several transformations, Nietzsche contends—from vital to distant and attenuated; and therefore the "real world" ultimately turns out deflated and worthy only of being discarded altogether, since it has lost its meaning and strength as a ruling idea. But if we abolish "reality," he continues, we also abolish "appearance"—that previously inferiorized realm charted by sense experience and the body, the other part of the appearance/reality dichotomy. We are then free to move into new territory and redefine the world. At this point, Zarathustra begins (the meaning of the Latin "*incipit*"), which is a cryptic way of alluding to the revaluation Nietzsche wishes to undertake. In short, a new voice, a new narrative takes over.

Below is a summary of Nietzsche's perspective on past values.

ORIGINAL VALUATION OF VALUES	FIRST REVERSAL OF VALUES	NIETZSCHE ENTERS THE SCENE	NEW REVALUATION
Noble ones, aristocrats of dim past (hypothetical)	Plato, Christianity, other philosophers	Nihilism	Zarathustra, overman
Affirmation of sense-experience No appearance/reality division	World (i.e., the earth and what we experience via the senses), becoming and appearance: devalued, denigrated; we feel unworthy as mere mortals "Heaven" or where "Forms" dwell, being, reality: praised, exalted; we hope to feel worthy one day	Appearance and reality reversed	Reaffirmation of sense experience Appearance/reality division abolished
Master Morality	Slave morality	Immoralism	New tablets of value

The new values. Even though I have stressed that Nietzsche's nihilism is only provisional, it is nonetheless more difficult to say what he stands *for* than what he stands *against.* This puzzle is framed by Nietzsche himself:

> "You call yourself free? Your dominant thought I want to hear, and not that you have escaped from a yoke. Are you one of those who had the *right* to escape from a yoke? There are some who threw away their last value when they threw away their servitude.
>
> Free *from* what? As if that mattered to Zarathustra! But your eyes should tell me brightly: free *for* what?
>
> Can you give yourself your own evil and your own good and hang your own will over yourself as a law? Can you be your own judge and avenger of your law?"[66]

As a consequence of the death of God, we have won the right to choose our own value system and posit the meaning of life. This reward has a high cost, however, for we have witnessed the collapse of established foundations on which to ground meaning and values, and we have even forfeited the ability to believe in shared meaning and values. The more positive idea in this speech of Zarathustra's is that freedom must be earned and deserved in order to be valuable. And those who earn and deserve it are those who are self-mastering, self-creating, self-actualizing beings. They are individuals who are capable of inventing themselves according to a plan of their own—one that affirms life and is power-enhancing. "No one is responsible for man's being there at all, for his being such-and-such, or for his being in these circumstances or in this environment."[67] That being the case, it is up to us to assume the burden of "playing God," so to speak (a theme taken up dramatically, though quite differently, by Sartre, as we shall see in chapter 7).

Where should we begin in seeking to sketch such an ideal person? We have already recognized that positing new values requires the strength to abandon the old and to actively revolt against them. Like the Phoenix of mythology, new birth springs from the ashes of the past. But more than this: the Nietzschean creator must deliberately cut the shackles of tradition and shed the weight of human mediocrity before moving ahead.

This movement is better understood as a single chain of events that involves at one and the same time the rejection of habitual, internalized norms and the salvaging of that which has been thoroughly scorned and slandered but which is actually the source of what is most productive of human well-being. In this way, an inversion of values is accomplished—or perhaps one should say that the ancient subversion of the values of the strong is undone, reversed; the damage to the human spirit is repaired. Zarathustra asserts that "'*Sex, the lust to rule, selfishness:* these three have so far been best cursed and worst reputed and lied about. . . .'"[68] Because these are alleged to be "evil" by Christianity and mainstream Western thought, they now need to be revalued; that is, they need to be infused with positive value in order to cancel out the past misjudgment of human potential and to set us free to shape the future as we see fit. As far as "sex" is concerned, Nietzsche seeks not just to celebrate sexual activity in the usual sense but also to validate and valorize the body and physical experience in general, to liberate the senses and the sensual. "The lust to rule" brings us back to his basic concept of will to power in all of its various meanings, but especially that of self-mastery and self-direction, so important for taking a fresh look at life. Finally, "selfishness" does not refer to narrow, egoistic, isolated concerns; Nietzsche condemns egoism just as much as altruism. Rather, what he has in mind is glossed by Zarathustra himself: "'the wholesome, healthy selfishness that wells from a powerful soul. . . .'"[69] As many besides Nietzsche have pointed out, healthy self-love, or feeling positive about oneself, is not good for its own sake alone; it is also necessary for being able to give fully to others. One gives from a position of strength and fullness, not from that of weakness, negativity, and emptiness.

A PHILOSOPHY FOR THE FUTURE

Thus Spoke Zarathustra, which is Nietzsche's manifesto for breaking with the past and venturing boldly into the unknown future, announces in its subtitle that it is "A Book for Everyone and No One." We have already encountered this theme—that the future is for the strong and daring, who shall inherit the earth because they deserve to. And we can now understand better why Nietzsche says, "Philosophy, as I have so far understood and lived it, means living voluntarily among ice and high mountains—the seeking out of everything strange and questionable in existence, everything so far placed under a ban by morality."[70] Philosophy should strive, according to him, to undo the bondage of the past and deliver a liberating message that creates a new cultural vista in which there is room to grow and flourish uninhibited by ressentiment and the tired old judgments issuing from it. Out of this thought, Nietzsche's philosophy of the future unfolds.

The overman. The central figure on which Nietzsche focuses discussion of the future is the overman. Sometimes, this term is left in its German original, *Übermensch* (literally: "overperson" or "aboveperson"). Definitely, we should avoid the English rendering, "Superman," for two reasons. First, "Superman" cannot help but make us think of the cartoon (and movie) character who is locked into the morality Nietzsche rejects. (We could also say that Superman is largely concerned with foiling crimes against property, such as bank robbery, rather than with preventing wars, child abuse, rape, environmental ruin, and other, more major wrongs.) Second, Superman generally solves problems by brute force, thus exhibiting the kind of mastery Nietzsche was least interested in.[71]

So who or what is this overman? Clearly, this person will "remain faithful to the earth" in the sense explained previously. That is, she or he will not be afraid to tap into instinctual energies, gain control over these for healthy purposes, posit new values for her- or himself, and, from a foundation of self-mastery, provide leadership and a model for others to follow. It is arguable that the overman will help others in rising to the level of accomplishment of which they are capable rather than seeing them merely as obstacles to be trampled into the dust and left behind: "'And there is nobody from whom I want beauty as much as from you who are powerful: let your kindness be your final self-conquest.'"[72] The relationship between overmen will be one of positive competition, a quest to attain degrees of excellence: "'Let us strive against one another like gods'"[73] shall be their motto.

Like utopian philosophers, Nietzsche is difficult to pin down about the new order that is to come. This is because it lies in the realm of the experimental, of the imagination, and of that which exceeds our ability to predict or fully determine: "'what is good and evil *no one knows yet*, unless it be he who creates. He, however, creates man's goal and gives the earth its meaning and its future. That anything at all is good and evil—that is his creation.'"[74] Those who are suitable for this task will be the new "'chosen people,'"[75] the "'new nobility,'"[76] a self-selected, self-positing class of superior beings, who, Nietzsche sometimes disturbingly conjectures, might be purposely bred for this role.

The overmen will be the earth's salvation, first in the sense that they will save humans from themselves by advancing beyond humankind along the evolutionary trail: "'Man is a rope, tied between beast and overman—a rope over an abyss. . . . What is great in man is that he is a bridge and not an end. . . .'"[77] Second, overmen will re-establish the earth as a place of creative accomplishment rather than destructive pettiness and meaningless violence in the pursuit of egoistic ends. One could hardly object to such a vision, at least in general terms. But inasmuch as Nietzsche is incredibly vague about the road to this new order, skepticism concerning it may prevail in many minds. Then again, Zarathustra cautions, like other gurus or spiritual leaders, that there are numerous possible pathways to the future: "'This is *my* way; where is yours?'—thus I answered those who asked me 'the way'. For *the* way—that does not exist.'"[78] What this entails, evidently, is that there must be minimal or no restrictions on self-development in the interest of an improved version of our species; it will eventuate from the free interplay of advanced beings.

It will strike many readers that unleashing human instincts as Nietzsche proposes can only lead to trouble, that the lack of guidelines in his vision of a world in which the new aristocracy of overmen prevails occasions more than a little anxiety. On the other hand, we need to remember that Nietzsche is a polemicist—he is trying to change things, to stir us up—and that views into the unknown and untried future are bound to be sketchy at best. Furthermore, he has a point in observing that if the imperative we should follow is something like: "Be yourself; live fully and adventurously," then this is very hard to encapsulate in general rules of morality. And last, it is worth recalling that the overman is going to be someone who has purged her- or himself of ressentiment, which is the source of antagonisms and aggression toward others.

Eternal recurrence. Interestingly, those who dismiss religion as cultural mythology are often those who cannot refrain from erecting their own substitute mythologies. Nietzsche is a case in point. He toys repeatedly with the idea of "eternal recurrence," or the fateful, unending return of the same, an idea that in the West first surfaced in the philosophy of the ancient Roman Stoics. While Nietzsche's version of the myth is relatively crude, he claims in *The Will to Power* that the doctrine amounts to a respectable scientific hypothesis. One might find this somewhat difficult to credit, and yet, according to inflation theory, a relatively new form of cosmology, the universe is spatially infinite and contains an infinite number of observable alternate universes, in each of which history repeats itself endlessly.[79] Whatever the fate of inflation theory and this admittedly counterintuitive result eventually turns out to be, Nietzsche's expresses his own version of the theory in a momentous and powerful way:

> "Behold . . . this moment! From this gateway, Moment, a long, eternal lane leads *backward*: behind us lies an eternity. Must not whatever *can* walk have walked on this lane before? Must not whatever *can* happen have happened, have been done, have passed by before? . . .
> And this slow spider, which crawls in the moonlight, and this moon-

light itself, and I and you in the gateway, whispering together, whispering of eternal things—must not all of us have been there before?

And return and walk in that other lane, out there, before us, in this long dreadful lane—must we not eternally return?"[80]

Nietzsche speaks of this idea as the one that will either make or break the strongest spirits: "If this thought gained possession of you, it would change you as you are or perhaps crush you. . . . Or how well disposed would you have to become to yourself and to life *to crave nothing more fervently* than this ultimate eternal confirmation and seal?"[81]

What we have here, quite simply, is a guiding myth and acid test for the overman, an elaborate "What if . . . ?" designed to make us say "Yes" to life, no matter what it brings our way. Those who accept and survive thinking about the eternal return of the same will be twice blessed; those who shrink away will be damned in their own sight. Now one might be forgiven for inferring that if everything is fated to recur eternally there is no freedom to change anything and therefore no point in trying to do or not do anything, for what will happen, will happen regardless of what we intend and decide. We may not be able to see into the past in order to discover what we are about to do next, but it is no less fully determined than if we *could* do so. This seems to reduce our lives to a trivial, puppet-like process of repeating the past and, thus, also to eradicate originality. Nietzsche doesn't shy away from these consequences, but he seems nevertheless to put a different spin on eternal recurrence. For him, the significance of accepting the doctrine is that in spite of its potentially devastating implications, the strong will accept and even celebrate it (perhaps because they too cannot see into the past?), using it to their advantage. The advantage I am referring to is that of being *empowered by self-assertion even in the face of fate.* For where there is the threat of the meaninglessness of existence, one must *make meaning.* But more than this: one must be able to affirm and rejoice at the thought of repeating the present moment eternally. (Nietzsche often speaks of *amor fati* or "love of fate" as the overman's creed. And those who can accept fate, he urges, will learn to "fly" and "dance" through life.) This kind of affirmation entails willing that the present moment represent an experience, an achievement of the highest value, so far as we think it within our power to make it so. This power may be illusory—we can never know—but if we succeed, then it must be because success has always been possible.

Yet if we succeed, isn't the reality that we are merely acting out a script that has been acted out before, and which we are only fooling ourselves into thinking we have crafted? This is the big question that cannot be answered, and perhaps it only arises when we take the doctrine of eternal return too seriously. Nietzsche wants it to be a *willed belief* of the overman and, like belief in God, with all its internal tensions and contradictions, it must be taken on faith or not at all.[82]

AFTERWORD: PERSPECTIVES AND VALUES

If, as Nietzsche urges, there are no facts but only interpretations made from some "perspective," we have the right to ask whether there is any reason to prefer the interpretations made from any particular perspective over those made from all the rest. He evidently thought so, for his revaluation of values is put forward as a privileged interpretation. By this I mean that Nietzsche clearly thinks his own view is true, or at least "truer" than the rest, especially those traditional valuations whose genealogy he has traced to their roots in the devious machinations of the weak. Nietzsche may be willing to concede that no such deliverances are true, strictly speaking, given that what is true, in his opinion, is just those errors we have come to rely on and that through reinforcement over time have become established. But he nonetheless has a commitment to certain beliefs over others. (And in any case, if what is true is only that which has a long tradition of being accepted as such, it seems impossible to understand how any *new* truth can even get launched.)

Can perspectivism be consistently maintained, however? Nietzsche seems to have knocked the props from under the platform we know and trust as "objectivity," which we generally rely on. He was neither the first nor the last to do so, of course, but his challenge is worrying all the same. He may take pleasure in speaking of "the gay science of fearless experimentation" and in thinking of his challenge to truth as just such an experiment. Everyone today would have to admit that what counts as firm knowledge sometimes changes and that there seem to be fewer certainties today than ever before, both in everyday life and in science and other fields. This admission is all well and good, for it indicates there is a pragmatic aspect to knowledge: beliefs are accepted as true if they produce results we can detect and make use of. When such beliefs cease to have these effects or are challenged by those that are more fruitful, we abandon the former and move on to the latter. In this very spirit, Nietzsche boldly testifies that his own criterion ("there are no facts, but only interpretations") is itself merely an experimental idea, presumably ripe for abandonment if a superior one comes along: "Supposing that this [perspectivism] also is only interpretation—and you will be eager enough to make this objection—well, so much the better."[83]

But somewhere the buck has to stop. He can't really say, "So much the better." For if the principle that there are no facts but only interpretations is *itself* just an interpretation, then it has no greater claim on acceptability than the rival interpretations it wishes to unseat (such as: "There are objective truths that everyone must accept" or "Nothing is true or can possibly be known"). Equally worrying, one must wonder whether we can ever escape from the subjectivity of our own interpretations except by happening fortuitously to share similar perspectives with each other.

You may have begun to see where this is all heading. If value judgments, such as those Nietzsche prefers, have no objective foundation, then what is their force and why should we subscribe to them? When he tells us that certain ways of life, attitudes, beliefs, and actions are empowering and others are weakening and lead to decadence, this is meant to command our attention and assent. But has Nietzsche left himself anything firm on which to base these evaluations? If so, it seems he must be making a covert appeal to some second-level theory or source of values when he makes his claims. But if any such hidden ground of values itself *lacks* objectivity, then it cannot lend the support to Nietzsche's judgments that he requires in order to convince us of their truth or preferability. And if the hidden ground of values *does* have objectivity, then perspectivism is refuted. We are therefore left with the quandary that when Nietzsche argues that X (some value) is "power-enhancing," he can only mean "Nietzsche approves of X" or "Nietzsche thinks X is better than Y." Surely, however, he had hoped to be saying something more important than this. Anybody can make value recommendations, but in and of themselves, they provide no reason why we should accept them.

There is no easy way out of this dilemma, and we cannot resolve it on Nietzsche's behalf—or likely at all. We seem, then, to have the following options: (1) endorsing Nietzsche's perspectivism, with all of its problematic features; (2) toning it down so that there are truths we all accept and build upon but also those which are perspectival in nature; or (3) rejecting the doctrine altogether. The present state of human knowledge, being what it is, however—there was never before as much *of* it, nor as much uncertainty *about* it—I think we would be foolish to choose (3). (That, of course, is only *my* interpretation!)[84]

NOTES

1. Friedrich Nietzsche, *Twilight of the Idols, or How to Philosophize with a Hammer/The Anti-Christ*, trans. R. J. Hollingdale (London: Penguin Books, 1990), p. 32.

2. Friedrich Nietzsche, *On the Genealogy of Morals*, trans. Walter Kaufmann and R. J. Hollingdale, and *Ecce Homo: How One Becomes What One Is*, trans. Walter Kaufmann (New York: Vintage Books/ Random House, 1989), *Ecce Homo*, "Why I Am a Destiny," sec. 1.

3. Ofelia Schutte, *Beyond Nihilism: Nietzsche Without Masks* (Chicago: University of Chicago Press, 1984).

4. Friedrich Nietzsche, Letter to Georg Brandes, April 10, 1888, *Selected Letters of Friedrich Nietzsche*, ed. and trans. Oscar Levy (London: Heinemann, 1921).

5. Nietzsche, *Ecce Homo*, "Why I Am So Wise," sec. 2; see also "Maxims and Arrows," in *Twilight of the Idols*, trans. Hollingdale, sec. 8.

6. Nietzsche, "Why I Am So Wise," sec. 1 (emphasis in original).

7. Ibid., secs. 1, 2.

8. Friedrich Nietzsche, "What Is Religious," in *Beyond Good and Evil: Prelude to a Philosophy of the Future*, trans. Walter Kaufmann (New York: Vintage/Random House, 1966), sec. 45 (emphasis in original).

9. This is the subtitle of Nietzsche's *Ecce Homo* (see above, note 2), and a recurring theme in his works.

10. Nietzsche, *Beyond Good and Evil*, "On the Prejudices of Philosophers," sec. 9 (emphasis in original); "We Scholars," sec. 205 (emphasis in original); "What Is Noble," sec. 292.

11. Nietzsche, *Ecce Homo*, Preface, sec. 3 (emphasis in original).

12. Friedrich Nietzsche, *Daybreak: Thoughts on the Prejudices of Morality*, trans. R. J. Hollingdale, ed. Maudemarie Clark and Brian Leiter (Cambridge: Cambridge University Press, 1997), sec. 547.

13. Nietzsche, "On the Prejudices of Philosophers," in *Beyond Good and Evil*, secs. 1 and 2; Friedrich Nietzsche, "We Fearless Ones," in *The Gay Science*, trans. Walter Kaufmann (New York: Vintage Books/Random House, 1974), bk. 5, sec. 344.

14. Nietzsche, Preface, in *Human, All-Too-Human: A Book for Free Spirits*, trans. Helen Zimmern (New York: Russell and Russell, 1964), *The Complete Works of Friedrich Nietzsche*, vol. 6, ed. Oscar Levy, pt. 1, sec. 1 (emphasis in original); cf. "On the Prejudices of Philosophers," in *Beyond Good and Evil*, sec. 4.

15. Nietzsche, *Ecce Homo*, "Why I Am So Wise," sec. 8 (emphasis in original).

16. Ibid., sec. 6 (emphasis in original).

17. Nietzsche, "Why I Am So Clever," in ibid., sec. 1.

18. Friedrich Nietzsche, "The Philosopher as Cultural Physician," in *Philosophy and Truth: Selections from Nietzsche's Notebooks of the Early 1870's*, ed. and trans. Daniel Braezeale (Atlantic Highlands, NJ: Humanities Press International, 1979), pp. 69–76.

19. Nietzsche, Preface, in *Human, All-Too-Human*, pt. 1, secs. 2ff.

20. Friedrich Nietzsche, *Thoughts Out of Season*, pts. 1 and 2, trans. Anthony M. Ludovici, vols. 4 and 5 of the *Complete Works*.

21. Friedrich Nietzsche, "We Fearless Ones," in *The Gay Science*, trans. Walter Kaufmann (New York: Vintage/Random House, 1974), bk. 5, sec. 343.

22. Ibid., sec. 377.

23. Friedrich Nietzsche, Letter to Hans von Bülow, October 22, 1887, in *Selected Letters*.

24. Nietzsche, *Anti-Christ*, trans. Hollingdale, Foreword.

25. Walter Kaufmann, *Nietzsche: Philosopher, Psychologist, Antichrist*, 3rd ed. (Princeton, NJ: Princeton University Press, 1968), p. 82.

26. Arthur Danto, *Nietzsche as Philosopher* (New York: Macmillan; London: Collier-Macmillan, 1965), pp. 12–13.

27. Nietzsche, "We Fearless Ones," in *Gay Science*, bk. 5, sec. 381 (emphasis in original).

28. Nietzsche, "'Reason' in Philosophy," in *Twilight of the Idols*, trans. Hollingdale, sec. 1.

29. Nietzsche, "Expeditions of an Untimely Man," in ibid., sec. 51 (emphasis in original).

30. Nietzsche, "Truth and Lies in a Nonmoral Sense," in *Philosophy and Truth*, sec. 1.

31. Ibid., sec. 2.

32. Ibid., sec. 1.

33. Friedrich Nietzsche, "Attempt at a Self-Criticism," in *The Birth of Tragedy out of the Spirit of Music*, trans. Shaun Whiteside (London: Penguin, 1993), sec. 5 (emphasis in original).

34. Friedrich Nietzsche, "Belief in the 'Ego'. The Subject," in *The Will to Power*, ed. Walter Kaufmann, trans. Walter Kaufmann and R. J. Hollingdale (New York: Vintage/Random House, 1968), bk. 3, sec. 481 (emphasis in original).

35. Friedrich Nietzsche, *The Antichrist*, in *The Portable Nietzsche*, trans. Walter Kaufmann (New York: Viking Press, 1954), bk. 1, "Nihilism," sec. 51 (emphasis in original).

36. Nietzsche, *Gay Science*, bk. 3, sec. 125 (emphasis in original).

37. For a fascinating and delightfully written brief statement on the eventual demise of all gods, see H. L. Mencken, "Memorial Service," in *A Mencken Chrestomathy* (New York: Vintage Books/ Random House, 1982), pp. 95–96.

38. Nietzsche, "Nihilism," in *The Will to Power*, bk. 1, sec. 55 (emphasis in original).

39. Friedrich Nietzsche, *Twilight of the Idols*, in *Portable Nietzsche*, trans. Kaufmann, "The Four Great Errors," sec. 7.

40. Nietzsche, *Anti-Christ*, trans. Hollingdale, sec. 39.

41. Nietzsche, "Discipline and Breeding," in *The Will to Power*, bk. 4, sec. 983.

42. Friedrich Nietzsche, *Thus Spoke Zarathustra: A Book for All and None*, in *Portable Nietzsche*, trans. Kaufmann, pt. 3, "On Old and New Tablets," sec. 20.

43. Donald A. Crosby, "Nihilism," *Routledge Encyclopedia of Philosophy*, ed. Edward Craig (New York: Routledge, 1998), 7: 1–2.

44. Nietzsche, "On the Three Metamorphoses," in *Thus Spoke Zarathustra*, pt. 1.

45. John 3:3; see also I Peter 1:23 and 2:2.

46. Nietzsche, "Of Self-Overcoming," in *Thus Spoke Zarathustra: A Book for Everyone and No One*, trans. R. J. Hollingdale (London: Penguin, 1969), pt. 2.

47. Nietzsche, *Gay Science*, bk. 3, sec. 126.

48. Nietzsche, *Antichrist*, trans. Kaufmann, sec. 2.

49. Nietzsche, *Gay Science*, bk. 3, sec. 126.

50. Nietzsche, *Beyond Good and Evil*, sec. 19 (emphasis in original).

51. Nietzsche, "The Four Great Errors," in *Twilight of the Idols*, trans. Kaufmann, sec. 3.

52. Nietzsche, Preface, in *Human, All-Too-Human*, pt. 1, sec. 4 (emphasis in original).

53. Nietzsche, "On Self-Overcoming," in *Thus Spoke Zarathustra*, trans. Kaufmann, pt. 2.

54. Friedrich Nietzsche, "Of the Thousand and One Goals," in *Thus Spoke Zarathustra*, trans. Hollingdale, pt. 1.

55. Nietzsche, "Natural History of Morals," in *Beyond Good and Evil*, sec. 187 (emphasis in original).

56. Nietzsche, "Our Virtues," in ibid., sec. 225 (emphasis in original).

57. Ibid., sec. 228.

58. Nietzsche, "Attempt at a Self-Criticism," in *Birth of Tragedy*, sec. 5.

59. Nietzsche, "The Birth of Tragedy," in ibid., sec. 1.

60. Nietzsche, "Why I Am a Destiny," in *Ecce Homo*, sec. 9. See also Nietzsche, "Discipline and Breeding," in *The Will to Power*, bk. 4, sec. 1052.

61. Footnote 5 to Nietzsche, *Beyond Good and Evil*, sec. 260, p. 204.

62. Nietzsche, "What Is Noble," in *Beyond Good and Evil*, sec. 260 (emphasis in original).

63. Nietzsche, "Zarathustra's Prologue," in *Thus Spoke Zarathustra*, trans. Kaufmann, pt. 1, sec. 3 (emphasis in original); and pt. 1, "On the Gift-Giving Virtue," sec. 2.

64. Nietzsche, "'Reason' in Philosophy," in *Twilight of the Idols*, trans. Hollingdale, sec. 1 (emphasis in original).

65. Nietzsche, "How the 'Real World' at Last Became a Myth," in ibid. (emphasis in original).

66. Nietzsche, "On the Way of the Creator," in *Thus Spoke Zarathustra*, trans. Kaufmann, pt. 1 (emphasis in original).

67. Nietzsche, "The Four Great Errors," in *Twilight of the Idols*, trans. Kaufmann, sec. 8.

68. Nietzsche, *Thus Spoke Zarathustra*, trans. Kaufmann, pt. 3, "On the Three Evils," sec. 2 (emphasis in original).

69. Ibid.

70. Nietzsche, *Ecce Homo*, Preface, sec. 3.

71. For a fascinating and entertaining deconstructive analysis of Superman, see Umberto Eco, "The Myth of Superman," in Umberto Eco, *The Role of the Reader: Explorations in the Semiotics of Texts*, trans. Natalie Chilton (Bloomington: Indiana University Press, 1979), pp. 107–24.

72. Nietzsche, "On Those Who Are Sublime," in *Thus Spoke Zarathustra*, trans. Kaufmann, pt. 2.

73. Nietzsche, "On the Tarantulas," in ibid., pt. 2.

74. Nietzsche, "On Old and New Tablets," in ibid., pt. 3, sec. 1 (emphasis in original).

75. Nietzsche, "On the Gift-Giving Virtue," in ibid., pt. 1, sec. 2.

76. Nietzsche, "On Old and New Tablets," in ibid., pt. 3, secs. 11, 12.

77. Nietzsche, "Zarathustra's Prologue," in ibid., pt. 1, sec. 4.

78. Nietzsche, "On the Spirit of Gravity," in ibid., pt. 3, sec. 2 (emphasis in original).

79. Steve Nadis, "Why You Live in a Multiverse," *Astronomy*, Collector's edition 2006: 32–37.

80. Nietzsche, "On the Vision and the Riddle," in *Thus Spoke Zarathustra*, trans. Kaufmann, pt. 3, sec. 2 (emphasis in original).

81. Nietzsche, "*Sanctus Januarius*," in *Gay Science*, bk. 4, sec. 341 (emphasis in original).

82. For careful and intelligent discussions of eternal recurrence, see Joan Stambaugh, *Nietzsche's Thought of Eternal Return* (Baltimore, MD: John Hopkins University Press, 1972); and Lawrence J. Hatab, *Nietzsche's Life Sentence: The Literal Meaning of Eternal Recurrence* (New York: Routledge, 2005).

83. Nietzsche, "On the Prejudices of Philosophers," *Beyond Good and Evil*, sec. 22.

84. Some scholars argue that in works Nietzsche published after *Beyond Good and Evil* (i.e., post-1886), he moves to a more objectivist position while still questioning the value of truth and endorsing perspectivism. For example, in *Genealogy of Morals* (III, sec. 12) he states: "There is *only* a perspectival seeing, *only* a perspectival 'knowing'; and the *more* affects [feelings] we allow to speak about one thing, the *more* eyes, different eyes, we can use to observe one thing, the more complete will our 'concept' of this thing, our 'objectivity,' be" (emphasis in original).

QUESTIONS FOR REFLECTION:

1. Is there a problem with reading Nietzsche in the various ways in which he seems to want us to read him? Should we require of a philosopher that she or he just be that and nothing else? Why or why not?

2. How can truth be defined in terms of error, illusion, and metaphor? How can we know the world in light of this definition?

3. Is God dead? How should this idea be interpreted in today's world?

4. What is "will to power?" Does this notion have the explanatory force that Nietzsche thinks it does?

5. Is Nietzsche's "genealogy of morals" a plausible account?

6. Is it sense or nonsense to ask, "What is the value of value?" Can values be "revalued"? How do we go about doing this?

7. The idea that we should "remain faithful to the earth" would seem to be of special importance at present. How best can we understand and apply this concept?

8. Does Nietzsche have a coherent "philosophy of the future"?

5

A BRIEF LOOK AT PHENOMENOLOGY

Although slowly evolving from the mid-eighteenth century onward, phenomenology did not really take shape in its specialized modern form until the time of Edmund Husserl (1859–1938). For historical reasons, then, it is a philosophical outlook and method that was not widely adopted until the twentieth century. A working knowledge of phenomenology helps us understand its major influence on the later development of existentialism.

PHENOMENOLOGY IS WHAT PHENOMENOLOGISTS DO

The existentialism of Heidegger, Sartre, and de Beauvoir cannot be fully appreciated without reference to phenomenology. While it is useful to develop a general understanding of what phenomenology is, it is even more instructive to look at how it is used in actual practice. Both approaches will be followed in this chapter. Joseph Kockelmans, a leading contemporary interpreter of phenomenology, argues that "Phenomenology is neither a school nor a trend in contemporary philosophy. It is rather a movement whose proponents, for various reasons, have propelled it in many distinct directions, with the result that today it means different things to different people."[1] Not only this, phenomenology has been used to throw light on a bewilderingly large array of subjects. A survey of topics addressed includes the phenomenology of: everyday life, internal time consciousness, sexual difference, landscape, music, nursing, past-life experiences, perception, electronic mail, therapeutic art expression, speech acts, music, men's experience of masculinity, astonishment, theater, film, religion, and geography. There is also phenomenological feminist philosophy, philosophy of mind, psychology, and psychotherapy. Phenomenology has even been given the unlikely characterization of being "applied philosophy."[2] In spite of this diversity of themes and directions, we shall take "phenomenology" to be the name of *a method of analytically describing different modes of experience—whether transient or enduring—in meticulous detail*, which is utilized in one form or another by twentieth-century existential thinkers such as Heidegger, Sartre, Merleau-Ponty, and de Beauvoir, and continues being influential.

WHAT CONSCIOUSNESS IS

For as long as human beings have speculated about what makes them unique in the natural order, consciousness has been placed front and center in their discussions. Today there are some who believe consciousness cannot be described, others who are trying to make sense of it in terms of physical (brain) processes alone, and still others whose research aims at showing that a variety of nonhuman species also manifest consciousness of a significant sort. We will not enter into these interesting controversies here, for the phenomenologists' position (rightly or wrongly) is that consciousness is a human endowment that is both describable and something to be studied on its own terms.

The story of phenomenology goes back to Franz Brentano and Edmund Husserl, as noted in chapter 2. Defining consciousness has been a perennially elusive goal of philosophers, and Brentano is noted for his novel proposal that, whatever other properties might be attributed to consciousness, its salient feature is *intentionality*. We have to be careful here, however, because philosophers also use "intention" to refer to one's purpose in acting in a certain manner, pretty much as we use the term in everyday life, and they have also introduced "intension" (with an "s") to refer to meaning or connotation. "Intentionality," for phenomenologists, following Brentano, designates what it is about consciousness that makes it a distinctive state, condition, attribute, potentiality, ability, or (better still) activity. In this technical sense, intentionality designates the "aboutness" or "directedness" of consciousness—the characteristic of its being concerned with something, which determines its momentary quality (as thinking about X, perceiving Y, and so on, and doing so in a certain way). Whatever it is that consciousness is occupied with, in turn, is the "intentional object" of its activity at that time. We could refer to the intentional object of consciousness as a "mental object," for example, an idea, except for the fact that phenomenologists are interested, among other things, in sidestepping the ancient mind-body problem. That is, they don't want to get into issues about the ontological status of objects of consciousness (though this has proved to be difficult, if not impossible for them to avoid); furthermore, as mentioned above, they are committed to only describing consciousness, not explaining or theorizing about it. Now, although Brentano seeks to avoid the mind-body problem, he nevertheless ventures to assert that intentionality is what sharply distinguishes conscious states from any kind of physical states whatsoever. (No physical state can be "about" or "directed at" anything else; conscious states alone can be.)

The term "intentionality" originated with medieval Scholastic philosophers, but Brentano brought it back into currency in his 1874 book, *Psychology from an Empirical Standpoint*. (Remember that at this time philosophy and psychology were inseparable, and even when they began to go their own ways, psychology was first called "mental philosophy.") Brentano thought that every act of consciousness is intentional in the special sense just explained, and of course has an intentional object. This means that conscious states are always *about, directed at, or pointed toward something*, an intentional object, which is "within" yet not identical to consciousness. Phenomenologists do not consider that ideas and other mental entities literally reside in consciousness; nor do they accept the image of consciousness as a container. Accordingly, Brentano borrows an expression from the Scholastics—"intentional inexistence"—in order to attribute a different kind of being to the objects of consciousness. For example, when I think of my old Granny, she is present in my thought in some fashion, yet what I am thinking about is not some homunculus situated in my consciousness but rather someone who exists (or existed) in the real world. This all makes sense; but you will easily understand how ontological problems arise from even this simplest account. What is it, exactly, that *does* inhabit my consciousness at this moment? What is the relationship between the intentional object and the real object (Granny herself)? And if Granny is no longer with us, what sort(s) of objects are we talking about then? These are intriguing questions, and they led Brentano to make major changes in his theory that posed challenges for later phenomenologists to deal with.

One additional feature of consciousness that Brentano singled out as definitive is that all of its acts are *accompanied by reflexive self-awareness.* In other words, consciousness is, in some manner, always aware of itself engaged in the process of doing what it does. To desire something is both to desire and to be aware of one's desiring; to see something is also to be aware that one is seeing, and so on. Even if we don't explicitly attend to this secondary awareness, it hovers in the background, so to speak. Sartre, in particular, makes a good deal of this feature of consciousness in his examination of "bad faith," which we'll investigate in chapter 7. (But see appendix G, "A Problem about Consciousness.")

THE STRUCTURE OF CONSCIOUSNESS

Husserl, a student of Brentano's, began the modern phenomenological movement. He dedicated himself to the concept that the task of philosophy should be to describe accurately and in fine detail the various ways in which things appear to us in experience and in everyday sorts of mental activity. Philosophy should avoid the temptation to offer grand theoretical accounts and should concentrate instead on what is concrete, providing a descriptive analysis of both the objects of consciousness and the structure of consciousness in regard to its object—its intentional stance, as it were. While both the object and the structure of consciousness are interrelated, Husserl insists that neither is reducible to the other. Many of his discussions take on the character of thought experiments, and he believed that by concentrating on different components of what he was investigating, its most characteristic properties (or essence) would eventually shine forth. This he held to be true of both the objects of consciousness and the intentional modalities of consciousness itself (such as perception, imagination, memory, judgment, and anticipation). He further argued that we must suspend or "bracket" our ordinary engagement with things, our "natural attitude" toward them, in order to conduct phenomenological investigations. Husserl attempted to explain how this suspension (or *epoché*,[3] as he called it) could be achieved, but it remains problematic whether one can truly disengage from the powerful sway of basic beliefs just as he would wish us to do. Be this as it may, what is central in Husserl's phenomenological approach is the attempt to grasp and articulate the character of experience as it exists before reflection begins, or *pretheoretically.* That is, phenomenology strives to gain access to and present experience as it is in itself, without taking into account its psychological origin, causal explanation, or the overlay of concepts and second- and higher-order beliefs that usually accompany it.

Now what more, exactly, is the subject matter of phenomenological philosophy? As one commentator states:

> It should analyze, e.g., how visual objects are perceived and how they depend on our cognitive activity of seeing, focusing, moving about, on the correlation of seeing with touching and grasping, and so on. Philosophy should describe the different ways in which such "regions of being" as material objects, living things, other persons, and cultural objects are given, how the past and the present are intended, how speech, numbers, time and space, and our own bodies are given to us, and so on.[4]

Thus, phenomenology is concerned with how consciousness displays itself by means of its specific acts, and how it constructs "the world." One can readily discern that for Husserl and those who followed his lead, experience is not the passive receptivity of sensations but something more like what we might call "participatory construction," in which an active mind responds to what's presented to it. And a more adequate model of cognition reveals that it encompasses many kinds of apprehending (literally: "laying hold of") or "taking," in which intentional objects are positioned and manipulated in relation to one another.

Although Husserl sought after certainty in his phenomenological investigations (thus retaining the ancient credo that philosophy is an avenue to absolute and objective truth), he also affirmed that experience is much too rich and complex ever to be exhaustively described. Not only does it surpass the limits of language, it also has dimensions (ways of presenting itself) that we cannot know or even completely absorb. Part of the reason for this is that there are infinite numbers of perspectives we can assume toward things; and part is owing to the fact that "the world" comprises both presences and absences. A simple geometrical solid, for instance, can be viewed from many angles, but not from all at once. Those features we now view are present (or presented) to us, the rest are absent (or absented) from us, but they contribute nonetheless to the total picture we have of the object in question. When we shift perspectives, the now absent features will be visible and the ones formerly on view will become absent. We can appreciate this better if we think of variations in lighting, patterns, shadows, and the like as important and defining aspects of what we experience when moving around objects. Not only this, but we also *experience* absence and presence, Husserl would suggest, as when an object itself moves through space from one place to another. Indeed, for an object to come into a place where we can now view it when formerly we could not is to be understood as presence ("manifestness," "closeness," or "givenness") replacing absence ("hidenness," "distance," or "emptiness"). Thus, Husserl notes, "perception must have a mixture of empty and filled intentions."[5] In a similar vein, expectations can be characterized as absences waiting to be filled and mere beliefs can be characterized as requiring substantiation in order to give them the content (or credibility) that turns them into knowledge. As we shall see, ideas such as these were of special importance to both Heidegger and Sartre in their own separate ways.

CONSCIOUSNESS AND THE WORLD

We know right away from considering phenomenology in general terms that those who practice it recommend a view of consciousness that sees it not as something occult and undiagnosable, not as a property or faculty of some "inner self," but rather as something that occurs *out in the world* and engages with it. This is a monumental shift in emphasis and conception that required a complete reorientation of philosophy. We can appreciate this more clearly by examining the thought of Maurice Merleau-Ponty (1908–61), who was not only one of Husserl's more prominent followers but also a high school classmate of Sartre and de Beauvoir in Paris and later part of the same French intellectual scene. As one of the relatively accessible philosophers of his time, Merleau-Ponty helped to popularize phenomenology and make its precepts more readily understood. He maintains that phenomenology is "a philosophy for which the world is always 'already there' before reflection begins. . . . It is [1] the search for a philosophy which shall be a 'rigorous science,' but it also offers [2] an account of space, time and the world as we 'live' them."[6] Although Husserl was devoted to (1), most of his followers (like Merleau-Ponty) have been more greatly attracted to (2), or what we might call the practical applications of phenomenology, deriving from Husserl's commitment to immersion in experiential subjectivity and the descriptive analysis of it. Merleau-Ponty adds that, historically speaking, phenomenology "has been long on the way," and that traces of it can be found in Kierkegaard and Nietzsche, among others.

What each of us is, according to Merleau-Ponty, is not something that can be captured by the abstract categories of science, for every individual human being represents a viewpoint on the world, an opening into existence. "I am the absolute source, my existence does not stem from my antecedents, from my physical and social environment; instead it moves out toward them and sustains them. . . . [C]onsciousness . . . [is that] through which from the outset a world forms itself round me and begins to exist for me."[7] The main thing to note here is that from the idea of the immediacy and self-sufficiency of experience comes that of consciousness in general (and each specific consciousness) being embedded in the world, and the world itself being a construction of consciousness. This does not entail that the world is merely a collection of our ideas, that it has no existence independent of minds. Rather, what the phenomenologist is getting at is that what we call "the world" is where we first discover ourselves to be; it is therefore the ground of all else that takes place in our lives. Thus, my consciousness is my point of view on the world, and from this position I then go on to give the world overall meaning, to imbue specific encounters with significance, and, most importantly, to act. As Merleau-Ponty writes:

> The real is a closely woven fabric. It does not await our judgement before incorporating the most surprising phenomena, or before rejecting the most plausible figments of our imagination. Perception is not a science of the world, it is not even an act, a deliberate taking up of a position; it is the background from which all acts stand out, and is presupposed by them.
>
> The world is not an object such that I have in my possession the law of its making; it is the natural setting of, and field for, all my thoughts and all my explicit perceptions. Truth does not "inhabit" only "the inner man," or more accurately, there is no inner man, man is in the world, and only in the world does he know himself.[8]

The lesson of phenomenology, then, is that human beings are "in the world" and "of the world" in the fundamental sense that the world is the inescapable context of our being. "I" is not the name of some metaphysical entity that transcends the world or resides in the depths of a psyche that has its own plane of existence independent of the material realm; I am, precisely speaking, "out there."

How it happens that each of us experiences the *same* world may be a matter of both the constitution of the world itself and of human consciousness in general, and various phenomenologists have debated this problem, just as have previous philosophers (for example and most notably, Kant). We will not pursue this topic further here, however. So far as existentialism is concerned, what is paramount is that "each person experiences the world in particular aspects that are exclusively one's [own] aspects of always the same world. . . . [Hence, the world is that] in relation to which one is constantly situating oneself."[9] What this means is that consciousness (or conscious experience), which is a human's way of being in the world, is always embedded in the world, as stated above, and, in an ultimate sense, cannot unanchor or alienate itself from that world. I must therefore constantly take account of the world and its relationship to me, as well as my relationship to it and to the other consciousnesses that cohabit the world with me. This is a powerful premise that not only echoes Nietzsche's pronouncement that one should "remain faithful to the earth," but also foreshadows the doctrines of Heidegger, Sartre, and de Beauvoir, insofar as they concern our presence in the world with others and advocate ultimate personal responsibility for our being who we are.

The moral of the story, for Merleau-Ponty as for Husserl, is simply that "the world is there before any possible analysis of mine. . . ."[10] It is a given, a backdrop, that provides the opportunity for there to be things that happen at all, or for people to be at all. In this way, phenomenology and existentialism together undercut some very basic and persistent old philosophical "problems," such as whether there really is a world that exists independent of minds; whether anything can ever be reliably known about the world; and whether there are minds other than my own. These vanish because of the starting point that is posited: We exist and are bodily implanted in the world, which is no less obviously there and presupposed by our existence than our biological parents can be said to be. "Our relationship to the world, as it is untiringly enunciated within us," Merleau-Ponty urges, "is not a thing which can be any further clarified by analysis; philosophy can only place it once more before our eyes and present it for our ratification."[11] In other words, the fact of our being in the world is constantly impressed upon us; it neither can be proven nor does it need to be proven. It is only something we can assent to when what we take for granted is made the object of attention. Beyond this, "true philosophy consists in re-learning to look at the world. . . ."[12] and phenomenology is "a disclosure of the world. . . ."[13] This implies that the proper job of philosophy is to employ the procedures of phenomenology in order to reveal what we in a sense already know—the deeper subtleties of lived, worldly experience.

THE BODILY PRESENCE OF HUMAN BEINGS

Merleau-Ponty's application of phenomenology is most noteworthy in relation to the concrete embodiment of human beings. That is, he seeks to understand what it is for us to be in, or a part of, the world, and from there, to orient our thinking about other facets of living in the world by viewing them as projections of consciousness expressed in physical behavior.

Humans are, first of all, "incarnate subjects" or embodied consciousnesses. Thus, once again, the initial assumption he makes undercuts the long-standing philosophical puzzle about how a unity or harmony of mind and body—two supposedly disparate things—can occur within us. To call humans "incarnate subjects" is just to say that we are given to ourselves (and to others, by the way) as a unity of body-and-consciousness within the world, and it is only the weirdness of philosophical speculation that can tear this unity apart. Merleau-Ponty cleverly elaborates this thought as follows:

> We must therefore avoid saying that our body is *in* space, or *in* time. It *inhabits* space and time. . . . In so far as I have a body through which I act in the world, space and time are not, for me, a collection of adjacent points nor are they a limitless number of relations synthesized by any consciousness, and into which it draws my body. I am not in space and time, nor do I conceive space and time; I belong to them, my body combines with them and includes them. The space and time which I inhabit are always in their different ways indeterminate horizons which contain other points of view. The synthesis of both space and time is a task that always has to be performed afresh. . . . My body has its world, or understands its world, without having to make use of my "symbolic" or "objectifying function."[14]

Notice how Merleau-Ponty continually mingles descriptions of subjectivity and embodiment so that we get the clear message that these are not to be ontologically distinguished (that is, understood as divergent kinds of being). Consciousness is a viewpoint located in physical space; and our bodies, as one commentator puts it, are "living centres of intentionality" through which "we choose our world and our world chooses us."[15] Also, from the very opening sentence, we are told (or perhaps reminded?) that the physical or material world is a *dwelling place*, not some sterile sphere into which we are indifferently placed.

This determined emphasis on lived experience and embodiment as equally fundamental signifies the phenomenologists' refusal to consider questions about the "reality of the physical world." These questions are peculiarly self-cancelling because they can only be posed by persons who already exist in the world and are aware of themselves as parts of it. Likewise, the concept of the "outside" or "external" world (cherished by many philosophers) is bogus, a kind of denial of the obvious. An interesting comparison can be made here with Camus. In the section of *The Myth of Sisyphus* he calls "An Absurd Reasoning," the first-person voice of the writer asks and answers his own question: "Of whom and of what indeed can I say: 'I know that!' This heart within me I can feel, and I judge that it exists. This world I can touch, and I likewise judge that it exists. There ends all my knowledge, and the rest is construction." We can, he continues later on, really be sure of "no general notions, but merely a few clear insights."[16] Camus is not advocating a brand of skepticism here—that too would be a "construction"; instead, he reiterates the idea, shared by Merleau-Ponty, that we are situated first and foremost within the experiential world as phenomenologically described. Everything else is an overlay at some level removed from it.

PHENOMENA

No discussion of phenomenology would be complete without some account of what it studies, namely, phenomena. This word has been used by philosophers in many different ways, having to do with perception, some aspect of perception, point of view, or experience in a broader sense. What is salient about phenomenology is that it takes "phenomena" to comprise not just what we normally think of as objects, but in equal measure such things as appearances (how things appear), symbols, images, mathematical entities, illusions, presences, absences, differences, and other items. Many of these have been "excommunicated" (as Nietzsche would put it) by the philosophical tradition, which placed its stress on spatiotemporal objects, eternal ideals, and entities that exist of necessity. Whatever contrasted with these was deemed to be unworthy of study or else nonexistent. However, "For phenomenology, there are no 'mere' appearances, and nothing is 'just' an appearance. Appearances are real; they belong to being. Things do show up. . . . Things that had been declared to be merely psychological are now found to be ontological, part of the being of things. . . . There is much to think about in the way things manifest themselves and in our ability to be truthful, our ability to let things appear."[17] So phenomenology is telling us that what happens *in* consciousness is of central importance to philosophy—but this is consciousness *immersed in the world,* not consciousness as a realm of private ideas or as something radically distinct and distanced from the world. Furthermore, reality is much richer and more filled with fleeting beings than any but poets and artists had previously imagined and credited it with.

Finally, the various intentionalities of consciousness give rise to diverse phenomena, or at any rate different ways in which something can appear and, hence, to different ways in which experience can be "taken." For instance, the same house can be seen, remembered, imagined (as it is, or as transformed somehow), dreamt about, and so on. Each of these modalities of consciousness can be examined in its own right, and each contributes to the fabric of the world as we live in it.

PHENOMENOLOGY AS A SOURCE OF ILLUMINATION

We now have a working idea of what phenomenology is and what it attempts to study and accomplish. Probably the best way to really capture the flavor of phenomenology, though, is to see it in action. In this section, therefore, we'll have a look at some examples of phenomenological descriptive analysis. These speak for themselves insofar as they have a certain intuitive appeal and force. (As Merleau-Ponty remarks, "We shall find in ourselves, and nowhere else, the unity and true meaning of phenomenology.")[18] But I shall also provide some commentary on each passage.

Example #1: Lived-space.

> All live movement in space occurs as a going away or a coming back. If I sit in the café, I can rise to fetch a newspaper and afterwards return to my place. But this place in the café is only a passing point of rest. After I have read my newspaper, I arise and go "home." But after I have returned to my place of residence, am I really "at home" there? Where is my *real* home? . . . [H]owever we look at it, in some sense we can certainly say that man is home somewhere, and that his *house* is the reference point from which he builds his spatial world.
>
> But it would certainly be exaggerated and wide of the mark to call the individual house the center of a man's space. As the individual does not live alone but has a certain position as a member in a community, so also his house stands in a membered spatial surrounding. . . .
>
> [E]ven today, if I live on the edge of a city I look to some perhaps not too localizable central point in "the city." Difficult as it may be to find it in a particular instance, there is such a middle point of life-filled space which is no longer the space of the individual man, but of the group and ultimately of the nation to which he belongs.[19]

Here, the author is playing with the theme of "home" and "being at home"—not just in the sense of being where one resides, but in the larger sense of being somehow rooted in existence. "Rootedness," as I am calling it, is clearly at least in part a function of spatial location, but not of being in just any old place. The house (a particular house) is a special place because one dwells in it and, furthermore, orients oneself spatially from that "center" outward. Lived-space, therefore, has both ontological and existential meaning (it helps define who and what one is), plus purely geometrical or navigational significance. As the author goes on to argue, however, the house as center is not an absolute reference point because it is, as it were, de-centered by larger centers (city and nation) that compete with the house for designating "where one is" and where "home" is and that make rival claims on one's sense of being *in* a specially identifiable place.

Example #2: Seeing an object.

> When I do concentrate my eyes on [an object], . . . I close up the landscape and open the object. . . . [T]o look at the object is to plunge oneself into it, and . . . objects form a system in which one cannot show itself without concealing others. More precisely, the inner horizon of an object cannot become an object without the surrounding objects' becoming a horizon, and so vision is an act with two facets. . . . To see is to enter a universe of beings which *display themselves*, and they would not do this if they could not be hidden behind each other or behind me. In other words: to look at an object is to inhabit it, and from this habitation to grasp all things in terms of the aspect which they present to it. . . . [E]very object is the mirror of all others. When I look at the lamp on my table, I attribute to it not only the qualities visible from where I am, but also those which the chimney, the walls, the table can "see"; the back of my lamp is nothing but the face which it "shows" to the chimney. I can therefore see an object in so far as objects form a system or a world, and in so far as each one treats the others round it as spectators of its hidden aspects which guarantee the permanence of those aspects by their presence. Any seeing of an object by me is instantaneously repeated between all those objects in the world which are apprehended as co-existent, because each of them is all that the others "see" of it.[20]

There are several interesting features of this analysis by Merleau-Ponty. First, in seeing, the object of attention gets singled out by an act of mine, which at the same time casts surrounding objects in the role of visual "horizon." This is an instance of the figure and ground phenomenon: the object of concern to me is the figure, everything else is the ground against which it stands out. Objects are thus arranged in a system of contingently dependent relations or, more accurately, they are so organized by perception. Second, Merleau-Ponty suggests that objects "display themselves": they are what they are and they show themselves to be such; but they also are what they aren't (or aren't what they are), in that much of what we suppose ourselves to be perceiving is construction. We fill in what is missing by means of assumptions and projections from what we see to what we don't see (at the moment, at least). This is the point of all the talk in the passage above about objects "seeing" or "mirroring" one another; each background object spatially occupies the assumed perspective from which I *could* (but at present *do not*) view the object I am involved with just now. In this way, each object supports the multiple perspectives that make up the world of visual knowledge, which is a compendium of what is present and what is absent to the viewer at any one time. Third, and implied by the foregoing, what we call "the world" is defined by both what is manifest and what is concealed—by presence and absence. We can now understand why Merleau-Ponty states that "there is nothing in the world which is foreign to the mind. The world is the ensemble of objective relations borne by consciousness."[21] It follows that all knowledge of the world is both perspectival (as Nietzsche argued) and inevitably incomplete. The world's richness, like that of great literature, art, or music, always surpasses our ability to capture it in words and formulas.

Example #3: The power of a human face.

> I am alone in a closed room, submerged in the present. The future is invisible; I imagine it vaguely beyond the armchairs, the table, the walls, all these sinister and indifferent objects which hide it from me.
>
> Then someone enters, bringing me his face; everything changes. In the midst of the stalactites hanging in the present, the face, alert and inquisitive, is always ahead of the look I direct upon it. It hastens toward countless private conclusions, toward a glance cast on the sly, toward the end of a smile. If I want to decipher the face, I must anticipate it, must aim at where it is not yet, as a hunter does with swift game.
>
> I must even plant myself in the future, right in the midst of its scheme, if I want to see it advance toward me from the depths of the present.
>
> A bit of future has now entered the room; a mist of futurity surrounds the face: its future. Just a little trail of mist, only enough to fill the hollows of my hands. But I can only see the faces of men through their future. And this visible future is in itself a kind of magic.[22]

I have included this wonderfully written passage both because it demonstrates an ingenious use of phenomenological analysis and because it offers a sample of Sartre's highly original and rather unusual perspective on human life. The narrator is "submerged in the present," being evidently preoccupied with his own concerns of the moment. Everyday objects, personified as "sinister and indifferent," somehow enclose him in the present and insure that the future is blocked from view. But another person intrudes into the scene, "bringing me his face." This curious expression makes it sound as if the face is something detached from the body. In a way, for Sartre, it is, for while both body and face can be vehicles for action in the world, the face alone possesses "the look," whereby one organizes space and time and interacts with others (wordlessly), such that they are likewise engaged. The face is an enigma, says Sartre, and in order to comprehend the meaning of its look, one has to "anticipate" what the face reveals of a person's intentions and how the plot will unfold. Hence, the appearance of another person's face in my room also introduces "a bit of future" into the environment. The face—and more importantly, its look—manifest an agent's freedom; so consequently, it is always projecting into the as-yet-indeterminate future. The freedom of another keeps the narrator guessing and somewhat off balance in contrast to the more or less predictable immersion in the present that he started with. (We will examine "the look" in more detail in chapter 7.)

Example #4: Aesthetic experience.

> Those of us who have been in Paris and have looked at the piece of marble called the "Venus of Milo" know this piece to have various properties which . . . obviously hinder . . . [aesthetic experience], in consequence of which we are inclined to *overlook* them, e.g., a dark stain on the nose . . . or various rough spots, cavities, and holes in the breast, corroded probably by water, etc. In an aesthetic experience, we overlook these particular qualities of the stone and behave as if we didn't see them. . . . We *supplement* "in thought," or even in a peculiar perceptive representation, such details of the object as play a positive role in the attainment of the *optimum* of aesthetic "impression" possible in the given case. . . . In an aesthetic perception, we see the *Venus*, i.e., a woman or goddess in a situation and in a psychic condition, which expresses itself in her countenance, her movement, etc. At the same time, however, it is for us no real woman's body and no real woman. . . . [T]he sense perception is here solely a *basis* for the further peculiar psychic acts, built over it, which lead us to the "Venus of Milo" as an object of aesthetic experience.[23]

The main point of this passage is that aesthetic appreciation may involve some very subtle and more or less automatic shifts and maneuvers made by our consciousness. Some of these involve substituting what is absent for what is present and bringing to bear on perception certain factors that enhance what we see in order to maximize the impact of what we are taking in. The author suggests that we more or less fool ourselves into believing that we behold something of greater significance than is contained in what we visually perceive. In a sense, we "know" in advance what we want to see here (the Venus of Milo), so we create the experience that corresponds to this expectation.

As we discover in this example, one of the things to which phenomenologists call our attention is the *structured* nature of experience. Influential in this regard has been the movement known as "Gestalt psychology," which flourished in the early twentieth century. The word "gestalt" has passed into regular English and refers to "an organized whole perceived as more than the sum of its parts."[24] Gestalt psychologists drove home the valid point that perceptions are not made up of isolated bits and pieces, and not even collections of these, but rather of configurations, forms, or patterns, which often depend on perspective, on what counts as foreground and background, on surrounding cues, and so on. For example, a drawing of a cube, showing all of its edges, will seem to have one surface pushing out toward the viewer, then suddenly things shift so that the same surface seems most distant.

Trick pictures, such as the young woman/old woman, duck/rabbit, or the vase that can also be seen as two faces looking at each other (see "Rubin's vase" below), likewise illustrate the gestalt principle, as do optical illusions, such as the photo of a distorted room in which a small dog looks larger than a boy or a child larger than an adult. The lesson gained from these examples is that perception is a holistic process, and that is the insight phenomenologists are determined to convey as well.

"Rubin's vase," named after Danish psychologist Edgar Rubin (1886–1951), who first devised this figure about 1915.

Example #5: Unintended behaviors.

> The comedy begins with the simplest of our movements, each of which carries with it an inevitable awkwardness. In putting out my hand to approach a chair, I have creased the sleeve of my jacket. I have scratched the floor, I have dropped the ash from my cigarette. In doing that which I wanted to do, I have done so many things I did not want. The act has not been pure, for I have left traces. . . . We are thus responsible beyond our intentions. It is impossible for the regard that directs the act to avoid the nonintended action that comes with it. . . . That is to say, our consciousness and our mastery of reality through consciousness do not exhaust our relation to reality, to which we are always present through all the density of our being. Consciousness of our reality does not coincide with our habitation of the world. . . .[25]

This passage tells us that even the simplest human actions produce unanticipated and unplanned (and sometimes unwished-for) consequences. Since we cannot help but be the agent of these effects, we are—to some extent at least—responsible for them, if only as the factor that brought them about. But the larger implication of the scenario sketched by the author is that one's presence in the world (as an embodied subject) is more pervasive ("dense") than we normally imagine, and that the domain one supposes oneself to be in control of is only a subset of the domain one actually and unwittingly influences. Therefore, conscious awareness of personal behavior is but a doubtful guide as to the true scope of one's environmental and social impacts.

Example #6: Kindness.

> When I perceive an act of kindness, I see the other as somehow influencing my life. I am simultaneously aware of myself as in need of the particular service performed. But I also judge the other's intervention as an act of generosity or of courtesy. I interpret it as a commitment to lighten my burdens coupled with a respect for my feelings.
>
> In other words, based on this judgment, I am aware of the other in basic sympathy with me, wanting to help me in the same manner in which I would help myself were it possible. The agent of the kindness takes my part as an actor unobtrusively slips into a role—in a nondominating and nonmanipulative way. In the same gesture, acts of kindness also become acts of gentleness with the latter being conceived as a moderation or, perhaps, a reasoned control in the use of power.[26]

This author carefully reveals the complex interplay of signs and empathetic gestures that constitute kind behavior toward another, but in this instance, as experienced by someone who gives a first-person account. The elements of the exposition include both self-perception (as a function of the interpersonal engagement) and awareness of how the other comports her- or himself vis-à-vis the recipient. As well, the analysis contains descriptions of both the affective (feeling) aspects of the situation and the beliefs and commitments implicit therein.

Example #7: The grace of a stranger.

Gabriel Marcel (1889–1973), an existentialist who specializes in describing the elusive richness that is hidden in interpersonal relations, turns his imaginative eye on:

> the shy young man who is making his first appearance at some fashionable dance or cocktail party. Such a young man is . . . to the highest degree *self-conscious.* . . . Let us suppose that some unknown person comes up at our party to say a word or two to the shy young man and put him at his ease. . . . [A]nd let us suppose that the ice is after all broken, and that the conversation takes on a more intimate character.
>
> "I am glad to meet you," says the stranger, "I once knew your parents," and all at once a bond is created and, what specially matters, there is a relaxation of tension. The attention of the young man ceases to be concentrated on himself, it is as if something gripped tight together inside him were able to loosen up. He is lifted out of that stifling here-and-nowness in which, if I may be allowed a homely comparison, his ego was sticking to him as an adhesive plaster sticks to a small cut.
>
> He is lifted right out of the here and now, and, what is very strange surely, this unknown person whom he has just met accompanies him on this sort of magic voyage. They are together in what we must call an elsewhere, an elsewhere, however, which has a mysteriously intimate character.[27]

This is a setting we can all easily identify with, and that is part of the power the description has over us. We know how readily we can work ourselves into feeling "out of it" when faced with an unfamiliar or novel situation, or when inserting ourselves into a social scene full of unknown people. But we know too how a small gesture from someone else can provide a catalyst for transforming the whole experience, and how important friendships, or at any rate memorable moments, can grow out of or hinge upon the serendipitous way in which our lives may be touched by strangers. Things don't always happen so, but sometimes they do. The genius of Marcel is to capture so concisely and delicately the special kind of interpersonal space that such an encounter creates, if only for a fleeting instant.

Example #8: Relational existence.

Similar thoughts have been expressed by the other great interpersonal existentialist Martin Buber (1878–1965), whose famous expression "I and Thou" designates the unique, often fragile and transitory engagement between persons, and occasionally between persons and other living things. Here is a sample of his prose.

> The life of human beings is not passed in the sphere of transitive verbs alone. It does not exist in virtue of activities alone which have some *thing* for their object.
>
> I perceive something. I am sensible of something. I imagine something. I will something. The life of human beings does not consist of all this and the like alone.
>
> This and the like together establish the realm of *It*.
>
> But the realm of *Thou* has a different basis.
>
> When *Thou* is spoken, the speaker has no thing for his object.
>
> For where there is a thing there is another thing. Every *It* is bounded by others; *It* exists only through being bounded by others. But when *Thou* is spoken, there is no thing. *Thou* has no bounds.
>
> When *Thou* is spoken, the speaker has no *thing*; he has indeed nothing. But he takes his stand in relation.[28]

Buber is preoccupied with relational existence. He holds that humans live much of their lives not so much surrounded by things (though indeed we are), but adopting a "thinglike" connection with various beings, often including other humans. In our transactions, we may make them into things, and vice versa. When we do so, we make ourselves into things as well. Buber doesn't question that it is normally appropriate to treat mere things in a thinglike fashion—as means to our ends. And he holds that it is also not wrong to treat other humans as means to our ends, provided two conditions are met (as Kant argued long ago in his ethical writings): (1) we do so only to a certain extent (for example, in particular roles); and (2) we don't treat them *merely* as means. Not treating other humans merely as means to our ends entails treating them respectfully at the same time, as ends in themselves or beings of independent worth, having purposes of their own. Buber builds on this idea, but he gives it a mystical, spiritual twist. For him, an elusive kind of connection is born when we enter the world of relations and abandon the world of things. When "Thou" is "spoken," thing-like connections are put aside in favor of something intimate and unbounded. This doesn't mean that we literally need to say "Thou," but rather that we come toward one another on a different plane—one of true humanity, generosity, acceptance, kindness, compassion, and mutual affirmation—even love. Buber goes on to say that this is a transient moment because of the busyness that dominates our lives. He also believes that there can be times when, in the proper frame of mind and soul, we can at least come close to saying "Thou" to another sort of living thing, for instance a tree. What Buber is trying to get at is very hard to express in words, though we can, if we are willing, intuitively grasp his phenomenological description and confirm that he is capturing something familiar to us all.

Example #9: The significance of existence.

Ralph Harper (1915–96) was a philosopher and theologian who is generally credited with introducing existentialism to the United States. He wrote a number of books in which he tried to capture some of the more sensitive and elusive dimensions of the experience of being human. In the following passage, he probes what it means to exist.

> First things first: existence does precede everything else, and yet how can one speak of existence without speaking of this or that existing life? Indeed, existence is not only the first fact, it is both simple and complex: simple because undefinable, if not ineffable; complex because it is the deposit for everything else, both security and insecurity, depending on the vantage point of the intuition of existence. It may be that some people never look at themselves from any vantage point but that of other people on the outside, and we should not expect them to understand this most peculiarly personal of all experiences, the experience of the self. . . .
>
> If all we could say about our existence as human beings is that we are, and that, like everything else we experience, we some day will cease to be, it would be impossible to convince anyone that the word "existence" is worth bothering about. . . . [But] the question of existence is not only whether to be or not to be, but rather whether to be oneself or not be oneself. . . . Of course, there is an obvious sense in which one cannot be other than what one is—one's identity guarantees that. But it is just as obvious that because our ideas and even personalities change as we grow older, we do have apparent alternative ways of behaving.
>
> An accumulation of changes of one sort or another adds up often to a transformation of self.[29]

There are several themes being presented here. First of all, existence is something we intuit or know directly, without any intervening concepts, steps of inference, and so on. We do not just know it objectively, as we know that we (like all other things) will eventually perish. Second, this intuition is an intensely personal revelation of existence (of *my* existence). Third, the intuition that the existentialists are trying to specify is one telling us that each has the sole responsibility of self-making. This involves actualizing some of the various possibilities that are uniquely ours ("becoming what we are," as explained earlier with reference to Kierkegaard and Nietzsche). Finally (although Harper makes this point first in the above passage), existence is intuitively understood by us as the ground for all else—that is, as the primitive space in being, the raw material, the assumption on which we build a life and realize a life plan.

AFTERWORD: PHENOMENOLOGY AND TRUTH

Many examples of phenomenology in action, like some of the above, have the quality of creative writing, such as one finds in novels, short stories, and plays. It is no surprise, then, that a number of existentialists work comfortably in the medium of fiction as well as philosophy—most notably Camus, Sartre, and de Beauvoir. But this fact raises an interesting question: What is the test of truth for phenomenological descriptions? I've mentioned several times that they possess an intuitive appeal, but is that enough to verify their accuracy? After all, people notoriously have different intuitions about many things, and we can seldom, if ever, settle disputes at this level.

I think that no wholly satisfactory answer to our question about phenomenology can be given, for the same reason that no wholly satisfactory answer is available for the question: How do we know when fictional works speak the truth? Fictional works are, after all, meant to take place in the realm of imagination, so it seems hard to understand that they can reach beyond themselves to make firm contact with the real world in which we live. And yet few seriously doubt that they do. We know this when they resonate with our lives and perceptions. What about phenomenology? First, we must note that phenomenologists argue that the lived world of subjective experience enjoys primacy over the world as understood objectively through science. This does not mean that the former is "right" and the latter somehow "wrong"; but it does mean two things: (a) that experience (even when reflected upon) provides a more immediate view of the world than any theory-derived perspective; and (b) that abstract models of truth are inappropriate to at least some aspects of basic experience. Robert Sokolowski draws a contrast between "two kinds of truth that occur in our rational life: the truth of correctness and the truth of disclosure." The first of these is what we look for when we are trying to test a statement, proposition, or belief against experience, evidence, facts, or a body of accepted knowledge to see whether it accords with it or them. The second type of truth has more to do with revealing, showing, displaying, or as Sokolowski goes on to say, "It is the simple presencing to us of an intelligible object, the manifestation of what is real or actual." When so "presented to us, the object or the situation simply unfolds."[30]

It follows, then, that phenomenological descriptions can claim to be true—in the sense appropriate to them—if they disclose something meaningful to us; that is, if they hold some feature of the world or experience up to us so that we gain fresh insight into its nature. Husserl thought that by doing so, phenomenology taps into the essences of things, which is a contentious supposition. It would seem to be enough just to assert that we learn through phenomenological descriptions to see things in a new way, to deepen our understanding of them, and to grow richer in ourselves as a consequence. We don't always find ourselves agreeing completely with the phenomenologists' take on experience or situations, but we may find insight nonetheless or at least a bold challenge to produce a different kind of disclosure that strikes us as more truthful. Sartre serves up very powerful descriptions that reveal disturbing facets of human relationships, and we find these virtually impossible to disregard, even if we don't like his conclusions. Heidegger adopts an approach that is more one of letting things show themselves, or as we might alternatively put it, letting the truth shine forth or emerge. In either case, however, we, the active observers and involved participants, are invited to join in with an open mind on a project to let things speak to us or become more clear. This is a process whereby we become receptive to the nuances of experience that are frequently invisible to us in the absence of a more insightful individual to expose them to our view.

Perhaps the best we can do, then, is admit that phenomenology, like most other forms of philosophy, offers arguments, not proofs, where the word "argument" must be understood in the broader sense I have developed in discussing Kierkegaard (in chapter 3). One commentator suggests that

in point of fact, all interpretive phenomenological inquiry is cognizant of the realization that no interpretation is ever complete, no explication of meaning is ever final, no insight is beyond challenge. Therefore, it behooves us to remain as attentive as possible to life as we live it and to the infinite variety of possible human experiences and possible explications of those experiences.[31]

Thus, phenomenology pays homage to the fact that there is no privileged standpoint from which to view the world. And if we accept this insight, we are likewise obliged to concede that the descriptive analyses of experience that it offers do not constitute tidy packages but instead testify to the absence of closure in human experience and the unfinished character of human existence.

NOTES

1. Joseph J. Kockelmans, "Phenomenology," in *The Cambridge Dictionary of Philosophy*, 2nd ed., ed. Robert Audi (Cambridge: Cambridge University Press, 1999), p. 664.

2. See Thomas Attig, "Existential Phenomenology and Applied Philosophy," in *Phenomenology in Practice and Theory*, ed. William S. Hamrick (Dordrecht, The Netherlands: Martinus Nijhoff, 1985), pp. 161–76.

3. Husserl uses Greek words, which are transliterated here. The *epoché* is introduced in Edmund Husserl, *Ideas: General Introduction to Pure Phenomenology*, trans. W. R. Boyce Gibson (London: George Allen & Unwin; New York: Macmillan, 1931), secs. 31, 32.

4. Robert Sokolowski, "Husserl, Edmund," in *The Cambridge Dictionary of Philosophy*, p. 405.

5. Ibid.

6. Maurice Merleau-Ponty, *The Phenomenology of Perception*, trans. Colin Smith (London: Routledge and Kegan Paul, 1962), p. 357.

7. Ibid., pp. 357–58.

8. Ibid., p. 359.

9. W. Kim Rogers, "World," in *Dictionary of Existentialism*, ed. Haim Gordon (Westport, CT: Greenwood Press, 1999), p. 497.

10. Merleau-Ponty, *Phenomenology of Perception*, p. 358.

11. Ibid., p. 363.

12. Ibid., p. 364.

13. Ibid., p. 365.

14. Ibid., pp. 139, 140–41 (emphasis in original).

15. Richard Kearney, *Modern Movements in European Philosophy* (Manchester, UK: Manchester University Press, 1986), p. 74.

16. Albert Camus, *The Myth of Sisyphus and Other Essays*, trans. Justin O'Brien (New York: Vintage Books/Random House, 1959). pp. 14, 41.

17. Robert Sokolowski, *Introduction to Phenomenology* (Cambridge: Cambridge University Press, 2000), p. 15.

18. Merleau-Ponty, *Phenomenology of Perception*, p. viii.

19. O. F. Bollnow, "Lived-Space," trans. Dominic Gerlach, in *Readings in Existential Phenomenology*, ed. Nathaniel Lawrence and Daniel O'Connor (Englewood Cliffs, NJ: Prentice-Hall, 1967), p. 180 (emphasis in original).

20. Merleau-Ponty, *Phenomenology of Perception*, pp. 67, 68 (emphasis in original).

21. Maurice Merleau-Ponty, *The Structure of Behaviour*, trans. Alden L. Fisher (London: Methuen, 1965), p. 3.

22. Jean-Paul Sartre, "Faces, Preceded by Official Portraits," trans. Anne P. Jones, in *Essays in Phenomenology*, ed. Maurice Natanson (The Hague: Martinus Nijhoff, 1966), p. 161.

23. Roman Ingarden, "Aesthetic Experience and Aesthetic Object," trans. Janina Makota with the cooperation of Professor Shia Moser, in *Readings in Existential Phenomenology*, ed. Lawrence and O'Connor, pp. 306–308 (emphasis in original).

24. *The Australian Concise Oxford Dictionary*, 4th ed., ed. Bruce Moore (South Melbourne: Oxford University Press, 2004), p. 584.

25. Emmanuel Levinas, "Is Ontology Fundamental?" in *Emmanuel Levinas: Basic Philosophical Writings*, ed. Adriaan T. Peperzak, Simon Critchley, and Robert Bernasconi (Bloomington: Indiana University Press, 1996), p. 4.

26. William S. Hamrick, "Kindness," in *Phenomenology in Practice and Theory*, ed. Hamrick, p. 210.

27. Gabriel Marcel, *The Mystery of Being*, vol. 1 (Chicago: Henry Regnery, 1951), as reprinted in *Phenomenology and Existentialism*, ed. Robert C. Solomon (New York: Harper and Row, 1972), pp. 432–44 (emphasis in original).

28. Martin Buber, *I and Thou*, 2nd ed., trans. Ronald Gregor Smith (Edinburgh, UK: T. and T. Clark, 1958), pp. 16–17 (emphasis in original).

29. Ralph Harper, *The Existential Experience* (Baltimore, MD: Johns Hopkins University Press, 1972), pp. 20, 22–23.

30. Sokolowski, *Introduction to Phenomenology*, pp. 158, 159.

31. Max von Manen, "Writing Phenomenology," in *Writing in the Dark: Phenomenological Studies in Interpretive Inquiry*, ed. Max von Manen (London, ON: Althouse Press, 2002), p. 7.

QUESTIONS FOR REFLECTION

1. Why is it important to view experience holistically? Give an example from your life in which you found that doing so was especially significant and explain why.

2. Do you agree that intentionality is what uniquely distinguishes consciousness from anything else? If you agree, how would you deal with the problem of identifying intentional objects for acts of imagination, dreaming, and thinking about what is nonexistent? If you do not agree, then what (if anything) *does* uniquely distinguish consciousness from all else?

3. Explain Merleau-Ponty's view of "embodied consciousness" and discuss its implications for the way philosophers think about the world.

4. Select one example from the section "Phenomenology as a source of illumination" and give your own interpretation of what the quoted author is trying to get at.

5. From what you have learned about phemonemology, how do you think it can enrich your understanding of your own life? Of film, theater, music, or art?

6

HEIDEGGER

THE QUEST FOR BEING

*Martin Heidegger (1889–1976) revolutionized existentialism in several ways: by intro-
ducing phenomenological descriptions, by sidestepping the theism-atheism conflict, and
by focusing on detailed consideration of our everyday experience of "being-in-the-
world." Because of his focus on Being and his claim to have moved beyond traditional
metaphysics, he takes on the persona of an "anti-philosopher." Heidegger's influence
has been enormous in a variety of fields.*

PHILOSOPHY AS AN OPENING OUT

Whatever else philosophers might say about their subject, one
theme that constantly recurs is its discovery of the unfamiliar
within the familiar and its ability to show us what we already
know in a new and more intense light. For Heidegger, philosophy teaches
us to look and listen as we have not done before and to cultivate a fresh
sensitivity and receptivity so that things can speak to us on a different
plane. He writes, provocatively, "It is absolutely correct and proper to say
that 'You can't do anything with philosophy'. It is only wrong to suppose
that this is the last word on philosophy. For the rejoinder imposes itself;
granted that *we* cannot do anything with philosophy, might not philos-

ophy, if we concern ourselves with it, do something *with us?*"[1] Whether or not he actually believes it to be so, Heidegger concedes here that philosophy is an impractical subject because he wants to get beyond this supposition to his real point: that philosophy can change us, radically altering or reorienting our lives. It's almost as if there were an independent agent, Philosophy, wielding power over us, just as we sometimes hear music, art, or spiritual enlightenment described.

What is the power of philosophy, then? Aside from its being a form of inquiry that "breaks paths," "opens perspectives," and "threatens all values," for Heidegger it serves a more important function; that is, *philosophy helps us recover our roots in Being.* If done properly, it creates a clearing in which Being can disclose itself to us. As Arno Baruzzi comments, "Philosophy was and is ontology; it interprets being by unfolding, disentangling, analysing it. . . ."[2]

Heidegger's orientation needs to be appreciated in its own terms. We can understand better what he is up to by noting that his philosophy circles round a radically different problematic. ("Problematic," used as a noun, is a technical term that refers to the way in which a question or debate is framed.) The problematic of most philosophers (and especially modern philosophers from Descartes onwards) can be expressed as follows: "How can I (or just: can I) know anything reliably?" Instead of adopting the same approach, Heidegger's problematic is this: "What is it for something—anything—to be?" (or just: "What is Being?"). But it's not merely that Heidegger takes off in an unexplored direction; he also believes that the more commonly posed basic question about knowing presupposes his newer one, and is therefore subsidiary to it.

Let's bring this down to the personal level. One could say that the issue expressed when we ask, "What is it for *me* to be?" precedes and underlies (makes possible) the asking of all questions pertaining to knowledge. As Michael Gelven suggests, "To-be-in-a-world is the ultimate presupposition of knowledge."[3] This is such a simple statement as to appear a truism, but it should not be despised for that. In any case, Heidegger asks, not only, "Mustn't I first exist in order to know?" but also, "What does it *mean* for me to exist?" His point is that we take our existence for granted in raising questions about knowledge (ethics, metaphysics, and the other fields of philosophy—and, for that matter, all fields of knowledge outside philosophy, too), and perhaps we ought *not* to, lest we miss something of paramount importance. What could this be? Nothing less than our situation in Being, our place in the scheme of things. Heidegger's persistent question can now be stated in this way: "Shouldn't we be taking this (our situation in Being) as the most vital issue of them all, the true starting point for *any* thinking?"

Now that you've had a taste of Heidegger's approach, it should be clear that he's no ordinary thinker. In fact, owing to his preoccupation and his offbeat, experimental approach to philosophizing, some commentators have been reluctant even to classify Heidegger as an existentialist. But we shall find, I think, that there are good and sufficient reasons for doing so.

METAPHYSICAL HOMESICKNESS

In chapter 2 we considered "metaphysical homelessness" as a metaphor for the human condition, with special reference to Pascal. In a similar vein, Heidegger posits that modern humans have lost their way in the universe. Reflecting on a comment by the Romantic poet Novalis (pseudonym of Friedrich von Hardenberg, 1772–1801), he asserts that philosophy is a kind of "homesickness," and (potentially) a response to this affliction. But "to be at home everywhere"—which is Heidegger's interpretation of the remedy we need—"means to be at once and at all times within the whole. . . . This is where we are driven in our homesickness: to being as a whole."[4] We are, in other words, directed to seek something we have apparently lost, namely, a primordial placement in the scheme of things.

It is characteristic of Heidegger to present an occasion like this, in which questioning is focused on the nature of philosophy, as a stage in the quest for Being. Philosophy is something that "happens" when we are "gripped" and turned toward a "fundamental attunement" with Being, which itself waits to be known and understood.[5] Philosophical questions are asked by, and from the standpoint of the only entity that is both *able* to interrogate Being and unable *not* to do so—the human being.

Heidegger takes Nietzsche's nihilistic dilemma (see chapter 4) with the utmost seriousness: With the collapse of the Judeo-Christian worldview as a solid framework for interpreting existence, a chasm of meaninglessness looms before us. We must either rise to this challenge or be claimed as the victims of nihilism. But Heidegger's response to the problem of metaphysical homesickness moves in a startlingly different direction from Nietzsche's. While remaining "faithful to the earth," like Nietzsche, Heidegger plunges into the heart of everyday life to seek there a window into Being that leads to a new ground or center where the rift in the human spirit can be healed. This *sounds* like a religious appeal, but Heidegger, though raised a Catholic, is cautious to not commit himself on this score, and he is generally considered to be neither a theist nor an atheist. This makes his philosophical approach attractive to a very wide audience, for we can all appreciate and understand that there is a contemporary spiritual crisis and, without too much additional effort, we can relate to the idea of metaphysical homesickness as its chief symptom.

BEING AND EXISTENCE

"Being" is the umbrella term philosophers since the beginning have used to denote what is: Whatever is, has being, or is part of being. "Existence," for existentialists, as indicated previously, refers to that special kind of being that humans have, or live. The insight might therefore suggest itself that existence is an avenue into understanding being as a whole—if there is any such avenue. And, indeed, this is exactly the route Heidegger takes. We will return to this plot in a moment, but first, a little relevant historical background is necessary.

In his metaphysical theorizing, Aristotle distinguished between entities and "being as such." Many things—of this kind and that—exist, each after its own fashion, he reasoned; but they all have something in common, which is being. It is difficult enough to define what it means for something to exist, harder still to think about being pure and simple. Yet Aristotle held that it is "being *qua* being" (or being as such, in itself, in general, in its own right) that the metaphysician wishes to know and understand. That is, what the metaphysician (or the ontologist, a metaphysician specializing in the study of being) wants to grasp is the essence or nature of being, not being as manifested one way or another in the sundry things that are. General knowledge and the diverse branches of science may classify the things that are, but metaphysics alone aims to answer questions lying beyond the boundaries of ordinary knowledge and science, such as that concerning the "is-ness" of what is, and how this "is-ness" can be comprehended. (For ontology, its business is "is-ness," we might say.)

Now some may find (and some philosophers have found) that all of this sounds like nonsense or, at any rate, like the raising of questions that are deeply unanswerable. More significantly, however, some major philosophers who have taken ontology seriously have drifted far from Aristotle's target of concern. For centuries, their objective had been to identify and characterize the permanent, unchanging substance(s) that lies (lie) behind all that is changeable. By the time of the Renaissance, not much difference remained between the concepts of existence and being. By the eighteenth century, Kant (arguing against the standard proofs of God's existence) was able to declare that existence is not a property or attribute of anything and that it makes no difference to our concept of a thing. And by the nineteenth century, Hegel had drawn the conclusion that "being," in the abstract, is an empty notion, entirely equivalent to "nothing," in support of which he cited Heraclitus (flourished c. 500 BCE), a philosopher who lived over a century before Aristotle.[6] (As one commentator points out, for Heidegger, Being is not opposed to Becoming; "Being is itself temporalised and has itself a history."[7] Heidegger pursues the theme of the history of Being in great detail in *Contributions to Philosophy*.)[8]

Where does this leave the debate? In Heidegger's view, it is greatly lamentable that the fortunes of Being should have sunk so low. This only shows, he believes, how alienated and uncoupled we have become from our true source of orientation in the universe after which philosophers once sought. "Being," he urges, "is still waiting for the time when it will become thought-provoking to man."[9] How can this problem be redressed? For Heidegger, the answer lies in finding some point of access into Being, as already indicated. Since we humans are immersed in existence, and since existence is a sub-species of Being, then the evident path to our goal is through an analysis of existence.

DASEIN

Heidegger's special term for human existence is "Dasein," a German word that literally means "there (*da*)-being (*sein*)." Dasein is usually left untranslated in English-language editions of his texts. The initial characterization of existentialism in chapter 1 included the idea that humans are placed in existence and simply discover themselves there. They must face the silent imperative: "Deal with it." Heidegger calls this peculiarity of existence "thrownness," which suggests being dropped into a situation or condition and hitting the ground running, so to speak. It also suggests that what we encounter is not of our own making or choice—though it can become so to a large extent as life unfolds and if we willingly take charge of it for ourselves. The concept of "Dasein" reflects all this, for it embodies the meaning that humans are just *there*, and that their form of being is to *be there*.[10] Where is "there"? In existence, to begin with, but also in a place or space of responsibility for self-making. Where we are, in a broader sense, it is our task to discover and, as explained above, this will turn out to be within Being, awareness of which we may or may not succeed in fully achieving.

Here is Heidegger's definition of Dasein:

> Dasein is an entity which does not just occur among other entities.
>
> Rather it is ontically distinguished [made unique as an entity] by the fact that, in its very Being, that Being is an *issue* for it. But in that case, this is a constitutive state of Dasein's Being, and this implies that Dasein, in its Being, has a relationship towards that Being. . . .
>
> That kind of Being towards which Dasein can comport itself in one way or another, and always does comport itself somehow, we call "*existence.*" And because we cannot define Dasein's essence by citing a "what" of the kind that pertains to a subject-matter, and because its essence lies rather in the fact that in each case it has its Being to be, and has it as its own, we have chosen to designate this entity as "Dasein," a term which is purely an expression of its Being.[11]

Heidegger argues here that Dasein doesn't just occur as a matter of fact, doesn't just have the same mode of being that pertains to all other things; instead, it has the singular feature of being disposed to question itself, especially where and how it belongs in the universe. Since Dasein's "place" (whatever it may be) is within Being as a whole, it follows, Heidegger holds, that Dasein has a fundamentally intimate relationship to the totality of Being, or being as such. Dasein's way of behaving, or "comporting itself," with respect to Being is its existence and the character of this existence it is Dasein's mission to work out and define. How it engages in doing this at any given stage represents its evolving relationship to Being.

Lastly, "Dasein" sounds like an abstract entity that is difficult for us to relate to. But although an "it" grammatically speaking, "Dasein" is meant to signify *who* we are; *each of us is Dasein*, and each one of us should put her- or himself in its place in Heidegger's text. Heidegger often seems to be repetitious in his remarks about Dasein, but one could say that he is doing variations on a theme, much as Kierkegaard does, aiming at a deeper form of understanding each time. He's also reminding us what we're after so that we stay attentive to the task at hand.

WORLD

Dasein exists in a world; more properly speaking, Dasein exists or spreads itself out in *its* world. But what is it to "exist in a world"? "World," for

Heidegger, is not a technical term, but he does give it a special, enriched meaning. The world Dasein inhabits is a set of relationships and possibilities that are worked out in interaction with the things that surround us, with certain goals and projects in view. Understood thus, the world gives meaning to human lives played out within it. In Heidegger's sense, each of us inhabits a plurality of "worlds" that correspond to our roles and situations. Hence, expressions like "the world of the poet," "the world of parents," or "the world of everyday Dasein" take on added significance and designate areas ripe for phenomenological investigation. "'I reside' or 'dwell alongside' the world, as that which is familiar to me in such and such a way," says Heidegger.[12] Dasein does not merely occupy space as objects do; it continuously changes and defines things and itself in relation to them.

EVERYDAYNESS

Each reader of Heidegger, we've seen, is a stand-in for Dasein. You will infer from the account I have given thus far that Dasein is not doing particularly well in seeking after Being, since we have fallen away from it (Being is a nothing, a vapor, an empty concept, and so on); because of this we have slid into metaphysical homesickness. But Heidegger should not be thought of as merely a judgmental, censorious voice. For his method is one of cautious hope, designed to utilize the phenomenological description of everyday life as a route from existence to Being.

A group of scholars observes that "although existentialism began somewhat earlier than phenomenology, it was not until the advent of phenomenology that existentialism was provided with a method appropriate to its concerns. . . . It is not until Heidegger that the two are combined into a single project—that of describing everyday human existence in uniquely human ways."[13] Indeed, Heidegger asserts that we may consider "every way of indicating things as they show themselves in themselves [as] 'phenomenology.'"[14] He also adds a few lines later that "*ontology is possible only as phenomenology.*" Describing existence, then, is a phenomenological mission, and it is also a form of ontology, a study of what is, to the extent that Heidegger seeks an understanding of what it is to be human.

The project just summarized occupies Heidegger's major work *Being and Time,* and its larger purpose is to enable us to take charge of ourselves or become "authentic." His teaching, as we shall see, is that clues for how to do this are there for discovery within the fabric of everyday life. (Note, however, that authenticity is not an end in itself; it is not the object of our existential yearning. That role is filled, once again, by Being. And so "authenticity" refers to a way of conducting our lives rather than a doctrine concerning what we should aim at becoming.)

Some salient characteristics of everyday life are now ripe for attention. These are the key elements that influence Dasein both negatively and positively in relation to its quest for self-understanding and for a revelation of Being.

The "they." We are each members of the general public and to varying degrees we let ourselves be shaped by others and defer to their opinions. In the busyness, confusion, conflicting demands, and din of everyday life, we tend to lose sight of ourselves and "go with the flow" or "follow the path of least resistance." When we do so, we let ourselves in for what Heidegger calls "inconspicuous domination by Others." His description of this anonymous reference group is interesting and subtle: "'The Others' whom one thus designates in order to cover up the fact of one's belonging to them essentially oneself, are those who proximally and for the most part '*are there*' in everyday Being-with-one-another. The 'who' is not this one, not that one, not oneself, not some people, and not the sum of them all. The 'who' is the neuter, the '*they*.'"[15] Notice that Heidegger is implicating no one in particular, not "them" and not "myself." We *all* need to be cognizant of this natural, social process of absorption in the commonplace, in taking things for granted, so as to avoid loss of self. This implies refraining from shifting responsibility onto others for what we should take charge of ourselves and avoiding self-justification by appeal to anonymous and amorphous opinion-makers (for example, "the media," "the average person," "they") and shadowy decision-makers (for example, "society," "scientists," "experts," "bureaucrats").

Idle talk, curiosity, and ambiguity. Our daily conversation is often fairly inconsequential, dealing with very ordinary concerns such as the weather, family doings, the latest gossip, sports events, and so forth. Much of this talk springs from curiosity, which appears to be motivated by attraction to, or fascination for, its subject matter, but it is also essentially an indifference toward it. Heidegger also refers to "the ambiguity of the way things have been publicly interpreted,"[16] by which he means to call attention to the fact that idle talk covers topics and events that are really not as clear-cut as they are represented. Gossip, for instance, does not reveal what is information and what is disinformation, what the spoken words mean to those who speak them, what the narrative (if true) means to those living through the situation being narrated, whether the intent of the narrative is malicious or shows genuine concern, and so on. Idle talk in general, then, is chatter without clear meaning.

Fallenness. Despite the obvious association with the "Fall of Man," Heidegger does not intend by referring to "fallenness" that there is some perfect or ideal condition or state of grace from which humans have willfully and defiantly departed. Indeed, he insists, "this term, which does not express any negative value judgment, means that Da-sein is initially and for the most part *together with* the 'world' that it takes care of."[17] Fallenness is a way of being in the world that exhibits what Kierkegaard had previously designated as forgetting what it means for oneself to exist. This type of oblivion is aggravated by immersion in the "they," and it is identified by Heidegger with "inauthenticity." Fallenness is also the temptation to lapse into a mode of acceptance and passivity in the face of "things we cannot change." There is no debating that our condition as human beings includes dimensions of fixity, which Heidegger designates by the umbrella term "facticity" (refer to chapter 1 for a full definition of this term). However, Dasein is the kind of entity that unfolds itself and is not predestined to be this or that but, rather, is the potential for becoming what it will, notwithstanding the given situation of human life in general, and as it is served up in particular to each of us. Therefore, fallenness is (or should be) the beginning of the story, not the end—the stimulus to growth and attainment.

Heidegger finds within everyday experience a contrasting kind of awakening that will lead in a different, more constructive (or "authentic") direction, as we shall soon see. Unlike Nietzsche, though, he does not prescribe that superior beings alone can take this path. Instead, prompts are available for all to act upon in the context of our everyday lives; what we need is a phenomenological account of them so that they are easier to discern. Furthermore, Heidegger's quest for Being does not end in a leap away from the world-with-others. His solution to the problem of existential forgetfulness and the "hiddenness" of Being is not that one should become a solitary guru but that one must aim at a clear apprehension of existence, personal responsibility for how one lives, and cautious protectiveness against merging too much into the "they."

Heidegger is also very well aware, as we shall see later on, that being "together with" and "taking care of" the earth may, and does, become a warped and dangerous process when humanity loses its way in Being.

FURTHER CHARACTERISTICS OF DASEIN

Human existence contains other facets of importance, which we must take into account as well.

Existentiality/Understanding. "Existentiality" refers to the feature of human life that has already been marked out for special attention by the philosophers with whom we are concerned in this book, from Kierkegaard onward; this is, as Marjorie Grene states, that the "human being exists as anticipation of its own possibilities: it exists in advance of itself. . . ."[18] But human possibilities cannot transcend the world in which we are situated, and are always to be understood and actualized (if at all) within this setting. Thus, when Dasein projects beyond itself (even when not aware of so doing), it always *takes a stand in the world.* This is because all action is choosing and shaping oneself, and doing so in relation to how one gets a grip on the world. Heidegger summarizes the point by declaring that Dasein is "*ahead-of-itself-in-already-being-in-a-world.*"[19] Thrownness is emplacement; however, Dasein is not a static entity but rather a process, an event in Being. Just as we are familiar with facticity as a component of our lives, we have moments during which possibility and effective agency are illuminated for our understanding—for example, when we see our plans realized, when we solve problems, or when we build satisfying relationships.

Speech/discourse. There is nothing very original in regarding humans as preeminent language users, but Heidegger's perspective is unique in the sense that he believes "language speaks us" as much as we speak it. That is, language is some kind of gift that facilitates contact with Being. For language and discourse (articulated language or speech) enable us to name, evaluate, order, and examine the significance of the things that constitute our "world." Spoken language is also a social dimension of Dasein's existence. Discourse situates Dasein within Being and gives meaning to this emplacement. It also situates us with respect to one another. Furthermore, it discloses how Dasein is faring: as it actively develops, it consolidates our understanding of the world and our place in it. Language, as spoken, is a dynamic, self-creative process that unfolds through time. It is a kind of attunement to Being and should be thought of as a "listening" activity.[20] (Heidegger's views on language will be considered in greater detail later in this chapter.)

Moods. Moods are more durable emotional states than feelings, which are transient. Moods, unlike feelings, have no fixed object that occasions or "causes" them. Heidegger thinks that moods are peculiarly human and that they direct us toward Being as a whole. Three moods are of special interest to him: joy, anxiety (dread), and boredom. When we are in one of these moods, everything is colored by it, everything slides together under this dominant aspect of experience. Thus, when one is joyful, the world looks good, the spirit is buoyant, all things seem possible, pleasantness abounds. When one is bored, everything strikes one as tedious, not worth the trouble, flat, gray, heavy.

Anxiety has the additional feature that it arouses in us an awareness of ourselves as Dasein. Here is how Heidegger describes it:

> That in the face of which one has anxiety is not an entity within-the-world. . . .
>
> Accordingly, when something threatening brings itself close, anxiety does not "see" any definite "here" or "yonder" from which it comes. . . . What threatens is *nowhere*. Anxiety "does not know" what that in the face of which it is anxious is. "Nowhere," however, does not signify nothing. . . .
>
> That which threatens cannot bring itself close from a definite direction within what is close by; it is already "there," and yet nowhere; it is so close that it is oppressive and stifles one's breath, and yet it is nowhere. . . .
>
> That which anxiety is anxious about is Being-in-the-world itself.[21]

In ordinary usage, one can feel anxious about an exam, a job interview, or some such event. But Heidegger is talking about a pervasive state of consciousness that he (like other existentialists) supposes to shift between hovering in the background of our experience and at moments being quite intrusive and overwhelming. We can get a better idea of what is distinctive about existential anxiety by comparing it with fear.

Fear	Anxiety
Is an emotion	Is a mood
Has a definite object	Has no particular object*
Is transient	Is a permanent feature of the human condition†
	*Can it be an intentional state, then? Heidegger would answer yes; its "object" is "the nothing" (as discussed later in this chapter).
	†This does not mean that we are always consciously aware of it; it is, rather, an ever-present possibility of experience.

The major conclusion Heidegger wishes to draw is that this more durable kind of anxiety, which we all no doubt experience, reveals Dasein as an issue for itself, namely, as "thrown," as always overreaching itself, and as mortal. Like other moods, anxiety gives us a way of monitoring our being-in-the-world; but what is special about anxiety is that it accompanies awareness of our condition and the ongoing need to respond creatively to it. Simply put, *existential anxiety is the way we experience being humanly alive.* Dasein has a sense of the "uncanny"—a vague discomfort that is the measure of its basic condition, that awakens or recalls it to authenticity. In everyday life, our sensibilities are dulled and we are absorbed in projects that have shared significance. There is nothing wrong with this, except that it can easily turn into denial of, and turning away from, our own individual destiny. Anxiety calls us back from this forgetfulness.

Temporality. As the title of *Being and Time* makes crystal clear, time is of equal importance to Being in Heidegger's preoccupations. Or to be more precise, time is Dasein's mode of being and route to Being. Dasein exists (stands out from itself) in time. Time is usually conceived of as an endless progression of instants in which things will eventually happen, but not now. Heidegger sees this as an inauthentic conception of time. Instead, time for him is the medium in which Dasein develops: "temporality makes up the primordial meaning of Dasein's Being."[22] (We shall explore, in the next main section on "Death," the way in which Heidegger encourages Dasein toward an authentic understanding of time.)

Care. Dasein's stand in the world is marked by care, an involvement that springs from the temporal unfolding, "eventfulness," or "happening" sort of being that Dasein is. Care, like temporality, is a unifying structure within the being of Dasein. Dasein's existence, as we've learned, is always an issue for it, and its task is to figure out the meaning of Being. Therefore, Dasein's engagements in the world are caring in that Dasein either cares for or cares about something, or else caretakes or takes care of something or someone. The former type of caring, Heidegger calls "*concern,*" the latter, "*solicitude.*" He also maintains that "as a primordial totality, care lies 'before' every factical 'attitude' and 'position' of Da-sein, that is, it is always already *in* them as an existential *a priori.*"[23] This seems to imply that for Heidegger, caring about things in the world, about how we're faring in the world, and about how other people are faring is something close to instinctual. We discover ourselves as "Being-with-others"; that is, as existing in a social context in which we mutually and cooperatively define ourselves.

DEATH

The topic on which Heidegger's views are best known is undoubtedly death. This is for three reasons: (1) Death awareness, for him, is a kind of awakening to authenticity. (2) Dasein's being-in-the-world is a structure that is multiply constituted, and death awareness is what ultimately gives it unity. (3) His outlook on death has been so widely influential outside of philosophy.

I observed earlier that Heidegger understands Dasein in terms of temporality above all else. It's not just that Dasein *exists* in time; in addition, all the activities of Dasein are organized around a circular pattern of influence involving past, present, and future. The present is conceived against the background of the past, but it is also where we are busy mapping out the future. It is readily apparent to everyone that what happens in the past and present shapes the future for each of us. What is less readily acknowledged, however, is that the future, as much as the past, has an impact on the present. Some might object that the future can't influence anything because it does not yet exist; but this does not stand out as a problem in Heidegger's estimation, for the reason that the future, as a domain of imagination and anticipation, is fertile ground for phenomenological investigation from the standpoint of how it is thought about in the present. Likewise, both present and future color the past, for we interpret or appropriate what has happened in our lives against the backdrop of how we see things now, plus what we envision as yet to come. In modern terminology, we can visualize past, present, and future as a set of interacting feedback loops. We need to keep these ideas in mind as we approach Heidegger's discussion of death.

Readers will by now be familiar with the fact that Heidegger is especially interested in any experiences that reveal Being as such, or that at least point in its direction. Death awareness is the paradigm of this sort of experience. But there are several peculiarities that adhere to thinking about death, which must first be cleared away, and much of Heidegger's discussion is devoted to this task.

Some obstacles to death awareness. First, there is the ancient problem associated with Epicurus, who argued that death "does not . . . concern either the living or the dead, since for the former, it is not, and the latter are no more."[24] That is, death is not an issue for the living, while they are alive, because during this time death is unreal, at a distance, beyond life, unthinkable in any meaningful sense. Nor is death an issue for the dead because, being dead, they are not in a position to think about or fear anything. Hence, death is never anything to worry over for anyone. Heidegger would agree that it is unproductive and inappropriate to fret over the prospect of one's own death, though he strongly disagrees that death is not an issue for the living. But his idea of *how we should think about death* is quite different from simply worrying or obsessing about it, as we shall see shortly.

Second, it is important to note the difference between death and dying. It may be argued that these are two different sources of concern for the living. *Death* is an event that marks the loss of ego or self, the permanent cessation of consciousness and experience. *Dying* is a process that may go on for some time, which ends in death. (There are even those who contend that life is slow dying, so to speak. Tibetan Buddhist master Dudjom Rinpoche, for example, remarks, "You see we are all dying. It's only a matter of time. Some of us just die sooner than others.")[25] Some fear death, some fear dying, some fear both; and it is often held that while the fear of death is bad enough, that of dying is much greater because we know this process can be protracted and painful. Heidegger's perspective cuts across the distinction between death and dying, for death is, phenomenologically speaking, an active presence in life and, therefore, an ongoing event, and, in its own way, it is a process just as much as dying is—in fact more so.

Third, Heidegger remarks that "when Dasein reaches its wholeness in death, it simultaneously loses the Being of its 'there'. By its transition to no-longer-Dasein, it gets lifted right out of the possibility of experiencing this transition and of understanding it as something experienced."[26] This means that a human life is complete only when the possibilities of experience, choice, and self-making are terminated, when a person becomes an object or a thing. (No one can write your definitive biography until you are dead.) Dasein, at death, *is* "whole" in this sense, and consequently it is no longer "there"; in brief, it ceases being situated as "thrown into existence." But death also defeats the possibility of Dasein's knowing itself as something that has *become* whole, since death ends Dasein. Therefore, "As long as Da-sein *is* as a being, it has never attained its 'wholeness.'"[27] Heidegger here cleverly poses the following problem: Is there any actual opportunity for Dasein to grasp its wholeness during life? He wants to argue that his analysis of death awareness enables an affirmative answer to be given. Hence, for Dasein to *experience* itself as a totality or an integral unity—if this is possible at all—must be something different than for it merely to *achieve* wholeness.

Fourth, and most significant, Heidegger indicates that various inauthentic ways of thinking about or engaging with death block movement toward that type of wholeness he is attempting to extract from death awareness. We will examine several of these inauthentic moves in the next two subsections.

Death as what happens to others. Thinking about death on some level is inescapable, but we often do this in relation to others rather than ourselves. We realize that death is "going on" all around us, ponder mortality statistics, worry about and grieve over elderly friends and relatives; we notionally understand that death will come eventually to all life forms; we "know" that death will claim us, too, but "not yet"; we refer to death, but these references generally concern tragic events in the news, war in far-off lands, and the like—things that just "happen" and that we've become accustomed to hearing about. Heidegger maintains that all these ways of relating to death, distancing it from us, occur in the context of the "they." In other words, all of them represent our immersion in "Being-with-Others." As we saw earlier, "The 'they' is constituted by the way things have been publicly interpreted, which expresses itself in idle talk."[28] With these words, Heidegger suggests that how we are inclined to think about certain matters—even very important ones—is a social construct. This is truer of death than of anything else.

For the "they," death "remains in the inconspicuousness characteristic of everyday encounters." It gets talked about in a "fleeting" manner, which promotes turning away from death. Heidegger adds that "in such talk, death is understood as an indeterminate something which first has to show up from somewhere, but which right now is *not yet objectively present* for oneself, and is thus no threat. 'One dies' spreads the opinion that death, so to speak, strikes the they. . . . Thus, the they makes sure of a *constant tranquillization about death*."[29] Fear of death (and dying) is neutralized by various acts of covering up and misrepresentation, linguistic and otherwise, all of which have the effect of anaesthetizing our sensibility and keeping us looking at the phenomenon of death (which we can scarcely avoid doing) without seeing what it really means to us as individuals.

Popular culture yields many examples that support the conclusions Heidegger is trying to frame. Death is not exactly a taboo subject, but it is something to be ignored, evaded, not talked about, or else joked about, as in sick or black humor. When talk is necessary, we have elaborate euphemistic and figurative language for referring to death: "the big sleep," "the great leveller," and as personified, "the Grim Reaper"; to dying: "passing away," "going to a better life," "departing," "leaving us," "biting the dust," "cashing in one's chips," "giving up the ghost," "meeting one's maker"; to an undertaker: "mortician," "funeral director," "grief counsellor." Denial, disassociation, and concealment are regular ways of dealing with death and dying. These range from the extreme emphasis on youthful images in the media; to bizarre services like the drive-through funeral parlors springing up in California, cryogenics (corpse freezing), "virtual grieving" at memorial Web sites and "burial" in outer space; to cosmetic surgery; to pills and remedies designed to vanquish old age and guarantee longevity. Meanwhile, myths of immortality and reincarnation across the ages have helped neutralize death's sting.

At the same time, there are abundant signs of necrophilia (literally: "love of death") in contemporary culture—an apparently opposite tendency. Some examples are: fascination with "death-defying" stunts and extreme sports; gothic and S & M influences in fashion chic; huge consumption of murder mysteries and horror films; violence, murder, and the death (of others) as obsessive media and pop music themes; the fetish for weapons (both for personal use and for the state's use); and voyeuristic displays of revenge sentiment (such as the cheering, souvenir-laden ugly mobs awaiting the execution of Timothy McVeigh, the "Oklahoma City bomber," in the United States during 2001). Besides these, ritual and other practices (voodoo, the Mexican Day of the Dead, and Halloween) seem to illustrate that death is a powerful magnet for the imagination.

Polly Toynbee, writing in *The Guardian Weekly*, expresses points similar to those I've just been making: "There is a growing disproportion and incoherence in public attitudes toward death, with a curious blend of indifference about deaths that should concern us, prurience about deaths that don't, and a squeamishness and fear verging on denial about mundane dying." She also goes on to speak of the "near-pornographic fascination with the gory details of a meaningless madman's murders in Virginia. . . ."[30] (Her reference here is to the mass killings at Virginia Tech University during April 2007, which made news headlines everywhere.) The contrast between attraction to death and repulsion by it, then, is a very real part of our culture.

How is this discrepancy to be explained? Perhaps it's the case, just as Heidegger observes, that what draws us *toward* death and dying is also, at the same time, the ability to postpone, deny, or narrowly escape their impact on us personally, in short, to *evade* them within the "they" framework. At any rate, it has to be said that many cultures have an enormous emotional, economic, and social investment in keeping death hidden but simultaneously titillating. The ways in which we socially construct death determine how we personally and emotionally relate to it. The odd thing is that such inauthentic behavior simply confirms what it seeks to deny— our own mortality.

Death as what individuates. The topic of death grows more curious the more we investigate it, as I'm sure you will agree. Heidegger brings matters to a crunch by pointing out that standard opinion actually inverts the truth concerning what is healthy and self-affirming about confronting death openly and honestly: "It is already a matter of public acceptance that 'thinking about death' is a cowardly fear, a sign of insecurity on the part of Dasein, and a sombre way of fleeing from the world. *The 'they' does not permit us the courage for anxiety in the face of death.*"[31] Death, in traditional Western culture at least, is not thought of as a phase of life; it is discontinuous with life, and something from which we should divert our attention; something about which we should maintain the proverbial "stiff upper lip," or stoic indifference. Heidegger, by contrast, urges us to recognize that "anxiety in the face of death" is normal and something to be worked with, not against. Thinking about death is not fleeing from the world; *refusing* to think about death, rather, is fleeing from life and from oneself. In this way, Heidegger returns to the wisdom taught long ago by Socrates: Life is a process of learning how to face death properly.[32]

But, of course, there is thinking and there is thinking. Heidegger distinctly denies that thinking about death existentially amounts to some sort of neurotic brooding on it. He strives to articulate a kind of thinking that will lead to a sense of wholeness in Dasein's view of itself, and, as observed earlier, he also strives to open a vista onto Being. We can say, then, that death awareness reveals Dasein as a being within Being. Let's see how this works.

Heidegger indicates "what is peculiar to the certainty of death, *that it is possible in every moment.* Together with the certainty of death goes the *indefiniteness* of its when."[33] He relishes conceptual subtleties and convolutions such as we see here: death's certainty resides in its possibility and indefiniteness. But, however paradoxical this may sound, it's no doubt true. The point is that death isn't just certain as a *fact* that exists somewhere *over yonder* (in the world, in the lives of others). Yes, it is that, but, more importantly, it's something that touches on *me*, something about *my life*, which uniquely concerns *me.*[34]

This last reflection takes us directly to the "existential-ontological conception of death," which Heidegger states in this way: "*As the end of Da-sein, death is the ownmost nonrelational, certain, and, as such, indefinite and not to be bypassed possibility of Da-sein.*"[35] The three characteristics of personal death are now clearly set forth. (1) It is "*ownmost*" and "*nonrelational,*" meaning that no one else can die my death or share its meaning for me; I alone "own" it. Nor can my death-possibility be disguised and distanced by the interpretations of "they"-consciousness. (2) It is "*certain and as such indefinite*"; that is, death hovers as an ever-present eventuality that I project ahead of me as part of the imprecisely known future. (3) It is "*not to be bypassed*" or, in other words, death is unavoidable and incapable of being evaded—as an event and as a passage of life.

Being-towards-death. Heidegger draws the conclusion that the phenomenological analysis of Dasein spirals in on the possibility of death and the way we relate ourselves to it. What is at stake here, for Dasein, is nothing less than "the possibility of the measureless impossibility of existence."[36] Again, Heidegger juxtaposes opposites within the same phrase, nicely illustrating the tension within this mode of awareness. The outcome is that Dasein needs to understand itself as "Being-towards-death"—as something that, in its existence, knowingly and willingly extends itself toward nonexistence. This is a positive feature, however, not a negative one:

> But anticipation does not evade the impossibility of bypassing death . . . but *frees* itself *for* it. Becoming free *for* one's own death in anticipation frees one from one's lostness in chance possibilities urging themselves upon us, so that the factical possibilities lying before the possibility not-to-be-bypassed can first be authentically understood and chosen.
>
> Anticipation discloses to existence that its extreme inmost possibility lies in giving itself up and thus shatters all one's clinging to whatever existence one has reached.[37]

Heidegger speaks here of liberation, which he means in two senses. First, by experiencing the existential awareness (including the accompanying outlook and attitude) of Being-towards-death, Dasein gains insight into the vital need to choose and act carefully (with care for oneself and others) because, crudely put, any moment may be one's last. Second, Dasein learns not to cling to and linger in the past too much, for within the act of choosing a future at each present instant meaningful existence may be found. The central idea seems to be that self-making is given an increased urgency, exhilaration, and ethical import by the anticipation of death. This is why Heidegger ends by characterizing Dasein's Being-towards-death as a "*passionate anxious* **freedom towards death** *which is free of the illusions of the they,* *factical, and certain of itself.*"[38] Existential death-awareness releases the potential of individual self-making from obedience to the "they"—from anaesthetized and sterilized thoughts about one's mortality, finitude, and responsibility, and from various modes of procrastination. It reenergizes or invigorates oneself and creates a new horizon for behavior.

The influence of Heidegger's thoughts on death. Heidegger's philosophizing about death has had a monumental impact—probably greater than his ideas on any other topic. All of those contemporary theorists and practitioners who take death seriously owe a debt to him, and most acknowledge this openly. The work of Elisabeth Kübler-Ross, which has been a catalyst to the hospice and death-with-dignity movements, as well as the entire burgeoning field of "thanatology" (death-related studies), is impossible to imagine without reference to Heidegger.

Irvin Yalom, a prominent American psychiatrist and novelist, expresses the basic insight that

> the concept of death plays a crucial role in psychotherapy because it plays a crucial role in the life experience of each of us. Death and life are interdependent: though the physicality of death destroys us, the *idea* of death saves us. Recognition of death contributes a sense of poignancy to life, provides a radical shift of life perspective, and can transport one from a mode of living characterized by diversions, tranquilization, and petty anxieties to a more authentic mode.[39]

Pure Heidegger, I think you will agree—even if it substitutes the somewhat static "*idea* of death" for what I call "the existential awareness of death."

Psychologist Herman Feifel remarked some time ago that the existentialism of Heidegger (among others)

> has placed the experience of death near the center of its analysis of the human condition. It has accented death as a constitutive part rather than the mere end of life, and highpointed the idea that only by integrating the concept of death into the self does an authentic and genuine existence become possible. The price for denying death is undefined anxiety, self-alienation. To completely understand himself, man must confront death, become aware of personal death.[40]

Feifel directly credits Heidegger with arousing this kind of perception in the West, though, again, he renders the philosopher's doctrine rather tame by alluding to "the concept of death" as what we must lay hold of.

Speaking to a more popular audience, the existential psychiatrist Viktor Frankl (see appendix B, part 2) observes that

> in the face of death as absolute finis to our future and boundary to our possibilities, we are under the imperative of utilizing our lifetimes to the utmost, not letting the singular opportunities—whose "finite" sum constitutes the whole of life—pass by unused.
>
> Finality, temporality, is therefore not only an essential characteristic of human life, but also a real factor in its meaningfulness. The meaning of human existence is based upon its irreversible quality.[41]

Again, pure Heidegger. But what is good about this passage is that it serves to remind us that it's because Dasein is temporally defined (as an unfolding process situated in time) that death is an issue in the first place.

More recently, these perceptions have been reaffirmed by psychologist Kate Douglas, who argues that humans' self-awareness of their own mortality is a major preoccupation, and that success in adjusting to life's challenges depends on how we take this dimension of experience into account.[42]

Convergence with Buddhism. Before we leave the present topic, it is worth noting that there is significant common ground between Heidegger's discussion of death and those that spring from the Buddhist tradition, making his thought of special interest to those who would forge ties between philosophies of East and West. Geshe Kelsang Gyatso remarks on how "the best way to avoid wasting our precious life is to become acutely aware of our impermanence by meditating on death."[43] But as Stephen Batchelor adds, "Reflective meditation is a way of translating thoughts into the language of feeling. . . . [D]eath meditation is not a morbid exercise at all. . . . Over time such meditation penetrates our primary sense of being in the world at all."[44] These ideas can be traced back to fundamental Buddhist notions of the impermanence or perishability of all things, mutual dependence (life requires death and death gives rise to life), and the power of the mind to quell suffering and produce equanimity.

CONSCIENCE, GUILT, AND RESOLUTENESS

In line with the recurring existentialist theme of knowing oneself and taking responsibility for the course of one's life in a spirit of honesty, Heidegger introduces the concepts that give this section its title. Conscience is often interpreted as a voice within that keeps us on the right track, especially in relation to moral behavior. As we might expect, Heidegger takes up part of this understanding but gives his own special twist once again to the matter. Inauthentic Dasein listens to the voice of the "they"; "it *fails to hear* its own self in listening to the they-self." Therefore, what Dasein needs to do in order to become authentic is to heed its own voice instead. This amounts to "the possibility of another kind of hearing that interrupts that listening [and] must be given by Da-sein itself."[45] So Dasein is both the voice that is listened to and the listener receiving its message. Heidegger gives the name "conscience" to the "call" to authenticity that emanates from within Dasein and is heard by Dasein when it listens properly. The subject matter of this "call" is Dasein's life as it will be chosen by it. "And to what is one summoned?" Heidegger asks. The answer he provides is simply: "To one's *own self*."[46] This is pretty straightforward, except that what's different in Heidegger's treatment of the topic is that he thinks there is a kind of latent authenticity within the self to which the conscious self must become attuned. As with receptivity to an awareness of Being (which he also describes as manifested by a "call"), one needs to cultivate a new kind of sensibility—rather like that which disciplines of the self such as meditation and yoga have taught for centuries. The upshot is that conscience, in this unusual sense, is not about being moral; it is about authentically being oneself. Perhaps the implication is, however, that conscience in the narrower, usual sense is strongly derivative from the act of being true to oneself.

Next, Heidegger speaks of "guilt," which he likewise perceives in a special way. We normally think it is a bad thing to be (or feel) guilty and that this is a sign of wrongdoing. Heidegger has in mind, however, a more basic state of being, which he calls "*being responsible for*."[47] It is easy to see that guilt in the narrower, more familiar sense follows from this capacity for being responsible and, indeed, he acknowledges this reversal of perspectives. Guilt, then, signifies the ability to take up a responsible stance with respect to one's Dasein, one's self-in-the-world.

Finally, the Dasein that is responding to the call of conscience and is "guilty" will take a stand in relation to its own "*self-projection*" into the future. What is this stand? Readers will by this time have little trouble ferreting out the meaning of what Heidegger labels as "resoluteness,"[48] namely, the determination to define oneself through one's own honestly-arrived-at choices, made with the "freedom-toward-death" that has been won by raising oneself beyond the confines of everydayness.

BEYOND *BEING AND TIME*

In his other (mostly later writings), Heidegger develops different approaches to Being from within Dasein's arena of self-examination. These all presuppose the relationship shown below, which is implicit in the analysis of Dasein we have been considering.

What kind of being Dasein is → 〈〉 ← How Being discloses itself to Dasein

Two sides of one coin

Truth. It is no secret that philosophers since the beginning have been in search of the truth. What kind of truth? At first, this encompassed the whole range of possible answers, since philosophy started off as "the mother of all disciplines" (and was also known as "the queen of the sciences"). We now tend to think of there being different kinds of truth, appropriate to each modern field of study as it has developed according to its own methods of investigation. Thus, there are historical truth, scientific truth, logical truth, psychological truth, and (some would argue, at any rate) aesthetic, literary, and ethical kinds of truth. Whether these are really different and/or incompatible sorts of truth we need not get into here. Not coincidentally, Heidegger harks back to what he thinks is the original conception of truth, in which he hopes to discover its "essence." There may yet be different varieties of truth, relative to the ways in which truth is now sought, but he argues that at a certain level, there is something common to them all. In effect, philosophy comes full circle when it latches onto this essence. (Remember too that Husserl's project in phenomenology—see chapter 5—was to identify essences in some quasi-empirical manner.)

Given his profound interest in ancient Greek philosophy, the origins of philosophical questioning, and the nuances of language, one can readily appreciate that an etymological inquiry is at the heart of Heidegger's investigation of truth. He had already begun this in sections 7(b) and 44 of *Being and Time*. The word he focuses on is *alétheia*, which the Greeks used for "truth." Heidegger replaces "truth" with "unconcealment" as his preferred version of the meaning of this term, contending that his rendering "is not merely more literal; it contains the directive to rethink the ordinary concept of truth in the sense of the correctness of statements and to think it back to that still uncomprehended disclosedness and disclosure of beings."[49] What he means here is that a more imaginative translation—one that resonates with the insight of those who first infused the word with significance—might recapture their sense of emplacement in Being, their perspective on what it means to be.

To identify truth with unconcealment suggests that obtaining the truth about something isn't just finding out that what we believe or assert corresponds to a state of affairs in the world; rather, it is a act of "letting beings be, which is an attuning, a bringing into accord. . . ."[50] Heidegger has the fascinating idea that we face the world as a domain of concealment and that our efforts to win the truth (true insight or knowledge), if conducted properly, bring what was hidden in darkness into light, or, as it were, permit correctness to happen. This is both a learning of what is so and also an emancipation of ourselves from ignorance. He writes that "in general, mystery (the concealing of what is concealed) as such holds sway throughout man's Da-sein."[51] But on the other hand, in establishing what is true, "Man's comportment is brought into definite accord throughout by the openedness of being as a whole."[52] I interpret this as follows. We approach the world (individually and collectively) as strangers seeking to understand it and feel at home there. In the slow and painful process by means of which we gain truth over time, our orientation to the world becomes steadily more secure, insofar as we succeed in placing ourselves in receptive readiness for Being to disclose itself to us. So truth is an event in which we first must prepare ourselves correctly and then become able to experience what Heidegger is calling disclosure or unconcealment. In sum, *truth is a discovery process featuring movement from concealment to disclosure, from untruth to truth, from mystery to knowledge and insight, in which Being opens up to partially reveal itself.*

The pursuit of truth is a free act of Dasein, which has this unique capacity, and, as we've seen above, the attainment of truth itself amounts to a kind of liberation. Therefore, Heidegger finds that freedom is part of the essence of truth. But with all free acts of human beings there also comes the possibility of getting things wrong, of erring, which he charmingly labels "passing the mystery by."[53] The world (and more importantly, Being) do not always reveal themselves readily, and so both concealment and unconcealment are integral aspects of the story of truth. What Being is has to be teased out gradually and with careful dedication by methods that can help us figure out its message.

Art and technology. These are two cultural areas in which Heidegger finds his theory of truth confirmed. Representational art, which preoccupies

Heidegger, does not create a world; rather, it enters into it and lets it shine forth. While the work of art is a thing and depicts things, it is much more than this, as we recognize by assigning it aesthetic value. Vincent Van Gogh's painting of a peasant's rugged shoes draws us into a world of hard-working people of the earth. It reveals to us how a world takes shape and is preserved by the doings of those whose world it is. It allows and encourages us to think about, and feel ourselves into, a way of being and thus, indirectly, to think about how Being reveals itself therein. Any work of art (for instance, a painting, a sculpture, or a poem) can do this from its own perspective and from within the world it holds up to view.

Yet there is still more going on within the work of art, according to Heidegger. As Thomas Sheehan points out, a work of art discloses "the radical tension. . . . between the self-expanding urge of a set of human possibilities and the rootedness of such possibilities in a specific natural environment."[54] Dasein, as we've learned, always exists in advance of itself and, that being the case, human life, in order to be portrayed accurately, must capture this feature. But most art is frozen in time. Therefore, successful artworks will somehow convey human potential or the fact that human activities are complex and ongoing, although to achieve this they must also be situated (as human life is) and not purely abstract or idealized.

Clearly, there is much art that does not fit this description and even flouts it intentionally. Whether Heidegger would judge that this variety of creative work is not art, bad art, or just that he's uninterested in what it has to offer, is uncertain. What is fairly evident, however, is that his discussion of art is quite selectively focused on works of the imagination that can be interpreted so as to confirm his wider philosophical theories.

In discussing the philosophical significance of technology, Heidegger again engages in etymological reflection. This time, it is the ancient Greek word techné (the root of "technology") that draws his attention. He notes that techné "is the name not only for the activities and skills of the craftsman, but also for the arts of the mind and the fine arts." It therefore signifies "bringing-forth . . . something poetic."[55] It turns out that technology, in Heidegger's rendering, is closely associated with—indeed, is an example of—the kind of disclosure of Being that truth represents. Technology is not just a means to an end, the production of useful objects and processes. Nor is it to be celebrated as the dominance and mastery of nature in the service of humanity. Rather, technology is in a fundamental sense a way of discovering how things are, what it is possible to envision because of what is so. "It is as revealing, and not as manufacturing, that techné is a bringing-forth."[56]

This thought leads into Heidegger's critique of technology, which has also been very influential. Modern technology has gone astray, he believes, and needs to be re-directed by the inspiration derived from its original meaning. Technology today transforms nature into a reservoir of resources (a "standing-reserve") that is treated as unlimited, and land becomes merely the place to plunder such resources. Hence, "the revealing that rules throughout modern technology has the character of a setting-upon, in the sense of a challenging-forth."[57] Technology seeks to conquer all, which tendency Heidegger labels "enframing." Getting quickly to the core of the matter, he asks, "Does not man himself belong even more originally than nature within the standing-reserve?"[58] By changing nature into a set of instrumentalities, humans make themselves dependent upon these as well, and thereby define themselves accordingly as producers, consumers, and cogs within a vast, rapacious industrial/commercial machine, while at the same time they pose as lords and masters of the natural world. In the ensuing turmoil, they lose themselves as Dasein.

Modern technology threatens the disclosure of Being Heidegger thinks we ought to be pursuing. But because of the fact that technology—of whatever type—is a *revealing*, this leaves open the possibility of doing things differently. Technology is not some abstract, tyrannical enemy; if there is an enemy, it is the choices we have made. We can, then, choose another way. He points out quietly that "precisely the essence of technology must harbor in itself the growth of the saving power."[59] Once again, if we can re-think and re-vision technology, we can save not only nature but also ourselves. (Technology—part of the problem—must also be part of the solution, as we often hear today.) Heidegger elsewhere juxtaposes against modern technology's antagonistic relationship to nature an interpretation of nature as "earth," as a place of "dwelling"[60]—a favorite concept of his. Theorists of environmental ethics, among others, have been inspired by this perspective to forge a new, more sustainable outlook on the natural world.

Nothing. In 1928, Heidegger was appointed to the chair of philosophy at the University of Freiburg, from which Husserl had just retired. In the following year, Heidegger delivered his inaugural lecture *What Is Metaphysics?* One can only imagine, with considerable amusement, what must have been going through the heads of those in his audience, learned though they obviously were, when he informed them that the subject of his speech was—"nothing."

A professor of mine once observed that the difference between science and philosophy is that "science gets to know more and more about less and less, until it knows everything about nothing. Philosophy gets to know less and less about more and more, until it knows nothing about everything." In this way, he illustrated the point that Heidegger makes in his lecture: We frequently refer to nothing, but when we do so, what is it we refer to? As we saw in chapter 5, absence, nonexistence, imaginary objects, and the like posed problems for the theory of intentionality as the defining property of consciousness; and how to make sense of referring to what does not exist has challenged philosophers and logicians since the beginning, but especially during the past century. We all know that negation is an indispensable feature of language and thought. "This is not that," "This is, that is not," "This is here and now, that isn't," and so on—these are the general forms by which we express negation. Heidegger, however, is interested in something much more than how these kinds of locutions are constructed and how they can be analyzed. He believes that the crucial question is one of metaphysics and concerns the origin of negation as such. Consequently, he makes the following bold pronouncements: "We assert that the nothing is more original than the 'not' and negation. If this thesis is right, then the possibility of negation as an act of the intellect, and thereby the intellect itself, are somehow dependent upon the nothing."[61] Notice that he speaks here, peculiarly, about "*the* nothing." It is necessary to look at this phrase to grasp the full meaning of his claims.

For Heidegger, "nothing" signifies a dimension of awareness, which is what phenomenologists generally (in large part following his lead) insist upon. But for him, "the nothing" is analogous to the ground of a figure-ground drawing of the kind that the Gestalt psychologists highlighted. Thus, *nothing* is the backdrop, the dark night, as it were, from which *Being* stands forth. At the end of *What Is Metaphysics?* Heidegger floats the following question: "Why are there beings at all, and why not rather nothing?"[62] This may seem an odd and unanswerable query and, indeed, Heidegger posits no answer. But his purpose is to underline the astonishment we might feel (when in the right state of mind) that anything exists at all. Starting with oneself—Why should I exist at all?—and moving on from there, everyone is capable of experiencing awe in the face of the world, the universe, even Being as such. And this is precisely the effect Heidegger wants to create.

There is more to the matter, however. Each living thing, and especially Dasein, has its lifespan, and then becomes part of that vast nothingness of all absent and negated things. This realization is not too difficult to digest. But Heidegger goes on to assert that "the nothing" is *an absence that is a presence*, an active presence, if you will: "The nothing itself nihilates."

(Alternative translation: "The nothing itself 'nothings.'") This means that nothingness manifests itself in the background of Being; it has its effect upon us, pulsating or vibrating all the time. The representation here is not merely metaphorical, for Dasein's possible nothingness is the source of anxiety. Anxiety, as a key existential mood, leads to insight, and what is gained is twofold. First, "In the clear night of the nothing of anxiety the original openness of beings as such arises: that they are beings—and not nothing. . . . Only on the ground of the original revelation of the nothing can human existence approach and penetrate beings." The being of beings—that they exist at all—is impressed upon us by the experience of anxiety and the nothing, and it is only by having this experience that we are prepared to begin grasping what Being is. Second, "Da-sein means: being held out into the nothing."[63] That is, human existence projects into, is defined by, the possibility of its own nonbeing. Therefore, because Dasein in a sense contains the nothingness of its own "not-yet" (the future, death), its mode of existence is a region, field, clearing, or opening in Being where Being as such can disclose itself.

Heidegger provides another particularly interesting phenomenological account of anxiety that complements the definition we examined above in the subsection on moods. He states that

> a peculiar calm pervades it. . . . In anxiety, we say, "one feels ill at ease." What is "it" that makes "one" feel ill at ease? We cannot say what it is before which one feels ill at ease. As a whole it is so for one. All things and we ourselves sink into indifference. This, however, not in the sense of mere disappearance. Rather, in this very receding things turn toward us.
>
> The receding of beings as a whole that closes in on us in anxiety oppresses us. . . . We "hover" in anxiety. . . . Anxiety robs us of speech. Because beings as a whole slip away, so that just the nothing crowds round, in the face of anxiety all utterance of the "is" falls silent.[64]

Anxiety of this kind is (thankfully) not a constant experience, at least in its fully developed form. But it can break out at any time, and when it does, we may be deeply unsettled. This state signifies our being torn away from the everyday and forced to examine things afresh and on the intuitive level. We encounter the awareness that Being and "the nothing" are mutually dependent and determining, like Yang and Yin.

Language. Heidegger's views on language are well worked out and derive consistently from his general position on the task of philosophy and Dasein's relationship to Being. George Steiner explains that from Heidegger's standpoint our use of language is highly problematic, considering what we take for granted: "In every sentence we utter, being is stated. But we do not stop to ask ourselves what *it is* that we *are* saying or, more exactly, what it is that allows, indeed that compels us to say *what is*."[65] Thus, when Heidegger reflects on language, he is recapitulating his whole project of inquiring into the state of Being in the modern world and how we can recover a more intimate connection with Being in our lives.

It will not be difficult to find widespread agreement on the proposition that language is, most of all, what defines humans. Heidegger asserts this in a much stronger sense than is commonplace, however, when he says that "language is the house of Being, . . . the home of man's essence."[66] He then goes beyond this sort of grounding statement to perform the type of reversal of perspectives of which he is fond, and which is probably inspired by his study of Nietzsche (see chapter 4). "Man acts as though he were the shaper and master of language, while in fact language remains the master of man,"[67] he says. Language is expression and communication, but it is much more than these. It is an *event* because it is first and foremost the spoken word. But at this point, Heidegger accelerates, leaving conventional theories of language in the dust, for he maintains that "*language speaks*"; and if we place ourselves correctly regarding language, then "language will call to us from there and grant us its nature."[68] No "merely logical description of language"[69] is ever adequate. Analysis of rules, sounds, meanings, symbols, and the like all fall short of capturing, singly or collectively, the essence of language. Why this is, Heidegger claims, has to do with the origin of language in human speech: the speaking of language "takes place as that which grants an abode for the being of mortals."[70] In other words, language creates a shelter, a region of being, a dwelling place in which humans can exist and discover themselves as what they are and what they are capable of.

Now we enter truly rarefied territory. "Poetry is what first brings man onto the earth, making him belong to it, and thus brings him into dwelling."[71] Heidegger should not be thought to be asserting here that poetry, in the full-blown sense, is how language first manifests itself. But one is tempted to recall Nietzsche's theory that: (a) humans' relationship to the world around them is basically an aesthetic one; and (b) language is essentially a metaphorical medium. What Heidegger wants to express is that imagistic use of language—and poetry proper, when it comes along— is what truly gives the world its meaning and value, and conveys a sense of belonging to it. In saying this, he is thinking at least in part of myths, epics, and the time-honored wisdom of oral traditions.

Poetry, then, stands as the model for the power of language to call into significant presence the things of the world. If the use of language is sufficiently masterful, "the things named are called into their thinging"[72] and present the world to us as that to which we are existentially bound. The world is enlivened by things, and things are given to us as populating a world in which we move, act, and affirm ourselves. Thus, language "expropriates world and things into the simple onefold of their intimacy."[73] (The lyric poet Friedrich Hölderlin [1770–1843] is Heidegger's personal favorite, and he is often cited by Heidegger in support of his generalizations about poetic language.)

In sum: "Man speaks first when, and only when, he responds to language by listening to its appeal. . . . Language beckons us . . . toward a thing's nature. . . . But the responding in which man authentically listens to the appeal of language is that which speaks in the element of poetry."[74] Therefore, the measure of language use is not correctness but *evocativeness*. Heidegger is interested here and throughout solely in the capacity of language to summon up a human world and to deliver awareness of Being to us. But, as with truth, this process is both concealing and revealing; humans, being finite, have only a limited and struggling grasp of the mystery that envelops them and that their best efforts can but partially penetrate.

Thinking. Another way in which Heidegger's project can be summarized is by reference to his very important reflections on thinking. One might suppose that philosophers are adept at thinking, if nothing else, and that Heidegger would celebrate this fact and illustrate it himself. But to our surprise, we find him saying, in a rare, candid moment of modesty, "It arises from the region of what is most thought-provoking—that we are still not thinking; none of us, including me who speaks to you, me first of all."[75] What are we to make of this startling revelation? Heidegger's point is that although, quantitatively speaking, a huge amount of thinking goes on, it doesn't amount to much, and this is because the kind of thinking that really matters is absent.[76] Not only is it absent, it hasn't yet been perceived as necessary, understood, learned, and mastered. This charge is compounded by an additional claim: "it could be that prevailing man has for centuries now acted too much and thought too little."[77] Considering the state of the world—especially of armed conflict and of the environment—one can hardly disagree.

Yet so many questions push themselves forward when we reflect on Heidegger's words: How can there be no thinking that "really matters," given all the great thinkers of the past and present? How can Heidegger know that there *is* a kind of thinking that's missing, if, as he states, we don't even know what this kind of thinking is? How can an existentialist possibly believe that there is too much action, if action is essential for self-making? As usual, Heidegger is presenting issues enigmatically, forcing us to puzzle through them. This exercise makes us think for ourselves rather than be thought for by him. Let us now look at the questions above. First of all, it is obviously an exaggeration to assert that there has been *no* real thinking or that no one "gets" what is required to think properly about Being and humans' relationship to it. But perhaps no one has yet quite entered into the sort of dedication that Heidegger finds appropriate to the subject—not even he, because in a way his role is to be the herald who arouses others to do so, in equal measure to his being himself the one who does so. By deliberately overstating the case, he goads us into reacting. Second, Heidegger could reasonably claim—as an article of faith, if nothing more—that there is a different (even if not new) form of thinking that needs to be applied to the problems he poses. And this is because he has laid them out in a careful and convincing manner. We might dispute whether such problems as obtaining knowledge of Being are solvable, but if it is our ultimate destiny to be able to do so, then there must be (one supposes) a pathway to this coveted goal. Furthermore, in spite of the "absence" of genuine thinking he assails, Heidegger spends much of his time and energy (as did Nietzsche) combing through the work of past philosophers and poets, looking for clues to what he is after. With this in mind, he says, "We are all on the way together, and are not reproving each other."[78] Third, of course self-realization depends upon action, but meaningful action is more than busyness; it requires guidance by the right kind of thinking.

The structure of Heidegger's thinking about thinking is by now familiar. He asks, "What is it that directs us into thought and gives us directives for thinking?" "What makes a call upon us that we should think and, by thinking, be who we are?" And he ponders "what intrinsically desires to be thought about in an essential sense."[79] A pointer to the answer is also placed among the questions: "In the widest sense, 'to call' means to set in motion, to get something under way—which may be done in a gentle and unobtrusive manner, and in fact is most readily done that way."[80] So what occasions thinking in the first place, and to which we must inevitably return, is something primordial, something foundational to our existence, something that moves us to posit our unique kind of "beingness" in the larger whole of Being. This is the "call" of Being.

In another pair of essays, Heidegger identifies the kind of thinking he seeks as "meditative" thinking, which he contrasts with thinking that is

Original illustration by David Greenhalgh.

"logical-scientific," "calculative," or "representational." The latter is characteristic of everyday and more technical, rational modes of thought, such as those by which we run our lives. The former is harder to define and, in fact, cannot be described, only pointed at. Yet Heidegger hints that to engage in meditative thinking does not require one to be a poet or guru: "Meditative thinking need by no means be 'high-flown'. It is enough if we dwell on what lies close and meditate on what is closest; upon that which concerns us, each one of us, here and now; here, on this patch of home ground; now in the present hour of history."[81] This statement resonates with another, to the effect that "thinking itself is man's simplest, and for that reason hardest, handiwork. . . ."[82] Philosophers have frequently indicated that, paradoxically, what lies closest at hand (or is taken for granted as best known) turns out to be quite difficult to understand, define, or rationalize when we focus on it for the first time. (Aristotle associated philosophical inquiry with wonder;[83] Wittgenstein proposed that "a philosophical problem has the form: 'I don't know my way about.'")[84] So, it would seem, Heidegger is telling us that we can only learn how to think about Being and our relationship to it by *trying to do it*, just as he himself engages in all sorts of experiments that work around the circumference of the problem and perhaps in time spiral in on the target.

The end of philosophy. Rightly or wrongly, Heidegger asserts that philosophy—as hitherto understood and practiced—is coming to an end in the present age.

> What is meant by the talk about the end of philosophy? We understand the end of something all too easily in the negative sense as mere cessation, as the lack of continuation, perhaps even as decline and impotence. In contrast, what we say about the end of philosophy means the completion of metaphysics. . . . The end of philosophy is the place, that place in which the whole of philosophy's history is gathered in its uttermost possibility. End as completion means this gathering.[85]

Briefly, Heidegger means that the tasks of understanding and sorting beings that philosophy has traditionally undertaken are now going to be taken over by the sciences (which were, of course, initially forms of specialized philosophy). Heidegger mentions cybernetics, in particular, but would probably include cognitive science, were he writing today. Thus, for example, some hold cognitive science will eventually solve (or resolve) the ancient mind-body problem and explain the riddle of consciousness. Heidegger thinks that a technology-driven society, of the Western model, is the outcome of philosophy's long journey. But if so, then does not some method or practice need to stand in for philosophy in order to prepare the opening where Being can disclose itself? Heidegger ponders this issue: "Perhaps there is a thinking outside of the distinction of rational and irrational, more sober-minded still than scientific technology, more sober-minded and hence removed, without effect, yet having its own necessity."[86] What could this possibly be? Heidegger admits that we don't yet know and that thinking about thinking, and about what its ultimate purpose is, may eventually lead us to the answer.

AFTERWORD: GETTING A GRIP ON HEIDEGGER

When I was doing graduate studies in philosophy in the 1960s, it was fashionable among English-language philosophers to ridicule Heidegger by taking sentences or passages from his work and holding them up to scorn for their obscurity and the odd use of language they often embody. That this is no longer the case shows how much trends in the discipline have changed for the better, and, more specifically, how much of an inroad European ways of thinking have made elsewhere, and how great Heidegger's influence has been. But there are still those on both sides of the Atlantic who wonder aloud about his accomplishments and sometimes aloud (but perhaps more often silently) whether his profundity is more apparent than real. There's no doubt Heidegger can be a difficult read; but, on the other hand, several of his works are relatively easy to digest, and the experience of reading at least substantial sections of *Being and Time* has been found by many to be surprisingly straightforward and illuminating. And he is certainly not the only philosopher whose theorizing delves into new areas, requiring the invention of new terminology (neologisms). He also remains a problematic individual because of his frequently authoritarian pronouncements about things and his historical involvement with Nazism in World War II Germany. Yet if we want philosophers to be exemplary people as well as good thinkers, we may find ourselves very disappointed by what the record offers.

Walter Kaufmann, one of the most astute commentators on nineteenth- and early twentieth-century German philosophy, gives this assessment:

> That Heidegger is, for all his faults, one of the most interesting philosophers of our time, there can be no doubt. What stands between him and greatness is . . . his lack of vision. After everything has been said, he really does not have very much to say. . . . Heidegger built on the expectation that he would unravel Being and accomplish what Western ontology since Aristotle had been unable to do. . . . But, having given his account of human existence [in *Being and Time*], Heidegger had, as a matter of fact, *not* unravelled Being. . . . and is still unable to do it. . . . [The questions he raises] are exciting but utterly vague—not really questions at all in the ordinary sense, but labels for vast complexes of problems that must be distinguished before any answers can be attempted. . . . When we ask in the end what has really been said, we come up either with nothing or with trivialities. . . . Heidegger . . . looks for a chimera, "Being"—the shadow of God.[87]

What are we to make of this somewhat-more-than-faint praise followed by damnation? I think it has to be admitted that Heidegger does ask peculiar questions ("How is it with Being?" and "What is called thinking?" for example). But this is owing to the fact that he comes at philosophical problems from such a novel angle and is making a self-consciously crafted attempt to break with tradition while at the same time preserving with meticulous care the intellectual heritage he builds upon. Furthermore, he puts the onus on his readers to try new ways of thinking—one might rather say, meditating or exercising mentally and spiritually—as Eastern sages have always done. It would be easy enough to dismiss Zen Buddhism (and many have done just that) because of the koans (mental puzzles, such as the sound of one hand clapping) that its devotees are asked to contemplate. Of course, that would be an unfortunate mistake that would gain nothing for the one who acts superior. A more constructive response is to let the questions sink in and see, in the fullness of time, whether there is a message in them that in our normal scurrying, practical way of approaching things we might otherwise miss.

The issue about Being is more worrying, however. Heidegger has written immensely on this subject, but are we any clearer about what Being is and how we are related to it? Consider the following perspectives. Charles Guignon observes that "in the later writings, being is not something humans do, but something that happens to humans."[88] And Joseph Kockelmans amplifies, noting that "Being is shown as sending itself toward *Dasein*; it sends itself in different epochs in different ways which consign *Dasein* to its privileged destiny, which is to be 'the Shepherd of Being.'"[89] So it seems that Being, which in *Being and Time* had the profile of a thing (perhaps the Thing of things) that we should be seeking to know, is, in the later writings, declared to be an event, a beacon (of truth?), something that emanates from a source (much like the power and grace of God, according to some theologians); and maybe Being "happens to humans" or maybe humans "happen" too, in the sense that they must somehow—wittingly or unwittingly, thoughtfully or unthoughtfully—take care of Being. What is Heidegger on about?

If someone chooses Being as her or his theme, then we might reasonably expect two things: (1) an account of why this is of central importance and what we can look forward to discovering in studying it along with the author; and (2) a definitive treatment of the subject, or at least some discernible progress toward solving the problem(s) set out by the author. Some (like Kaufmann) would judge that Heidegger fails to deliver on either score. Others, however, believe he has succeeded, if only because he has defined the modern condition of "waiting"—so poignantly depicted in the "tragicomedy" *Waiting for Godot* by Samuel Beckett (1906–89)[90]—better than any other philosopher. This waiting is the historical-cultural situation we occupy in the wake of the death of God, wherein we experience the quandary of how to find new roots in _____. What can one use to fill in this blank other than "Being"? Heidegger seems right about that. And it scarcely seems that he is to blame for an answer not springing forth in spite of his many efforts. Perhaps, as some complain, he has replaced sober reason with poetry and intuition. But reason may not be able to solve this problem, at least unassisted. Many have written and spoken at length of the need for new types of consciousness for an apocalyptic age, in which we must make some radical changes in direction or else our species (and lots of others) will not survive. Heidegger steps into the gap opened up by Nietzsche and leaves us with, not solutions, but issues that, as even Kaufmann concedes, "haunt the mind."[91] Can we demand more? Has anyone else surpassed this point? Still, Heidegger's critics may rightly respond that my rhetorical questions do not constitute an argument. Furthermore, they might reiterate that raising questions (which philosophers do best) is sometimes only learned throat clearing and takes us nowhere.

In this vein, Kaufmann laments that Heidegger has not "unravelled Being," and that it is, in his hands, "a chimera." Yet, according to Daoism (and some forms of mystical Western religion), the ultimate *is* unnameable and not rationally describable. The Dao is both the source of what is and the way that we should follow in order to be in harmony with the universe. Whether a comparison between one elusive theory and another is helpful, each will have to judge for her- or himself. But the verdict one passes on a philosopher is always a function of prior expectations, and it may be that some of these provide an inappropriate measure not only of Heidegger's contribution, but also of what philosophy can, and ought to, achieve.

NOTES

1. Martin Heidegger, *An Introduction to Metaphysics*, trans. Ralph Manheim (New Haven, CT: Yale University Press, 1959), p. 120 (emphasis in original).

2. Arno Baruzzi, "Heidegger, Martin," in *Handbook of Metaphysics and Ontology*, vol. 1, ed. Hans Burkhardt and Barry Smith (Munich: Philosophia Verlag GmbH, 1991), p. 347.

3. Michael Gelven, *A Commentary on Heidegger's "Being and Time"* (New York: Harper Torchbooks, 1970), p. 55.

4. Martin Heidegger, *The Fundamental Concepts of Metaphysics: World, Finitude, Solitude*, trans. William McNeill and Nicholas Walker (Bloomington: Indiana University Press, 1995), p. 5 (emphasis in original). Compare another remark of Hei-

degger's: "Homelessness is coming to be the destiny of the world. Hence it is necessary to think that destiny in terms of the history of Being" (Martin Heidegger, "Letter on Humanism," trans. Frank A. Capuzzi in collaboration with J. Glenn Gray, in Martin Heidegger, *Martin Heidegger: Basic Writings—From "Being and Time" [1927] to "The Task of Thinking" [1964]*, rev. exp. ed., ed. David Farrell Krell [New York: Harper & Row, 1993], p. 243).

5. Heidegger, *Fundamental Concepts of Metaphysics*, p. 7.

6. G. W. F. Hegel, *The Encyclopaedia Logic (Part 1 of the Encyclopaedia of the Philosophical Sciences)*, trans. T. F. Geraets, W. A. Suchting, and H. S. Harris (Indianapolis: Hackett, 1991), sec. 88.

7. George Pattison, *The Later Heidegger* (London: Routledge, 2000), p. 16. See also note 4 above.

8. Martin Heidegger, *Contributions to Philosophy (from Enowning)*, trans. Parvis Emad and Kenneth Maly (Bloomington: Indiana University Press, 2000). This work was written during the period 1936–38 and not published in German until 1989. Some consider it to be next in importance to *Being and Time* among Heidegger's writings.

9. Heidegger, "Letter on Humanism," p. 227.

10. Heidegger takes the ancient Greek verb "to be" (*einai*) as meaning "to be present" (Martin Heidegger, *What Is Called Thinking?* trans. Fred D. Wieck and Glenn Gray [New York: Harper & Row, 1968], p. 235).

11. Martin Heidegger, *Being and Time*, trans. John Macquarrie and Edward Robinson (Oxford: Blackwell, 1967), sec. 4 (emphasis in original).

12. Ibid., sec. 12.

13. Howard R. Pollio et al., *The Phenomenology of Everyday Life* (Cambridge: Cambridge University Press, 1997), p. 5.

14. Martin Heidegger, *Being and Time*, trans. Joan Stambaugh (Albany: State University of New York Press, 1996), sec. 7.

15. Heidegger, *Being and Time*, trans. Macquarrie and Robinson, sec. 27 (emphasis in original).

16. Ibid, sec. 37.

17. Heidegger, *Being and Time*, trans. Stambaugh, sec. 38 (emphasis in original).

18. Marjorie Grene, "Heidegger, Martin," in *The Encyclopedia of Philosophy*, vol. 3, ed. Paul Edwards (New York: Macmillan and The Free Press; London: Collier-Macmillan, 1967), p. 460.

19. Heidegger, *Being and Time*, trans. Macquarrie and Robinson, sec. 41 (emphasis in original).

20. Martin Heidegger, "Language," trans. Albert Hofstadter, in Martin Heidegger, *Poetry, Language, Thought* (New York: Harper Colophon Books, 1975), pp. 189–210.

21. Heidegger, *Being and Time*, trans. Macquarrie and Robinson, sec. 40 (emphasis in original).

22. Ibid., sec. 45.

23. Heidegger, *Being and Time*, trans. Stambaugh, sec. 41 (emphasis in original).

24. Epicurus, "Letter to Menoeceus," in *Epicurus: The Extant Remains*, trans. Cyril Bailey (Oxford: Oxford University Press, 1929).

25. Dudjom Rinpoche, cited by Sogyal Rinpoche, *The Tibetan Book of Living and Dying*, rev. and updated ed., ed. Patrick Gaffney and Andrew Harvey (San Francisco: HarperSanFrancisco, 1994), p. 30.

26. Heidegger, *Being and Time*, trans. Macquarrie and Robinson, sec. 47.

27. Heidegger, *Being and Time*, trans. Stambaugh, sec. 46 (emphasis in original).

28. Heidegger, *Being and Time*, trans. Macquarrie and Robinson, sec. 51.

29. Heidegger, *Being and Time*, trans. Stambaugh, sec. 51 (emphasis in original).

30. Polly Toynbee, "Private Grief, Public Places," *Guardian Weekly* 176, no. 19: 14.

31. Heidegger, *Being and Time*, trans. Macquarrie and Robinson, sec. 51 (emphasis in original).

32. Socrates, in Plato, *Phaedo*, 64a.

33. Heidegger, *Being and Time*, trans. Stambaugh, sec. 52 (emphasis in original).

34. Compare, for interest, Kierkegaard's thoughts on relating to one's own death subjectively. See Søren Kierkegaard, *Concluding Unscientific Postscript to "Philosophical Fragments,"* vol. 1, trans. Howard V. Hong and Edna H. Hong (Princeton, NJ: Princeton University Press, 1992), pp. 166–70.

35. Heidegger, *Being and Time*, trans. Stambaugh, sec. 52 (emphasis in original).

36. Heidegger, *Being and Time*, trans. Macquarrie and Robinson, sec. 53.

37. Heidegger, *Being and Time*, trans. Stambaugh, sec. 53 (emphasis in original).

38. Ibid. (emphasis in original).

39. Irvin Yalom, *Existential Psychotherapy* (New York: Basic Books, 1980), p. 40 (emphasis in original).

40. Herman Feifel, "Death—Relevant Variable in Psychology," in *Existential Psychology*, 2nd ed., ed. Rollo May (New York: Random House, 1969), p. 62.

41. Viktor Frankl, *The Doctor and the Soul: From Psychotherapy to Logotherapy* (New York: Vintage Books/Random House, 1973), p. 64.

42. Kate Douglas, "Death Defying," *New Scientist*, 183, no. 2462: 40–42.

43. Geshe Kelsang Gyatso, *Introduction to Buddhism: An Explanation of the Buddhist Way of Life*, 2nd ed. (Ulverston, UK: Tharpa Publications, 2001), p. 48.

44. Stephen Batchelor, *Buddhism Without Beliefs* (New York: Riverhead Books, 1997), pp. 32, 33.

45. Heidegger, *Being and Time*, trans. Stambaugh, sec. 55 (emphasis in original).

46. Ibid., sec. 56 (emphasis in original).

47. Heidegger, *Being and Time*, trans. Macquarrie and Robinson, sec. 58 (emphasis in original).

48. Ibid., sec. 60 (emphasis in original).

49. Martin Heidegger, "On the Essence of Truth," trans. John Sallis, in *Basic Writings*, p. 125.

50. Ibid., p. 129.

51. Ibid., p. 130.

52. Ibid., p. 129.

53. Ibid., p. 133.

54. Thomas Sheehan, "Heidegger, Martin (1889–1976)," in *Routledge Encyclopedia of Philosophy*, vol. 4, ed. Edward Craig (London: Routledge, 1998), p. 318.

55. Martin Heidegger, "The Question Concerning Technology," trans. William Lovitt, in *Basic Writings*, p. 318.

56. Ibid., p. 319 (emphasis in original).

57. Ibid., p. 321.

58. Ibid., p. 323.

59. Ibid., p. 334.

60. Martin Heidegger, "Building Dwelling Thinking," trans. Albert Hofstadter, in *Basic Writings*, pp. 347–63.

61. Martin Heidegger, "What Is Metaphysics?" trans. David Farrell Krell, in *Basic Writings*, pp. 97–98.

62. Ibid., p. 110. Heidegger cherished this question and thought that his posing of it was original. But the rationalist philosopher Gottfried von Leibniz (1646–1716) had asked it more than two centuries earlier: "*nothing happens without a sufficient reason.* . . . This principle laid down, the first question which should rightly be asked, will be, *Why is there something rather than nothing?* For nothing is simpler and easier than something. Further, suppose that things must exist, we must be able to give a reason *why they must exist so* and not otherwise" (*The Principles of Nature and of Grace, Based on Reason* [1714], in Gottfried von Leibniz, *Leibniz: Selections*, ed. Philip P. Wiener [New York: Charles Scribner's Sons, 1951]).

63. Heidegger, "What Is Metaphysics?" p. 103.

64. Ibid., pp. 100–101.

65. George Steiner, *Heidegger* (Hassocks, UK: Harvester Press, in association with Fontana Books, 1978), p. 41 (emphasis in original).

66. Heidegger, "Letter on Humanism," pp. 236, 237.

67. Martin Heidegger, ". . . Poetically Man Dwells . . . ," trans. Albert Hofstadter, in *Poetry, Language, Thought*, p. 215.

68. Heidegger, "Language," p. 191.

69. Ibid., pp. 190, 193 (emphasis in original).

70. Ibid., p. 192.

71. Heidegger, ". . . Poetically Man Dwells . . . ," p. 218.

72. Heidegger, "Language," p. 199.

73. Ibid., p. 210.

74. Heidegger, ". . . Poetically Man Dwells . . . ," p. 216.

75. Martin Heidegger, "What Calls for Thinking?" trans. Fred D. Wieck and J. Glenn Gray, in *Basic Writings*, p. 379. (This is an excerpt from *What Is Called Thinking?* [see above, note 10].) It is ideas such as this that led Heidegger to speak elsewhere of "the end of philosophy," which is equivalent to a manifesto for some new, as-yet-unnamed discipline. (See Martin Heidegger, "The End of Philosophy and the Task of Thinking," trans. Joan Stambaugh, in *Basic Writings*, pp. 431–49.)

76. Compare the following colorful observation: "Thoughtlessness is an

uncanny visitor who comes and goes everywhere in today's world. For nowadays we take in everything in the quickest and cheapest way, only to forget it just as quickly, instantly" (Martin Heidegger, *Discourse on Thinking*, trans. John M. Anderson and E. H. Freund [New York: Harper & Row, 1966], pp. 44–45). Although Heidegger's remarks here were first published in German in 1959, they perfectly capture the superficial aspects of our so-called "information age."

77. Heidegger, "What Calls for Thinking?" p. 370.

78. Ibid., p. 379.

79. Ibid., pp. 384, 390, 372.

80. Ibid., p. 386.

81. Heidegger, *Discourse on Thinking*, p. 47.

82. Heidegger, "What Calls for Thinking?" p. 381.

83. Aristotle, *Metaphysics*, bk. 1, 980a.

84. Ludwig Wittgenstein, *Philosophical Investigations*, trans. G. E. M. Anscombe (Oxford: Basil Blackwell, 1953), pt. 1, sec. 132.

85. Heidegger, *End of Philosophy*, pp. 432–33.

86. Ibid., p. 449.

87. Walter Kaufmann, *From Shakespeare to Existentialism*, rev. eds. (Garden City, NY: Anchor Books/Doubleday, 1960), pp. 365, 366, 367, 368 (emphasis in original).

88. Charles Guignon, "Heidegger, Martin," in *A Companion to Metaphysics*, ed. Jaegwon Kim and Ernest Sosa (Oxford: Blackwell, 1995), p. 205.

89. Joseph J. Kockelmans, "Heidegger, Martin," in *Thinkers of the Twentieth Century*, ed. Ronald Turner (Chicago: St. James Press, 1987), p. 335 (emphasis in original).

90. Samuel Beckett, *Waiting for Godot: A Tragicomedy in Two Acts*, trans. by Samuel Beckett (New York: Grove Press, 1954). See also Robert McAfee Brown, "Four Ways of Waiting: A Case Study (J. D. Salinger, Samuel Beckett, Franz Kafka, W. H. Auden)," in Robert McAfee Brown, *Persuade Us to Rejoice: The Liberating Power of Fiction* (Louisville: Westminster/John Knox Press, 1992), pp. 41–52.

91. Kaufmann, *From Shakespeare to Existentialism*, p. 367.

QUESTIONS FOR REFLECTION

1. What do you think of Heidegger's diagnosis of the human condition?

2. Explain some ways in which we merge in everyday life with the "they" (or "they-self"). Can we avoid this entirely? Should we attempt to?

3. Heidegger claims that death awareness individuates and liberates us more than any other experience. Do you agree or disagree? Why? What impact do his theories about death have on you?

4. How are death, the nothing, and existential anxiety related? How are Being and nothing related? How are existential anxiety and authenticity related?

5. Heidegger holds that in the search for truth and in the disclosure of Being, every unconcealment is also a concealment. Why does he say this? What does this doctrine mean to you personally?

6. "Language speaks." How? What are the implications of this view?

7. "We are still not thinking." Explain what this means to you. Didn't you have to think in order to answer this question? What would Heidegger say in reply?

8. Is Heidegger a religious philosopher? If not, why not? If so, in what sense?

7

SARTRE

FREEDOM WITHOUT EXCUSES

Jean-Paul Sartre (1905–1980) brought existentialism to the popular consciousness of his time but also fused it with political and ethical concerns that transcend his moment in history. His mode of thought is often weird, quirky, "off the wall"; however, the descriptions he gives of human self-assertion and failure can't be matched for their inherent interest and truth. Sartre is one of the modern era's most ingenious and vigorous defenders of the human capacity for free action.

OWNING EXISTENTIALISM

Most people associate or even identify existentialism with Sartre, and this is in no small part due to his propagandizing on behalf of the movement, as well as to the image he created of the engaged intellectual, which became an indelible feature of the twentieth century. An acquaintance with Sartre's thought usually begins with his 1945 lecture *Existentialism Is a Humanism* (also translated as *Existentialism and Humanism*), in which he made several key assertions that he wanted to be taken as definitive and that have been so taken by a wide variety of readers. (Later on, Sartre had cause to regret the somewhat simplistic view of existentialism that this essay generated and then did not wish it to be understood as the final word on the subject.) In the essay, originally delivered as a lecture to Le Club Maintenant ("The Now Club") in Paris, Sartre makes a basic distinction between religious and atheistic existentialists, including Heidegger and himself among the latter. He floats the doctrine that "existence precedes essence": There is no God or human nature to serve as a reference point for self-definition and, hence, we all emerge out of nothingness, and only after we exist do we make something of ourselves.[1] Subjectivity is therefore the origin of self-knowledge, as well as of self-affirmation, and the ultimate responsibility for becoming what we are stems from the freedom of self-choice.

The reader may recall a certain example of graffiti that illustrated Nietzsche's perspective on the existence of God. Another updates this from Sartre's viewpoint:

> *God is dead.* —Nietzsche
> *Nietzsche is dead.* —God
> *God and Nietzsche are dead.* —Sartre

Whether *Existentialism Is a Humanism* is meant to be the "official" statement of existentialist ideas, or is taken or not taken to be so, there are some important and abiding ideas in it that help gauge accurately what Sartre stands for. To begin with, he argues that in being responsible for ourselves, we are also "responsible for all men. . . . [T]here is not a single one of our acts which does not at the same time create an image of man as we think he ought to be. . . . [T]he image is valid for everybody and for our whole age. Thus, our responsibility is much greater than we might have supposed, because it involves all mankind."[2] One might think that Sartre has in the back of his mind here some sort of Kantian principle—that a person ought to do whatever she or he could consistently want everyone else to do in the same circumstances—for he says, "one should always ask himself, 'What would happen if everybody looked at things that way?'"[3] But the temptation to impose Kant on Sartre should be resisted, as it leads to a superficial and misleading interpretation. Sartre's view, rather, is something like this: that for each of us, the question is, "What mark am I prepared to leave upon the world? What contribution am I going to make to the quality of life in general?" Humanity should be thought of as a collective experiment in living, with each doing her or his part to fashion the world "as it should be," one might say.

In addition, freedom is always at issue, for Sartre, its scope being either expanded or contracted by our decisions and actions. Each choice projects an image of humanity, of human possibility. Choices are what make a world and posit values. When we choose, we act as beings who enjoy reciprocity with one another, who take each other's "images of human possibility" into account, sometimes positively (when we build upon them), sometimes negatively (when we reject and move beyond them), sometimes neglectfully (when we ignore or shortsightedly flout them). Whatever we do, freedom is always put to the test.

Still, there is some ambiguity in Sartre's above remarks. For when he says, "[T]here is not a single one of our acts which does not at the same time create an image of man as we think he ought to be," he is presumably not trying to persuade us that *all* of our actions—regardless of the principles they embody or their outcome or what we think of them later on—express ideals we endorse. Such a sweeping assertion would be obviously untenable. This is why I've interpreted him as making a somewhat exaggerated statement to the effect that human actions are exploratory and experimental: Singly and collectively they set out the range of values among which we choose to build a shared future world. We also have to keep in mind that for Sartre all acts are spontaneous and do not follow logically from a process of deliberation as in the traditional model of value-governed behavior. As we shall see in this chapter, deliberation does occur, but it is not the "cause" (logically or psychologically) of what we do.

Anguish (which we shall return to later) is also singled out for attention in *Existentialism Is a Humanism*, and Sartre maintains that it "is evident even when it conceals itself,"[4] as in the case of Kierkegaard's Abraham (see chapter 3) making a momentous decision before God (Sartre's own example). Anguish "is not a curtain separating us from action, but is part of action itself."[5] It is the way we experience the weight of our freedom and responsibility. We don't (and can't, in principle) know what the outcome of our choices will be, and whether, in any case, they are the "right" or "best" ones; and with each choice we are positing values that challenge us to accept responsibility for ourselves in the world. These are scary and unsettling aspects of the human condition that we simply have to live with. If we seek to evade them, we betray our humanity. Sartre captures the burden of choice with one of his most famous slogans: "man is condemned to be free."[6]

In his characteristic way of turning things on their heads, Sartre substantiates his theories about freedom and ethics by describing two young men trying to work their way through personal decision-making quandaries. The first was a student of Sartre's in the early 1940s, who came to seek his advice on whether he should look after his emotionally dependent mother in German-occupied Paris or go to England and join the self-exiled Free French Forces waiting indefinitely to take part in the liberation of France. Sartre observes that "he was wavering between two kinds of ethics. On the one hand, an ethics of sympathy, of personal devotion; on the other, a broader ethics, but one whose efficacy was more dubious. He had to choose between the two." But Sartre reflects, "Who could help him choose? . . . No book of ethics can tell him. . . ." In situations like this, Sartre adds, sounding very much like Camus, "the only thing left for us is to trust our instincts."[7] This is perhaps a very unsatisfactory conclusion to reach if one is committed to a more classical approach to ethics, wherein, as noted earlier, we supposedly derive our choices by inference from some universally applicable principle or rule. However, for Sartre, there is no anchor point either within or outside oneself that will generate answers to ethical dilemmas in a purely rational or mechanical fashion. And so (here comes the reversal of perspectives) he points out that by choosing Sartre as his adviser (rather than, say, a priest), the young man *has already made the choice* about which he had sought advice— presumably to join the Free French, given Sartre's own well-known position as an intellectual leader within the resistance movement.

What, then, *was* Sartre's advice? Simply: "'You're free, choose, that is, invent.'" He explains this as follows: "No general ethics can show you what is to be done; there are no omens in the world. The Catholics will reply, 'But there are.' Granted—but, in any case, I myself choose the meaning they have."[8] Perhaps this is not very helpful or illuminating, but Sartre is eager to avoid turning ethics into preaching or making up others' minds for them.

Surely, in any case, we all face the kind of circumstances that Sartre sets up. Should I tell a white lie in this or that situation? How can I best honor a dead person that I cared about when living? What values should I raise my child with? What obligations do I have to my friends, my permanent partner, my working colleagues? Should I have an abortion? Should I become an activist against violence, against the mistreatment of animals, against threats to the environment? How far should I be prepared to go in expressing and defending my basic values? Some claim (wrongly, as I argue) that existentialism has no ethics or, at any rate, that it cannot generate a coherent and convincing ethical doctrine. But at one level, what's going on here is that the critic is begging the question by insisting that any form of ethics must conform to a standard model that stresses rational procedures and strives for precise answers and systematic completeness.

TWO SARTRIAN PIGS IN THE
DAYS OF THE RESISTANCE.

And Sartre is specifically denying the appropriateness of this very model for the situations that humans typically find themselves in. At the very least, he is himself insisting that whatever general ideas we bring to bear on situations that call for responsible decision-making require interpretation, validation, and appropriation by the agent whose situation it is, if they are meaningfully to come into play at all. Not only that, but as Sartre points out especially well in his play *Dirty Hands*, moral situations are often far from clear-cut, with compromises or lesser-of-evil solutions having to be settled for. Everyone has "dirty hands" in the sense that moral choices are exactly that—choices—where "the right choice" may only be "the better choice from a certain standpoint" or "given an unattractive range of options" or "because of expediency." In an increasingly complicated world such as ours, this lesson comes home to us daily, as we make consumer, lifestyle, political, parenting, workplace, and other choices.

Sartre's second example of personal choice in this essay concerns someone who experienced several kinds of adversity in childhood and made a number of blunders such that he might well have considered himself a total failure and "taken refuge in bitterness or despair." Instead, he saw these events collectively as a sign from God that the path he should follow was a religious rather than an earthly one. He therefore joined the Jesuits. Sartre's gloss is: "Who can help seeing that he alone decided what the sign meant?"[9] Hence, when the question "What ought I to do with my life?" arose, the answer was again to be found in the individual's personal, self-generated response to his unique situation, not in some "higher principle"—although (for him) *God* had spoken. (But even if one *were* to receive a divine command, which is not the case here, strictly speaking, one could still choose to disobey or obey it.) In short, the individual in this example has doubly chosen: to interpret events in his life as a sign from God and, further, to interpret this as meaning he should take up a religious vocation.

THEORY OF CONSCIOUSNESS

In a short early book published in 1936, *The Transcendence of the Ego*, Sartre began to establish a foundation for the theory of consciousness that underlies (and is further developed in) the themes of his best-known book *Being and Nothingness* (1943). Sartre adopts the now-familiar stance that all consciousness of the world and consciousness of self ("reflective consciousness") is intentional and also "positional." What this means is that (a) consciousness has an object on which it directs its attention (it is an arrow of awareness or attentiveness); (b) consciousness occupies a standpoint on the world; and (c) intentional objects are objects in relation to consciousness. But consciousness, in all of its activities, has a more basic, "non-positional" awareness of itself as well. This he describes as "immediate" and "non-cognitive" and, here, "consciousness is not for itself its own object." At this point, the reader may be thinking, "You've lost me already." So let's take a closer look at this distinction.

Sartre wants to convey the fact that consciousness has an ongoing sense of its own being at work; he points out that our ordinary awareness includes a continuous monitoring of awareness, but this occurs in such a manner that consciousness is not turned into an explicit object of inspection for itself. I don't need to rehearse to myself, "I am thinking (or perceiving, imagining, and so on)" in order to be thinking (perceiving, imagining, and so on). I just do it, and I am one with my awareness. If someone were to ask me, "What are you doing?" I would reply, "I'm thinking about my plans for the day," or some such. Even at that time, I am not really reflecting on my thinking, I am simply reporting my fundamental awareness of my own conscious activity as it occurs. Normally, it takes a further inquiry of the kind, "Well, what are you planning, then?" to make me genuinely reflect on what I am doing. More on this in a moment. But first, notice some conclusions Sartre draws about consciousness.

1. "[T]he type of existence of consciousness is to be consciousness of itself."[10] This has already been explained: consciousness is aware of itself without the need to make itself into an object, intentional or otherwise.

2. "All is therefore clear and lucid in consciousness. . . ."[11] It follows that (a) consciousness is always "translucent" to itself;[12] (b) because of (a), consciousness is a unity; and (c) because this unity is one in which all is "clear and lucid," there is no "unconscious mind."[13]

3. Since consciousness just *is*, it does not require that there first be a "subject" to have it; therefore, it is an "impersonal spontaneity."[14]

4. Owing to this spontaneity, consciousness is free to determine and direct itself; hence "each instant of our conscious life reveals to us a creation *ex nihilo* [out of nothing]. Not a new *arrangement*, but a new existence."[15] Consciousness is always a potentiality and is not bogged down by a "subject" that "has" it, by the past, the condition of the world, or any other factor. As this quotation affirms (and as *Being and Nothingness* subsequently reiterates), consciousness is a "nothingness," a self-propelled wheel, an ability to posit meaning, value, and relationships to others and to the world starting from scratch. Indeed, Sartre goes much further, as we've just seen, insisting that my consciousness is reborn, not only each day of my awareness, but "each instant." It can always strike off in a different direction and define itself afresh. This is doubtless the single most important implication of Sartre's theory of consciousness.

5. Consciousness, being self-renewing in the way Sartre claims, forever transcends, "flies beyond," or "overflows" itself.[16]

6. Because of the previously listed features of consciousness, it has the capacity to give itself its own specific properties (that is, to define itself, to create a self as such). It also has the power to *negate*: to differentiate present from past, present from future, self from other, desirable from undesirable, and so on. In each case, the operative implicit judgment is: "This is not that"; "This is not as worthy as that"; or something akin to these.

7. Since consciousness emerges from the abyss of nothingness, Sartre holds that it is "anguished."[17] Before freedom can even be enacted, consciousness must possess the spontaneity of which Sartre speaks; thus, freedom, if it has any ground at all, is only anchored in the volatile potentiality that is consciousness. Another expression Sartre uses to capture this aspect of conscious-

ness is "'vertigo of possibility.'"[18] To refer, metaphorically, to the spontaneity of consciousness and the freedom that it represents as "vertigo" suggests that being free is experienced similarly to the dizzying sense of instability encountered by someone who is fearful of heights or precipices.

8. What we call "I" or "me" and the "ego" or "self" properly exists only when our becoming is momentarily arrested; only then *am* I such-and-such or do I have an *essence* or *identity*. Thus, for example, it's just at times when I sum up myself—what I have been up to now—that I can say who or what I am. The reason is that only then do I arrest the spontaneous movement of my consciousness in order to reflect on it *as an object*. An example will help here. Suppose I am listening to a church bell chiming the hour. I am counting the bongs and am (unreflectively) aware that I am doing this. Along comes someone who asks me, "What are you doing?" I answer, without really thinking about it, "Counting the hours by the church bell." Sartre believes I give this response without interrupting consciousness' immediate flow of awareness of its own activity. However, the person persists: "What is it, *exactly*, that you are doing?" or: "How do you go about that?" Now, I'm forced to stop, step back from the activity, and examine it on a second-order level. I then make my first-order awareness (plus my immediate awareness of awareness) an object of examination and discussion. In like manner to reflecting on who I have been up to now (who I "really" am, we often say), I sum up my previous activity. And the thing to note is that I lose my original focus; I lose count of the bongs because instead of being immersed in the activity, I'm now being asked to account for it. I am engaged in meta-consciousness, second-order, or reflective consciousness, which makes spontaneous, first-order consciousness into its intentional object. Another way of putting Sartre's point about the self is that the self (such as it is) exists for consciousness only when it is backward looking, looking on (as a spectator in relation to itself), when freedom is "idling," as it were. We shall see that that is also the point when we sit in judgment on ourselves. One can understand the distinction Sartre is making as a version of the contrast existentialists draw between becoming and being. Becoming (or doing) is my engagement in present activities; being is the sum total of my completed activities and projects.

---

becoming ————————————————————>
    flux, flow of freedom through time, ongoing self-creation
        (I am what I do)

being: becoming stops or is arrested
        (I am someone or something—at least momentarily)

It will readily be appreciated that in Sartre's theory of consciousness, he is dramatically departing from some well-established ideas. While he affirms that consciousness is the starting point for philosophy, there is no need for a substantial self to have it or to be the permanent or essential entity that endures through the various changing moments of mental activity and experience. He colorfully expresses this thought as follows: "For most philosophers the ego is an 'inhabitant' of consciousness. . . . We should like to show . . . that the ego is . . . outside, *in the world*. It is a being of the world, like the ego of another. . . . My *I*, in effect, is *no more certain for consciousness than the I of other men*. It is only more intimate."[19]

Because there is no unconscious for Sartre, everything that occurs in consciousness must be available to it in principle. Nothing is hidden, although some things may be less well attended to than others. (I will consider these claims further when investigating what Sartre calls "bad faith.") In Sartre's view, then, agency entails taking full responsibility for who or what we are at any given moment; we cannot flee from accountability (in our own eyes and those of others) by seeking refuge in excuses that in any way undermine the "transcendence" of consciousness. (The key to what I am is what I make of myself, and this is always up to me. Consciousness is the vehicle by means of which this takes place.)

Consciousness has no inherent properties of its own, other than its negating (or "nihilating") power, beginning with its ability to differentiate itself from other things (including other consciousnesses). Sartre sometimes describes it as a kind of subtle and invisible "breeze" blowing out into and inhabiting the world.

We can summarize Sartre's theory of consciousness in this manner (listing various alternative terms that occur in translations of his texts):

CONSCIOUSNESS =

consciousness₁
(primary/unreflected/prereflexive/prereflective/unreflective)
characteristics: spontaneous, engaged, positional, intentional; but also possesses a nonreflexive, nonpositional, or nonthetic awareness of itself

*   *   *

consciousness₂
(secondary/reflected/reflexive/reflective)
characteristics: unspontaneous, disengaged (that is, it "spells out" or halts ongoing conscious₁ activity), positional, intentional; but also features a reflexive awareness of consciousness₁

There is something a bit troubling in all this, for it seems that Sartre has helped himself to saying a great deal about consciousness while still maintaining that it has no essence. Surely, one supposes, to describe it as free, spontaneous, translucent, anguished, and all the rest, suggests essential qualities belonging to consciousness. Without these, it wouldn't be what it apparently is. Even to describe consciousness as a nothingness might be said to assign it an essence, and thus, to turn it into a thing, which is what he had wished to avoid. Sartre would no doubt reply, however, that since one can only *hint* at what consciousness is, one has to do this by saying what it is *not*, and by describing it metaphorically (for example, as a "breeze" or an "arrow"). Yet some would respond by arguing that defining something negatively is still defining it. Let us leave Sartre with the final word here: *insofar as consciousness can be defined at all,* he has done his best to render intelligible *what it is,* mostly in terms of *what it does.* We will revisit this issue in the next section.

BEING AND NOTHINGNESS

Sartre's book *Being and Nothingness* is subtitled *An Essay on Phenomenological Ontology.* This tells us that the phenomenological descriptions he offers in it are meant to convey an understanding of what exists, at any rate so far as experience reveals this. To this end, he distinguishes between two kinds of being: *being-in-itself* and *being-for-itself.* Being-in-itself represents the mode of being of a thing, the essence of which is given to it or completely defined by internal and external factors. Its essence and existence coincide, Sartre likes to say. The brute factuality or facticity of objects, of the object-world as such, is disturbingly captured in Sartre's impressive novel *Nausea,* when his protagonist Roquentin experiences the overwhelming and overbearing materiality of things.[20] Another feature of a thing is that it is a "center of opacity for consciousness."[21] This means that every object presents an unlimited number of facets or perspectives, to catalogue which would be an inexhaustible task (recall example #2: "Seeing an object," in chapter 5). Being-for-itself applies to human consciousness and, as we already know, its existence precedes its essence. Consciousness first exists (it is "thrown" into the world, as Heidegger puts it), then it becomes something. It is a "nothing" that becomes "something" by defining itself through its own acts. In contrast to the opacity of objects, consciousness is "clear and lucid," we have been told.[22]

It's pretty obvious that consciousness is not a thing; it is unlike other

things that lack consciousness. But what is Sartre getting at when he identifies consciousness with nothingness? Part of the answer is contained in
what has been said in the previous section, but much more needs to be
added for a full picture. Let's review for a moment. Consciousness—is
free; has the power of negation; is spontaneous; posits meanings, values,
and relationships; is always self-transcending; reinvents itself at each
instant. All of these properties entail that what we are dealing with makes
itself what it will be; or, in opposition to things, which just are what they
are, *consciousness is a process of being-on-the-way-to-having-an-essence.* This "not
yet" quality is crucial, for it signifies the nothingness of consciousness
quite plainly: Consciousness is *not yet* what it will be, and what it will be is
up to it to determine. Sartre likes to say things such as: (1) "I am what I
am not, and am not what I am," and (2) "I am what I will be, in the mode
of not being it." These formulations and others of a similar sort can be
very confusing to first-time readers, but they actually follow readily from
his views about consciousness. The meaning of (1) is that "you can't pin
me down because what I am is always changing; I'm always moving beyond
what seems to be true of me at the moment to a new point in my life. What
anyone (even myself) declares me to be is not a resting place and cannot
exhaust my potential." In (2) we find a more direct statement: "Whatever
I will be, I am not now, because I have yet to choose and become that."
Another way to look at all of this is via the distinction between being
(having an essence) and becoming (moving toward an essence). Thus, the
sense of both (1) and (2) from this perspective is: "What I *am* now constitutes the process of becoming what I am not but yet will be; I *am not* (really
or fully) the person I appear to be now and am already overreaching; I am
my 'future self' in the mode of projecting it as a possibility and moving
toward realizing it." On reflection, it seems appropriate to give three different readings to Sartre: (a) temporal (I am always changing); (b) epis-
temic (No one, including me, can distill my identity into a formula); and
(c) metaphysical (My unactualized possibilities constitute who I am *now*).
Sartre's view of the ever-emerging self can be diagrammed in this manner:

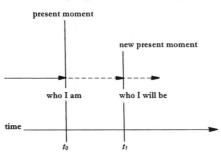

Notice that in these attempts to "translate" Sartre, as well as in his own type of formulation, it is strongly asserted that the choice of myself is enabled by my capacity to overleap the present (to become what I am not) and to envision now a state of affairs that is yet to come (the future, which will emerge in time). To speak of "what I am not yet" indicates the negating power of consciousness, which derives from its nothingness. Negating does not merely display the ability to say "No" or "This is not that." It also signifies what we today call "thinking beyond the box," or pushing past limits that restrict our growth and development. When I think of options for my future, envision the world as a different and better place, imagine flying through the universe and meeting aliens on distant planets, or anything that moves me beyond the time and place of the present, I am *nihilating* what is (or appears to be) the case and exerting my freedom to remake myself or the conditions around me. But, equally, when I recall the past, I *nihilate* (overleap) the present in order to reconnect with what used to be. Simply put, *all acts of freedom, choice, and vision are energized by the nothingness that belongs to consciousness.*

Because consciousness begins as nothing, a pure potential directed only by its own intrinsic freedom, Sartre speaks of humans (or being-for-itself) as "gratuitous" or "superfluous" (*de trop*). There is no reason why we exist and there is no justification outside of ourselves for our existence. We inherit the world we find ourselves in and are left to do what we can and want to do with it. Thus, he repeats the existentialist theme of abandonment or "thrownness," but with a stern, yet positive twist: It's up to us to make the world our oyster. In short, I am what I do, and what I do is a perpetual coming-to-be or emergence. Once again, a piece of graffiti explains the difference between Sartre and some other important thinkers:

> *"To do is to be."* —Heidegger
> *"To be is to do."* —Sartre
> *"Do-be-do-be-do."* —Sinatra

NOTHINGNESS AND THE STRUCTURE OF EXPERIENCE

Among the collection of very memorable statements by Sartre are the following: "*nothingness haunts being*" and "Nothingness lies coiled in the heart of being—like a worm."[23] What are we to make of these curious remarks? Their explanation lies in Sartre's theory of consciousness. Inasmuch as consciousness is itself "empty" and is only a capacity for freely transcending the world (in thought) and altering it (through choice leading to action), consciousness expresses itself as a nihilating stance toward the world. Another way of saying this is that consciousness is fundamentally transformative: it is experimental and forward-looking; it juts out into the unknown; it searches for new solutions. Sartre argues that there are what he calls "*négatités*" ("nonentities" or "pools of non-being") throughout existence,[24] and this is because there are "types of human activity which while not obviously involving a negative judgment nevertheless contain negativity as an integral part of their structure; e.g., experiences involving absence, change, interrogation, destruction."[25] Each of the foregoing examples is a mode of consciousness in relation to the world that illustrates negation: Detecting the *absence* of something or someone signifies an expectation that is *not* met; *change* makes something or some state of affairs *not* to be (cancels it) in favor of another that had previously *not* been the case (brings about a new state of affairs); *interrogation* (or questioning)—of one kind, at any rate—issues the challenge why something is *not* so when it might be, or is so when it might *not* have been; *destruction* obviously is intended to make something that is, *not be*. Sartre sums up by characterizing "nothingness as a sort of geometrical place for unfulfilled projects, all inexact representations, all vanished beings or those of which the idea is only a fiction. . . ." It also embraces "those negations which include non-being in their being." All of these "possess as much reality and efficacy as other beings."[26]

One of Sartre's brilliant ministudies of consciousness in action concerns absence.

> I have an appointment with Pierre at four o'clock. I arrive at the café a quarter of an hour late. Pierre is always punctual. Will he have waited for me? I look at the room, the patrons, and I say, "He is not here." . . .
>
> It is certain that the café by itself with its patrons, its tables, its booths, its mirrors, its light, its smoky atmosphere, and the sounds of voices, rattling saucers, and footsteps which fill it—the café is a fullness of being. . . . I am witness to the successive disappearance of all the objects which I look at—in particular of the faces, which detain me for an instant (Could this be Pierre?) and which as quickly decompose precisely because they "are not" the face of Pierre. . . .
>
> But now Pierre is not here. . . . In fact Pierre is absent from the *whole* café; his absence fixes the café in its evanescence. . . . This figure which slips constantly between my look and the solid, real objects of the café is precisely a perpetual disappearance; it is Pierre raising himself as nothingness on the ground of the nihilation of the café.[27]

As we see here, and as he explicitly states elsewhere in the text from which I am quoting, Sartre fully accepts the phenomenological idea that experience is always constructed in terms of figure against ground. In this specific case, the figure of attention is, not Pierre, but Pierre as *missing* (the *absence* of Pierre), and the ground or context that sets this awareness off, and is in turn set off by it, is the café. But notice that Sartre goes still further, referring to the "nihilation of the café." The idea he's trying to get at is that against the disappointed expectation of finding Pierre in this place, the café itself becomes structured, not as "fullness of being," but rather as "the scene where Pierre is not to be found" or "the locale that at this time is of no interest to me because it is minus Pierre." Both elements exist in tandem and color one another. And Sartre's point is that this structure doesn't just tell us something about me but also reflects a kind of momentary reality.

Many more such examples pepper Sartre's work, for as he observes, "We see nothingness making the world iridescent, casting a shimmer over things."[28] And like Heidegger, Sartre insists that it is because we apprehend nothingness in the world that negation enters our thought processes, not the reverse.

SARTRE VS. HEIDEGGER

While Sartre followed Heidegger in a temporal sense and borrowed ideas from him, he cannot be called Heidegger's disciple. There were important differences between the two, and both Heidegger and Sartre sometimes felt the impulse to distance themselves from one another's doctrines. One thing to note is that for Sartre, nothingness is the active element of human consciousness and choice. For Heidegger, the nothing is more of a brooding backdrop to Being—that by contrast to which the questionable presence of beings (and especially of Dasein) is highlighted.

Sartre and Heidegger are both concerned with self-making and the pursuit of authenticity in the process, but Sartre seems to have little or no interest in being-toward-death as a defining aspect of human awareness. As well, Sartre has much more to say (albeit generally of a negative tone) about concrete engagements between people than Heidegger, whose analyses of interpersonal behavior often strike one as rather abstract in comparison.

And, of course, Sartre is unabashedly atheistic in a way that Heidegger is not. Heidegger is not afraid to speak of "gods" as formative cultural possibilities and of "the holy" as a dimension of experience. Sartre thinks that a commitment to atheism is pretty much the starting point of existentialist discourse, while Heidegger deliberately chooses to dwell in his thought somewhere between atheism and theism, notwithstanding Sartre's inclusion of him among atheist existentialists (see first section of this chapter). As Heidegger frankly observes, "The statement that the essence of man consists in being-in-the-world . . . contains no decision about whether man in a theologico-metaphysical sense is merely a this-worldly or an otherworldly creature."[29]

The most important disagreement between the two philosophers, perhaps, is that which we find reflected in Heidegger's reaction to Sartre's *Existentialism Is a Humanism*. This essay prompted Heidegger to publish his *Letter on Humanism* two years later. Originally a response to some questions put to him by a French intellectual, Heidegger's letter pinpoints a few of his crucial departures from Sartre's manifesto, with its pretense at becoming the standard by which existentialist principles should be understood and judged. Basically, Heidegger wishes here to refocus on the study of Being as a way of getting at what humans are and where they might and should be heading. "Thinking comes to an end when it slips out of its element," Heidegger contends, from which one may readily infer that Sartre's kind of thinking is guilty of exactly this error.[30] Even though he concentrates on Being, with which metaphysics was traditionally occupied, Heidegger's project is to go *beyond metaphysics*, whose tendency is to freeze forms of awareness into sterile categories of thought, and to seek for an experience- and discourse-based engagement with Being (see chapter 6). According to him, "Every determination of the essence of man that already presupposes an interpretation of being without asking about the truth of Being, whether knowingly or not, is metaphysical." And he later adds that "Sartre. . . . [in asserting that existence precedes essence] stays with metaphysics in oblivion of the truth of Being." Hence, "the highest determinations of the essence of man in humanism still do not realize the proper dignity of man."[31] This announces a clash of ideas that cannot be mediated, for Heidegger is saying that, in his view, Sartre starts off on the wrong foot because he grounds himself in the Western philosophical tradition in a major way rather than throwing it into question and starting over. An alternative view, however, might profile Sartre as the thinker who ventures forth in a new direction by trying to create an analysis and practical philosophy of life that responds affirmatively to the death of God, while Heidegger is left to wallow around in uncertainty and endless preliminaries, waiting for the call of Being.

RADICAL FREEDOM

Sartre makes no secret of the fact that his commitment to the scope of human freedom is quite extreme. Everything we do is an expression of our freedom. Thus, to take but one example—a rather charming one—he claims that skiing on fresh snow represents not merely the freedom we all know to be inherent in playfulness and sport. It also signifies the desire to imprint our freedom on the in-itself (in this case, the snow)—to be, in a way, the snow's raison d'être.[32] Yet it would be a mistake to describe Sartrean freedom as "total" or "absolute," as is often done. I prefer the adjective "radical" for various reasons, which will now be explained.

To begin with, Sartre does not make absurd claims, such as that we can make time stand still, defy gravity, alter the past, make 2 + 2 equal to 5, transform the world with a snap of our fingers, or magically change ourselves into nonhuman beings. These things might be assumed to lie within the power of someone who had "absolute" freedom. (Whether they would lie within the power of God, as traditionally conceived, has been much debated, as has the issue of whether, if they did not, God's power would be limited, making him less than omnipotent.) The point is that Sartre endorses the common-sense position that human freedom is limited, not all powerful.

In particular, we cannot change or control what falls within the realm of what Heidegger calls *facticity*. Sartre adopts the term and therefore fully acknowledges the given elements of our situation (refer to chapter 1 for a full definition of facticity). But although we do not have power over these things, *it is always up to us to determine how we will react to them and what attitude we will take up toward them.* This is a fundamental belief of Sartre's. Another is that *no matter what we have been up to the present, we have the ability to strike off in a new direction at any time.*

Let me illustrate these two ideas. First of all, things do happen to us that we might wish had not. An individual may have been the victim of childhood physical or sexual abuse; she or he may have been born and raised in an environment of civil war or of ghetto poverty and crime. There are those who cannot move past these events and thus succumb to their devastating impact. But there are also those who do rise above them and make their lives dramatically better through their own efforts. Sartre holds that the former have chosen to give up or pack in their lives while the latter have chosen to say "No" to their former lives, using their freedom to craft new ones. This is an easy pronouncement on the part of someone raised in middle-class comfort (namely, Sartre), one might think. But Sartre would reply, "How else are we to explain why people raised in almost identical circumstances—often even in the same family—turn out differently, given their beginnings? The tough truth is that we make our choices and then live them out, often without accepting any responsibility for this."

We will explore this topic further under the heading of "bad faith"; but for now, note that Sartre divides the world between those who evade responsibility and those who take it. Both start off equally free, but whereas some choose to live in the attitude of excuse, others live without excuses. For example, consider two young people with the same family experience who are raised in a degrading and demoralizing urban ghetto, with all that that entails. One becomes a drug dealer and pimp while the other uses sports as an avenue to escape, earning a university scholarship, graduating, then becoming a prominent and ethical professional. The first forever blames parents, teachers, "circumstances," "bad breaks," "society," the behavior of "others," and everything else for the way things have turned out. The second acknowledges having received some "lucky breaks" but also expresses a steadfast determination to achieve something to be proud of, in spite of adversity. Why is there such a big difference here? No one can tell with certainty, and neither heredity nor environment provides a plausible account, nor do both taken together. We are therefore left, Sartre maintains, to appeal to the agent's own initiative or lack of it in order to find the source of these two responses to life's challenges. The person whose attitude is one of excuse denies her or his freedom and adopts instead a framework of being a victim, of being acted upon like a thing. The person who lives without excuses shoulders the burden of freedom in a productive, autonomous fashion. That is really all we can say.

Finally, as noted in chapter 1, everyone always exists in a situation, which is a set of circumstances that are given but at the same time contain a challenge to transform them. Thus, in a person's situation of the moment, facticity meets freedom and the outcome is a function or interplay of the two; but, more importantly, the outcome is whatever freedom makes of the facticity with which it is presented.

These ideas have been put into practice by a number of existential psychotherapists, psychologists, counselors, and sociologists. To take but one example, William Glasser (b. 1925) developed "reality therapy," a method of dealing with behavioral change that emphasizes personal responsibility and willingness to plan differently for the future. Clients are not allowed to shift responsibility away from themselves and onto others, dwell on the past, or procrastinate in other ways. Instead, the task is to figure out what one is going to do now and tomorrow to chart a new course in life. Notable success in treating alcoholics and juvenile delinquents was reported early on by Glasser, and the approach (later incorporated into "choice theory") has since been applied to many other areas.[33]

We cannot end this discussion of radical freedom without some reference to Sartre's views on determinism and fatalism. Briefly, he sees these as attitudes of excuse. They are prototypes, as it were, for modes of thinking designed to evade responsibility for choosing who we are to be. (As Kierkegaard held, they are limitations one places on "possibility.") They also solidify human existence and turn it into a passive object, something merely acted upon—in short, a thing. Determinism, whatever else it may be, is generally the position that my choices and the course of my life as a whole are not "up to me" because extraneous conditions and factors hold sway over me. My behavior is caused, and the causes can be traced beyond me to things that are out of my control. From this it would seem to follow that not only can I not be blamed for what I do, I am not even responsible for it in the first place. Few, I think, would wish to advocate such a sweeping form of nonresponsibility; for along with it comes lack of reward or praise for our deeds, credit for our positive personal traits, and so on, which are too valuable—perhaps impossible—to forgo. But many would and do seek self-excuse when it is convenient and, for Sartre, determinism signifies the theoretical possibility of pushing this to its logical conclusion.

Fatalism, the view that whatever happens or will happen in the future is timelessly predetermined (or "in the cards"), provides an even more rigid template for the attitude of excuse. This is because for a fatalist it doesn't even matter what causal factors chance to appear—"what will be, will be" in spite of any empirically discoverable circumstance or effort on the part of a human agent. In chapter 9, we will examine determinism as a threat to existentialism in more detail. For now, let it just be noted that Sartre, like Kierkegaard before him, sets up his outlook on human life in strong opposition to that which is believed to flow from deterministic thinking.

ANGUISH

Whereas death awareness is for Heidegger the paradigm experience by which our own possible nothingness is revealed to us, for Sartre anguish fills this role. Anguish, one might say, is the raw awareness of freedom or possibility; that is, of the open-endedness of human existence. Sartre offers this perceptive account:

First we must acknowledge that Kierkegaard is right; anguish is distinguished from fear in that fear is fear of beings in the world whereas anguish is anguish before myself. Vertigo is anguish to the extent that I am not afraid of falling over the precipice, but of throwing myself over. A situation provokes fear if there is a possibility of my life being changed from without; my being provokes anguish to the extent that I distrust myself and my own reactions in that situation.[34]

Here, fear and anguish are both spoken of as feelings because Sartre has specific situations in mind. He does not deny, and in fact affirms just prior to the above passage, that anguish is a "mode of being." It would be incorrect, however, to infer that anguish, for Sartre, is what I have (in chapter 6) called a mood, for, as he states somewhat earlier, "it is in anguish that freedom is, in its being, in question for itself." Freedom is not always conscious of itself as such; generally it is just engaged with whatever situation engulfs it at the moment. There are times, though, when we have a reflective awareness of freedom, and it is then that anguish blossoms in us. *Anguish is a possibility of awareness that unceasingly hovers in consciousness.*

Neither I nor anyone else knows exactly what I am going to do until I do it. In making this claim, Sartre does not mean to imply that freedom is a loose cannon but rather that it is the potential to decide and act in many different ways. The facticity that confronts a person in her or his situation can evoke fear but it cannot determine the person's response; only freedom can do that. The distinction between fear and anguish is underlined by Sartre's comment that "consciousness . . . senses [its own] spontaneity as *beyond* freedom";[35] that is, as a restless, ever-present energy—the possibility of choice itself. Anguish lies in the potential for choosing even before freedom activates the choice.

Sartre selects a metaphorical example to illustrate further the difference between fear and anguish. A dangerous cliff edge can inspire fear; there's the concrete possibility (not up to me) that it might collapse under my feet. But anguish arises when I realize that it *is* up to me not to fall if I don't want to; or to take risks that might be fatal if I choose to; or to deliberately make myself fall if that is my plan. According to a popular old folk song, God "has the whole world in his hands." But from Sartre's standpoint, it is true for each of us that "I have the whole world in my hands"—at least *my* world.

Anguish comes to the fore in relation to both one's personal past and future. Sartre uses the example of a gambling addict to illustrate the former. Let us suppose this person has firmly resolved to give up gambling. The problem is that such a resolution lies in the past and the situation faced (to gamble or not *now*) is in the present. The gambler would like to be able to rest in confidence that a past intention will govern what is about to happen, but, unfortunately, life does not work that way; *now* is when her or his personal freedom to decide selects between the two alternatives. Anguish resides, as it always does, in the accompanying awareness that it is for me to make this choice, and that I could make the choice go either way, despite past resolutions, self-regard, special counseling, pleas from family members, promises, and the like. Thus, the past by itself carries no weight because the game of life is constantly beginning afresh.

Anguish haunts the future too in an analogous manner. Sartre remarks as follows: "the future which I am remains out of my reach. . . . I await myself in the future, where I 'make an appointment with myself on the other side of that hour, of that day, or of that month.' Anguish is the fear of not finding myself at that appointment, of no longer even wishing to bring myself there."[36] In other words, anguish exists when I understand, if only momentarily, that the future is "up to me," but in a sharply different sense from how I relate to the past. I embark on a project, such as writing this book. I envision the steps it takes to bring the task to completion and possibly even the state of completion and what lies beyond. Yet I may equally well decide to abandon the project somewhere along the way and to turn to something else instead. Anguish lies in the realization of the contingency of all such plans, and of my ability to radically alter them. The future, which I plan now, may seem to be the stable foundation of my life, but this stability is merely illusory. It is always under threat by me, as it were, because I may choose to be a different "self" than the one I previously thought I wanted to be. Sartre isn't saying that there's anything wrong with this state of affairs, just that the wide scope of possibility freedom provides makes us full of unease when we contemplate it.

One final point Sartre makes about anguish is that it pervades our value structures. Normally, we think and act as if our values have a foundation of some kind. Even if we don't suppose that they have certainty or are guaranteed by the word of God, we may still believe in them more or less firmly for one reason or another. Sartre claims, however, that "when I consider myself in my original relation to values" I realize that even if I did not in the first instance choose to hold those I do (I may have acquired them uncritically from my parents or my cultural group, for example), as an adult it is nonetheless a matter for me alone, once again, whether to accept or reject them. From this standpoint, "My freedom is anguished at being the foundation of values while itself without foundation."[37] My values, like my future, are therefore always in question in the spotlight of freedom. The problem with all this is that one first needs to adopt Sartre's atheistic framework and to affirm the consequences he draws from it (for example, in this case, that if values don't come from God, then they can have no other source outside ourselves) before his argument will work. Of course, the same kind of challenge confronts us in reading any philosopher's (or novelist's or essayist's) work: the extent to which we must accept the author's premises or depiction of the world. As I pointed out at the beginning of the present chapter, atheism is a premise, not a conclusion, of Sartre's position. But at least he develops a consistent and forceful view of this type, which, one might suggest, constitutes an argument of sorts for his outlook.

This issue notwithstanding, Sartre leaves us with a striking reflection on value, or perhaps we might better say, significance; that is, in pondering the basis of value in my freedom, "I discover myself suddenly as the one who gives its meaning to the alarm clock, the one who by a signboard forbids himself to walk on a flower bed or on the lawn, the one from whom the boss's order borrows its urgency, the one who decides the interest of the book which he is writing, the one finally who makes the values exist in order to determine his actions by their demands."[38] This is another instance where Sartre intriguingly inverts the expected order of things, in this case locating imperatives within consciousness that are usually thought to emanate from outside of it. But he is, after all, right: I could decide one day to throw the alarm clock against the wall and go back to sleep instead of heeding its call; I could tell my boss, "Take this job and shove it!" I could decide to opt for the life of a beach bum or a hermit in the forest. However unlikely, implausible, or self-undoing these choices might be isn't the point. That they are possible is enough to demonstrate that freedom does have the underlying, dominant role Sartre assigns to it.

BAD FAITH

We now have the basic tools needed to understand Sartre's celebrated doctrine of bad faith. Two things are central here: anguish and negation. However "anguish" may be defined, we know that it is something unpleasant, something we would prefer to avoid, if possible. On Sartre's account, "Anguish is precisely my consciousness of being my own future, in the mode of not-being."[39] And because this form of consciousness yields a raw awareness of my freedom and its awesome scope, I am inclined to shrink away from it and instead go into a state of denial. We see this happen when people either affirm what is *not* the case in regard to themselves or else refuse to acknowledge what *is* the case. In ordinary language, we refer to these as examples of self-deception (see appendix H, "Self-Deception"); but Sartre, because he dismisses the idea of a substantial self, invents his own label, calling them instances of "bad faith." Bad faith, as we shall observe, amounts to negation directed toward oneself in a particular way. Generally speaking, bad faith has the structure and purpose of either promoting positive ideas of oneself or displacing and neutralizing negative ideas. It has a similar effect on oneself and on others who potentially sit in judgment on oneself.

Interestingly and ironically, bad faith is possible for the same reason that any kind of self-judgment is possible. Not all self-judgment is negative and destructive, of course. Indeed, much is of a positive variety. But it all hinges on the power of negation, for whenever I say, "I am good (bad), friendly (unfriendly), generous (stingy), moral (immoral)," and so on, I am only assessing what I've been until now. In Sartre's terms, I *am not* any of these things; perhaps I *have been* this or that, but my essence derives from my existence, which is ongoing and always up to me to choose as I project myself into the future. *Bad faith is just an exaggerated form of negation that is self-targeted and that either affirms what is untrue or denies what is true of me in a way that abrogates the freedom to choose and change.*

First, let's consider a few commonplace examples of self-deception. No one has any difficulty recognizing that a person who angrily pounds a desktop with his fist while declaiming, "I am *not* angry!" is deluding himself about his emotional state of the moment. The tone of voice, facial expression, and body language all contradict the verbal report that is simultaneously given, and all add up to overwhelming evidence for the opposite conclusion. Now consider someone who has lost out to a rival in an affair of love and who portrays the beloved as "unworthy after all." We readily identify this as an act of rationalization, like that which features in Aesop's famous fable of "The Fox and the Grapes." The fox found the grapes to be beyond reach and consequently decided that they were probably sour anyway, and hence a waste of time to pursue any further. Iain Fletcher points out, in the context of gambling, that "we are habitually inclined to be rather lenient on ourselves when examining our motivation and judgement in most things we do. So, although we are quick to attribute *mistakes* that others make to failings in their character or skills, when we suffer the same fate, the reason has to be external factors, most typically attributed to *bad luck*, for instance."[40] Another kind of bad faith aims to protect oneself from the painful truth about something that's of great concern. Thus, a mother whose son is caught cheating on an exam maintains, in the face of all indications to the contrary, that he couldn't have done it: "I know him, and he's not like that." There are those we are all familiar with who display an unassuming character, which we see rather as "false modesty" parading before us, as an effort to draw praise that will remedy insecurity and self-doubt. Finally, readers who are old enough to remember former US president Richard Nixon, or have seen him on video clips, may recall him shaking his jowls and sweating before the cameras while—wanting to project sincerity but dripping insincerity—protesting, "Let me be perfectly clear," or "I am not a crook!" Great literature is full of examples of the kind discussed here, as are the works of Shakespeare, Freud, and other insightful psychologists. But everyday life provides plentiful material to ponder as well.

What exactly is bad faith and how does it do its work? Sartre begins by distinguishing between lying and acts of bad faith. In lying, the objective is to deliberately conceal from others something that I know (and generally am in no doubt that I know). Thus, what I tell to them is the opposite of what I am withholding. The liar and the lied-to are distinct individuals and possess different information. I control the information flow to produce the desired effect. In bad faith, by contrast, the model of lying is inappropriate; literally or by definition, I cannot succeed in lying to myself. This is because the same person (namely, me) is both the subject and the object of the act, and to try to represent it as lying undermines the meaning of the term, for I must both know and not know the same thing. Yet we believe we must somehow be able to conceptually capture the phenomenon in question (bad faith or self-deception) for the reason that it actually does occur. So what we begin with is this contrast:

BEHAVIOR	SUBJECT	OBJECT
lie	oneself	others
bad faith	oneself	oneself, but also others

Bad faith is a puzzle, for how can it happen that I deceive myself about what I am well aware is the case (or not the case)? It is really insufficient for Sartre to declare that "the project of bad faith must be itself in bad faith."[41] And the problem is compounded since he has declared that consciousness is always translucent to itself while rejecting any idea of an unconscious mental realm. It follows from his model of bad faith that consciousness must at all times know, or at least be capable of being aware of, what is going on within it. His solution is to invoke the distinction between first-order and second-order consciousness explained earlier in this chapter. The operations of self-deception occur in prereflexive consciousness, with the usual spontaneity that this entails. The rationalizations, reports on myself, and public disavowals of my own duplicity occur in reflexive consciousness as acts of self-evaluation or self-summation. It is in the latter sort of act that I can preserve or shore up a certain image of myself before others, facilitate my own moral cynicism, avoid difficult situations, evade responsibility, and otherwise protect myself from criticism or condemnation, garner unwarranted praise, and perhaps even attempt to psych myself up to face some kind of overt threat. Now, because bad faith holds contradictory tendencies within the unity of a consciousness that is translucent to itself, it is, as Sartre admits, bound to be a shifting and inherently fragile structure, subject at each moment to breakdown. Sartre uses the word "metastable" to describe this feature of bad faith.[42]

Patterns of bad faith, then, have the complex organization shown below:

SARTREAN BAD FAITH

prereflexive activity {
1. I deceive myself.

2. I deceive myself about deceiving myself.

3. I am nevertheless "aware" of maneuvers 1 and 2.

reflexive activity   4. I relate to myself as *not* deceiving myself (for example: "I am perfectly sincere"; "I'm being completely honest with you").

all this occurs in one consciousness (unitary but "metastable")

It should be clear that what we have here is not just a ruse, but a very elaborate apparatus, and the question is whether the gain in understanding offsets the complexity of Sartre's account, or whether we pay too high a price for maintaining, with him, the consistency of his theory of consciousness. But one thing to notice is that rendering bad faith intelligible seems to require that both "orders" of conscious activity (prereflexive and reflexive) be invoked. And one is bound to wonder whether, in the end, this is no less problematic than Freud's appeal to conscious and unconscious systems of mental activity, which he uses to explain repression (and by extension, self-deception) and which Sartre had sworn to displace by a better approach.

Be this as it may, we will turn now to a consideration of the six scenarios of bad faith Sartre offers in *Being and Nothingness* in order to illustrate the prevalence of bad faith in human affairs. The first concerns a woman who is not prepared for the sexual advances of her male companion on a first date. The crunch comes when he says how attractive he finds her and takes her hand in his. She adopts a strategy that amounts to a denial of her freedom.

> The aim is to postpone the moment of decision as long as possible. . . . [T]he young woman leaves her hand there, but she *does not notice* that she is leaving it. . . . because it happens by chance that she is at this moment all intellect. She draws her companion up to the most lofty regions of sentimental speculation; she speaks of Life, of her life, she shows herself in her essential aspect—a personality, a consciousness. And during this time the divorce of the body from the soul is accomplished; the hand rests inert between the warm hands of her companion—neither consenting nor resisting—a thing.[43]

This is no ordinary instance of indecisiveness, wherein alternatives seem either equally weighty or equally insignificant, for the purpose here is to evade commitment and an honest appraisal of the fledgling relationship. Freedom, in a way, gets suspended and the body (or part of it) is treated like a thing, not just symbolically but also psychologically. The for-itself (freedom) can never really become the in-itself (a thing), and this is why Sartre thinks of bad faith as subject to collapse at any moment. He uses other examples, however, to suggest that some forms of bad faith can and do congeal into a way of life, a more or less permanent role, as we'll see. Sartre amplifies his comment about body and soul in the passage about the dating woman by immediately adding: "But bad faith does not wish either to coordinate them or to surmount them in a synthesis." Bad faith holds apart aspects of our make-up that naturally belong together, and, in creating a rift within the psyche, it also displays itself as a precarious enterprise.

The second example depicts Sartre's famous café waiter. Here is someone definitely locked into a role—that of obsequious subservience.

> His movement is quick and forward, a little too precise, a little too rapid. He comes toward the patrons with a step a little too quick. He bends forward a little too eagerly; his voice, his eyes express an interest a little too solicitous for the order of the customer. Finally, there he returns, trying

to imitate in his walk the inflexible stiffness of some kind of automaton while carrying his tray with the recklessness of a tight-rope-walker. . . . All his behavior seems to us a game. . . . But what is he playing? . . . [H]e is playing at *being* a waiter in a café.[44]

The clue to identifying bad faith here lies in the last sentence. The waiter adopts a certain mode of being and, in a kind of mimicry dictated by some notion he has of the mechanical role-playing required by the occasion, curtails his freedom. Yet the waiter can only "play at *being* a waiter" because his freedom prevents him from actually being one. Another way to understand this scenario is shown below.

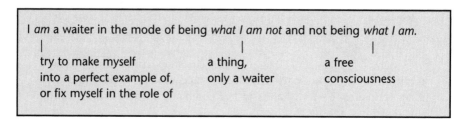

I *am* a waiter in the mode of being *what I am not* and not being *what I am.*

try to make myself into a perfect example of, or fix myself in the role of	a thing, only a waiter	a free consciousness

Sartre's description may be a bit simplistic, yet we all know of cases where we speak of a caricature, of someone's being a parody of her- or himself, and so on. And even less extreme versions of role-playing are nevertheless illuminated by Sartre's perspective.

Third, Sartre offers a cluster of examples, which go under the heading of "tradesmen," whose "condition," he contends, is "wholly one of ceremony." Again, we have an exaggeration, but one which contains a grain of truth. Consumers do expect those who serve their daily needs to be fully at their disposal and to have a certain deferential and formal—even subordinate—manner. Following on this comes one of the most acute remarks to be found anywhere in Sartre's works: "There are indeed many precautions to imprison a man in what he is, as if we lived in perpetual fear that he might escape from it, that he might break away and suddenly elude his condition."[45] One is immediately reminded here of Jean-Jacques Rousseau's celebrated statement that "Man was born free, and everywhere he is in chains."[46] In any event, the political side of Sartre is wholly evident in what he says, for it is not only we ourselves who shirk the responsibility of our freedom, there is also a high social investment (cross-culturally) in excessively restricting the freedom of the individual to be an individual, to think for her- or himself, and the like.[47]

The fourth and fifth cases revolve around a "paederast" (whom we would now call a "gay man") struggling against admitting that he is a homosexual and instead blaming his past, others, and various circumstances for his being the way he is. Sartre also introduces "the champion of sincerity," who seeks to wring from the gay man a confession of what he is so that he might achieve some sort of forgiveness and a chance to move beyond his past.[48] This procedure may even sound as if it's in line with Sartre's campaign for being honest with oneself. But this is only an appearance. In the tableau that is laid out before us, "the critic demands of the guilty one that he constitute himself as a thing, precisely in order no longer to treat him as a thing"; that is, "the champion of sincerity" wishes the gay man to take on an essence—gayness—and then become indebted to him as the apostle of the freedom to express oneself. I would paraphrase the dynamics of the situation in this way: The "champion of sincerity" in effect says, "I'll play God to your Sinner and I will give you back your freedom as a gift or an act of grace." However, no one can force another to be honest with her- or himself or "own" another's act of "coming out" in this way. This interesting case study helps us discern a model for all acts of absolution, which Sartre views as creating the double bind of liberation and enslavement. It raises, in addition, the question of whether sincerity, as such, is in bad faith, for the meaning of "sincerity" is that I am *just* this and nothing more; inside I am really what shows overtly: "What you see is what you get." But each of these formulations seems to be a recipe for freedom denial and misleading self-representation.

Scenario number six concerns a coward who can only transcend cowardliness by at the same time admitting it.[49] Otherwise, it appears there is nothing concrete to be denied in the first place. Sartre traps the coward into both being and not being one, which makes it very mysterious how this person can ever change in the way Sartre wants us to be able to. Perhaps the solution is just that the cowardly individual must be able to say that she or he has been a coward up to now but that no one is destined to continue along the same path. But note that denial of (previous and/or present) cowardliness can in fact only succeed in blocking movement forward into a new future.

All of these examples are meant to expose bad faith as a condition that features the entrapment of freedom and its transformation into a thing that spins its wheels and does no work. This outcome can be brought about solely by oneself or else with the aid of others; in either case, the individual is responsible for it and for not resolving the internal contradiction it represents. Sartre suggests metaphorically, and I think correctly, that "one *puts oneself* in bad faith as one goes to sleep and one is in bad faith as one dreams."[50] People who adopt a pose of bad faith as a way of life (for example, the cynical, world-weary academic or the businessperson who blames others for her or his shortcomings) gets into this state by perfecting a certain persona until, as we say, it "becomes second-nature." Going along with Sartre's metaphor, and bearing in mind his explanation of the structure of bad faith, however, it makes sense that those who are in bad faith may have occasional "awakenings" from it. Hence, no one is ever so conditioned or has such totally ingrained traits as to totally lack self-awareness, be unable to change, or completely evade responsibility for being the person she or he is. Following Kierkegaard, Sartre holds that we are always called back from the forgetfulness of our freedom, no matter how well we try to hide it from ourselves. Yet bad faith seems clearly to predominate in Sartre's thinking. Could there ever be "good faith"? This is a question I will examine at the end of the chapter.

SELF AND OTHER

A great many of Sartre's most valuable insights and most controversial scenarios concern interpersonal behavior. When people interact, a different organization of consciousness occurs, according to Sartre, because of the intrusion of the other's consciousness into my own. This destabilizes my consciousness in that I am objectified in and through the eyes (and judgment) of the other, and my transcendence (or freedom) has to re-establish itself on a new ground. The basic pattern of interaction between humans, for Sartre, is one of conflict, whether at the phenomenological/ontological level of asserting or preserving a perceptual field or at the sociopolitical level.

We should remember two things about all this, however. First, as Joseph Catalano observes, "Sartre's insistence on conflict does not result from a historical analysis of man's inability to cooperate with his fellowman, but on his insistence that each for-itself is freedom."[51] Freedom is a force that is bound to meet resistance from a counterforce of like kind; it's as simple as that. Second, as Sartre affirms, "at the same time I need the Other in order to realize fully all the structures of my being."[52] Indeed, he remains true to this dictum in spite of the rather gloomy picture of human relations he paints.

Shame is the feeling Sartre identifies as the paradigm for our presence before others.[53] Shame, an emotion present in all cultures, represents two things: (a) my appearing as an object before others (as someone judged to be "shameful," a "loathsome person," "nothing but a thief," and so on); and (b) the prereflexive awareness of myself that is immediately aroused by "the presence of another in my consciousness."[54] The effect of this "presence of another" in my field of existence and perception is illustrated by Sartre, in the first instance, by the example of someone entering into a public park where I had previously been alone. In Sartre's phenomenological description of what transpires, the entire field undergoes alteration and reorganizes itself around the stranger, who takes on the character of an alien intruder:

> Instead of a grouping *toward me* of the objects, there is now an orientation *which flees from me.* . . . The distance [between us] appears as a pure *disintegration* of the relations which I apprehend between the objects of my universe. . . . Thus suddenly an object has appeared which has stolen the world from me. . . . [I]t appears that the world has a kind of drain hole in the middle of its being and that it is perpetually flowing off through this hole. . . . [which is] an internal hemorrhage. . . . My original fall is the existence of the Other.[55]

Sartre's peculiar cast of mind is clearly on display here. His main thought seems perfectly valid: The presence of another alters the structure of my more or less daydreamy immersion in my environment of the moment. But his description is couched in terms of threat, loss, collapse, and the gobbling up of my world by some sort of weird black hole created by a rival vantage point. This rhetoric strikes one as over the top and betrays an almost paranoid, fearful fantasy of aggressive encounter and universal competition. Nevertheless, Sartre insists that the presence of the other inevitably challenges the stability of my perception and construction of the world at that time, and the situation requires that I re-establish this stability on a new footing. This is because—as with Nietzsche—the interaction between free beings is always a power relationship in which all seek to assert themselves and/or extend their domain of control. For Sartre, freedom is forever vulnerable to being eroded, either by oneself (in an act of bad faith) or by the other (in some form of contestation or subjugation). Therefore, the other is, at one level or another, my nemesis, and vice versa.

Oneself and the Other

a subject who sees me as an object
in the world that is also a subject

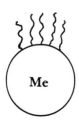

aware of myself as an object for
the Other, as defined by that Other

The important and fascinating aspect of personal interactions, in Sartre's version, is that while people may attempt to control each other's freedom, this effort is doomed to failure. As he asserts, "I can not be an object for an object," but only for another subject.[56] An object (a thing, an in-itself) is an object for a subject and nothing more. A subject, however, as we commonly say, may be "objectified," as when we treat someone according to a stereotype, as nothing but a source of sexual gratification, and so on, but it cannot really be divested of its subjectivity (consciousness and freedom), or, at any rate, not completely so.

Sartre's most well-known example of the interaction discussed above also concerns shame before the other. We are asked to imagine a situation in which a certain individual is crouching in a dark hallway and peering through a keyhole at whatever unspecified activity is going on in the room on the far side of the door. Suddenly, this perhaps prurient absorption in the private behavior unfolding in the room beyond is interrupted by the sound of footsteps in the hall. Sartre writes:

> Someone is looking at me! . . . But here the self comes to haunt the unreflective consciousness. . . . I *am* indeed that object which the Other is looking at and judging. I can be ashamed only as my freedom escapes me in order to become a *given* object. . . . I flow outside myself. . . . Everything takes place as if I had a dimension of being from which I was separated by a radical nothingness; and this nothingness is the Other's freedom. . . .

Shame reveals to me that I *am* this being, not in the mode of "was" or of "having to be" but *in-itself*.[57]

Here we have "the Look," a justly famous moment in Sartre's work. The look is what makes me aware of myself, at first unreflexively, as "experiencing shame" or as "shamed," and then, one assumes, reflexively, as "someone shameful," when I objectify myself through the eyes of the other and realize my possibility as "having been caught doing the sort of thing that perverts do," or some such. I then become a self, as my involvement with the activity of looking is replaced by reflection on (a) what I have done, and (b) how that activity was frozen and myself "thingified" by the other's judgment that (c) I now take on and re-express as "my *essence*" or "who I *am*." Sartre explains that "for the Other I have stripped myself of transcendence [freedom]. . . . The Other as a look is only that—my transcendence transcended." The struggle of life—not only for the peeping Tom here but for all of us—is in some way to re-establish freedom and the alternative possibilities it makes available. We have to do this in the face of social pressures that tend to construct us according to certain generalized norms and preconceived notions. How this will be done is not scripted in advance; we make it up as we go along.

Notice, too, that in this example there is wordless interaction; no judgment need be spoken in order to create the incident in question. In his complex analysis of the look, Sartre suggests that "the Other's look hides his eyes; he seems to go *in front of them*."[58] And we surely understand what he means. We *know* what it's like to be judgmentally scrutinized (by a parent, a teacher, or an employer, for example). The keyhole case shows that a look can convey a judgment without any verbal communication whatsoever. Furthermore, as Sartre points out, "the look will be given just as well on occasion when there is a rustling of branches, . . . or the slight opening of a shutter, or a light movement of a curtain. During an attack men who are crawling through the brush apprehend as a *look to be avoided*, not two eyes, but a white farm-house which is outlined against the sky at the top of a little hill."[59] Thus, many things, events, or circumstances can serve as surrogate looks because of associations we have formed through experience. This does not entail that our assessment of such situations is infallible, only that the presence of others is frequently suggested or implied rather than plainly evident. Those who enjoy good novels or films will be aware how regularly devices of this kind are utilized to build suspense or narrative tension.

As a postscript to this discussion, I would like to relate a piece of psychological research that I ran across while writing this book. Experimenters at the University of Newcastle in England found that in an office environment, people were much more likely to pay for coffee, tea, and milk on an honor system—and even to pay more—when a poster showing a pair of eyes was displayed at the cash box than when a poster showing flowers was substituted.[60] No credit to Sartre was given, but he'd certainly rejoice in this empirical confirmation of his theories!

HUMAN RELATIONSHIPS

Sartre's general view of human interactions is fairly grim: "With the Other's look the 'situation' escapes me. . . . I *am no longer master of the situation*."[61] Moreover, the other threatens with "decomposition" both my relation to objects in the world and to my own freedom. Hence, there is also an ontological dimension to the struggle between individuals, which makes it ever necessary to exert oneself in order to recover the integrity of consciousness and its independent standing in the world.

This dynamic infects all relationships between people—so much so that one wonders whether Sartre might not be projecting and universalizing his own struggle to be someone, particularly when he was a child. Be that as it may, he does provide a consistent theory with many intriguing applications. A few examples follow.

Love and desire. Sartre interprets love as the need to have one's contingent existence validated by the free act of another. Love requires the complete devotion of the other to me and also signifies my attempt to possess the other's freedom through this devotion. The physical side of love signifies my objectification of the other; it is part of the process by which I lay hold of her or his freedom. When the other freely gives her- or himself to me physically, I capture—if only momentarily—the other's freedom, and vice versa. Thus, there is a constant tension between (a) the assertion and recognition of freedom that takes place between lovers; and (b) their objectification of one another, which tends to reduce each to a mere body. Sartre regards these components as inseparable parts of the whole encounter.

Desire (that is, sexual desire), according to Sartre, is equivalent to my freedom expressed through my body (that is, grounded in a thing and given a foundation in the world by it). The desire of another to whom I feel attracted is likewise her or his freedom expressed as embodied. The "project of desire" (or its ontological significance) is to possess the other's freedom in its embodied state or to "transcend [the other's] transcendence."[62] In this process, the other experiences personal freedom as objectified in her or his body because of me (that is, because of the physical attraction between us). I want the stability afforded by the other's embodied freedom; I want the other to freely offer her- or himself for the purpose of physical gratification *because I am desired.* But to desire the other, in turn, is to have the dynamic reversed, with me freely offering myself in the same fashion. So, while each wants the other to serve as the ground of her or his own freedom, each also wants *not* to have personal freedom negated in the process; therefore, each seeks to gain the upper hand. At a deeper level of analysis, "My goal is to cause [the other] to be incarnated as flesh in *his own eyes.* . . . [which act yields] the ensnarement of consciousness in the body."[63] Both parties present themselves to their sexual partner as the object of desire, and this cannot be avoided when sexual attraction is mutual; but this tends toward reducing both myself and the other to things.

It's easy to see that as a "project," in Sartrean terms, "desire is doomed to failure"[64] because there is no room in his vision for creative give and take. Sexual desire must express itself as either dominance or submission, both of which are in bad faith because they treat freedom—in oneself or the other—as a thing. It also seems that I must always be engaged in either self-indulgence or selflessly pleasing my partner; there seems to be no point in between where a different kind of interaction can thrive, at least according to Sartre. But of course there is: During sexual intimacy, partners can shift back and forth from being passive receivers to active givers, or if you prefer, from being submissive to dominating, even if they cannot be both simultaneously.

The obscene. Sartre moves effortlessly to several further applications of his ideas. He conjectures that what we call "obscene" is simply "when the body adopts postures which entirely strip it of its acts and which reveal the inertia of its flesh."[65] In other words, the obscene is not the dead body but the living body treated as immobile and as not animated by free agency, as not embodying freedom and all that that entails. One can hardly disagree with Sartre's assessment, which seems spot on, at least if one thinks of older-style pornography featuring passive, disinterested, disengaged, vapid subjects-who-are-objects.

Hate, masochism, and sadism. Hate is equivalent to mutual repulsion, wherein the other is fixed in the rigid mold of a thing from which no positive behavior can emanate. Masochism prevails when I willingly allow my freedom to be totally controlled. Sadism is manifested when the other's freedom is forcibly suppressed. But at least Sartre is consistent; and, in a sense, he sounds a hopeful note when he declares that these relationships, too, like desire and love, are failures to one degree or another, and for basically the same reason: "Consciousness . . . can *freely make itself* akin to things, but it cannot *be* a thing."[66]

A pair of interesting sub-applications are worth noting. The first is that Sartre claims extreme sadism, culminating in torture, fails as a project for two specific reasons: (1) the victim can always resist total domination, even if it is only for one second longer; and (2) if torture leads to the victim's death, then the torturer is dealing with a thing, and the whole point of the "project" (to enslave or "thingify" *a person*—a freedom that still exists in some form) collapses and self-destructs.[67] The second sub-application pertains to racism, about which Sartre wrote in *Being and Nothingness*, *Anti-Semite and Jew*, and elsewhere. Racism also is a failed "project" because it attempts to discriminate against a certain class of people, making them into objects through stereotyping, persecution, and other tactics. But, once again, freedom cannot be completely dominated without being eradicated. It would seem, then, that racism, along with its other ugly and objectionable features, is caught in the same irresolvable conflict between a wish to annihilate freedom and the resilience of freedom itself.

THE PROJECTS OF FREEDOM; EXISTENTIAL PSYCHOANALYSIS

A thorny question that arises in studying Sartre is this: How can something (consciousness) that has no essence define itself? And in relation to what? There seems to be a need for a fixed point somewhere in this sea of formlessness. These questions are never really answered by Sartre, it must be admitted. But he does have a story to tell that to some extent fills the bill. It starts with the assertion that "fundamentally man is *the desire to be.* . . ." And he continues: "The original project which is expressed in each of our empirically observable tendencies is then the *project of being.* . . . Thus human reality is the desire of being-in-itself."[68] In short, because we are unsettled, self-determining beings with an open-ended future, who experience anguish in the face of our radical freedom, we seek the ideal comfort of a final resting place where we *are something* instead of suffering all this seemingly interminable *becoming*. Of course, this goal will be reached only in death, when becoming is truly and finally replaced by being, and, hence, to entertain such a goal during life is mere fantasy and wish fulfillment.

Sartre recognizes this but insists that all attempts to ground ourselves in existence derive from a "fundamental" or "original choice," which is the overriding project each of us separately engages in. We may view this as a decision concerning the kind of person I will be (or will to be): for example, someone who helps others and stands up for them in adversity or only "looks after Number One"; someone who is optimistic or pessimistic; someone who aims to change the world or just accepts the status quo; and so forth. Following on from this choice, a person then engages in life projects, such as being a writer, a professional athlete, a teacher, an environmentalist, a power broker, and so on. Based on this idea, Sartre makes the rather sweeping claim that each individual "expresses himself as a whole in even his most insignificant and his most superficial behavior. In other words there is not a taste, a mannerism, or a human act which is not *revealing*."[69] He also invents a discipline called "existential psychoanalysis," the purpose of which is phenomenological/explanatory, not therapeutic. This has as its aim the discovery of the meaning of a life through the ways in which particular behaviors express the original choice one has made. For the original choice, he asserts, "is the center of reference for an infinity of polyvalent meanings."[70] In his biographical works—on Gustav Flaubert, Charles Baudelaire, Stéphane Mallarmé, and Jean Genet—he employs this procedure with powerful effect.

One may well be skeptical about the original choice. While it is true that some people say they "always knew" what they were going to do with their lives and seem to have singular dedication, others take a long time to find themselves or never do. We could say that the latter have as their fundamental project to lack direction in their lives, but this sounds rather like an empty, self-fulfilling, ad hoc way of preserving Sartre's theory, not like an explanation with any substance. It clearly is grossly implausible that everyone should have made such a momentous choice when merely a child, especially when many have no recollection or evidence of their having done so. And perhaps Sartre does not mean to imply this, for there are many instances of consolidation of character that happen later in life—witness the case of John Newton (1725–1807), whose decision to renounce his involvement in the slave trade is so movingly described in the well-known hymn *Amazing Grace*.

But Sartre has something even more dramatic up his sleeve: that in wanting to *be* something or other, humans seek not only to express their freedom but also to possess the determinacy and finality of thinghood. They want to have their cake and eat it too. Realizing that we can't deny our freedom, we nonetheless yearn to be both for-itself and in-itself at the same time and in the fullest sense of both. This impossible goal Sartre calls *the desire to be God* because God (whom he thinks of as an ideal only) represents both ultimate freedom and total self-realization or essence achieved, all rolled into one. Consequently, "man is the being whose project is to be God."[71] Clearly, people really are, to an extent, both kinds of being (for-itself and in-itself) in that sometimes we act, sometimes we are acted upon; we play roles, but we aren't identical to these; and so on. But what we cannot accomplish is the trick that God allegedly performs, of having both kinds of being at all times, in a harmonious and complete manner. Because of this, Sartre famously declares: "But the idea of God is contradictory and we lose ourselves in vain. Man is a useless passion."[72] In brief, we are the kind of entity that strives to be what is forever and in principle unattainable by it.

I'll end this section with a diagram that summarizes the order of derivation of human behavior discussed above.

SARTRE'S EXISTENTIAL PSYCHOANALYSIS

the desire to be (God)
↓
the fundamental project (original choice)
↓
life projects, vocations
↓
specific projects or ongoing commitments
↓
individual actions and gestures

EXPLAINING BEHAVIOR

Existential psychoanalysis, along with his denial of the unconscious mind, can be understood as part of Sartre's attack on, and departure from, the ideas of traditional psychoanalysis. But he also goes in a different direction from psychology more generally, owing to his theories of consciousness and freedom. Thus, for example, Sartre considers explanations of behavior in terms of motives as constructions after the fact. A person may have any number of motives for acting in various ways at a given moment of time, but a particular motivational account makes sense and is convincing only retrospectively. One might be tempted to conclude that this is because human behavior, being free, cannot be predicted in advance by me or anyone else. For me, prediction is the same as decision; for others, even if a piece of behavior happens to be correctly predicted, the values and meanings expressed in it cannot be, and there is always the possibility of my making a different choice. However, Sartre urges on us an even more radical position, namely, that any piece of behavior "is a human act only in so far as it surpasses every explanation which we can give of it. . . ."[73] That is, motives do not determine behavior, period. This statement may appear extreme and indefensible, and perhaps it is. But Sartre's concern is to argue that one's actions always "overflow" both past and present and, therefore, that explanations of behavior cannot be reduced to citing essential character traits or dispositions or generalized patterns of conduct, as when we say, "He's nothing but a criminal, so what could you expect?" There is always room for change, and even "criminal" behavior can spring from many factors or be done *as* or *to express* (or *act out*) many different things.

An additional aspect of purposeful behavior that Sartre fastens onto is that while all such behavior (as opposed to accidental behavior or mere bodily movement such as a reflex) results from prior reasons, for something to count as a reason it must involve an interpretation of experience. Two implications follow from this. Meaningful behavior (a) cannot just be the product of mechanical causes lying outside human agency; and (b) must be holistically viewed as a temporal process of before, during, and after, not simply as one member of a chain of events.[74] Behavior relates to a human life and all that that entails; it is not merely something that happens.

Another prominent aspect of Sartre's approach is that he steadfastly refuses to give credit for good intentions. Everybody knows of situations in which someone says something like this: "Oh, I really meant to call you, but I couldn't for such and such reasons," "I wanted to be at the demonstration, but something came up," or "I had every intention of being a better Dad, but life's so complicated, you know." Each of us has probably made up excuses like these many times. The object of these disclaimers is to neutralize or soften criticism from others as well as our own feelings of guilt in ourselves. But for Sartre, we don't get off the hook that easily. One can "intend" to do millions of things, but we only know where we (or others) truly stand when an action puts values into practice; that is, when some result in the world makes a difference, however small. Garcin, in Sartre's play *No Exit* (which concludes that "Hell is—other people!"), even though he is now speaking from the afterlife, still tries to establish that he was not a coward when living. But since you are what you do, this will not wash, which is the point Sartre's other characters mercilessly drive home.

POLITICAL ENGAGEMENT; THE WRITER'S MISSION

One of the best-known facts about Sartre is that he was the exemplar of an "engaged" philosopher. True to his teachings, he believed that the intellectual's calling is to use personal freedom to create values by acting in the world, to take responsibility for so doing, and to explore in the public sphere what is humanly possible. Sartre's political involvements ranged from journalism to joining demonstrations; from endorsing radical forms of communism to being a strong supporter of Israel and a vociferous critic of Stalin, Soviet interventions in Eastern Europe, and, later on, of Castro's Cuba. Although strongly left wing in his opinions, he never joined the French Communist Party and had a stormy relationship with it spanning many years. Sartre involved himself deeply in the Algerian struggle for independence (1954–62) and in the anti–Vietnam War movement (1959–75), among others. Because of his outspoken encouragement of desertion among French Foreign Legion forces occupying Algeria, some called for him to be jailed. General Charles de Gaulle, who was then French president, rebuffed this appeal, allegedly stating: "One does not arrest Voltaire."[75] Sartre's apartment in Paris was bombed twice by right-wing opponents of Algerian independence. At his state funeral in 1980, a crowd of fifty thousand people was present. This testifies not only to a celebration of the life of a philosopher whom many considered to be a national treasure—something very French and very remote from the North American experience—but also to Sartre's influence as a cultural icon and prominent political figure for decades from World War II onward.

Sartre's publications discussing how he conceived of the writer's task amount to manifestos about political engagement as well. "One of the chief motives of artistic creation," he states, "is certainly the need of feeling that we are essential in relationship to the world."[76] Thus, the writer cannot just be writing for her- or himself; rather, writing is directed to "the reader's subjectivity," and this is because "the writer appeals to the reader's freedom to collaborate in the production of his work."[77] This is true, he thinks, not just in the aesthetic sense of the artist's being a catalyst to reader response, which makes the work come to life, but also, and more importantly, in the political sense: "You are perfectly free to leave that book on the table. But if you open it, you assume responsibility for it."[78] And if the book should describe a disturbing situation of social injustice, for example, then the reader is challenged to become engaged by doing something about it or else to face the consequences of turning away in bad faith. In sum, "whether he is an essayist, a pamphleteer, a satirist, or a novelist, whether he speaks only of individual passions or whether he attacks the social order, the writer, a free man addressing free men, has only one subject—freedom."[79] As we have seen elsewhere, for Sartre the sole topic that is worthy to be described and studied is freedom, and all else is simply the context that makes this process possible and that assists in activating the phenomenon of interest—freedom in the world.

MARXISM AND EXISTENTIALISM

For about two decades, starting in the late 1950s, Sartre tried to develop his own version of Marxism.[80] Having come to the conclusion that the world had entered an age of scarcity, in which many lacked the luxury of self-determination exalted in his earlier theories, he decided to put pure existentialism temporarily on hold, as it were, until circumstances might make it universally applicable. Instead, he fashioned what is generally understood as a fusion of existentialism and Marxism. In the *Critique of Dialectical Reason* and *Search for a Method*, he analyzes various forms of oppression and acknowledges the economic factors that produce them. But Sartre maintains that humans can, through coordinated action, rise above their historical condition in order to create a better world. In a situation of scarcity, individuals tend to treat each other as things; but a world of abundance—the product of some form of socialism—would be the result of, and would exemplify, people's willingness to join forces and work together for a common purpose. They would then win back their radical freedom.

SARTRE AND ETHICS

I noted at the beginning of this chapter that Sartre considers the ethical position of existentialism, albeit briefly and not altogether satisfactorily, in *Existentialism Is a Humanism*. In the very last paragraph of *Being and Nothingness*, he promises a future work devoted exclusively to ethics. This book was never published within his lifetime, and the closest thing to it, his *Notebooks for an Ethics*, only appeared in English translation more than a decade after his death. In addition, there are evidently several other ethical manuscripts—a few quite substantial—that to this day remain unpublished even in French. Some suppose that existentialism has (and can have) no ethics because it is so strongly focused on the individual. And, of course, the absence in his published body of work of Sartre's promised book on ethics only reinforces this view. Nor has the availability today of the *Notebooks* settled the issue for everybody, since it does, after all, represent a collection of thoughts rather than a unified theoretical account.

It seems unlikely that we shall ever know exactly what Sartre's considered views on ethics were, but a reasonable inference would be that, for him, ethics is more a matter of concrete examples than of theorizing about universals, prescribing rules and principles, and the like. Or, at any rate, it is about the "singular universal," an expression he once used to describe Kierkegaard.[81] That is, ethics concerns the specific predicaments facing the individual whenever either personal freedom or that of others is at stake. Unacceptable as this conclusion may be to traditionalists, it is nonetheless an approach to ethics that cannot just be derisively swept aside. After all, in *Being and Nothingness*, his novel sequence *The Roads to Freedom*, and indeed throughout Sartre's works, there is a constant exploration of morally charged situations and observations on resolving them (consistently with a fundamental commitment to freedom) or on the failure to resolve them.

One of Sartre's comments about ethics in the *Notebooks* is quite illuminating as to where he stands:

> Ethics is by definition an abstract fact. It is the goal one gives oneself when there is no goal. It is a certain way of treating others when one has no other relation to others except the purely ontological relationship [such as the self/other relationship we explored earlier in this chapter]. It appears, therefore, when my relation to the other is defined by the purely formal recognition of his universal personhood. But his universal personhood is itself defined by his freedom, it is abstract recognition of his freedom as potential, not as actual. In other words, it obliges respect for freedom in general as a pure potentiality and it leaves undetermined the relation we ought to have with the content of this freedom. . . .
>
> In this sense, ethics, not having any real content, can only be conceived of in terms of some status quo.[82]

It's evident from this excerpt that Sartre has no use for abstract ethical theorizing—which we already knew. But it's equally apparent that his philosophy is deeply ethical in tone and application, inasmuch as he is always returning to these themes: (1) facing up to one's freedom; (2) utilizing one's freedom constructively (being honest with oneself; being "authentic" in Heidegger's sense); and (3) taking responsibility for one's choices and actions, including the example one continuously sets for others. Hence, Sartre's work, arguably, is rich in its ethical implications.

But if he wants to argue, as above, that "ethics can only be conceived of in terms of some status quo," then it seems we are back to envisioning moral behavior in a purely situational fashion, with the corresponding sacrifice that it seems to lose real universality. Sartre's additional remark in the *Notebooks* that he is searching for "a concrete ethics that is like *the logic of effective action*"[83] is hardly reassuring on this score, and it is also uncomfortably vague. Is ethics, then, no more than pragmatism? Or perhaps, more generously interpreted, has Sartre in mind that means and ends must be evaluated contextually and that actions must be judged according to some overall doctrine of freedom such as I've summarized in the previous paragraph before any ethical pronouncements can be issued?

I think it's fair to say that Sartre (so far as we can tell from his published work, at any rate) never settled these questions. In the next chapter, however, we'll see how Simone de Beauvoir, Sartre's lifetime partner and close philosophical ally, attempted to do so.

AFTERWORD: THE POSSIBILITY OF LIVING IN "GOOD FAITH"

Although Sartre wrote at length on bad faith, he has very little to say about good faith. Just as Freud considered nearly everyone to be neurotic, so that one wonders whether there is any room left for normalcy in his theory, one is also led to ponder whether for Sartre there is the practical possibility of honesty toward oneself and honest, fulfilling interactions with others. First, we have to recall that Sartre dismisses sincerity as a goal, for in his interpretation, sincerity (not in regard to the past, but to the present moment) means objectifying oneself ("I *am* just what I appear to you to be"), which is neither honest nor admirable. Second, Sartre argues that even those who live in bad faith have episodes of more honest self-awareness, but these are fleeting and evidently of little significance to them. Hence, it seems he knocks the props out from under good faith rather effectively and completely.

Still, there must be some sense to Sartre's talk of good faith, and this for two reasons: (a) unless there were, there would be no way to explain why he introduces the term; and (b) for the expression "bad faith" to be meaningful, there must be something that "good faith" signifies in contrast to it. If everything is ultimately an example of bad faith, then this expression becomes devoid of significance—because what explains everything, explains nothing. We do not necessarily need a conception of good faith as a total way of life. But a criterion that will enable us to single out the phenomenon is what we're after here. Joseph Catalano observes that

> in good faith we start with the realization that we are freedom; we recognize, however, that we can exist only by tending in the direction of being, only by trying to become what we freely choose to be. We also recognize that our very flight toward being will never be achieved as an identity. In good faith we do not flee our freedom, and in particular, we do not flee the very fact that our good faith is always in question. . . . [G]ood and bad faith [must be seen] as initial projects of facing our freedom or avoiding it.[84]

Thus, good faith is an unending project in that although freedom directs itself toward the wholeness of *being something* (the in-itself of complete self-realization), it can never get there. But this is quite different from the failure bad faith exemplifies when it denies freedom and shrinks away from the task of shaping human existence through honest choices and genuine actions. Both projects fall short of attainment, but their different starting points make all the difference to our understanding of their relative value.

This is a positive line of elucidation; however, we are seemingly left with empty hands in spite of it, for it seems that Sartre has concocted a theory of human life that features the failure of bad faith and concedes both the rarity of good faith and the struggle against huge odds that it represents. But, then, he is not the first or the last thinker to portray humanity as a glorious yet tragic experiment.

NOTES

1. Jean-Paul Sartre, *Existentialism Is a Humanism*, trans. Bernard Frechtman and reprinted under the title *Existentialism*, in *Existentialism and Human Emotions* (New York: Citadel Press/Kensington, 1987), pp. 13–15.

2. Ibid., pp. 16, 17.

3. Ibid., pp. 18–19.

4. Ibid., p. 19.

5. Ibid., p. 21.

6. Ibid., p. 23.

7. Ibid., pp. 25, 26.

8. Ibid., p. 28.

9. Ibid., p. 29.

10. Jean-Paul Sartre, *The Transcendence of the Ego: An Existentialist Theory of Consciousness*, trans. Forrest Williams and Robert Kirkpatrick (New York: Octagon Books, 1972), p. 40.

11. Ibid., p. 40.

12. Ibid., p. 42.

13. See Jean-Paul Sartre, *Being and Nothingness: An Essay in Phenomenological Ontology*, trans. Hazel E. Barnes (New York: Philosophical Library, 1956), pp. 50–54.

14. Sartre, *Transcendence of the Ego*, p. 98.

15. Ibid., pp. 98–99 (emphasis in original).

16. Ibid., p. 99.

17. Ibid., p. 102.

18. Ibid., p. 100

19. Ibid., pp. 31, 104 (emphasis in original).

20. Jean-Paul Sartre, *Nausea*, trans. Lloyd Alexander (London: Hamish Hamilton, 1962), pp. 170–82.

21. Sartre, *Being and Nothingness*, p. li.

22. Sartre, *Transcendence of the Ego*, p. 40.

23. Sartre, *Being and Nothingness*, pp. 16, 20 (emphasis in original).

24. Ibid., p. 21. "There is an infinite number of realities which are not only objects of judgment, but which are experienced, opposed, feared, etc., by the human being and which in their inner structure are inhabited by negation, as by a necessary condition of their existence. We shall call them *négatités*" (p. 19, emphasis in original).

25. Hazel Barnes, translator's "Key to Special Terminology," in Sartre, *Being and Nothingness*, p. 631.

26. Sartre, *Being and Nothingness*, pp. 19, 21.

27. Ibid., pp. 9, 10 (emphasis in original).

28. Ibid., p. 23.

29. Martin Heidegger, "Letter on Humanism," trans. Frank A. Capuzzi in collaboration with J. Glenn Gray, in *Martin Heidegger: Basic Writings—From "Being and Time" [1927] to "The Task of Thinking" [1964]*, rev. exp. ed., ed. David Farrell Krell (New York: Harper & Row, 1993), p. 252.

30. Ibid., p. 220.

31. Ibid., pp. 225–26, 232, 233.

32. See Sartre, *Being and Nothingness*, pp. 581–85.

33. See William Glasser, *Reality Therapy: A New Approach to Psychiatry* (New York: HarperPerennial, 1990). (Originally published in 1965.) See also http://www.journalofrealitytherapy.com/realitytherapy.htm.

34. Sartre, *Being and Nothingness*, p. 29.

35. Sartre, *Transcendence of the Ego*, p. 100 (emphasis in original).

36. Sartre, *Being and Nothingness*, p. 36.

37. Ibid., p. 38.

38. Ibid., p. 39.

39. Ibid., p. 32.

40. Iain Fletcher (with Jamie Walters), *The Rough Guide to Poker* (London: Rough Guides, 2005), p. 120 (emphasis in original).

41. Sartre, *Being and Nothingness*, pp. 67–68.

42. Ibid., p. 50.

43. Ibid., pp. 55–56 (emphasis in original).

44. Ibid., p. 59 (emphasis in original).

45. Ibid., p. 59.

46. Jean-Jacques Rousseau, *The Social Contract* (1762), chap. 1.

47. Sartre elsewhere presents an exaggerated but striking image to reinforce his claim: "There are even men (e.g., caretakers, overseers, gaolers) whose social reality is uniquely that of the Not, who will live and die, having forever been only a Not upon the earth" (*Being and Nothingness*, p. 47; emphasis in original).

48. Sartre, *Being and Nothingness*, pp. 63–65.

49. Ibid., p. 66.

50. Ibid., p. 68 (emphasis in original).

51. Joseph S. Catalano, *A Commentary on Jean-Paul Sartre's "Being and Nothingness"* (New York: Harper Torchbooks, 1974), pp. 180–81.

52. Sartre, *Being and Nothingness*, p. 222.

53. Why not pride? Sartre gives no answer. Pride (together with fear) does come in later on as one of "my original reactions," but Sartre equates pride with vanity and insists that it must be in bad faith (*Being and Nothingness*, pp. 290–91).

54. Sartre, *Being and Nothingness*, p. 221.

55. Ibid., pp. 254, 255, 256, 257, 263 (emphasis in original).

56. Ibid., p. 257.

57. Ibid., pp. 260, 261, 262 (emphasis in original).

58. Ibid., p. 258 (emphasis in original).

59. Ibid., pp. 257–58 (emphasis in original).

60. Ian Sample, "Honestly, the Eyes Have It," *Guardian Weekly* 175, no. 3: 19.

61. Sartre, *Being and Nothingness*, p. 265 (emphasis in original).

62. Technically, "transcend" only means "go beyond" or "surpass"; Sartre could therefore have chosen a better word to convey his meaning here, such as "dominate" or "capture."

63. Sartre, *Being and Nothingness*, pp. 395, 397 (emphasis in original).

64. Ibid., p. 396.

65. Ibid., p. 401.

66. Jean-Paul Sartre, "The War Diaries: November 1939–March 1940," trans. Quintin Hoare, in *Existentialist Philosophy: An Introduction*, 2nd ed., ed. L. Nathan Oaklander (Upper Saddle River, NJ: Prentice-Hall, 1992), p. 322 (emphasis in original).

67. See Sartre, *Being and Nothingness*, pp. 403–406.

68. Ibid., pp. 565–66 (emphasis in original).

69. Ibid., p. 568 (emphasis in original).

70. Ibid., p. 570.

71. Ibid., p. 566.

72. Ibid., p. 615.

73. Ibid., p. 35.

74. See ibid., pp. 433–38, 445–51.

75. Widely reported in different versions, as in *Encounter* magazine's June 1975 issue.

76. Jean-Paul Sartre, "Why Write?" in Jean-Paul Sartre, *What Is Literature?*, trans. Bernard Frechtman (New York: Philosophical Library, 1949), pp. 26–27.

77. Ibid., pp. 31, 34.

78. Ibid., p. 34.

79. Ibid., p. 46.

80. Perhaps it doesn't need to be said, but someone can be a Marxist without being a Communist Party member—something that many people (especially those in political office) seem unable to grasp.

81. Jean-Paul Sartre, "The Singular Universal," trans. Peter Goldberger, in *Kierkegaard: A Collection of Critical Essays*, ed. Josiah Thompson (Garden City, NY: Anchor Books/Doubleday, 1972), pp. 230–65.

82. Jean-Paul Sartre, *Notebooks for an Ethics*, trans. David Pellauer (Chicago: University of Chicago Press, 1992), p. 103.

83. Ibid., p. 104 (emphasis in original).

84. Catalano, *Commentary on Sartre's "Being and Nothingness,"* pp. 88, 89.

QUESTIONS FOR REFLECTION

1. What does Sartre mean by saying that we are "condemned to be free"? Are we?

2. What is the "nothingness" that belongs to or defines consciousness? What is the relationship between this and the "nothingness" that Sartre claims we find "in the heart of being"?

3. Can we make sense of "bad faith" without resorting to the idea of unconscious mental activity? Who is right here: Freud or Sartre—or neither?

4. Do you agree or disagree with the notion that human relationships are always characterized by conflict? If you agree, how is this fact to be explained? If you disagree, what alternative characterization would you offer?

5. Why does Sartre think that love is a project doomed to failure? Does this outlook rest on particularly male-oriented assumptions?

6. Sartre's doctrine of "the Look" suggests that we are socially conditioned to experience shame before others, for example. But this seems quite inconsistent with his view of "radical freedom." Is there a way to resolve this problem?

7. "Man is a useless passion." Explain and discuss.

8. Do you think Sartre was right to "suspend" the existential conception of freedom until the problem of scarcity in the world is dealt with? Explain your answer.

8

DE BEAUVOIR

FREEDOM MATURING

Simone de Beauvoir (1908–1986) played an important part in the development of exis-tentialism. Her distinctive philosophical and literary voice has come to be more widely appreciated in the decades since her death as scholars have taken a closer look at her body of work. De Beauvoir's emphasis on the social dimension of freedom and mutual respect marks an advance in moral philosophy, just as her better-known work on women contributes to modern feminist theory in a major way.

INTRODUCTION

In addition to being a brilliant writer and philosopher, Simone de Beauvoir was also a highly influential feminist theorist, as well as an essayist, novelist, author of short stories and travel diaries, political activist, and journalist. Notwithstanding all of these endeavors and her many achievements, as a philosopher she has remained in Sartre's shadow until relatively recently. Perhaps this was partly her own choice, as she often denigrated her philosophical efforts even though Sartre publicly professed to consider her his equal as a thinker. In any event, since her death in 1986 there has been a reassessment of her philosophical contri-bution, with the result that de Beauvoir stands today in the forefront of the existential movement.

De Beauvoir acquired the nickname "Castor" (the French word for "beaver") from the group of Parisian intellectuals she socialized with. Whether this was because she was such a hard worker, because of a play on words ("Beauvoir" and "beaver"), or both, remains unsettled. Several of Sartre's books—including *Nausea, Being and Nothingness, Search for a Method*, and *Critique of Dialectical Reason*—bear the simple dedication: "au Castor" ("to the Beaver").

This chapter will focus on de Beauvoir's two principal philosophical works: *The Ethics of Ambiguity* (1947) and *The Second Sex* (1949). I want to highlight three themes: (1) De Beauvoir had her own interesting perspective on the human condition. (2) She developed an ethical theory that is original and of lasting value, which departs from the philosophical ideas she shared with Sartre while surpassing the boundaries set by his ethical outlook. (3) This ethical theory helped shape the feminist viewpoint for which she is most widely known.

AMBIGUITY

"Ambiguity" is the special term that de Beauvoir uses to describe the human condition, and it is the concept that anchors her major contribution to moral philosophy, *The Ethics of Ambiguity*. In speaking of ambiguity, she has in mind something rather like what Kierkegaard meant when he called existence "paradoxical" (see chapter 3). Humans, as physical beings, are part of nature, but the power of the mind enables them to go beyond the limits imposed by the material world. In consciousness, we can venture anywhere, entertain alternative courses of action, think of the future, dream, imagine, and so on. But while we have this capacity to "transcend," everyone "escapes from his natural condition without, however, freeing himself from it."[1] This is the fundamental ambiguity of which de Beauvoir speaks: that we rise above being mere objects and life-forms through the action of consciousness, yet we do not thereby cease being vulnerable members of the natural order. She draws out further features of the ambiguity of human existence: (1) It hovers between freedom and facticity (refer to chapter 1 for a full definition of this term). (2) We are both subjects (agents and perceivers) and objects (of others' as well as our own perceptions and actions). (3) Each of us is both an individual and belongs to a "collectivity" that includes all others. (4) Freedom is pure possibility and nothing more. (5) Existence is always open-ended. (6) Existence, however glorious, ends in death. (7) There are no externally discoverable values or reference points to guide us. (8) In a godless universe we nevertheless desire to be God (see chapter 7). (9) Life is a series of experiments with only uncertain outcomes. From this set of observations, de Beauvoir sets out by arguing that in order to come to terms with existence as well as to approach the task of framing an ethics appropriate to the human situation, we must "try to assume our fundamental ambiguity."[2] The message here is that we should accept the given parameters of existence and learn to work within them. Again, one may recall Kierkegaard's caution that all philosophical problems begin with existence and must be addressed within existence; existence is the context to which we always return. His warning against "forgetting" that we exist also comes to mind. In a similar manner, de Beauvoir suggests that ethical thinking hitherto "has been a matter of eliminating the ambiguity" of existence in one way or another. Rule-governed moral theories, utopian plans for the future, and grand religious sagas about life and history are examples of such thinking. But it is no longer possible to defend these approaches because "men of today seem to feel more acutely than ever the paradox of their condition."[3] There are many reasons why de Beauvoir might have reached this conclusion, including the loss of credibility of religion for a large number of people, general cynicism concerning utopian views, and doubts about objectivity in knowledge and in ethics. Whether one agrees with her appraisals, certainly it seems correct to say, as she does, that ethics is one of the major ways in which we take up our ambiguous existence and deal with it.

Unlike Sartre, though, de Beauvoir sounds a note of optimism from the outset. She agrees with him that our purpose in existing, if there is one, must be self-justifying. Life has the quality of "tragic ambiguity"[4]— tragic, because the contradictions that characterize it do not yield to our attempts to resolve them. But it remains the case that *we ourselves* are responsible for making life meaningful and worthwhile and for validating the norms we choose to live by, for in the nature of things, we cannot expect the valorizing of life and the legitimizing of values to come from a source external to us.

At this juncture, de Beauvoir diverges significantly from Sartre. Insofar as we "desire to be," as he put it, we may be considered failures, for we cannot be God or God-like. If we suspend this desire (in the manner of Husserl, see chapter 5) and shift perspectives (in the manner of Heidegger, see chapter 6), however, and instead think of an equally fundamental yearning, the "desire to disclose being," we may see ourselves as succeeding.[5] In short the stress should lie not on the impossible task of incorporating both becoming and being into our nature (like God) or acquiring an essence (like a thing or like God), but rather on revealing the world to ourselves and finding constructive projects within it that are ends in themselves. De Beauvoir suggests, therefore, that we need to find a fresh perspective that will help us avert the "failure" toward which Sartre's philosophy seems to predispose us, and then open up new horizons of achievement. "This means that man, in his vain attempt to *be* God, makes himself exist *as* man, and if he is satisfied with this existence, he coincides exactly with himself," she writes.[6] There are three points being advanced here: (1) With the dawning awareness that we cannot be God, we are thrown back on being human and exploring fully what that entails. We need to reverse the tendency to see ourselves as failures and to experience the fulfilment, the accomplishment, of being human. (2) In human terms, we need to find within existence values and patterns of living that are self-sufficient. De Beauvoir observes, in a manner reminiscent of Camus (see appendix D, "The Absurd"), that "it is a matter of knowing whether [each of us] wants to live and under what conditions."[7] Here, she reiterates the existential lesson that we must come to ethical conclusions from within ourselves as an expression of the stance in the world we have chosen. (3) We "coincide exactly with ourselves," not by actualizing an essence (becoming a thing) but by "becoming who we are" (as both Kierkegaard and Nietzsche put it); that is, by tapping into our potential and expressing ourselves in the ongoing process of self-making.

So far as ethics is concerned, de Beauvoir is insistent that the first lesson is to "abandon the dream of an inhuman objectivity."[8] Before proceeding, let us take a moment to investigate the meaning of this claim.

INTERLUDE: REFLECTIONS ON OBJECTIVITY IN ETHICS

Most varieties of ethical theory assume that objectivity in our judgments on moral matters is an attainable goal, that there is always (or nearly always) a way of "getting the right result" (that is, right for anyone in that situation). De Beauvoir obviously seems to be denying this. So let us ask, what would it mean to say that our values and principles of conduct are "objective"? Below are the major contenders for an answer, with an indication of which philosophical tendencies are associated with each standpoint.

Values and principles of conduct are objective if they are:

- independently rooted or grounded in the world; discoverable by ordinary or scientific observation (naturalism)
- prescribed by God or some other supreme authority (divine command theory)
- shared uniformly (cross-culturally) by everyone (universalism)
- grounded in truths about human nature (utilitarianism; sympathy/compassion theories; ethics of care)
- derived from reason (Kantian or deontological ethics)
- self-evident (intuitionism)
- dictated by society (relativism, conventionalism, social constructionism)

De Beauvoir's strategy is not to refute each of these, nor will I attempt to do so here. Instead, she adopts the position that the free choices of the existing individual alone can give birth to values. Certain consequences follow: (a) There is no reason outside of ourselves and the purposes we posit why we should do this or that or consider anything useful or useless. (b) There can be no absolutes, whether external or internal, that ethically compel us. (c) Values cannot be understood as things we must either simply appropriate or not. It is "because [freedom] makes itself a lack that value appears."[9] Freedom, as you will recall, is *the way consciousness projects into nothingness, enabling us to envision how things might be otherwise.* And it is in relation to what is not, or to what is but may be changed into something else, perhaps a better state of affairs, that freedom energizes us for action.

But, de Beauvoir asks, if objectivity in the above senses is rejected, then do we pay the price of having ethics collapse into subjectivism, even solipsism? Subjectivism is the view that whatever I believe is right (good, valuable, etc.) is so just for that reason. (Believing something's so makes it so.) And if each of us thinks accordingly, one can see that it will be only a matter of chance that our opinions should coincide, and ethics will be a shambles. It might even be the case that we all exist within our own private value bubbles, as individuals who don't take each other's worlds and outlooks seriously. We then become ethical solipsists. Certainly, existentialism is often saddled with the accusation of subjectivism. De Beauvoir responds, however, as follows: "not only do we assert that the existentialist doctrine permits the elaboration of an ethics, but it even appears to us as the only philosophy in which an ethics has its place."[10] Such a generalized statement is not likely to win many friends for existentialism. But one has to understand it within the context of de Beauvoir's notions of ambiguity and freedom. Ambiguity includes the absence (nonexistence) of God, and freedom entails responsible agency—that humans autonomously express themselves in their actions, whatever moral character and consequences these may have. Now a critic might reply, for example, that an ethics "has its place" within a religious context too; it is just a different place. Within a secular context, as well, there are other forms of ethics each of which "has its place," given the particular humanistic assumptions it rests upon. I suggest that de Beauvoir deliberately exaggerates the power of an existentialist ethics in order to take the offensive in her argument and thereby counter anticipated criticisms such as these. As part of this argumentative strategy, she insists that there is another form of objectivity located within freedom, which will form the basis of her ethical theory. This we will now examine.

THE ETHICS OF AMBIGUITY

As she recommended earlier, de Beauvoir actively grasps the ambiguity of the human condition herself, and now she begins to construct an existentialist ethics. It is easy to suppose that freedom in a Godless universe must be unstructured, undisciplined, rudderless, and, as Dostoevsky suggested (in *The Brothers Karamazov*), capable of condoning any conduct whatsoever. But de Beauvoir is unhesitant in declaring this to be a mistaken perception. "On the contrary, it appears to us that by turning toward this freedom we are going to discover a principle of action whose range will be universal."[11]

As we saw in the previous section, finding an objective reference point for ethical values and judgments may be a matter of controversy or even a hopeless cause. But it does not follow that, even if they lack an agreed-upon objective foundation, such values and judgments must also lack universality. There are many universal principles without ethical content, for example: "Everyone ought to have an adequate number of hours of sleep per night;" "Shoelaces should always be tied like this;" and "Whoever wants to become a citizen must fill out these forms." Similarly, there are principles with ethical content that are not universalizable, or, at any rate, they do not appear to be so, such as: "Thieves ought not to steal from one another"; "Men with hair should not make jokes about those who are bald"; and "In the present situation, where you have made conflicting promises to your children, you must honor the promise made to the older one." Yet it is commonly accepted among philosophers that a hallmark of ethical significance is universal applicability. This means that even principles of con-

duct that do not appear in any obvious way to apply universally nevertheless derive from a general principle that everyone should accept, for here,
they would say, we find the essence of getting the right answer in ethics.
Identifying principles that are universal in the sense of being applicable to
all people, at all times and places, is a very tall order. But it seems clear that
we cannot cavalierly toss universality out of ethics just because specific situations may be complex and involve unique individuals, for: (a) not all
details of a situation are relevant to making an ethical judgment about it;
and (b) more importantly, even though no two people are exactly alike,
there may be a value or values that can be directly intuited from reflection
on the human condition. Sartre recognized these points in his talk of setting an example for others (see first section of chapter 7), and de Beauvoir
plainly does as well (refer to quotation ending previous paragraph).

The stage is set for de Beauvoir to develop her universal ethical principle, which she elaborates as follows: "Freedom is the source from which
all significations and all values spring. It is the original condition of all jus-
tifications of existence. The man who seeks to justify his life must want
freedom itself absolutely and above everything else. At the same time that
it requires the realization of concrete ends, of particular projects, it
requires itself universally. . . . To will oneself moral and to will oneself free
are one and the same decision."[12] De Beauvoir returns here to the idea
that freedom is the origin of meaning and value, from which it follows, she
holds, that freedom must always aim to preserve and assert itself. Since
ethics is a primary domain of value, this "will to freedom" is manifested
therein. If I take on the responsibility of acting morally, of moral agency,
then this is predicated on a commitment to my own freedom. More basically still, if I want life to have meaning and purpose, I must also want
freedom to flourish, since it is the source of all value. To fail to acknowledge this is not merely an ethical mistake but an existential one as well.

But what about others, since ethics largely concerns the social impact of
one's conduct? Importantly, de Beauvoir veers away from the Sartrean view
(in *Being and Nothingness*) that the freedom of each is bent on devouring the
freedom of every other agent it comes into contact with, that conflict
between people is ontologically grounded and therefore both inescapable
and seemingly insurmountable. For her, as Kristana Arp indicates, "these
conflicts are seen as having concrete social and political causes, not metaphysical ones. . . . [of the sort that leave] not much hope for an ethics."[13]
Accordingly, de Beauvoir searches for an ethical insight that will counteract
conflict, positing that "the precept will be to treat the other . . . as a freedom
so that his end may be freedom. . . ."[14] Just as my own freedom is always in

the process of being renewed by me, so it is with others. And in order to nurture freedom, there must be an environment favorable to this project, which consequently becomes a joint endeavor and responsibility. So de Beauvoir's first point is that individual freedoms are interdependent because the flourishing of each is contingent upon that of other freedoms. This being the case, what I will for myself I must will for others too: "To will oneself free is also to will others free."[15] But this is not just a matter of helping myself out by assisting others so that they will assist me in return. Instead, freedom can only be understood properly as a joint project.

Following from the above, de Beauvoir's second point is that there is an important inconsistency in not advancing the freedom of others. She argues that "action can not seek to fulfill itself by means which would destroy its very meaning."[16] In saying this, she appeals to an idea reminiscent of Kantian ethics, namely, that actions that contravene ethical principles are not just wrong but also in some way self-contradictory, self-stultifying, or self-nullifying. De Beauvoir illustrates the point in considering (a) how one relates to oneself and (b) how one's actions impinge upon others. Speaking of oneself, she observes, "In laziness, heedlessness, capriciousness, cowardice, impatience, one contests the meaning of the project at the very moment that one defines it."[17] When, through sloth, carelessness, or bad faith, I let decisions be made for me by others or by circumstances, I yield up my freedom and in effect I make it, or allow it to be made, into an object. But this defeats the cause of my project, which is to use freedom in a way that is creative and beneficial to myself. In relation to others, if I do things that deprive them of their freedom, or limit it, then I am using freedom (my own) to objectify freedom (that of others). I am asserting freedom as a value, on the one hand, in order to deny that same value, on the other—and, hence, my act turns back on itself to undermine its own meaning. The end of all this is that when one acts wrongly, by either doing or failing to do something, the commitment to freedom has failed.

Elsewhere, de Beauvoir treats this theme in more general terms, noting that "only the freedom of others keeps each one of us from hardening in the absurdity of facticity."[18] Our own humanity and agency require an environment that keeps freedom alive, and to secure this environment in turn requires that we celebrate and reinforce the freedom of others whenever we possibly can. De Beauvoir seems to be suggesting that if this project falls short, individuality will be replaced by some other, more mechanical expression of existence, such as conformism, stimulus-response behavior, role-playing, and the like. Sartre argued (see chapter

7) that for one freedom to struggle against another, the first must regard the second as a freedom, even at the same time as it wishes to subdue it and turn it into an object. If the first does succeed in turning the second into an object (say, in a relationship of total domination, or when one party is humiliated or ostracized), then this result represents a hollow victory, for freedom can express itself—in either a positive or a warped way—solely within a world of free beings, not in a world of unfree objects. In a similar vein, de Beauvoir maintains that freedom negates itself if it objectifies other freedoms by using them as mere means to its own ends, for within a realm of pure facticity (a world of objects), it cannot meaningfully exert itself. This kind of freedom would be comparable to that of someone lost on a remote island with no chance of ever making contact with other people again. It would be questionable whether we should even attribute freedom of action to such a person, since all they have to interact with is a collection of objects and food sources viewed as objects.

But de Beauvoir advances beyond Sartre's position here, too, as I will explain presently. In chapter 7, I cited Sartre's claim that "I need the Other in order to realize fully all the structures of my being."[19] Presumably, he meant this to apply to each of us: We need an interactive milieu in order to engage fully with the world and realize our plans and projects. However, his suggestion seems to be that my need for the other is more self-interested than anything else. For Sartre, dealing with others is just plain tedious and draining, even if necessary. De Beauvoir both avoids the negative slant Sartre puts on the matter and takes a much more holistic and contextual approach to human relations. "Respect for the other's freedom," she notes in an earlier work, "is not an abstract rule. It is the first condition of my successful effort. I can only appeal to the other's freedom, not constrain it. I can invent the most urgent appeals, try my best to charm it, but it will remain free to respond to those appeals or not, no matter what I do."[20] In other words, respect for other people's freedom is not derived from a prescription governing morally correct conduct. Nor is it just a matter of pragmatic or prudential behavior. Rather, it is, as she urges, an "appeal" designed to evoke a similar gesture in return, namely, a sign of trust, an act of faith, an overture that signifies mutual support and validation of my humanity. I cannot own, cajole, or dominate another person if I wish to nurture the delicate balance that allows both of us to thrive. Respect can only be solicited in the spirit of cooperation.

The contrast between de Beauvoir and Sartre is nowhere more plainly drawn than in her attitude toward the future. For both thinkers, projecting oneself into the future is what freedom and being human is all about. But de Beauvoir consistently sees this as a joint endeavor. To begin with, she explicitly defines what it is to be a person or agent in terms of an emergence from the present into the future: "I can not genuinely desire an end today without desiring it through my whole existence, insofar as it is the future of this present moment and insofar as it is the surpassed past of days to come."[21] She plainly has in mind here ends that relate to longer-term plans and projects, not merely to momentary whims or short-term desires. The quotation just given is a little tricky, owing to the care required in order to discern what each occurrence of the word "it" refers to. I understand her to be saying that desiring an end, in the longer-term sense, is freely willing that this end (first "it") be part of my emerging self in the future, just as it is in the present; and "my whole existence" (second and third "it") is both the transition of my present into the future that I effect through my commitment and choice and the continual transformation of present and future into past that I live through and shape into a meaningful life as time goes by.

In a later passage in *The Ethics of Ambiguity*, de Beauvoir links this movement into the future with the social context of freedom: "to be free is . . . to be able to surpass the given toward an open future; the existence of others as a freedom defines my situation and is even the condition of my own freedom."[22] We already know that the existence of others (or at least their actions, so far as they impinge upon us) is part of what is meant by "facticity"—what we can't change. But to say that others' freedom is "even the condition of my own freedom" suggests a very strong sense of reciprocal effect that we all have on one another in the process of seeking to attain our potential. De Beauvoir apparently intends that the project of "disclosing" the world as a place of meaning and value must be a social process, as I have previously indicated. We are not just solitary capsules or islands unto ourselves, but, rather, we are sources of freedom whose freedom is activated by mutual interaction. We swim—or we sink—together. In *Pyrrhus and Cineas* (1944), de Beauvoir offers a delightful image to get this point across: "Our freedoms support each other like the stones in an arch, but in an arch that no pillars support."[23] Healthy human relations, in short, form a self-supporting edifice.

De Beauvoir elaborates her theory of freedom as a social phenomenon by suggesting that freedom "regards as privileged situations those which permit it to realize itself as indefinite movement. . . . Thus, . . . freedom always appears as a movement of liberation. It is only by prolonging itself through the freedom of others that it manages to surpass death itself and to realize itself as an indefinite unity."[24] There are two main thoughts here. (1) Freedom seeks to assert itself, not as an end-in-itself, but as the source of all ends and purposes in life. Wherever there is an obstacle to freedom, therefore, freedom projects itself into a condition beyond that which constrains it at the moment. Hence, freedom is identified by de Beauvoir with self-liberation. (2) But no one's freedom exists in a vacuum; freedom is always interlaced with other freedoms, other "movements of liberation." It follows that in order to achieve its potential, preserve its unique identity, and continue developing, each freedom must also will the success of every other freedom in its struggle to overcome the material obstacles we all encounter, and to resist the freedom-denying acts of human beings themselves.

In discussing the conceptual background to de Beauvoir's ethics of ambiguity, Arp introduces distinctions that help clarify the different ways in which de Beauvoir conceives of freedom. Arp contrasts (a) "natural" or "ontological" freedom; (b) "power" or "concrete" freedom; and (c) "moral" or "ethical" freedom.[25] The first of these is a given—it is identifiable with the human condition—and only because of it are we "able to engage in any goal-directed activity at all."[26] The second is freedom instantiated in the world, in the acts that we do. The third is freedom that we take charge of, or take responsibility for, as autonomous agents in a social setting. Arp points out succinctly that "it is impossible . . . to base an ethics on freedom if freedom is equated solely with subjectivity," as it appears to be for Sartre.[27] De Beauvoir posits moral freedom, then, according to Arp, because "there are two different ways that one can respond to the fact of one's ontological freedom. Although one cannot will oneself *not* to be free, because freedom [in the most basic sense, or sense (a)] is an ontological structure of human existence, one can fail to choose to will oneself free. Since one is always free, one can, and indeed one must, freely choose what attitude to take to one's freedom."[28] We have already encountered this idea before—of the possibility of either fleeing from or seizing hold of one's freedom—in examining Sartre's notion of bad faith. De Beauvoir is elaborating this thought, then, in her argument that owning one's freedom and actively making use of it to assert oneself by engaging with the world and with others is precisely what being a moral agent amounts to.

LIBERATION

Those who live in more privileged parts of the world tend to take their freedom—both political and personal—for granted. If one hasn't experienced life in a situation of scarcity, oppression, violence, and daily degradation, she or he is unlikely to understand in as profound a way what de Beauvoir means by the need for mutual support of one another's freedom. As we've seen, though, she finds that freedom, even in the best of circumstances, is always a "movement of liberation." In some situations, however, this is much more strikingly apparent. And because freedoms are interdependent in the way she shows, it follows that "a freedom which is interested only in denying freedom must [itself] be denied."[29] For this kind of freedom is that of the oppressor.

What, exactly, is it to be an oppressor? De Beauvoir explains by reference to the impact of certain constraints placed on freedom by fellow human beings: "If, instead of allowing me to participate in this constructive movement [that is, defining my own future], they oblige me to consume my transcendence in vain, if they keep me below the level which they have conquered and on the basis of which new conquests will be achieved, then they are cutting me off from the future, they are changing me into a thing."[30] Substitute "oppressors" for "they" and you will have the meaning of oppression for de Beauvoir. Simply put, an oppressor is one who systematically blocks the movement toward self-definition that advances us into a meaningful and fulfilling future and who thereby stifles the freedom of emergence that not only makes us human but also makes each of us unique. This is why oppressors should be prevented from realizing their plans for the future, in order that the transcendence of the oppressed can be restored. (Plans for the future cannot be one-sided, as we have seen; they must involve participation by all concerned.) De Beauvoir follows Hegel and Marx in asserting that both the oppressed and the oppressor benefit from bringing an end to oppression, since "each one needs to have all men free."[31] Odd as it sounds, this conclusion is indeed entailed by her general theory of freedom, as discussed above. The trouble is, however, that oppressors do not realize that they need freedom in general to flower, nor do they give up their power over others reasonably or willingly. Hence, the only alternative for the oppressed is to take power away from the oppressors—often by force—in order to win back their own freedom.

Many questions arise at this point: How much intrusion on one's freedom is required to create a situation of oppression? By whose standard is this to be measured? How many people's freedom must be at stake? What is the distinction between legitimate constraint and oppression? Do we ever oppress ourselves or cooperate in our own oppression? Who is responsible for oppression anyway? What means are justifiably used to win freedom back? Can violence always—or ever—be avoided in this process?

It must be said that these are huge questions for anyone to answer, and de Beauvoir falls short of dealing adequately with them. But let us concentrate on what she does say rather than on what she doesn't.

De Beauvoir indicates that violence, lamentable though it may be, sometimes needs to be used in the struggle against oppression; but the worst thing about violence, according to her, is that "since we can conquer our enemies only by acting upon their facticity, by reducing them to things, we have to make ourselves things. . . ."[32] She seems to mean by this that those who fight for freedom often not only aim to cancel out opposing freedoms by the crudest of actions but also may themselves become mere instruments to advance a cause, and then become brutalized by the very liberation campaign in which they play a part. Another question de Beauvoir addresses is whether there can be a political order without oppression and violence. Her answer is no: "freedom will never be given; it will always have to be won. . . ." Here, we see that she is alluding to the second kind of freedom identified by Arp: power or concrete freedom, which, in the everyday human sphere is always contested. De Beauvoir continues: "But the truth is that if division and violence define war, the world has always been at war and always will be; if man is waiting for universal peace in order to establish his existence validly, he will wait indefinitely: there will never be any *other* future."[33] While some may disagree with this estimate, there is enough truth in Nietzsche's and Sartre's observation that freedoms will always oppose each other in important ways for us to accept the tenor of her argument. And the reasonable corollary on which de Beauvoir insists is that we need to deal with the world as it presents itself *now* and is likely to be for some time to come—to accept this as our collective condition—if we wish to get on with the task of freely defining ourselves. In line with this, she then maintains that: "The end justifies the means only if it remains present, if it is completely disclosed in the course of the present enterprise."[34] It might have been better had she phrased this as follows "the end *can* justify the means only if. . . ." But in any event, the position she takes here appears to be that efforts to make the world a better place are subject to moral appraisal in terms of what we now envision and not in relation to a utopian "future-myth" of some kind,[35] for, collectively, we act in ways whose effects carry over into a humanly shared future—but a future we will not live to experience fully. Therefore, we have to be as sure as we can *now* that we are making the best choices we can. This political argument applies equally soundly to environmental contexts, as we are learning today.

ON LIBERATION AND ETHICS

In view of her somewhat harsh but realistic appraisal of the ongoing struggle for liberation in the world, one might wonder whether de Beauvoir is backtracking on her ethical claims. I don't think so, for the purpose of any ethical outlook is both to express an ideal of behavior toward which we should strive and to explain why. If we routinely fall short of meeting the standard we have set, the best response is not to become cynical about it or repudiate it but to try harder. We may be a long way from having universal freedom of the kind de Beauvoir extols, but at least we do have something to build upon—a carefully thought-out ideal as well as practical examples, found within the moments of our lives, of how relationships can be at their finest.

A FEMINIST VIEWPOINT

Most people who have any acquaintance with de Beauvoir's work know her as the author of *The Second Sex*, which was an important catalyst to the development of contemporary feminist ideas and consciousness-raising. In this book, she considers the question, "What is woman?" and explores the ways in which social constructions of gender characteristics (masculine and feminine) determine our ideas of sex (male and female) and sexuality (how we express ourselves as sexual beings). In a much-cited passage, de Beauvoir explains that "one is not born, but rather becomes, a woman. No biological, psychological, or economic fate determines the figure that the human female presents in society; it is civilization as a whole that produces this creature, intermediate between male and eunuch, which is described as feminine."[36] Here, she states bluntly that there is no fixed or "eternal" female "nature"; yet even so, a woman has "a destiny imposed upon her"[37] from outside in relation to which there are two possible outcomes: she either conforms to it (as in the past) or may rebel against it (in the present and future). In any event, the possibility of change requires an understanding of the road already traveled and of how liberation might be pursued in light of this knowledge.

De Beauvoir uses the framework, with which we are already familiar, of the complex encounter between separate freedoms to forward her basic position. For her, men have not only controlled language and discourse about sexual matters, but have also created an ontology of the sexes grounded in various myths about men and women, which transforms the alleged difference between them into a timeless feature of reality. Within this ideology or story of how things are and are meant to be, men are "the essential," the standard of worthiness and self-affirmation in the world, and women, by contrast, represent "the Other" (the inessential, inferior, contingent, accidental, dependent, passive, dispensable, and so on). Men are active, rational, and creative doers; women are emotional or irrational beings, tied by their physical endowments to nature, childbirth, and domestic drudgery. Because this ontology has largely gone unnoticed and therefore unquestioned, men have benefited by having available to them many sources of fulfilment historically denied to women. Women, in equal measure, have suffered loss of freedom and oppression.

Another way in which de Beauvoir expresses the difference between men and women, according to the traditional model, is that men represent "transcendence" (self-choice) and women, "immanence" (fixity of character). Men have the inborn power of agency; women have an objectified status that allows little room for autonomy. Women's position of social inferiority is socially enforced, and it is experienced by them as deadening in relation to their freedom, personality, and sense of self-worth. In the following important passage de Beauvoir explains what is wrong with this situation, drawing upon her insights in *The Ethics of Ambiguity*.

> [T]hose who are condemned to stagnation are often pronounced happy on the pretext that happiness consists in being at rest. This notion we reject, for our perspective is that of existentialist ethics. Every subject plays his part as such specifically through exploits or projects that serve as a mode of transcendence; he achieves liberty only through a continual reaching out towards other liberties. There is no justification for present existence other than its expansion into an indefinitely open future.

Here, she starts with the idea that freedom needs to be actualized. The capacity for self-guiding behavior is what makes us human. De Beauvoir then associates freedom with emergence, with standing out into the unknown future. And lastly, she links one's quest for freedom with that of others. We need the reinforcement and alliance with other self-guided individuals in order to reach our full potential. All of these perspectives are then identified with existentialist ethics. The passage concludes as follows:

> Every time transcendence falls back into immanence, stagnation, there is a degradation of existence into the "*en-soi*" [in-itself]—the brutish life of subjection to given conditions—and of liberty into constraint and contingence. This downfall represents a moral fault if the subject consents to it;

if it is inflicted upon him [or in the present context, her], it spells frustration and oppression. In both cases it is an absolute evil. Every individual concerned to justify his existence feels that his existence involves an undefined need to transcend himself, to engage in freely chosen projects. . . . The drama of woman lies in this conflict between the fundamental aspirations of every subject . . . and the compulsions of a situation in which she is the inessential.[38]

When in a person's life freedom is prevented from unfolding itself, subjectivity lapses into objectivity and self-determination is suppressed. If we examine such situations, we discover either wrongdoing on the part of the agent or a situation of oppression (or perhaps both, as when the agent is complicit in her or his oppression). Women, who have the same fundamental need for freedom as men, strain against the oppression of sexual stereotyping, which prevents them from finding pathways toward becoming genuine, self-chosen persons.

As well as suggesting later on in *The Second Sex* that women have been complicit in their own oppression, de Beauvoir analyzes with care and subtlety the stratagems women have utilized to take advantage of their subordinate position or to put it better, to turn their supposed weaknesses into strengths in order to gain leverage in what we sometimes call "the war of the sexes." This is obviously a power struggle, which shows that women are not incapable of changing. Like other oppressed groups, women have realized that if they can assert themselves without upsetting the whole power structure of which they are a part (what we call "working within the system"), then there is motivation to make the best of the status quo and attempt to extract some benefits from it. Given an unsatisfactory situation, some degree of freedom can nonetheless be achieved, however small a victory this signifies. This does not, however, translate into the judgment that women "will" or "consent to" their position of inferiority or that they enjoy it any more than did African American slaves or Arabs subject to colonial rule (to whom de Beauvoir compares women in general). Within these parameters, though, women cannot expect to cast off their oppression, constitute society differently, or recover their freedom and establish their independence.

REVISIONING THE SEXES

Because de Beauvoir is committed to a philosophy of freedom, she is clearly dissatisfied with this state of affairs. She argues, first, that the relationship between the sexes *can* be improved because it is not derived from conditions over which humans have no control. Rather than being a permanent feature of reality, sex roles are socially constructed, or determined by the choices people have made. Therefore, we can look at how we are socially constructed and, if we don't like what we see, we are able to constitute ourselves differently. In other words, when we understand things from a new angle, we may learn that the status quo is not written in stone, and thereby acquire the insight to want change and the will to bring it about. De Beauvoir's work is aimed at bringing about these results for women.

Second, the relationship between the sexes *must* change because it is detrimental not only to women, whose potential is stunted, but also to men. This is because men lose out by experiencing impoverishment in their own lives from acting as oppressors and maintaining the institutions that inhibit freedom. By subordinating women and treating them as inferior, men miss out on what women really have to offer to relationships and to society at large. But by doing so, they also define themselves and their standards of accomplishment on false premises, which limits their own possibilities for growth and fulfilment. A better, more mutually beneficial sociopolitical order would remedy these problems.

Third, women, as free beings, have the most to gain by being able to assert their agency and independence and enhance their quality of life within the context of a new social order.

It's clear that for de Beauvoir, none of these outcomes follows from a mere reversal of male and female roles. Even if this were possible, it would only create a skewed set of power relations of an opposing sort. So what is needed instead is for a cooperative rethinking and transformation to take place in regard to all our ideas and ideals concerning male and female sexual identity. An unjust political and ideological system cries out to be changed. Men have to give up power and control over women and abandon myths about both themselves and women. They also need to accept that they have functioned in, and benefited from, an oppressive system, and redefine their notion of possibilities, privileges, and rewards according to a new vision that entails mutual respect for freedom, regardless of gender. Women, for their part, need to give up their inferior position and any advantages it brings them, move beyond myths such as "that of the feminine 'mystery,'"[39] and redefine their own potentialities, which in turn will lead to a new kind of empowerment and creative energy. Women's activism will serve to prompt and energize the changes that need to come from all sides.

Both sexes must detach themselves from the false belief that sexual equality means a society in which women would be less "feminine" and men less "masculine," and in which the monotony of androgynous clones would prevail. In truth, a greater range of options for self-expression, independence, and personal growth means wider vistas for both men and women than exist within a more rigidly role-governed framework. As de Beauvoir observes, "Let us not forget that our lack of imagination always depopulates the future. . . . New relations of flesh and sentiment of which we have no conception will arise between the sexes. . . . I fail to see that this present world is free from boredom or that liberty ever creates uniformity."[40] Although she affirms that "there will always be certain differences between man and woman," she also argues (correctly, in my opinion) that "the fact that we are human beings is infinitely more important than all the peculiarities that distinguish human beings from one another. . . ."[41] One can imagine how radical thoughts such as these would have been in the late 1940s. Indeed, it took a decade or more for the women's movement to catch up and for men to begin making any kind of constructive response.

POSTSCRIPT TO *THE SECOND SEX*

Feminist theory and scholarship have, of course, moved a long way since *The Second Sex* was written, and many of de Beauvoir's perspectives have been superseded. For example, socialist feminists see society not as a system in which men simply exercise power over women but as one in which some men (those who have the most political and economic power) dominate women *and* most other men. Marxist feminists and standpoint theorists would argue that authors like de Beauvoir, who, despite their hatred of the middle class, nevertheless exhibit in their analyses a privileged, middle-class bias, and that the struggle for equality looks quite different from the position of poor, genuinely working-class women, women who belong to racial or ethnic minorities, and so forth. Recent scholarship and translations reveal historical examples of women who have achieved greater success in asserting themselves against the norm than de Beauvoir perhaps allows for. The central issue raised by these perspectives is whether an emphasis on freedom and self-making really points us in the right direction for analyzing the major obstacles to equality. As you may recall, Sartre worried about this issue, and it occasioned his shift to a Marxist viewpoint in his later works.

Notwithstanding the limitations just noted, de Beauvoir learned from her experience of living through World War II in Paris that the connections between human beings are fundamental: "I renounced my individualist, anti-humanist way of life. I learned the value of solidarity," she writes, autobiographically, in *The Prime of Life*.[42] This more expansive and embracing view of self and other became increasingly central in her thinking, as did her awareness of world poverty and of the material requirements for a satisfactory human life. In spite of her self-assessment here, however, it can be noted that these kinds of awareness were at least somewhat apparent even in *Pyrrhus and Cineas* and *The Ethics of Ambiguity*.

AFTERWORD: DOING THE RIGHT THING

De Beauvoir never felt comfortable with her ethical writings, specifically with *The Ethics of Ambiguity*, which she later denounced.[43] However, not only did she chronically underrate herself, we have also seen that this work has much to recommend it. De Beauvoir hitched her ethical wagon to the existential theory of freedom. While it's arguable that Sartre does likewise, de Beauvoir's ethics clearly represents a new development that surpasses the conclusions reached by Sartre. We can see this very plainly by noting that whereas Sartre seems to be advocating some kind of universalistic, Kantian principle in *Existentialism Is a Humanism*, he goes on to espouse an apparently nihilistic principle in *Being and Nothingness*. In the latter, he writes that "my freedom is the unique foundation of values and . . . *nothing*, absolutely nothing, justifies me in adopting this or that particular value, this or that particular scale of values."[44] Here, Sartre states that values are grounded in freedom, but he adds, rather sweepingly, that no value or value system is, or can be shown to be, preferable to any other. It seems obvious, from his ethical and political judgments, however, that Sartre, no less than anyone else, thought some values were preferable to others. If this weren't the case, then there'd be no such thing as good faith or bad faith. Yet Sartre quite incautiously suggests, in the passage just quoted, that value choices are arbitrary and indefensible. De Beauvoir, on the other hand, deliberately grounds value choices, not only in the existential theory of freedom but also in the outlook that individual freedoms are intertwined and either mutually reinforcing or mutually degrading, as the case may be.

Although this is a philosophical improvement, it does not, by itself, tell us whether de Beauvoir's ethics can help us sort out the hard moral dilemmas of life. One has to look further into her works, both nonfictional and fictional, in order to form an opinion on this. And the review one gives of her attempts is likely to be mixed. Do we serve the cause of freedom if we use violence, even murder, to stop oppression? Arguably so, de Beauvoir tentatively and regretfully claims, but only when turned to as a last resort, and "only if it opens concrete possibilities to the freedom which I am trying to save. . . ."[45] Do we serve the cause of freedom by assisting a drug addict who asks for help in maintaining the habit? Or if we decline to prevent a suicide by someone who has made many serious previous attempts? De Beauvoir thinks so; but she also argues that we are involved in these people's lives and therefore accept some responsibility for looking after them.[46] These are no doubt difficult cases and controversial claims. Yet whatever we may think of her specific discussions, three important conclusions emerge from an examination of her theoretical work on ethics.

The first is that her view of freedom is much more positive than Sartre's in one respect. Sartre's metaphor for the human condition, once again, was: "man is condemned to be free."[47] This suggests that the world is a penal colony in which we unfortunately happen to be stuck and that freedom is not only imposed on us but is inescapable. While this may be something of a caricature of Sartre, it must be said that he invites the problem with his choice of words and his phenomenological descriptions of freedom unfolding and being evaded. De Beauvoir, by contrast, although not without flaws of her own, at least attempts to show how freedom makes existence meaningful and valuable by linking the sense of identity and the search for autonomy with ethics, and by showing how ethics depends on sensitivity to the needs of others and cooperative living.

The second conclusion is that there's a certain appealing humility in de Beauvoir's approach to ethics, deriving from her notion of the ambiguity of human existence. Because there are no certainties of conduct, she contends, there is always the possibility of error in our decision-making and choices. De Beauvoir underlines this at the beginning of *The Ethics of Ambiguity* when she offers the formula: "without failure, no ethics."[48] Ethics is neither a science nor a method of deducing what is right and wrong from fixed, objective, and/or eternally valid principles. So, although we cannot avoid making and acting upon them, ethical judgments are bound to be made with a degree of risk and trepidation. We can never be absolutely sure of the correctness of our conduct; we can only do our best in the circumstances and hope the outcome will justify in time what we have done. Existentialist ethics, like ethics in general, is a work in progress; but unlike ethics in general, it admits the fact.

The third conclusion is that ethics and politics are inseparable. De Beauvoir puts the point simply: "political choice is an ethical choice."[49]

This is because in her conception ethics always involves projects of mutuality that aim at increasing the possibilities for people's free self-determination. Given this feature of her thinking, it would be equally true to say that "ethical choice is a political choice." Thus, in defiance of the persistent tendency (discussed earlier in this chapter) to view existentialist ethics as excessively subjective, de Beauvoir situates herself among those who clearly discern and try to evaluate the larger social picture in terms of which choices—both ethical and political—are to be judged.

NOTES

1. Simone de Beauvoir, *The Ethics of Ambiguity*, new ed., trans. Bernard Frechtman (Secaucus, NJ: Citadel Press, 2000), p. 7.

2. Ibid., p. 9.

3. Ibid., pp. 8–9. For more on ambiguity, see Stacy Keltner, "Beauvoir's Idea of Ambiguity," in Margaret A. Simons, ed., *The Philosophy of Simone de Beauvoir: Critical Essays* (Bloomington: Indiana University Press, 2006), pp. 201–23.

4. De Beauvoir, *Ethics of Ambiguity*, p. 7.

5. Ibid., p. 12.

6. Ibid., pp. 12–13 (emphasis in original).

7. Ibid., p. 15.

8. Ibid., p. 14.

9. Ibid., p. 15.

10. Ibid., pp. 33–34.

11. Ibid., p. 23.

12. Ibid., p. 24.

13. Kristana Arp, *The Bonds of Freedom: Simone de Beauvoir's Existentialist Ethics* (Chicago: Open Court, 2001), p. 22.

14. De Beauvoir, *Ethics of Ambiguity*, p. 142.

15. Ibid., p. 73. Sartre advances the same thought at one point: "Of course, freedom as the definition of man does not depend on others, but as soon as there is involvement, I am obliged to want others to have freedom at the same time that I want my own freedom. I can take freedom as my goal only if I take that of others as a goal as well" (*Existentialism Is a Humanism*, trans. Bernard Frechtman and reprinted under the title "Existentialism" in *Existentialism and Human Emotions* [New York: Citadel Press/Kensington Publishing, 1987], p. 46). The difference between de Beauvoir and Sartre here is that de Beauvoir goes on to develop the idea thoroughly in her ethics and Sartre does not.

16. De Beauvoir, *Ethics of Ambiguity*, p. 131.

17. Ibid., p. 25.

18. Ibid., p. 71.

19. Jean-Paul Sartre, *Being and Nothingness: An Essay in Phenomenological Ontology*, trans. Hazel E. Barnes (New York: Philosophical Library, 1956), p. 222.

20. Simone de Beauvoir, *Pyrrhus and Cineas*, trans. Marybeth Timmerman, in *Simone de Beauvoir: Philosophical Writings*, ed. Margaret A. Simons, with Marybeth Timmerman and Mary Beth Mader (Urbana, IL: University of Chicago Press, 2004), p. 136.

21. De Beauvoir, *Ethics of Ambiguity*, p. 27.

22. Ibid., p. 91.

23. De Beauvoir, *Pyrrhus and Cineas*, p. 140.

24. De Beauvoir, *Ethics of Ambiguity*, p. 32.

25. Arp, *Bonds of Freedom*.

26. Ibid., p. 90.

27. Ibid., p. 54.

28. Ibid., p. 55 (emphasis in original).

29. De Beauvoir, *Ethics of Ambiguity*, p. 91; cf. p. 100.

30. Ibid., p. 82.

31. Ibid., p. 85.

32. Ibid., p. 99.

33. Ibid., p. 119 (emphasis in original).

34. Ibid., p. 125.

35. Ibid., p. 128.

36. Simone de Beauvoir, *The Second Sex*, trans. and ed. H. M. Parshley (London: Jonathan Cape, 1953), p. 273.

37. Ibid., p. 284.

38. Ibid., p. 27 (emphasis in original).

39. Ibid., p. 262.

40. Ibid., p. 686.

41. Ibid., pp. 686, 684.

42. Simone de Beauvoir, *The Prime of Life*, trans. Peter Green (Cleveland, OH: World Publishing, 1962), p. 285.

43. Simone de Beauvoir, *Force of Circumstance*, trans. Richard Howard (Harmondsworth, UK: Penguin Books, 1987), pp. 75–76.

44. Sartre, *Being and Nothingness*, p. 38 (emphasis in original).

45. De Beauvoir, *Ethics of Ambiguity*, p. 137.

46. Ibid., pp. 136–37.

47. Sartre, *Existentialism Is a Humanism*, p. 23.

48. De Beauvoir, *Ethics of Ambiguity*, p. 10.

49. Ibid., p. 148.

QUESTIONS FOR REFLECTION

1. Do you find de Beauvoir's idea of "ambiguity" helpful in understanding the human condition? In understanding ethics? Explain.

2. What do you think of basing ethics on freedom and "the will to be free"? Do you think freedom is defined carefully enough by de Beauvoir to carry this load?

3. Would you describe de Beauvoir's conception of freedom as specifically "feminist" in character? Why or why not?

4. Do you think personal freedom has the social dimension that de Beauvoir ascribes to it?

5. Take a couple of examples of moral dilemmas from your life, or that you know about, and analyze them in terms of an ethics of freedom such as de Beauvoir's. What are the results?

6. Is it ever justifiable to use violent means to win back freedom from oppressors? If so, when, and to what extent? If not, why not, and what are the alternatives?

7. Is there a fundamental difference between saying we are "condemned to be free" and saying that freedom is part of the "tragic ambiguity" of our condition? What is the difference and how significant is it?

9

EVALUATION OF EXISTENTIALISM

AND ITS LEGACY

There are many ways in which to end a book on existentialism. I have chosen to consider first some issues raised by its critics and what the response to these might be; next, I assess the cultural impact of existentialism; and, finally, I offer some observations on existentialism as a way of life.

THE CHALLENGE OF DETERMINISM

The issue of free will and determinism is one of the oldest and most intractable in the history of philosophy, and an incredibly wide range of theories has been offered to resolve it in one way or another. It is not my purpose to try doing so here, but only to say a few words on the original contribution of existentialism to the debate. Obviously, a philosophy of freedom such as existentialism must be able to make its case on behalf of human autonomy and choice, and to demonstrate that it provides a better framework for understanding human behavior than deterministic or compatibilist theories on offer. It may appear that existentialism assumes rather than argues for human freedom, given that it is such a basic premise of this style of philosophizing. While it is true that they are most interested in presenting a skilful portrait of the world of free action, I believe it can also be said that existential philosophers do successfully rise to the challenge of determinism. But we first need to see how they get past certain problems.

A persistent challenge to those who put forward very strong claims on behalf of human freedom (usually classified as libertarians) is that they transform the capacity for free action into something that is totally irrational and unaccountable. If my acts are spontaneously chosen and lack identifiable antecedent conditions, it is said, then they appear to come out of nowhere and to be merely bizarre, unexplainable, chance events, not the behaviors of a thoughtful, deliberative agent. Sartre, for one, attempts to meet head-on the challenge posed by this criticism. I have already noted (in chapter 7) that his view of freedom should be thought of as "radical" rather than "absolute" because he maintains neither that freedom can do anything nor that it is an end in itself, just that it is fundamental to fulfilling the human potential, which is to become something entirely through one's own efforts. This position resonates with the outlooks of Kierkegaard, Nietzsche, and Heidegger, as well. Even de Beauvoir, who states that the purpose of freedom is to choose freedom and to advance its frontiers, is not really arguing that freedom is an end in itself. Instead, she urges that the point of freedom is to find meaning and values in spite of the ambiguity of human existence, and, in doing so, to disclose the world (see chapter 8).

Returning to the problem with which we started above, Sartre comments that freedom does not need to be defended as "a pure capricious, unlawful, gratuitous, and incomprehensible contingency"; nor does being free "mean that my act can be anything *whatsoever* or even that it is *unforeseeable*."[1] In contrast, freedom, for him, is a "constantly renewed act [that] is not distinct from my being; it is a choice of myself in the world and by the same token it is a discovery of the world."[2] One might remark that Sartre is basically siding here with those who contend that an adequate characterization of human existence must prominently feature freedom. Sometimes this view is put forward more weakly in one of these forms: "I'm free because I believe I am" or "I choose freedom over determinism and make myself free by this very choice." We may admire these strident declarations to a certain extent, but they don't really prove anything. Much more persuasive is the claim that only free choice can account for the unlimited number of ways in which human beings express themselves and solve the problems of existence. This is the strong position advocated by existential philosophers and substantiated through the painstaking analyses of self-making that they offer. To be free, they assert, is to be able

to spontaneously transcend the past and present in order to craft the future. But how do we really know that we *can* do this, that it is *our own choice* that effectively shapes what is to come?

It strikes some as easy to dismiss belief in freedom and label it as illusory. Baruch Spinoza (1632–77) argued that feeling one's actions are free from causal influences beyond our control is deceptive; in this sense, we are no more free than a stone flying through the air (which we might imagine as suddenly endowed with consciousness) judging in mid-flight that it has chosen its trajectory.[3] Spinoza's image suggests that only out of ignorance do we suppose we are the unrestricted initiators of our own behavior.

But, as has often been replied, in terms of reasons to believe, plus what is to be gained from believing, plus what is lost by disbelieving, espousing belief in freedom is on balance a more attractive existential choice than endorsing determinism. And even the thought that we *can* opt for either of these opposing beliefs seems to reinforce the case for freedom. As Kierkegaard and Sartre would point out, the power of freedom also includes the choice to deny freedom, to self-negate, to sink ourselves into the mire of determinism, and to treat ourselves as the mere playthings of circumstance and facticity.

Recent empirical research demonstrates the extent to which belonging to a group whose members think alike, and basing one's own decisions on what others are saying and doing, can undermine autonomy. Psychologist Philip Zimbardo observes that "if you can diffuse responsibility so people don't feel accountable, they will probably do things they normally never would."[4] This appears as a new kind of challenge to belief in free will, but, at the same time, it reinforces the existentialists' plea for individuality and responsibility for who and what one becomes. If we consider de Beauvoir's view of freedom as the most well-rounded among the existentialists, however, then the task turns into a careful working out of the balance between mutually supportive activity and self-choice. Those who live up to the demands of freedom are the ones who steadfastly take responsibility for themselves; the rest allow themselves to slip into the "they" of which Heidegger speaks so eloquently (see chapter 6).

We must also ponder whether there may be some unfortunate people who have apparently been robbed of all capacity for free action by the acts of others (such as brutalizing parents), by psychotic illness, or by some kind of extreme trauma the effects of which they cannot escape. It is possible that these constitute cases where humanity is stalled and cannot be restarted. There is no triumph for determinism here, however, only a limitation on how widely disbursed radical freedom may actually be.

Still, looking back on the theories I've reviewed in this book, one must ask what kind of person or agent existentialism ultimately posits and presents. The answer is neither entirely clear nor completely satisfactory. If there is no permanent or abiding self that underlies experience and choice, then who I am is just what I do from moment to moment. That conception may be all right so far as it goes, but does it not leave in some kind of epistemological and metaphysical limbo the status of my memories, beliefs, commitments, and so on? (Do they persist, and, if so, where and in what form?) Granted, it is up to me how I relate to these and whether I reaffirm them as time goes on, but to suppose that I create myself totally anew at each instant (or even at the start of each day) seems an exaggeration. Perhaps the solution is that who/what I am is a process of development in which "I" am the active force of reconciliation, revitalization, and change that occupies the continuous "now," or situates itself "at the cutting edge" of my existence. This idea helps us understand how freedom functions as a factor in human life, even if it does not lay to rest the problem of freedom versus determinism.

ALLEGED SHORTCOMINGS OF EXISTENTIALISM

No comprehensive philosophical theory is free from defects, and many have been, or can be, identified in existentialism. I will only consider a few in this section.

A discouraging worldview. Some maintain that existentialism fosters a grim and gloomy outlook, that it is preoccupied with negative aspects of human life, such as anxiety, death, bad faith, absurdity, lostness, conformity, and so on. It is true that these dimensions of experience are often dwelt upon by existential thinkers. But I believe it is also true that we need to look beneath the surface at what is going on in their reflections. When we do this, we see that *existentialism is more diagnostic than remedial.* That is, it concerns itself more with understanding what it is to be human than with trying to prescribe how we should conduct ourselves in existence, which is something for each of us to figure out and implement in her or his own manner and time. In addition, it hardly needs to be said that existentialism did not invent, and can merely descriptively capture and discuss, our common condition. Furthermore, as I have previously noted (in chapter 8), de Beauvoir observes that "men of today seem to feel more acutely than ever the paradox of their condition."[5] As Stacy Keltner suggests, "Beauvoir . . . diagnoses late modernity as a technological-industrial destruction of the forms of thought that have traditionally functioned to provide meaning and coherence to existence." This crisis is one "resulting in the emergence of ambiguity as such in the historical loss of those discourses to account for modern experience."[6] I take this to imply that while human existence has always been ambiguous, in de Beauvoir's special sense, this awareness has become aggravated by the breakdown of those systems and frameworks to which people used to appeal in order to secure understanding and meaning in life. Existentialism and later postmodernism can both be seen as responses to this collapse.

Too high a standard of conduct. Some would posit that existentialism demands too much of us, as in their own way do the teachings of Jesus, for example. Whereas Jesus calls for complete humility, self-effacement, pacifism, obedience to God, and so forth, existentialists advocate equally impossible personal objectives, such as total honesty with oneself and others, facing death unflinchingly, maximizing one's freedom and responsibility, embracing uncertainty, and creatively coming to terms with absurdity, nothingness, alienation, the groundlessness of values, and God's nonexistence. Moreover, it may be said that although following Jesus is a difficult path, there is a reward that it leads to in the afterlife. But what is the payoff for an authentic existence? Surely part of the response to this challenge has to do with what we think the point of life is and what we expect of those who try to guide us by words, examples, or both. Along these lines, it is difficult to cite a moral outlook that has served as an inspiration or model for others to follow and did not make stringent demands on them. This is the essence of perfectibility—that we strive to fulfil certain ideals even if we know or at least suspect they will forever elude us in whole or in part. Having said that, it seems reasonable to state on behalf of existentialism that what it offers is not so much a path to a definite goal but rather an ongoing process of personal renewal and growth. Correspondingly, the "reward" lies in the benefits that derive from the kind of life we carve out for ourselves *now*, rather than from benefits that are postponed and removed to some remote place we can only dimly imagine. (I would suggest that an "existential" interpretation of Jesus' message would go along these same lines.)

Extreme individualism. Another limitation of existentialism is often thought to be its focus on the individual. We have seen in earlier chapters that this viewpoint contains some truth. If anyone ever stood for the individual, it is Kierkegaard. Nietzsche's Zarathustra enjoins listeners to follow their own path. Heidegger identifies authenticity with detaching oneself from the crowd. Sartre thinks of freedom as something to be won from the struggle with others, who seek to curtail it or to take it away from me. Yet de Beauvoir portrays freedom as a joint project in which each depends on others. It looks as if we have a yes and no answer to this criticism, then: Yes, existentialism is admittedly individualistic, even subjectivistic, some would add, but no, it is not exclusively so. Yes and no may not be all there is to the matter, however, for might it not be argued that we first need to know ourselves before we can truly go the distance with others? Or perhaps the origins of change are to be discovered within the self, such that self-improvement and enhancing the lot of others occur in tandem afterward? These are intriguing possibilities, and even if existentialism seems to swing too far toward individualism, this may be the necessary philosophical and psychological starting point for personal renewal and for contributing in a healthy way to the ongoing project of our species' development.

The nonhuman world. Scarcely ever talked about by either the leading figures discussed in this book or their commentators, critics, and apologists is the status of the nonhuman world in existential philosophy. Sartre asserted that "existentialism is a humanism," and this seems to sum up the attitude that prevails within the movement. Buber hints mysteriously at some kind of "Thou-experience" that might be had (fleetingly) with an animal or a tree. Heidegger talks of the need to treat nature as something more than a set of resources. But these small traces of concern do not in any way constitute genuine consideration for the natural world—as something that is of value and importance in its own right. Here, I think we find what is possibly the greatest omission of existentialism. In this respect, however, it is certainly a child of its times, since philosophy as a whole showed no greater tendency in this direction until the influence of existentialism had already passed its peak. The modern environmental movement began in earnest in the 1960s, and the field of environmental philosophy only arrived on the scene in the early 1970s. A somewhat different direction might have been pursued by existential thinkers had they received some of the input of environmentalism.

Inadequate argumentation. Related to the charges of subjectivism and excessive individualism that are sometimes lodged against existentialism is another, more serious one—perhaps the most serious of all. This is that it lacks the rigor and method characteristic of philosophy and is, in short, doomed to superficiality and lack of rational cogency. As Oxford University philosopher Mary Warnock reflects,

> There is no real possibility of *argument* with the deliverances of the concrete imagination. If I see significance in some feature of the world around me, I am at liberty to say so. . . . But philosophy without arguments is not possible, in the long run. We may be struck by the image of the man listening at the keyhole and caught in the act; we may be enlightened by it. But we cannot be expected to accept a whole theory of interpersonal relations, and therefore of morality, on the basis of this picture. The fact is that in philosophy we wish to theorize about the world. We do not wish merely to describe it, or have it described, even if, like Heidegger, the philosopher offers us a whole new vocabulary of description.[7]

This seems a rather surprising evaluation to find offered at the close of a book on existentialism, but be that as it may. There are three main points I would offer in response. First, Warnock's argument clearly pertains to those existential philosophers who have made phenomenology an integral part of their approach but much less obviously to others who have not (Kierkegaard and Nietzsche, in particular).

Second, and following from the above, as I discussed in chapter 3 (on Kierkegaard), there are many different ways of constructing arguments in philosophy, and often these are to be understood as converging toward and reinforcing the same conclusion rather than being self-sufficient. As a consequence, we shouldn't allow ourselves to be blinkered by a preconception that the formal structures of deductive and inductive argument, are the only respectable techniques of persuasion. Furthermore, alternative strategies of argument such as Kierkegaard's, do, in reality, very often plug into methods of reasoning with which we are quite familiar—when we begin to appreciate how they induce us to accept them. (For example:

"If faith offers a dimension of existence that contributes to greater wholeness of the self, as Kierkegaard claims, and I desire such wholeness in myself, then I ought to embrace faith as a dimension of my existence.")

Third, Warnock seems not to credit phenomenology with having a method at all, or, at any rate, she seems to be denying that powerful descriptions can sometimes convince us as effectively as more standardly recognized kinds of philosophical argument. However, I think this is a shortsighted judgment, if we appreciate what phenomenological accounts are trying to do, namely, that they attempt to explore interpersonal relations and relations between self and world from the standpoint of the experiencing subject. Granted, there can be different ways of doing this, with the result that any given phenomenological account will win over some readers and not others. But the same is true of deductive and inductive arguments. And just as some of these start out with premises that contest those used by others employing the same methods of argument, so is this the case with phenomenological arguments. Moreover, the penalty to be paid for adhering to Warnock's position is that we would also have to sacrifice the notion that truth can be found in the arts, particularly literature. This is in itself a big issue, but I believe we should not be too hasty in adopting an outlook that entails that fictional works cannot make truth claims about the world. Finally, with respect to Sartre in particular, he does not expect us to "accept a whole theory of interpersonal relations, and therefore of morality" on the basis of a single example, as I show in chapter 7. To sum up, the existential approach—whether or not it relies on the tools of phenomenology—is one of presenting a complex, multifaceted argument rather than a single, bone-crunching piece of logic.

THE ENDURING APPEAL OF EXISTENTIALISM

Any account of the history of philosophy in recent times would have to devote careful attention and space to existentialism. But how important it is, or was, in the overall development of ideas remains the subject of debate.

Conflicting viewpoints. Is existentialism a historical relic? Two perspectives on this issue are discernible. Some scholars hasten to answer in the affirmative, almost as if the disappearance without a trace of existentialism were a proposition that no reasonable observer of culture would contest. Anne Whitmarsh, for instance, simply states that "existentialism is outmoded and no longer dominates current thought."[8] Now there are two different claims being made here. And while the perception that it "no longer dominates current thought" is unquestionably true, is it so obvious that "existentialism is outmoded"? I think not; but in order to weigh this assertion properly, we need to unpack what it is supposed to mean. If a philosophy is outmoded, that presumably means (a) that no one adheres to or speaks on behalf of its principles anymore; (b) that its cultural influence is negligible; (c) that it has been superseded by some other mode of thought; or (d) all of the foregoing. But it's evident (as I shall explain in a moment) that (a) and (b) are false with respect to existentialism, at least in some reasonable interpretation of them (and therefore also [d])—even if (c) may well be true. So, in a way, Whitmarsh's ahistorical perspective misses the point, since a philosophy like existentialism always has its own history and is in turn part of the history of philosophical thought flowing onward from it.

Hence, a more realistic assessment is one given by Max Charlesworth: "I think most people would now agree that as a movement [existentialism] has lost momentum. No doubt its memory and influence linger on in all sorts of areas. . . ."[9] Charlesworth's comment, from a work published in 1975, is just as accurate today as it was then. And we can add the following, more recent (1998) observation of Charles Guignon: "Whether or not existentialism as such will continue to thrive, it seems that there will always be a place for the style of critique of society and the concern with concrete realities of life that are central to existentialist thought."[10] As Guignon points out here, the rebellion of existential writers against the dehumanizing tendencies of modern society and the existentialists' focus on the unique features of the human situation sound a note that thoughtful people will (so far as we can tell) always respond to. Thus, existential philosophy (as opposed to existential*ism*) is neither lacking in historical relevance nor historically left behind.

The special contributions of existentialism. Perhaps above all else, the label "existentialism" signifies the study of human beings as whole entities placed in existence and striving to come to terms with it. Facing the world and each other with limited knowledge, they must nevertheless make choices and take responsibility for these. As they do this, so too do they define themselves. Heidegger may have taken Sartre to task for an allegedly excessive commitment to humanism, arguing that a more spiritual dimension of existence also needs to be taken into account. Yet, in the end, all of the existentialists share the project of unraveling what it is to be an existing individual amid the uncertainties and frailties that characterize our lot. In a way, de Beauvoir sums this up best when she says, "Life is occupied in both perpetuating itself and in surpassing itself; if all it does is maintain itself, then living is only not dying, and human existence is indistinguishable from an absurd vegetation; a life justifies itself only if its effort to perpetuate itself is integrated into its surpassing and if this surpassing has no other limits than those which the subject assigns himself."[11] In order to live fully human lives, in other words, we must grasp and make use of the realization that we exist in advance of ourselves, that we choose in the face of many uncertainties, and that time is a rolling process of self-unfolding.

Another avenue toward considering the universal appeal of existential thought leads from the discussion of freedom earlier in this chapter. Because freedom is always at issue in one way or another in a complex social and political world, existential philosophers' treatment of the human being as something that is fashioned, not given or fixed, remains vital and relevant. Indeed, it is not too much to say that in some form or another, existential freedom lies at the core of all opposition to oppression, coercion, and totalitarianism—central issues of our time and of much of our collective past.

In its relatively short history as a major movement of thought, existentialism has to its credit having led the way in awakening philosophical interest in topics of everyday urgency. What this means is generally laid out in chapter 1. As a supplement to that discussion, it's worth noting that for a significant period during the last century, philosophy substantially (in the English-speaking world in particular) fell away from its traditional task of helping people clarify their thinking about basic questions of value, how to live, and where to find meaning in existence. Although there are a number of factors and modes of thought that have contributed to reversing this trend, I think it is fair to state that existential works provided the first model and inspiration. Thus, it may, in the end, be more in its personal application than in its historical influence that the value of existentialism is to be gauged most accurately.

Taking an even broader view, the pervasive influence of existentialist ideas can be discovered by looking at English usage. Here, we can trace changes that are akin to the way in which words from one language slowly emerge as established parts of another language's vocabulary. Alfie Kohn writes that

> our consciousness has been subtly changed by the presence of existentialism. This is clear whenever we speak of "absurdity" and mean more than simple silliness, whenever we talk of "a leap of faith" or "bad faith,"

whenever we refer to making someone into an object or having a "dialogue." As Maurice Friedman observes, "It's not always being named existentialism, but the thing that represents that spirit is very palpably there. It's had a very permanent impact that's growing, and people are growing through it."[12]

This association of existentialist thought and themes with personal growth is most significant in (and has been most appreciated by) the fields of psychology and psychiatry, into which this philosophy has been notably assimilated.

It is likewise important to cite the fact (also noted in chapter 1) that many—especially young people—now a generation or two on from the heyday of existentialism, are very much drawn to the ideas that spring from the movement. This can be seen, among other things, in the large number of well-subscribed university courses on the subject, in the films and dramas to which they give acclaim, and in the kinds of books they buy and read. Consider, for example, the popularity of *I Heart Huckabees*, *The Truman Show*, *The Matrix Trilogy*, *Crash*, *As It Is in Heaven*, and Woody Allen's movies, all of which have strong existential themes. And reflect on the following two comments found on the Amazon.com website under the listing for de Beauvoir's *The Ethics of Ambiguity*: Michael, from Minneapolis, writes: "This book changed my life. In precise but understandable terms, this book offers a compelling view of existentialism, devoid of the terminological wilderness of other books on the subject (e.g. *Being and Nothingness*)." And writing from Illinois, Christopher T. Paluch adds: "It is probably my favorite philosophy text, and I have read my share. . . . A wonderful exploration into the nature of humanity . . ." Whether de Beauvoir is the finest writer among the existentialists is not the issue here; the point is that these sorts of opinions are seldom stimulated by other contemporary philosophical works, even those read by a wider audience than the fans of de Beauvoir.

A similar kind of verdict is delivered by students taking existentialism courses. Here are a few excerpts from course evaluations I've received over the years. "I really liked the thought-provoking subject matter of this course. The subject of existentialism opened up a totally new way of thinking for me." "It was extremely applicable to my own life; this class was like therapy for me." "I found [the course] directly influenced my life and the way I thought about it." "Course content both interesting and relevant beyond classroom." "I really liked how what I learnt in this course was directly related to my life and encouraged me to question certain aspects of it. It was challenging for me in a personal way, unlike many other university courses. . . ." "It was enriching to take a philosophy class which was applicable to my everyday life, and also to learn how this philosophy can be applied, to topics like Buddhism and psychology." Clearly, these comments are not simply about how the course was taught and how the material was presented but also, more importantly, they are about the ideas of the remarkable existentialists themselves and the bearing those ideas have on the process of self-understanding students are engaged in. Do students say the same thing about philosophy courses overall? Speaking as someone who has taught a wide variety of courses over a long career, I answer no; this experience is quite unique to courses on existentialism.

Not only is personal engagement with existentialism intense, but scholarly interest in the principal figures—Kierkegaard, Nietzsche, and Heidegger especially—is great and still growing. It might be replied, of course, that the number of scholars is increasing and, in any case, that scholarship has become a self-propelling industry in its own right. While true, these facts alone do not explain why existential authors are of abiding concern, nor do they explain the variety of angles from which the existentialists are being approached by their interpreters. What *does* account for this activity is, first, the intrinsic interest of existential writers' works and their contribution to the opening up of philosophical inquiry and the study of both traditional and contemporary problems. The abiding value of these works lies in their originality, insightfulness, and compelling quality.

Second, since existentialism has been succeeded (or, some would have it, superseded) by other forms of thought, there is considerable incentive for today's thinkers to re-examine existentialist authors from their own theoretical perspectives and/or to appropriate these authors' ideas in some manner.

EXISTENTIALISM AND OTHER CONTEMPORARY MOVEMENTS OF THOUGHT

In what follows, I try to situate various movements in relation to existentialism and also historically. Although there is some kind of chronological order in this account, it must be borne in mind that there are interrelationships between these movements and sometimes they exhibit overlapping tendencies as well. Furthermore, certain figures are common to more than one movement; for instance, discussions of hermeneutics, deconstruction, post-structuralism, and postmodernism include references to the work of Jacques Derrida (1930–2004), while the writings of

Michel Foucault (1926–84) span the structuralist, post-structuralist, and postmodernist movements.

Hermeneutics (origins in ancient Greece; flourished in Middle Ages and Renaissance; revitalized in nineteenth and twentieth centuries). The study of interpretation and of the interpreter's involvement in the act is known as hermeneutics. In its modern form, hermeneutics draws heavily on the work of Heidegger, among others. This is owing to the fact that in his earlier philosophy he makes the interpretation of what it is to be human a central concern. Dasein's self-understanding and understanding of its world are the preoccupations of *Being and Time* (see chapter 6). Many of Heidegger's later writings engage with the project of interpreting canonical texts in the history of philosophy as well. Michael Inwood comments that "to understand a text we need to go beyond dictionaries and grammars to reconstruct the world of its author and the 'possibilities' it offered."[13] This perspective, which involves both historicism (situating the author in time and place) and hermeneutics, is very much in the spirit of what Heidegger tries to do. Finally, insofar as hermeneutics is also about the search for criteria by which to evaluate and revise interpretations, Heidegger's influence looms large once again.

Some other important figures in this movement include Friedrich Schleiermacher (1768–1834), Wilhelm Dilthey (1833–1911), Hans-Georg Gadamer (1900–2002), Paul Ricoeur (1913–2005), Karl-Otto Apel (b. 1922), and Jürgen Habermas (b. 1929).

The Frankfurt School (1920s to the 1960s). This interdisciplinary movement of social criticism developed an adaptation of Marxist and Hegelian thinking, known as "critical theory," which was used to expose prevalent ideologies that both reflect and perpetuate social inequalities. It promulgated self-enlightenment and rejection of the political status quo as vital steps toward breaking down such inequalities and building a better, rationally reorganized society. Existentialism was seen as masking a bourgeois ideology that stood in need of being overthrown, and it was specifically targeted by Theodor W. Adorno (1903–69) in his book *The Jargon of Authenticity.*[14] Although this work was mainly aimed at Heidegger, his critique of technology (see chapter 6) was influential on the later development of the Frankfurt School as it struggled to come to grips with the rise of Fascism and Stalinism. Some other important figures in this movement: Walter Benjamin (1892–1940), Max Horkheimer (1895–1973), Herbert Marcuse (1898–1979), and Jürgen Habermas.

Structuralism (flourished from the 1920s to the 1970s). Obviously, structuralism is the study of structures or, more exactly, the use of structural relations to illuminate thinking, experience, language, behavior, society, and culture. Structuralism began with the groundbreaking linguistic theories of Ferdinand de Saussure (1857–1913), which gave rise to semiotics, or the study of signs and symbols. Structuralists investigated human phenomena from the standpoint of the contexts and wholes (for example, conventions, rule systems, belief systems) of which they are a part, within which they function, or that make them possible. Its analyses emphasized the role played by difference and binary oppositions (such as hot/cold, male/female, culture/nature, being/nonbeing, reason/emotion) in the production of meaning. Overall, structuralism can be understood as standing in opposition to the existentialists' and phenomenologists' emphasis on the independent structures of consciousness and on the individual as the locus of meaning and signification. Other leading structuralist theorists include Jacques Lacan (1901–81), Claude Lévi-Strauss (b. 1908), and Roland Barthes (1915–80).

Deconstruction (1960s and continuing). This movement evolved a method of (re)reading philosophical and other texts that seeks to unearth and expose their inner contradictions and to analyze the ways in which distinctions relied upon by their authors tend to destabilize or subvert the stated or otherwise evident purpose of these very texts. The process just described may yield a quite different interpretation of the author's work than she or he might endorse. An important influence on this movement has been Heidegger's inquiries into what he takes to be the original meaning of Greek concepts and his rethinking of the Western philosophical tradition. (Indeed, the term "deconstruction" comes from his work *The Basic Problems of Phenomenology.*) Nietzsche's corrosive interrogation of a wide range of philosophical terms (see chapter 4) has also inspired deconstructionist efforts. Existentialist works have been and continue to be the subject of deconstructionist writings too. Deconstructionists argue that there is no privileged vantage point from which to analyze a text (such as identifying the author's intention in writing the work). This idea resonates strongly with Kierkegaard's technique of using pseudonyms, evading authorial responsibility, and declaring that his intentions are irrelevant to an understanding and evaluation of his texts (see chapter 3). Influential deconstructionists include Paul de Man (1919–83), Jacques Derrida, and Gayatri Spivak (b. 1942).

Post-structuralism (1970s and beyond). The notion that structures of any sort are self-sufficient and based on secure or certain foundations is attacked by members of this movement; in addition, they assail the assumption that opposing concepts can be clearly distinguished (for example, true and false, appearance and reality). Their belief, accordingly, is that thought can never reach or adequately represent reality. As many structuralists came to realize, the study of structures is bound to be culturally influenced (even biased). Therefore, a shift of attention is required—such that focus is placed on inquiries into the ways in which what passes for knowledge is generated. In post-structuralism, the death of subjectivity as an authoritative standpoint is proclaimed. The movement also "decenters" authors from their texts, preferring to look elsewhere for meanings and interpretations. Readers are embedded in their own cultural norms just as authors are, and this must be somehow factored into interpretations. (This position paves the way for the developing idea that "text" is a term applicable to a wide range of culturally constructed objects, including films, TV programs, political messages, and even the adorned human body.) The assault on systematic thought begun by Kierkegaard and Nietzsche is continued with a vengeance. Generally, the refusal of existentialists and others to reduce human behavior to instances of lawlike phenomena is taken up and reinforced by the movement. Foucault's post-structuralist attempts to integrate the analysis of power relations and the (non-legitimate) use of power into the study of institutions (such as prisons and mental hospitals) owes much to Nietzsche as well. Foucault, who initially made use of existential phenomenology under the influence of Merleau-Ponty and Heidegger, eventually defined his position in opposition to Sartre and what he took to be Sartre's extreme focus on the subject and the tendency, in his political writings, to set himself up as the universal judge of society. Some other prominent post-structuralists are Jacques Lacan (1901–81), Claude Lévi-Strauss, Roland Barthes, Gilles Deleuze (1925–95), Jacques Derrida, Luce Irigaray (b. 1930), Hélène Cixous (b. 1937), and Julia Kristeva (b. 1941).

Postmodernism (1980s and continuing). Movements amid which we find ourselves are notoriously difficult to define. Nevertheless, postmodernism is usually associated with a deep mistrust of the following: foundational (or anchoring) beliefs and truths; essentialism; transcendental explanations (such as God's plan, destiny, or appeal to a higher order of reality); grand justifying narratives (such as religion, systematic metaphysics, political ideology, sweeping theories of history, utopian vision, and the like); belief in progress; objectivity in knowledge; and the assumption that the world is an intelligible unity. Postmodernism embraces what is transitory (such as the products of popular culture) and/or viewed from a particular standpoint. Nietzsche's perspectivism and his aesthetic/metaphorical theory of language are important precursors to this movement. Much postmodernist writing about humans and the world asserts the lack of a fixed reference-point for interpretation and features ironic, oblique, and whimsical commentary. The multilayered philosophical approach of Kierkegaard—in which he utilizes irony, humor, storytelling, dramatization, "indirect communication," and other devices, and also exalts subjectivity over objectivity and expresses profound doubts about the efficacy of language and rational thought—must be seen as clearing the way for the full flowering of postmodernism. Camus' concept of absurdity (which itself owes a debt to Kierkegaard) helps prepare the ground as well (see appendix D). The assertion, by Kierkegaard and others, of human beings' rootedness in existence foreshadows postmodernist rejection of transcendental modes of explanation. Other inputs of interest are the breakdown of the distinction between subject and object in phenomenology and the rejection by existentialism of claims to objectivity and unconditional, timeless principles featured in conventional ethical and value theories. Sartre argued vigorously against these claims and also marshaled the case against essentialism (see chapter 7). The postmodern spirit, then—like existentialism itself—has been under way (or on the way) for a long time. Leading postmodern thinkers include Jean-François Lyotard (1924–98), Jean Baudrillard (1929–2007), Roland Barthes, Michel Foucault, Jacques Derrida, and Richard Rorty (1931–2007). Most of these are heavily indebted to the writings of Nietzsche and/or Heidegger.

Miscellaneous social, political, and cultural movements (1950s to 1970s, with echoes beyond). Existentialism was indisputably part of the nexus of ideas and influences and cultural ferment during this period, and it played a significant part in producing the ambience of these times. Developments like Theater of the Absurd, the Beat Generation, the beatnik phenomenon, and the 1960s counterculture cannot be fully appreciated without reference to existentialism. Included in what we call "the 1960s counterculture" are the civil rights movement in the United States; student revolts against government in various parts of the world; interest in alternative lifestyles; innovative (often anti-establishment) trends in popular music, film, literature, and other areas of creative endeavor; the anti–Vietnam War movement; the so-called sexual revolution; and psychedelic experimentation. The emphasis on freedom, self-examination, questioning of authority and norms, and thoughtful validation of individualism—which we identify with existentialism—all featured importantly in the way the history of these times took shape.

Recent North American philosophy (1970s and beyond). During the first half of the twentieth century, English-language philosophy and Continental (European) philosophy went in markedly separate directions for various historical and intellectual reasons. It is not too much to say that there was a relationship of antipathy between them that has only slowly (and not entirely) broken down. A rapprochement of sorts has occurred through the efforts of certain thinkers who began to take notice of other modes of philosophizing and to respectfully study them and sometimes integrate elements of them into their own work. Part of this process reveals the influence of existentialism on recent North American philosophy, a few examples of which follow. Hubert Dreyfus (b. 1929) launches a sustained and classic assault, derived from the existential (largely Heideggerian) view of embodied, context-dependent subjectivity, on claims made by some artificial intelligence (AI) researchers concerning the capacities of machines. Charles Taylor (a Canadian social and political philosopher, b. 1931) draws upon Heidegger and Merleau-Ponty in arguing that human being is bodily immersed in the world and must be understood from that position. In his neo-pragmatist writings, Richard Rorty takes off in part from Nietzsche's critique of the concept of truth as an absolute value. Thomas Nagel (b. 1937), a wide-ranging thinker, finds the meaning of life in forward-looking projects justified only within the parameters of one's own life. Meanwhile, Christine Korsgaard (b. 1952) makes use of the idea of "self-creation" in theorizing about ethics. Cornel West (b. 1953), a controversial and influential philosopher and social activist, applies existential concepts to the analysis of African Americans' historical struggle for equality, seeing existential freedom as the goal of their quest. Judith Butler (b. 1956), an important figure in the development of feminist theory and queer theory, offers a strongly anti-essentialist perspective on gender, affirming that gender is the result of what we do—how we choose to lead our lives—rather than being something fixed and given. And Sonia Kruks (b. 1947) draws ideas together from Merleau-Ponty, Marcel, Sartre, and de Beauvoir to fashion a new feminist political theory. All of this activity prompts one observer to suggest, provocatively, that "in some sense, existentialism's very notoriety as a cult movement may have impeded its serious philosophical reception. It may be that what we have most to learn from existentialism still lies before us."[15]

AFTERWORD: EXISTENTIALISM AS A WAY OF LIFE

Existentialism is about how we lead—and more accurately, how we construct—our lives. While I have suggested throughout that the existentialists do not wish to prescribe the same path for everyone or to tell us specifically how we ought to live, it is still the case that a way of life flows more or less directly from their teachings. This has already been touched upon in above sections of the present chapter. What needs to be added here is that existentialism speaks to the ancient idea that we should engage in self-examination and aim to know ourselves. With commitment and seriousness of purpose, we should always conduct this process, never allowing it to end, while acknowledging that growth in ourselves and likewise in others is unending. In addition, wisdom—if there is any to be attained—comes not from seeking certainty but in spite of, and even because of, the lack of certainty.

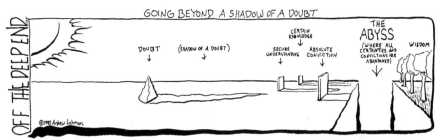

Reprinted by kind permission of Andrew Lehman.

Existential philosophers present their thoughts with passion and in a spirit of confrontation and mutual involvement with the reader. Ideas such as theirs—one could say *any* ideas—are there for appropriating and applying, for making into the vehicles of change and progression from one life state to the next. Therefore, ideas—the existentialists' in particular—are not merely static concepts we can review and leave alone; they are, instead, dynamic stimuli designed to precipitate reaction from us. "I think, therefore I am," Descartes famously said. But *what* we think and *how* we think about it tell the story of *who* we are on the way to becoming.

NOTES

1. Jean-Paul Sartre, *Being and Nothingness: An Essay on Phenomenological Ontology*, trans. Hazel E. Barnes (New York: Philosophical Library, 1956), p. 453 (emphasis in original).

2. Ibid., p. 461.

3. Baruch (Benedict) Spinoza, "Letter 58 to G. H. Schuller" (October 1674), in *The Correspondence of Spinoza*, trans. and ed. A. Wolf (London: Frank Cass, 1966), pp. 295–96.

4. Philip Zimbardo, cited in Michael Bond, "They Made Me Do It," *New Scientist* 2599: 44.

5. Simone de Beauvoir, *The Ethics of Ambiguity*, new ed., trans. Bernard Frechtman (Secaucus, NJ: Citadel Press, 2000), pp. 8–9.

6. Stacy Keltner, "Beauvoir's Idea of Ambiguity," in *The Philosophy of Simone de Beauvoir: Critical Essays*, ed. Margaret A. Simons (Bloomington: Indiana University Press, 2006), p. 203.

7. Mary Warnock, *Existentialism* (Oxford: Oxford University Press, 1970), p. 139 (emphasis in original).

8. Anne Whitmarsh, *Simone de Beauvoir and the Limits of Commitment* (Cambridge: Cambridge University Press, 1981), p. 168.

9. Max Charlesworth, *The Existentialists and Jean-Paul Sartre* (St. Lucia, AU: University of Queensland Press, in association with the Australian Broadcasting Commission, 1975), p. 1.

10. Charles Guignon, "Existentialism," *Routledge Encyclopedia of Philosophy*, vol. 3, ed. Edward Craig (London and New York: Routledge, 1998), p. 501.

11. De Beauvoir, *Ethics of Ambiguity*, pp. 82–83.

12. Alfie Kohn, "Existentialism Here and Now," *Georgia Review* 38 (1984): 397.

13. Michael Inwood, "Hermeneutics," *Routledge Encyclopedia of Philosophy*, vol. 4, p. 388.

14. Theodor W. Adorno, *The Jargon of Authenticity*, trans. Knut Tarnowski and Frederic Will (Evanston, IL: Northwestern University Press, 1973; reprinted New York: Routledge, 2006).

15. Thomas Crowell, "Existentialism," *Stanford Encyclopedia of Philosophy* (online), Spring 2006 edition, ed. Edward N. Zalta, http://plato.stanford.edu/archives/spr2006/entries/existentialism/.

QUESTIONS FOR REFLECTION

1. Does existentialism make a good case for freedom of action? Explain your view.

2. What criticisms of existential thought would you make? How might they be responded to by its defenders?

3. Has existentialism changed your life? In what way(s)? If not, why not?

4. Is existentialism a kind of perennial philosophy as Max Charlesworth contends? Carefully explain your answer.

5. On which contemporary movement(s) of thought do you see existentialism as having the most influence and why?

APPENDIX A

NOTHINGNESS

"If by 'abyss' we understand a great depth, is not man's heart an abyss? . . . Do not you believe that there is in man a deep so profound as to be hidden even from him in whom it is?"[1]

*   *   *

"For, after all, what is man in nature? A nothing compared to the infinite, a whole compared to the nothing, a middle point between all and nothing."[2]

*   *   *

"Dasein is an entity which does not just occur among other entities. Rather it is ontically distinguished by the fact that, in its very Being, that Being is an *issue* for it."[3]

*   *   *

"Where shall we seek the nothing? . . . In order to find something must we not already know in general that it is there?"[4]

*   *   *

"Without the original revelation of the nothing, no selfhood and no freedom."[5]

*   *   *

"Why are there beings at all, and why not rather nothing?"[6]

*   *   *

"Nothingness lies coiled in the heart of being—like a worm."[7]

*   *   *

"If man, as the existentialist conceives him, is indefinable, it is because at first he is nothing. Only afterward will he be something, and he himself will have made what he will be."[8]

*   *   *

"Anxiety is precisely my consciousness of being my own future, in the mode of not-being."[9]

*   *   *

"Nothing that happens to a man is ever natural, since his presence calls the world into question."[10]

*   *   *

"Nothing is more real than nothing."[11]

*   *   *

"That which arouses anxiety is nothing, and it is nowhere."[12]

*   *   *

"Man is an inexhaustible abyss."[13]

NOTES

1. St. Augustine, *An Augustine Synthesis*, ed. E. Przywara (New York, 1958), p. 421. Cited by John Macquarrie, *Existentialism: An Introduction, Guide, and Assessment* (London: Penguin, 1973), p. 47.

2. Blaise Pascal, *Pensées*, rev. ed., trans. A.J. Krailsheimer (London: Penguin, 1995), p. 61.

3. Martin Heidegger, *Being and Time*, trans. John Macquarrie and Edward Robinson (Oxford: Blackwell, 1967), sec. 4.

4. Martin Heidegger, "What Is Metaphysics?" trans. David Farrell Krell, in *Martin Heidegger: Basic Writings from "Being and Time" [1927] to "The Task of Thinking" [1964]*, rev. exp. ed. (San Francisco: HarperSanFrancisco, 1993), p. 98 (emphasis in original).

5. Ibid., p. 103.

6. Ibid., p. 110.

7. Jean-Paul Sartre, *Being and Nothingness: An Essay in Phenomenological Ontology*, trans. Hazel E. Barnes (New York: Philosophical Library, 1956), 21.

8. Jean-Paul Sartre, *Existentialism Is a Humanism*, trans. Bernard Frechtman and reprinted under the title *Existentialism*, in *Existentialism and Human Emotions* (New York: Citadel Press/Kensington, 1987), p. 15.

9. Sartre, *Being and Nothingness*, p. 32.

10. Simone de Beauvoir (original source unknown).

11. Samuel Beckett, cited by William Barrett, *Irrational Man: A Study in Existential Philosophy* (Garden City, NY: Anchor Books/Doubleday, 1962), p. 283.

12. Macquarrie, *Existentialism*, p. 168.

13. Ibid., p. 243.

APPENDIX B

MEANING

(1)

If the existentialists are right in saying that there is no fixed human nature, only a human condition, then it seems to follow that we are free to find our own meaning in life. Indeed (they would argue) we have no other choice, if any meaning at all is to be found. Atheistic, theistic, and non-aligned existentialists would agree: There are no ready-made answers.

But if we are beings who seem unable *not* to seek for and find meaning in life, then perhaps we have some kind of nature after all. At least it's difficult to see what the difference is between saying (a) that we are "condemned to be free" and are meaning givers; and (b) that there is a universal human nature.

Perhaps this issue will remain unresolved; however, what we *can* say is that for existentialists there are no fixed horizons to a human life, or to human life in general. We are extremely malleable creatures—not in the sense that outside forces can control and mold us, but in the much more interesting sense that we can fashion ourselves according to our own image of what we want to be.

280

How do we go about doing this? Our thinkers all agree that what counts, what constitutes our sense of value and worth, is just the daily process of working out a life for ourselves with certain goals in mind. The empowerment we receive from seeing things go well and from learning from our setbacks and sorrows—these are the experiences that shape our understanding of life. We either renew or change ourselves in relation to them.

This is a simple truth, and it may seem all too obvious and disappointing when what we are looking for is something profound. We may feel cheated. But the elements of everyday life contain as much mystery, surprise, and depth of significance as we could possibly hope for if we but tune in carefully and pay heed to them. Maybe we can also find meaning in making the world a better place, to whatever extent we are able.

Perhaps this is the central message of existentialism (as well as of Buddhism and Daoism): that just attending to the rhythms of living can teach us everything we need to know.

*   *   *

(2)

Viktor Frankl (1905–97) was an Austrian psychiatrist and a Holocaust survivor, who in his work applied many of the ideas of existentialism. Frankl created a branch of psychiatry he called "logotherapy," based on the search for basic meaning in life. In the Nazi concentration camp environment he came to realize a piece of existential wisdom for himself, and he also taught it to despairing inmates:

> Life ultimately means taking the responsibility to find the right answer to its problems and to fulfil the tasks which it constantly sets for the individual.
>
> These tasks, and therefore the meaning of life, differ from man to man, and from moment to moment. Thus it is impossible to define the meaning of life in a general way. Questions about the meaning of life can never be answered by sweeping statements. "Life" does not mean something vague, but something very real and concrete, just as life's tasks are also very real and concrete. They form man's destiny, which is different and unique for each individual. . . .[1]

Accordingly, the pursuit of meaning is not an exercise in intellectual construction but rather a response to life's questioning of us. Meaning is personal, individually shaped, contextual, and situational. The sense of meaning undergoes change over time, but generally we build up meaning rather than lose it if our lives are functioning well. Suffering and facing death are occasions for the discovery of meaning, as they are experiences that are unique to each of us.

Frankl believed that the "will to meaning" (or to find meaning) is the most fundamental human drive because if one gives up on the search for meaning, or finds life devoid of meaning, then living becomes impossible and death will likely not be far away.

NOTE

1. Viktor Frankl, *Man's Search for Meaning: An Introduction to Logotherapy* (New York: Washington Square Press, 1963), pp. 122–23.

APPENDIX C

ALIENATION

Hegel first introduced the term "alienation" or "estrangement" (German: *Entfremdung*) into philosophy in order to describe a regular—indeed essential—feature of change, which he understood or interpreted *dialectically*. From this perspective, the world is composed of forces, counterforces, and contradictory tendencies that vie with each other for supremacy. Ideas, schools of thought, and historical and political trends not only struggle for supremacy, but also turn into their opposites when analyzed carefully, or as time goes by. These opposites, which had been dormant potentialities at first, may emerge quickly or slowly, but now stand forth in relation to the original idea, position, or trend as a hostile force, a threatening and foreign "other." Progressive movement or creative, dynamic change occurs, however, only if and when this alien other is confronted and overcome, and it is only overcome when its "otherness" is subsumed or incorporated into a new, "higher" result. Dialectical processes of this nature energize all developments in the world.[1]

Hegel applies his theory of dialectical change not just to abstract events and entities but also to human beings and, in this context, he argues that it is *an act of the self* that causes alienation, that all alienation

283

within individual experience is in fact *self-alienation.* And it follows that alienation must be removed or mitigated by means of the self's own *labor.*[2] Through its own activity, a resolution is found, for example, when one finds a less conflict-ridden, more complete and satisfying way of life, outlook, or place in society.

Since Hegel's time, alienation has come to the fore as a major concept; it is even invoked to characterize the age in which we live ("the age of alienation"). This is largely owing to the early writings of Marx (*Economic and Philosophical Manuscripts of 1844*), who refined and developed Hegel's idea, and to the existentialists, who addressed the phenomenon in their various writings.

Alienation, following Hegel, is generally taken to refer both to a certain sort of conscious (subjective) experience and to a state of affairs in the world. In the first sense, it refers to things like loss of a sense of creativity or productivity, passive experience of oneself in the face of larger forces, loss of identity or relatedness to things and other people, dehumanization, feelings of worthlessness, and so on. One experiences oneself as an object, merely acted upon and controlled by external factors. Alienation, in this sense, has been defined (by psychiatrist Erich Fromm) as "a loss of the integrative power of the personality."[3] In the second sense, "alienation" (or "alienated") refers to the condition of detachment, or the relationship or state of affairs that produces the feeling of being undermined, estranged, or rendered ineffective. It also signifies the attribution of a certain property to something or someone, made by another observer (for instance, "Today's youth are alienated," "Assembly line work is alienating," and, more controversially, "You're alienated whether or not you feel you are.")

For Marx, the term "alienation" embraced several aspects of life in the industrial era. He thought that the worker in capitalist society is dehumanized and therefore alienated in several ways: (a) from the products of her or his labor; (b) in the act of production itself (this is self-alienation as a subjective experience); (c) from "species-life" (that is, human nature); (d) from other humans; and (e) from nature itself (because of the "unnatural" kind of work being performed). Not only is alienation present in the productive process and the relationships that it spawns, it is also a feature of the "fetishism of commodities" and the way in which money takes on a life of its own (becomes "reified," or materialized into an independent and powerful force), draining everything else of value. Marx held, in addition, that religion projects an alienated or distorted form of human nature into the concept of God, which then dominates and rules over us.

Note that the capitalist, for Marx, is likewise alienated in several of the same respects (particularly [c], [d], and [e] above). Alienation infects all sides of relationships under capitalism. But Marx did believe that alienation could be overcome once and for all. Hegel and the existentialists maintain, however, that it is rooted in the human condition.

NOTES

1. See G. W. F. Hegel, *Lectures on the Philosophy of World History: Introduction—Reason in History*, trans. H. B. Nisbet (Cambridge: Cambridge University Press, 1980).

2. See G. W. F. Hegel, *The Phenomenology of Spirit*, trans. A. V. Miller (Oxford: Clarendon Press, 1977).

3. See Erich Fromm, Introduction, *Marx's Concept of Man* (New York: Ungar, 1966).

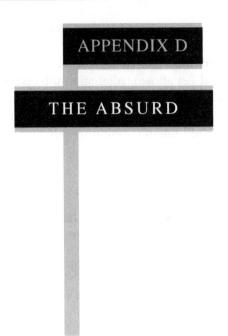

APPENDIX D

THE ABSURD

When we say that something is "absurd," what do we mean? We may mean any one or more of the following: that it is without reason, contrary to reason, beyond reason, meaningless, ridiculous, laughable, or impossible. Camus claimed that "at any streetcorner the feeling of absurdity can strike any man in the face."[1] In the "theater of the absurd" movement of the 1940s to 1960s, playwrights such as Adamov, Beckett, Ionesco, Genet, Pinter, and Albee sought to "convey their sense of bewilderment, anxiety, and wonder in the face of an inexplicable universe."[2] These writers put into practice the ideas of Camus, who is generally credited with being their inspiration.

According to Camus, "There is but one truly serious philosophical problem, and that is suicide. Judging whether life is or is not worth living amounts to answering the fundamental question of philosophy."[3] With these very dramatic words, he posited that the job of philosophy is to help us find meaning in existence and, consequent upon this, value in living. But for Camus, this process is one of thinking and feeling joined together, and it must inevitably unfold against the backdrop of a universe that is mute in response to our questionings and fundamental yearnings.

While Camus is the modern proponent of philosophical absurdism, the issues that drive it go back much further in time. Skepticism about knowledge, the scope and limits of philosophy, whether God exists, whether there is an afterlife, and whether there is any purpose in the scheme of things have as long a history as recorded human thought. Tertullian (c. 155–240), an early Christian church father of note from Carthage, described his faith in these famous words: "It is to be believed because it is absurd" and "it is certain because it is impossible."[4] While these mottos represent a frontal attack on rationality, they were evidently meant not to put an end to trustworthy belief and our sense of meaning but rather to shift us away from reason to faith. A similar doctrine was espoused nearly two centuries later by St. Augustine.[5] Kierkegaard picks up on this approach after almost a millennium and a half pass by, maintaining that Christianity is paradoxical and contradictory (and therefore "offensive") because it centers on the eternal God coming into finite existence in the person of Jesus. "This contradiction is the absurd, which can only be believed," asserts the pseudonymous author of one of his works, adding, much later in his discourse, that what makes being a Christian especially difficult is the need "for every human being to relinquish his understanding and his thinking and to concentrate his soul on the absurd. . . ."[6] Not everyone shares this perspective on Christianity, of course. But these authors have succeeded in laying down the gauntlet: If you do interpret Christianity in this way, then either you must take the religion on board despite its absurdity or you must reject it as nonsensical.

Is the absurdity of life to be denied, despaired over, or perhaps just accepted? Thomas Nagel has argued, under Camus' influence, that the sense of the absurd is a fact about us as much as it is a fact about the universe. That being admitted, he thinks the proper attitude to life is one of ironic acceptance, rather than Camus' stance of noble defiance, which Nagel regards as "romantic and slightly self-pitying."[7] Pascal would recommend a good dose of humility in addition. Whether the absurd haunts us constantly, as some philosophers hold, or only visits us intermittently, it seems to be an unavoidable dimension of existence.

NOTES

1. Albert Camus, *The Myth of Sisyphus and Other Essays*, trans. Justin O'Brien (New York: Vintage Books/Random House, 1959), p. 9.

2. *Grolier Multimedia Encyclopedia*, extract viewed at Crabb, Jerome P., "Theatre of the Absurd," Theatre Database, September 3, 2006, http://www.theatre database.com/20th_century/theatre_of_the_absurd.html.

3. Camus, *Myth of Sisyphus*, p. 3.

4. Tertullian (Quintus Septimius Florens Tertullianus), *De Carne Christi*, 5.

5. St. Augustine, *Confessions*, vol. 1, bk. 5, 1, ch. 5.

6. Søren Kierkegaard, *Concluding Unscientific Postscript to "Philosophical Fragments,"* trans. Howard V. Hong and Edna H. Hong (Princeton, NJ: Princeton University Press, 1992), vol. 1, pp. 211, 557.

7. Thomas Nagel, "The Absurd," *Journal of Philosophy* 68 (1971): 716–27.

APPENDIX E

ANGST/ANXIETY/ANGUISH

In *An Introduction to Existentialism,* philosopher Robert Olson defines three types or dimensions of the anxiety that, according to the existentialists, is a principal feature of the human condition.[1] His useful classification may be summarized as follows.

1. "The anguish of being." We exist in the face of nothingness and in full awareness of the radical contingency of everything in the world, everything that happens, and especially ourselves. We find ourselves in a human environment shot through with irrationalities and in a universe that not only surpasses our comprehension but also often seems hostile to our purposes.

2. "Anguish before the here and now." Human existence is transitory and our situation cannot be escaped or transcended in thought, but only confronted. There is sometimes a sense of unreality about all this. Becoming, change, flux, and instability are the ultimate principles of the universe, and any view to the contrary is a fantasy of denial.

3. "The anguish of freedom." Each of us is a self-making entity, having the burden of choosing for her- or himself and of discovering meaning in existence. There are no certainties to guide us and no guarantees of success in life. We must reaffirm who we are at every moment and constantly strive for what we believe in.

Psychiatrist Irvin Yalom draws upon clinical observations and existential philosophy in order to construct an account of the origins of anxiety.[2] He sees it as stemming from four factors: (1) fear of death; (2) a sense of groundlessness in existence; (3) feelings of isolation; and (4) a sense of life's inherent meaninglessness. These are not necessarily pathological symptoms (though they may become so if they are not dealt with, and therefore become obsessions). Rather, they are the parameters of awareness that we all share.

NOTES

1. Robert G. Olson, *An Introduction to Existentialism* (New York: Dover, 1962).
2. Irvin D. Yalom, *Existential Psychotherapy* (New York: Basic Books, 1980).

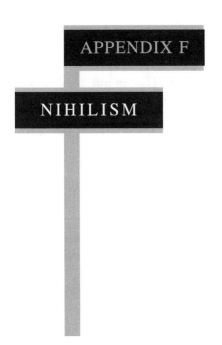

APPENDIX F

NIHILISM

The word "nihilism" derives originally from the Latin *nihil* ("nothing"), and many meanings of the term have evolved over time. To some, it labels any wholesale pattern of disrespect for people and/or of destructive behavior. To others, it suggests an entrenched attitude of negativism and world-weariness. But it also has more refined meanings in philosophy, as we shall see in a moment.

Historically, nihilism is linked to a Russian social and political movement of the nineteenth century. Your initial reaction might be to think of "Russian roulette," a dangerous game played by those whose lives are surely in disarray or in desperate straits. But this would be a mistake. Originally a species of radical thought in the decades leading up to the Russian Revolution of 1917, the nihilist stance featured several doctrines, such as opposition to religion, the state, and tradition, and also endorsed a not too well thought out materialist metaphysics. Its adherents promoted a rationally and scientifically planned, secular, maximally free, egalitarian society. Nihilists were young activists who believed it was necessary to sweep the way clear in order to build a better future, and this meant getting rid of old values, practices, and institutions. Over time, nihilism in Russia and elsewhere in Europe degenerated into a destructive, violent, aimless impulse, often (though wrongly) identified with anarchism and atheism.

Philosophically, nihilism has a long history, which stems from ancient Greek skepticism in its most extreme forms. This brand of skepticism decrees that the world and all of its features are impenetrable by the human intellect. The basic type of nihilism is *epistemological* in character: the view that nothing can be known and that truth is a myth. It follows that all efforts to communicate are doomed to failure, since these depend on the stability provided by things' being known and true. Next comes *axiological* nihilism: the claim that no values have any foundation, or that nothing has any value. Even if there were some genuine form of knowledge, it would not suffice to support any value judgments. This position entails that nothing is either good or bad, right or wrong, beautiful or ugly, and so on. Following closely on axiological nihilism is *political* nihilism, which denies the validity of any political outlook, institution, or way of life. *Cosmic* nihilism posits that the universe is wholly absurd, unintelligible, and either indifferent or hostile to human purposes. Finally, the despairing claim that life has no meaning, point, value, or justification is often identified as *existential* nihilism. We have to be especially careful here, however, for, as I argue throughout this book, existentialism is a concerted attempt to combat nihilism and move beyond it. So "existential" will be taken here in the same way that any interpretation of existence would come under this heading, and *not* as a reference to existentialism proper.

Common to all types of philosophical nihilism just distinguished is that they offer no hope for remediation or, indeed, any ideas of a positive sort by which to reassess or rebuild what they target for demolition. It will be readily understood that these philosophical forms of nihilism cannot be refuted, since they effectively demolish any grounds on which an argument against them could rest. They do this by announcing in advance that every consideration that could be brought to bear is invalid from the start. By the same token, however, it can be argued that the varieties of nihilism are *self-refuting* because there are no grounds left on which nihilists can base their own claims.

Many think that in our postmodern age, nihilism is a pervasive influence. If so, then this is worrisome because nihilism has always proved difficult for philosophy to deal with for the reasons just indicated. But as Nietzsche, Heidegger, and Camus all realized in different ways, the challenge of nihilism must be met somehow if we are to carry on with vision and at least some degree of optimism for the future. And perhaps the best response to it is, as the Russians themselves advised, to sweep the way clear for a new cultural beginning.

APPENDIX G

A PROBLEM ABOUT CONSCIOUSNESS

There is a problem about whether, in being self-aware, consciousness is an intentional object for itself. If it is, then does this entail that there is a secondary act of consciousness that is aware of the first (and a third that is aware of the second, and so on to infinity)? This is clearly an undesirable outcome. If I am thinking, for example, about the abstract question of what consciousness is or what the word "consciousness" means, then consciousness, as a conceptual entity, is, of course, the intentional object of my act of thinking. But what about when I am just being aware of something? Even if this act, like all other acts of consciousness, is assumed to be self-directed (i.e., there is always a consciousness of consciousness going on when I am conscious of something), does this necessarily make consciousness itself an intentional object?

Phenomenologists have much debated this issue. Brentano thought that "every act [of consciousness] . . . is an awareness of itself" (and Sartre agrees). "This awareness does not consist in a second mental act, but consists of the act itself," continues Brentano. However, another theorist disagrees, claiming that if I hear something, for instance, then according to Brentano's account, "there is a *hearing* of a *hearing*! It seems quite evident to me that one cannot hear one's acts of hearing." This critic therefore arrives at the conclusion that "no mental act is ever its own object, not even an act of awareness. . . . [Hence,] it is not true that a mind is aware of every act which occurs in it."[1] Yet we may question why being aware of one's act of hearing must itself constitute an act of hearing, thereby leading to the absurdity set up by this critic. Perhaps acts of consciousness are just more complex than is being allowed for. Perhaps the self-awareness component is just a background accompaniment to each act of consciousness—end of story. This solution would seemingly create the need for a revised doctrine of intentionality, however, according to which at least one activity of consciousness has no intentional object.

NOTE

1. Reinhardt Grossmann, *Phenomenology and Existentialism: An Introduction* (London: Routledge & Kegan Paul, 1984), pp. 52, 53.

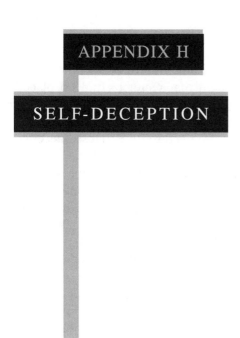

APPENDIX H

SELF-DECEPTION

Most philosophers who have discussed self-deception view it according to the following model: knowing X and at the same time believing not-X (or vice versa). The puzzle arises from our apparent inability to describe such a state of affairs coherently, since knowing X entails believing X to be the case. Well, then, *can* a person believe and disbelieve the same thing simultaneously? One commentator has pointed out that "logic prevents [contradictory beliefs] from both being true, but not from both being held."[1] Is it just, then, that self-deceivers for some reason believe both X and not-X simultaneously, however illogical it may be to do so? No, because there is more going on here than this approach alone can explain.

Freud's account of self-deception appealed to his notion of "the unconscious"—a hidden system of mental states and maneuvers. What went on there could, he thought, be quite different from (and, indeed, contradictory to) what goes on in normal consciousness. The trouble with this hypothesis is that it makes it very difficult to capture the apparent *purposiveness* of self-deception. Even in Freud's terms, self-deception was aimed at protecting one from the truth, from harmful thoughts, impulses to commit immoral or illegal actions, and so on. Purposiveness is the element missing in the "believing both X and not-X" view with which we began, and it is also the key ingredient that seems to find no place in Freud's somewhat mechanical explanation hinging on events in the unconscious.

Where do we go from here? First, we need to note that self-deception is not a matter of entertaining beliefs that conflict so much as it is one of conflict between overtly expressed intentions and beliefs, on the one hand, and unavowed or disavowed emotions, desires, wishes, and impulses, on the other. Herbert Fingarette proposes to make sense of this kind of conflict with a new theory of consciousness, according to which consciousness is an active process and a skill he calls "spelling-out." To spell-out "is to make . . . explicit . . . the particular features of an individual's engagement in the world. . . ."[2] Because this is a skill, a person can be better or worse at it but, more importantly, in the case of self-deception, she or he can adopt a "tacit policy" not to spell-out experiences.[3]

Fingarette's clever suggestion does succeed in exhibiting self-deception as something purposive but, unfortunately, it leaves us to ponder whether self-deception really goes on consciously, unconsciously, or as a combination of the two because to label self-deception as a "tacit" activity hints at its occurrence outside of awareness.

At this point, it becomes clear that Sartre's analysis of "bad faith," despite its complexities and enigmatic character, has a certain advantage; for Sartre maintains that we always know what is going on in our consciousness—things can't hide there, and there's nowhere else (such as the unconscious) for them to hide either. Therefore, all we can do is choose (in bad faith, as he says) to disregard or be inattentive to some things in consciousness and not others. But we can't escape from the responsibility for doing this or for any outcome that results.

It may be that what is needed is a combination of Sartre's and Fingarette's views. When a person is being self-deceiving, we (as common-sense observers of human behavior) normally discover this, not by examining the structure of her or his belief system, the evidence available to her or him, and so forth, but rather by noticing discrepancies between overt expressions of belief, feeling, desire, intention, or motivation and the subject's consciously stated or acted-out versions of these same things. Hence, we might indeed suspect that self-deception is a tendency resulting from the purposive (and therefore culpable) refusal to do that which can be described, not too imperfectly, as performing certain acts of self-disclosure.

NOTES

1. David Pugmire, "'Strong' Self-Deception," *Inquiry* 12 (1969): 344.

2. Herbert Fingarette, *Self-Deception* (New York: Humanities Press, 1969), pp. 39, 40.

3. Ibid., p. 48.

BIBLIOGRAPHY

ANTHOLOGIES OF EXISTENTIAL PHILOSOPHY AND PHENOMENOLOGY

Friedman, Maurice, ed. *The Worlds of Existentialism: A Critical Reader*. New York: Random House, 1964. Reprinted Amherst, NY: Humanity Books, 1991.

Gordon, Lewis R., ed. *Existence in Black: An Anthology of Black Existential Philosophy*. New York: Routledge, 1996.

Guignon, Charles, ed. *The Existentialists*. Lanham, MD: Rowman and Littlefield, 2004.

Guignon, Charles, and Derk Pereboom, eds. *Existentialism: Basic Writings*. 2nd ed. Indianapolis: Hackett, 2001.

Langiulli, Nino, ed. *European Existentialism*. Piscataway, NJ: Transaction, 1997.

Luper, Steven. *Existing: An Introduction to Existentialist Thought*. New York: McGraw-Hill, 1999.

MacDonald, Paul S., ed. *The Existentialist Reader: An Anthology of Key Texts*. New York: Routledge, 2001.

Marino, Gordon, ed. *Basic Writings of Existentialism*. New York: Modern Library/Random House, 2004.

Moran, Dermot, and Timothy Mooney, eds. *The Phenomenology Reader*. Oxford: Oneworld, 2002.

Oaklander, L. Nathan. *Existentialist Philosophy: An Introduction*. 2nd ed. Upper Saddle River, NJ: Prentice Hall, 1996.

Raymond, Diane Barsoum. *Existentialism and the Philosophical Tradition.* Upper Saddle River, NJ: Prentice Hall, 1998.

Solomon, Robert C., ed. *Existentialism.* 2nd ed. New York: Oxford, 2004.

———, ed. *Phenomenology and Existentialism.* 2nd ed. Lanham, MD: Rowman and Littlefield, 2001.

GENERAL WORKS ON EXISTENTIALISM, PHENOMENOLOGY, AND RELATED TOPICS

Barnes, Hazel E. *An Existentialist Ethics.* 2nd ed. Chicago: University of Chicago Press, 1978.

Barnes, Julian. *Nothing to Be Frightened Of.* New York: Knopf, 2008.

———. *Humanistic Existentialism: The Literature of Possibility.* Lincoln: University of Nebraska Press, 1959.

Barrett, William. *Irrational Man: A Study in Existential Philosophy.* Garden City, NY: Anchor Books/Doubleday, 1962.

Batchelor, Stephen. *Alone with Others: An Existential Approach to Buddhism.* New York: Grove Press, 1983.

Becker, Carol S. *Living and Relating: An Introduction to Phenomenology.* Newbury Park, CA: Sage, 1992.

Blackmore, Susan. *Consciousness: A Very Short Introduction.* New York: Oxford University Press, 2005.

Brosman, Catharine Savage. *Literary Topics: Existential Fiction.* Belmont, CA: Thomson Gale, 2000.

Carroll, John. *The Existential Jesus.* Carlton North, AU: Scribe, 2007.

Cerbone, David R. *Understanding Phenomenology.* Stocksfield, UK: Acumen, 2006.

Chalmers, David J. *The Conscious Mind: In Search of a Fundamental Theory.* New ed. New York: Oxford University Press, 1997.

Clarke, Randolph. *Libertarian Accounts of Free Will.* New York: Oxford University Press, 2003.

Collins, James. *The Existentialists: A Critical Study.* Chicago: Henry Regnery, 1952.

Cooper, David E. *Existentialism: A Reconstruction.* 2nd ed. Oxford: Blackwell, 1999.

Cotkin, George. *Existential America.* Baltimore: Johns Hopkins University Press, 2003.

Crosby, Donald A. *The Specter of the Absurd: Sources and Criticisms of Modern Nihilism.* Albany: State University of New York Press, 1988.

Daigle, Christine, ed. *Existentialist Thinkers and Ethics.* Montreal: McGill-Queen's University Press, 2006.

Detmer, David. *Freedom as a Value.* La Salle, IL: Open Court, 1986.

Earnshaw, Steven. *Existentialism: A Guide for the Perplexed.* New York: Continuum International, 2007.

Elliott, Anthony. *Concepts of the Self.* 2nd ed. Malden, MA: Polity Press, 2007.

Flynn, Thomas. *Existentialism: A Very Short Introduction.* Oxford: Oxford University Press, 2006.

Golomb, Jacob J. *In Search of Authenticity: Existentialism from Kierkegaard to Camus.* New York: Routledge, 1995.

Gordon, Haim, ed. *Dictionary of Existentialism.* Westport, CT: Greenwood Press, 1999.

Gordon, Lewis R. *Existentia Africana: Understanding African Existentialist Thought.* New York: Routledge, 2000.

Grossman, Reinhardt. *Phenomenology and Existentialism: An Introduction.* London: Routledge & Kegan Paul, 1984.

Guignon, Charles. *The Existentialists: Critical Essays on Kierkegaard, Nietzsche, Heidegger, and Sartre.* Lanham, MD: Rowman and Littlefield, 2004.

Hammond, M., J. Howarth, and R. Keat. *Understanding Phenomenology.* Oxford: Blackwell, 1991.

Harper, Ralph. *The Existential Experience.* Baltimore: Johns Hopkins University Press, 1972.

Kane, Robert. *A Contemporary Introduction to Free Will.* New York: Oxford University Press, 2005.

Koenig, Thomas R. *Existentialism and Human Existence: An Account of Five Major Philosophers.* 2 vols. Malabar, FL: Krieger, 1997.

Lee, Sander H. *Eighteen Woody Allen Films Analyzed: Anguish, God and Existentialism.* Jefferson, NC: McFarland, 2002.

Lingis, Alphonso. *The First Person Singular.* Evanston, IL: Northwestern University Press, 2007.

Luijpen, William A., and Henry J. Koren. *A First Introduction to Existentialism.* Pittsburgh: Duquesne University Press, 1969.

Luper, Steven. *Existing: An Introduction to Existentialist Thought.* New York: McGraw-Hill, 1999.

Macquarrie, John. *Existentialism: An Introduction, Guide and Assessment.* London: Penguin, 1973.

Matthews, Eric. *Merleau-Ponty: A Guide for the Perplexed.* New York: Continuum International, 2008.

McFee, Graham. *Free Will.* Stocksfield, UK: Acumen, 2000.

Meyerson, George. *Teach Yourself 101 Key Ideas: Existentialism.* New York: McGraw-Hill, 2001.

Michelman, Stephen. *Historical Dictionary of Existentialism.* Lanham, MD: Scarecrow Press, 2008.

Molina, Fernando. *Existentialism as Philosophy.* Englewood Cliffs, NJ: Prentice Hall, 1962.

Moran, Dermot. *Introduction to Phenomenology.* New York: Routledge, 2000.

Novak, Michael. *The Experience of Nothingness.* Rev. exp. ed. Piscataway, NJ: Transaction, 1997.

Olafson, Frederick A. *Principles and Persons: An Ethical Interpretation of Existentialism.* Baltimore: Johns Hopkins University Press, 1967.

Panza, Christopher, and Gregory Gale. *Existentialism for Dummies*. Hoboken, NJ: Wiley, 2008.

Park, James Leonard. *Our Existential Predicament: Loneliness, Depression, Anxiety, and Death*. 4th ed. Minneapolis: Existential Books, 2001.

Patrik, Linda E. *Existential Literature: An Introduction*. Belmont, CA: Wadsworth, 2000.

Pink, James Leonard. *Free Will: A Very Short Introduction*. New York: Oxford University Press, 2004.

Reynolds, Jack. *Understanding Existentialism*. Stocksfield, UK: Acumen, 2006.

Scarre, Geoffrey. *Death*. Stocksfield, UK: Acumen, 2007.

Schrag, Calvin O. *Existence and Freedom*. Evanston, IL: Northwestern University Press, 1961.

Sokolowski, Robert. *Introduction to Phenomenology*. Cambridge: Cambridge University Press, 2000.

———. *Phenomenology of the Human Person*. New York: Cambridge University Press, 2008.

Solomon, Robert C. *Introducing the Existentialists: Imaginary Dialogues with Sartre, Heidegger, and Camus*. Indianapolis: Hackett, 1981.

Sprigge, Timothy. *Theories of Existence*. Harmondsworth, UK: Penguin, 1984.

Tanzer, Mark. *On Existentialism*. Belmont, CA: Wadsworth, 2006.

Velmans, Max. *Understanding Consciousness*. 2nd ed. New York: Routledge, 2009.

Velmans, Max, and Susan Schneider, eds. *The Blackwell Companion to Consciousness*. Malden, MA: Wiley Blackwell, 2007.

Wahl, Jean. *Philosophies of Existence*. Trans. F. M. Lory. New York: Schocken, 1969.

Wartenberg, Thomas E. *Existentialism: A Beginner's Guide*. Oxford: Oneworld, 2008.

Wild, John Daniel. *The Challenge of Existentialism*. Bloomington: Indiana University Press, 1963. Reprinted Westport, CT: Greenwood Press, 1979.

Woelfel, James. *The Existentialist Legacy and Other Essays in Philosophy and Religion*. Lanham, MD: University Press of America, 2006.

Wrathall, Mark A., and Hubert L. Dreyfus, eds. *A Companion to Phenomenology and Existentialism*. Oxford: Blackwell, 2006.

Yalom, Irvin D. *Staring at the Sun: Overcoming the Terror of Death*. San Francisco: Jossey-Boss, 2008.

Young, Julian. *The Death of God and the Meaning of Life*. New York: Routledge, 2003.

BOOKS BY AND ABOUT KIERKEGAARD

Kierkegaard, Søren. *Concluding Unscientific Postscript*. Trans. David F. Swenson and Walter Lowrie. Princeton, NJ: Princeton University Press for American-Scandinavian Foundation, 1941.

———. *Concluding Unscientific Postscript to "Philosophical Fragments."* Trans. and ed. Howard V. Hong and Edna H. Hong. Princeton, NJ: Princeton University Press, 1992.

———. *Either/Or: A Fragment of Life*. London: Penguin, 1992.

———. *The Essential Kierkegaard*. Ed. Howard V. Hong and Edna H. Hong. Princeton, NJ: Princeton University Press, 2000.

———. *Fear and Trembling*. Trans. Alastair Hannay. New York: Penguin, 2006.

———. *The Humor of Kierkegaard: An Anthology*. Ed. Thomas C. Oden. Princeton, NJ: Princeton University Press, 2004.

———. *A Kierkegaard Anthology*. Ed. Robert Bretall. New York: Modern Library/Random House, 1978.

———. *The Last Years: Journals 1853–55*. Trans. and ed. Ronald Gregor Smith. London: Fontana/Collins, 1968.

———. *Papers and Journals: A Selection*. Ed. Alistair Hannay. London: Penguin, 1996.

———. *Parables of Kierkegaard*. Ed. Thomas C. Oden. Princeton, NJ: Princeton University Press, 1978.

———. *Provocations: Spiritual Writings of Kierkegaard*. Maryknoll, NY: Orbis Books, 2003.

———. *The Soul of Kierkegaard: Selections from His Journals*. Trans. and ed. Alexander Dru. New York: Dover, 2003.

* * *

Alex, Ben. *Søren Kierkegaard: An Authentic Life—The Life and Writings of an Extraordinary Christian Philosopher*. Kelowna, BC, Canada: Northstone, 2000.

Anderson, Susan Leigh. *On Kierkegaard*. Belmont, CA: Wadsworth, 1999.

Caputo, John D. *How to Read Kierkegaard*. New York: W. W. Norton, 2007.

Carlisle, Clare. *Kierkegaard: A Guide for the Perplexed*. New York: Continuum International, 2007.

Chamberlain, Jane, ed. *The Kierkegaard Reader*. Oxford: Blackwell, 2001.

Gardiner, Patrick. *Kierkegaard: A Very Short Introduction*. Oxford: Oxford University Press, 2002.

Giles, James, ed. *Kierkegaard and Freedom*. Houndmills, Basingstoke, Hampshire, UK: Palgrave Macmillan, 2001.

Graff, Joachim. *Søren Kierkegaard: A Biography*. Trans. Bruce H. Kirmmse. Princeton, NJ: Princeton University Press, 2005.

Hannay, Alastair. *Kierkegaard*. Reprint ed. London: Routledge, 1999.

———. *Kierkegaard: A Biography*. Cambridge: Cambridge University Press, 2001.

Hannay, Alastair, and Gordon Daniel Marino, eds. *The Cambridge Companion to Kierkegaard*. Cambridge: Cambridge University Press, 1997.

Kirmmse, Bruce H., ed. *Encounters with Kierkegaard: A Life as Seen by His Contemporaries*. Trans. Bruce H. Kirmmse and Virginia R. Laursen. Princeton, NJ: Princeton University Press, 1996.

Leon, Celine, and Sylvia Walsh, eds. *Feminist Interpretations of Søren Kierkegaard*. University Park: Pennsylvania State University Press, 1997.

Lippitt, John. *Routledge Philosophy Guidebook to Kierkegaard and "Fear and Trembling."* New York: Routledge, 2003.

Marino, Gordon. *Kierkegaard in the Present Age.* Milwaukee: Marquette University Press, 2001.

Mehl, Peter J. *Thinking through Kierkegaard: Existential Identity in a Pluralistic World.* Urbana: University of Illinois Press, 2005.

Mullen, John Douglas. *Kierkegaard's Philosophy: Self-Deception and Cowardice in the Present Age.* New ed. Washington, DC: University Press of America, 1995.

O'Hara, Shelley. *Kierkegaard within Your Grasp.* Hoboken, NJ: Wiley, 2007.

Ostenfeld, Ib. *Søren Kierkegaard's Psychology.* Trans. and ed. Alastair McKinnon. Waterloo, ON: Wilfrid Laurier University Press, 1978.

Pattison, George. *The Philosophy of Kierkegaard.* Stocksfield, UK: Acumen, 2005.

Pattison, George, and Stephen Shakespeare, eds. *Kierkegaard: The Self in Society.* Houndmills, Basingstoke, Hampshire, UK: Palgrave Macmillan, 1998.

Sontag, Frederick. *A Kierkegaard Handbook.* Atlanta: John Knox Press, 1979.

Stack, George J. *Kierkegaard's Existential Ethics* (Studies in the Humanities No. 16, Philosophy). Tuscaloosa: University of Alabama Press, 1977.

Thompson, Josiah, ed. *Kierkegaard: A Collection of Critical Essays.* Garden City, NY: Anchor Books/Doubleday, 1972.

Walsh, Sylvia. *Living Christianly: Kierkegaard's Dialectic of Christian Existence.* University Park: Pennsylvania State University Press, 2005.

Watts, Michael. *Kierkegaard.* Oxford: Oneworld, 2003.

BOOKS BY AND ABOUT NIETZSCHE

Nietzsche, Friedrich. *Basic Writings of Nietzsche.* Trans. and ed. Walter Kaufmann. New York: Modern Library/Random House, 2000.

———. *Beyond Good and Evil: Prelude to a Philosophy of the Future.* Trans. Walter Kaufmann. New York: Vintage Books/Random House, 1966.

———. *Friedrich Nietzsche: Selections.* The Collector's Library of Essential Thinkers. London: CRW Publishing, 2005.

———. *The Gay Science.* Trans. Walter Kaufmann. New York: Vintage Books/Random House, 1974.

———. *Hammer of the Gods: A Friedrich Nietzsche Reader.* Rev. ed. Trans. Stephen Metcalf. Gardena, CA: Solar Books/SCB Distributors, 2007.

———. *Nietzsche.* Ed. John Richardson and Brian Leiter. New York: Oxford University Press, 2001.

———. *The Nietzsche Reader.* Ed. Keith Ansell-Pearson and Duncan Large. Oxford: Blackwell, 2006.

———. *On the Genealogy of Morals/Ecce Homo.* Trans. Walter Kaufmann. New York: Vintage Books/Random House, 1967.

———. *The Philosophy of Nietzsche.* Ed. Geoffrey Clive. New York: Meridian/Penguin, 1996.

———. *The Portable Nietzsche.* Trans. and ed. Walter Kaufmann. New York: Viking, 1954.

———. *Thus Spoke Zarathustra: A Book for Everyone and No One.* New ed. Trans. R. J. Hollingdale. London: Penguin, 1969.

———. *Twilight of the Idols/The Anti-Christ.* New ed. Trans. R. J. Hollingdale. London: Penguin, 1990.

*   *   *

Ansell-Pearson, Keith, ed. *A Companion to Nietzsche.* Malden, MA: Blackwell, 2007.

Ansell-Pearson, Keith, and Simon Critchley. *How to Read Nietzsche.* New ed. New York: W. W. Norton, 2005.

Berkowitz, Peter. *Nietzsche: The Ethics of an Immoralist.* Cambridge, MA: Harvard University Press, 1995.

Conway, Daniel. *Nietzsche's "On the Genealogy of Morals": A Reader's Guide.* New York: Continuum International, 2007.

Danto, Arthur. *Nietzsche as Philosopher.* New York: Macmillan, 1965.

Diethe, Carol. *Historical Dictionary of Nietzscheanism.* 2nd ed. Lanham, MD: Scarecrow Press, 2006.

Elsner, Gary. *Nietzsche: A Philosophical Biography.* Lanham, MD: University Press of America, 1992.

Frisch, Shelley. *Nietzsche: A Philosophical Biography.* New York: W. W. Norton, 2003.

Hill, R. Kevin. *Nietzsche: A Guide for the Perplexed.* New York: Continuum International, 2007.

Hollingdale, R. J. *Nietzsche: The Man and His Philosophy.* 2nd ed. Cambridge: Cambridge University Press, 2005.

Kaufmann, Walter. *Nietzsche: Philosopher, Psychologist, Antichrist.* 4th ed. Princeton, NJ: Princeton University Press, 1974.

Leiter, Brian. *Routledge Guide to Nietzsche on Morality.* New York: Routledge, 2002.

Magnus, Bernd, and Kathleen Higgins, eds. *The Cambridge Companion to Nietzsche.* Cambridge: Cambridge University Press, 1996.

May, Simon. *Nietzsche's Ethics and His War on "Morality."* New York: Oxford University Press, 2004.

Morgan, George A. *What Nietzsche Means.* New York: Harper Torchbooks, 1965.

Myerson, George. *"Thus Spake Zarathustra": A Beginner's Guide.* London: Hodder & Stoughton, 2001.

Nehamas, Alexander. *Nietzsche: Life as Literature.* Cambridge, MA: Harvard University Press, 1985.

Reginster, Bernard. *The Affirmation of Life: Nietzsche on Overcoming Nihilism.* Cambridge, MA: Harvard University Press, 2006.

Sarles, Harvey B. *Nietzsche's Prophecy: The Crisis in Meaning.* Amherst, NY: Humanity Books, 2001.

Seung, T. K. *Nietzsche's Epic of the Soul: "Thus Spoke Zarathustra."* Lanham, MD: Lexington Books, 2005.

Solomon, Robert C., ed. *Nietzsche: A Collection of Critical Essays.* Notre Dame, IN: University of Notre Dame Press, 1980.

Spinks, Lee. *Friedrich Nietzsche.* New York: Routledge, 2003.

Steinhart, Eric. *On Nietzsche.* Belmont, CA: Wadsworth, 1999.

Tanner, Michael. *Nietzsche: A Very Short Introduction.* New York: Oxford University Press, 2000.

Welshon, Rex. *The Philosophy of Nietzsche.* Stocksfield, UK: Acumen, 2003.

Wicks, Robert. *Nietzsche.* New ed. Oxford: Oneworld, 2007.

Zeitlin, Irving M. *Nietzsche: Re-examination.* Cambridge: Polity Press, 1994.

BOOKS BY AND ABOUT HEIDEGGER

Heidegger, Martin. *Martin Heidegger: Basic Writings: From "Being and Time" (1927) to "The Task of Thinking" (1964).* Rev. exp. ed. Ed. David Farrell Krell. New York: HarperCollins, 1993.

———. *Being and Time.* Trans. John Macquarrie and Edward Robinson. Oxford: Blackwell, 1967.

———. *Being and Time.* Trans. Joan Stambaugh. Albany: State University of New York Press, 1996.

———. *Discourse on Thinking.* Trans. John M. Anderson and E. Hans Freund. New York: Harper Torchbooks, 1966.

*   *   *

Cerbone, David R. *Heidegger: A Guide for the Perplexed.* New York: Continuum International, 2006.

Clark, Timothy. *Martin Heidegger.* New York: Routledge, 2001.

Dreyfus, Hubert. *Being-in-the-Wold: A Commentary on Heidegger's "Being and Time."* Cambridge, MA: MIT Press, 1990.

Gelven, Michael. *A Commentary on Heidegger's "Being and Time."* New York: Harper Torchbooks, 1970.

Gorner, Paul. *Heidegger's "Being and Time": An Introduction.* Cambridge: Cambridge University Press, 2007.

Guignon, Charles. *On Being Authentic.* New York: Routledge, 2004.

———, ed. *The Cambridge Companion to Heidegger.* 2nd ed. Cambridge: Cambridge University Press, 2006.

Harman, Graham. *Heidegger Explained: From Phenomenon to Thing.* Chicago: Open Court, 2007.

Hodge, Joanna. *Heidegger and Ethics.* New York: Routledge, 1995.

Inwood, Michael. *Heidegger: A Short Introduction.* New ed. New York: Oxford University Press, 2002.

Johnson, Patricia. *On Heidegger.* Belmont, CA: Wadsworth, 1999.

King, Magda. *A Guide to Heidegger's "Being and Time."* Albany: State University of New York Press, 2001.

McDonough, Richard M. *Martin Heidegger's "Being and Time."* New York: Peter Lang, 2006.

Mulhall, Stephen. *Routledge Philosophy Guidebook to Heidegger and "Being and Time."* New York: Routledge, 2005.

Olafson, Frederick A. *What Is a Human Being? A Heideggerian View.* Cambridge: Cambridge University Press, 2002.

Pattison, George. *Routledge Philosophy Guidebook to the Later Heidegger.* New York: Routledge, 2000.

Polt, Richard F. H. *Heidegger: An Introduction.* Ithaca, NY: Cornell University Press, 1999.

Safranski, Rüdiger. *Martin Heidegger: Between Good and Evil.* Trans. Ewald Osers. Cambridge, MA: Harvard University Press, 1999.

Smith, Bruce Gregory. *Martin Heidegger: Paths Taken, Paths Opened.* Lanham, MD: Rowman and Littlefield, 2006.

Vallega-Neu, Daniela. *Heidegger's "Contributions to Philosophy": An Introduction.* Bloomington: Indiana University Press, 2003.

White, Carol J. *Time and Death: Heidegger's Analysis of Finitude.* Aldershot, Hampshire: Ashgate, 2005.

Wrathall, Mark A. *How to Read Heidegger.* New York: W. W. Norton, 2006.

Wrathall, Mark A., and Hubert L. Dreyfus, eds. *A Companion to Heidegger.* New ed. Malden, MA: Blackwell, 2007.

Young, Julian. *Heidegger's Later Philosophy.* Cambridge: Cambridge University Press, 2001.

BOOKS BY AND ABOUT SARTRE

Sartre, Jean-Paul. *Being and Nothingness: An Essay on Phenomenological Ontology.* Trans. Hazel E. Barnes. New York: Philosophical Library, 1956. Reprinted New York: Routledge, 2003.

———. *Existentialism and Human Emotions.* New York: Citadel Press/Kensington, 1987. (Includes *Existentialism Is a Humanism* under the title *Existentialism.*)

———. *Existentialism Is a Humanism; Including a Commentary on "The Stranger."* Trans. Carol Macomber. New Haven, CT: Yale University Press, 2007.

———. *Jean-Paul Sartre: Basic Writings.* Ed. Stephen Priest. New York: Routledge, 2001.

———. *Notebooks for an Ethics.* Trans. David Pellauer. Chicago: University of Chicago Press, 1992.

———. *The Philosophy of Jean-Paul Sartre.* Ed. Robert Denoon Cumming. New York: Modern Library/Random House, 1966.

*   *   *

Bernasconi, Robert. *How to Read Sartre.* New York: W. W. Norton, 2007.

Catalano, Joseph S. *A Commentary on Sartre's "Being and Nothingness."* New York: Harper Torchbooks, 1974.

Charlesworth. Max. *The Existentialists and Jean-Paul Sartre.* St. Lucia, AU: University of Queensland Press, in association with the Australian Broadcasting Commission, 1975.

Cohen-Solal, Annie. *Sartre: A Life.* Trans. Norman Macafee. New York: Pantheon, 1987.

Cox, Gary. *Sartre: A Guide for the Perplexed.* New York: Continuum International, 2006.

———. *Sartre Dictionary.* New York: Continuum International, 2008.

Detmer, David. *Sartre Explained: From Bad Faith to Authenticity.* Chicago: Open Court, 2008.

Flynn, Thomas R. *Sartre and Marxist Existentialism: The Test Case of Collective Responsibility.* Chicago: University of Chicago Press, 1984.

Hatzimoysis, Anthony. *The Philosophy of Sartre.* Stocksfield, UK: Acumen, 2007.

Hayman, Ronald. *Writing Against: A Biography of Sartre.* London: Weidenfeld and Nicolson, 1986.

Howells, Christina, ed. *The Cambridge Companion to Sartre.* Cambridge: Cambridge University Press, 2005.

Kamber, Richard. *On Sartre.* Belmont, CA: Wadsworth, 1999.

Law, David R. *Sartre's Existentialism and Humanism.* London: SCM-Canterbury Press, 2007.

Levy, Neil. *Sartre.* Oxford: Oneworld, 2002.

Manser, Anthony R. *Sartre: A Philosophic Study.* London: Athlone Press, 1966.

Martin, Thomas. *Oppression and the Human Condition: An Introduction to Sartrean Existentialism.* Lanham, MD: Rowman and Littlefield, 2002.

McCulloch, Gregory. *Using Sartre: An Analytical Introduction to Early Sartrean Themes.* New York: Routledge, 1994.

Santoni, Ronald E. *Bad Faith, Good Faith, and Authenticity in Sartre's Early Philosophy.* Philadelphia: Temple University Press, 1995.

Schilpp, Paul Arthur, ed. *The Philosophy of Jean-Paul Sartre.* La Salle, IL: Open Court, 1981.

Strathern, Paul. *The Essential Sartre.* New York: Virgin Books, 2002.

Warnock, Mary, ed. *Sartre: A Collection of Critical Essays.* Garden City, NY: Anchor Books/Doubleday, 1971.

Webber, Jonathan. *The Existentialism of Jean-Paul Sartre.* New York: Routledge, 2008.

BOOKS BY AND ABOUT DE BEAUVOIR

De Beauvoir, Simone. *The Ethics of Ambiguity.* Trans. Bernard Frechtman. Secaucus, NJ: Citadel Press, 2000.

———. *The Second Sex.* Trans. and ed. H. M. Parshley. London: Jonathan Cape, 1953. Reprinted New York: Vintage Books/Random House, 1989.

————. *Simone de Beauvoir: Philosophical Writings*. Ed. Margaret A. Simons, with Marybeth Timmermann and Mary Beth Mader. Urbana: University of Illinois Press, 2004.

*   *   *

Arp, Kristana. *The Bonds of Freedom: Simone de Beauvoir's Existentialist Ethics*. Chicago: Open Court, 2001.

Bergoffer, Debra B. *The Philosophy of Simone de Beauvoir: Gendered Philosophies, Erotic Generosities*. Albany: State University of New York Press, 1997.

Card, Claudia, ed. *The Cambridge Companion to Simone de Beauvoir*. Cambridge: Cambridge University Press, 2003.

Kruks, Sonia. *Situation and Human Existence: Freedom, Subjectivity and Society*. London: Unwin Hyman, 1990.

Moi, Toril. *Simone de Beauvoir: The Making of an Intellectual Woman*. Oxford: Blackwell, 1994.

Pilardi, Jo-Ann. *Simone de Beauvoir Writing the Self: Philosophy Becomes Autobiography*. Westport, CT: Greenwood Press, 1999.

Sandford, Stella. *How to Read Beauvoir*. New York: W. W. Norton, 2007.

————, ed. *Feminist Interpretations of Simone de Beauvoir*. University Park: Pennsylvania State University Press, 2008.

Scholz, Sally. *On De Beauvoir*. Belmont, CA: Wadsworth, 2000.

Simons, Margaret A., ed. *The Philosophy of Simone de Beauvoir: Critical Essays*. Bloomington: Indiana University Press, 2006.

Tidd, Ursula. *Simone de Beauvoir*. New York: Routledge, 2003.

Vintges, Karen. *Philosophy as Passion: The Thinking of Simone de Beauvoir*. Trans. Anne Lavelle. Bloomington: Indiana University Press, 1996.

INDEX

Abraham (Old Testament), 71–73, 189
absence, 127–28, 136, 172, 176, 199–200, 213, 217, 220, 223, 246–47, 270–72. *See also* presence; Sartre, *négatités*
absurd/absurdity, 40, 58, 61, 63, 76–77, 240, 259, 271, 286–87, 291, 293. *See also* Camus; Theater of the Absurd
actuality. *See* potentiality/actuality
Adamov, Arthur, 286
Adler, Alfred, 101
Adorno, Theodor W., 268
Aesop, 208
affects. *See* feelings/affects/emotions; moods
African Americans, 248, 272
agape, 73. *See also* love
Albee, Edward, 286
Ali, Muhammad (Cassius Clay), 52
alienation, 37, 41, 165, 283–85

ambiguity, 40, 48, 234–36, 257. *See also* absurd/absurdity; de Beauvoir, ethics
anarchism, 291
angst/anguish/anxiety, 54–55, 157–58, 173, 193–94, 196, 204–207, 220, 259, 276, 286, 289–90
Anselm. *See* St. Anselm
antirationalism, 36. *See also* absurd/absurdity; faith; irrational; rationality/reason
Anti-Semite and Jew (Sartre), 220
Apel, Karl-Otto, 268
appearance and reality, 109–10. *See also* reality
Aquinas. *See* St. Thomas Aquinas
argument, 52–53, 60, 143, 238, 262–63
Aristotle, 26, 31–32, 109, 143, 150–51, 177, 179, 181, 207, 238
Arnold, Matthew, 31
Arp, Kristana, 239, 243, 245

artists/art(s), 21, 48, 74, 90, 135, 170, 224, 263. *See also* Nietzsche, art
artificial intelligence, 272
As It Is in Heaven (film), 266
atheism, 14, 92–95, 111, 200–201, 207, 222, 280, 291. *See also* Sartre, God
Attack Upon "Christendom" (Kierkegaard), 65
Augustine. *See* St. Augustine
authenticity/inauthenticity, 27, 153–54, 158–59, 161–65, 167, 175, 219, 260

bad faith, 126, 195, 203, 225, 240, 243, 259, 295–96. *See also* Sartre; self/selfhood, deception
  defined, 208
  examples of, 211–13
Barnes, Hazel, 11
Barrett, William, 19, 28n8, 31
Barthes, Roland, 269–71
Basic Problems of Phenomenology, The (Heidegger), 269
Batchelor, Stephen, 166
Baudelaire, Charles, 221
Baudrillard, Jean, 271
Beat Generation, 271
beatniks, 16, 271
Beauvoir. *See* de Beauvoir, Simone
Beckett, Samuel, 40, 180, 286
becoming, 32, 110, 143, 151, 194, 220, 273, 289
  what one is, 74, 86, 118n9, 142, 239, 242–43, 271
being, 32, 148–60, 164, 167, 169–70, 172–74, 176–81, 194, 201, 235, 269, 275–76, 289. *See also* Heidegger, Being
  in-the-world, 24, 133–34
  towards-death. *See* Heidegger, death/Being-towards-death
Being and Nothingness (Sartre), 11, 28n14, 169, 192–93, 196, 211, 220, 225–26, 229n24, 230n47, 230n53, 239, 251

Being and Time (Heidegger), 153, 158, 168, 179–80, 268
Benjamin, Walter, 268
Bergson, Henri, 38
Berkeley, Bishop George, 109
Beyond Good and Evil (Nietzsche), 121n84
Birth of Tragedy, The (Nietzsche), 104
Bollnow, O. F., 133–34
Bonaparte, Napoléon, 56
Brentano, Franz, 38, 124–26, 293
Brothers Karamazov, The (Dostoevsky), 106, 238
Browning, Robert, 37
Buber, Martin, 14, 140–41, 261
Buddha/Buddhism, 36, 54, 77, 88, 160, 166, 267, 281. *See also* Zen
Butler, Judith, 272
Byron, George Gordon, Lord, 66

Caesar, Julius, 95
Camus, Albert, 11, 14, 131–32, 142, 190, 236, 271, 286–87, 292
Carlshamre, Staffan, 75
Castro, Fidel, 224
Catalano, Joseph, 214, 228
Catholicism/Catholics, 14, 150, 190
certainty, 273
Charlesworth, Max, 264
choice/choosing, 23, 35, 41, 69, 251–53, 257–59, 289–92, 296
  of self. *See* self/selfhood, as process of choice/self-making; Kierkegaard, "becoming what one is"; Kierkegaard, self/selfhood; Nietzsche, "how one becomes what one is"; Nietzsche, self-mastery
"Christendom." *See* Kierkegaard, "Christendom," attack on
Christian Discourses (Kierkegaard), 66
Christianity/Christians, 32, 46, 53, 55, 57, 59–60, 64–66, 73–78, 92–97, 102, 104, 149, 287. *See also* Catholi-

cism/Catholics; Protestant Reformation
civilization, 37–38, 105
Cixous, Hélène, 270
Concluding Unscientific Postscript (Kierkegaard), 50–51, 58–59, 66, 73–75, 78n4, 80n42, 80n54
Confessions (Rousseau), 34
Confessions (St. Augustine), 32
consciousness, 35, 124–33, 135, 138, 157, 164, 172, 178, 192–99, 205, 237, 269, 293–94
    defined 124–26, 196. *See also* intentionality; unconscious, the
contingency, 23, 206, 289. *See also* finitude; mortality
Contributions to Philosophy (Heidegger), 151, 182n8
Crash (film), 266
critical theory. *See* Frankfurt School
Critique of Dialectical Reason (Sartre), 225
Crosby, Donald, 96

Danto, Arthur, 89
Daoism, 181, 281
Dasein. *See* Heidegger, Dasein
death/dying, 11, 31, 36–37, 108, 159–67, 204, 259, 290. *See also* contingency; finitude; mortality
de Beauvoir, Simone, 12, 14–15, 27, 40, 73, 123–24, 128, 130, 142, 227, 257–61, 265–66, 272
    ambiguity, 234–36, 257
    and Camus, 236
    contrasted with Sartre, 235–36, 239–43, 251–53, 253n15
    death, 235, 242
    desire to disclose being, 235–36
    equality of others, 239–44, 247, 249–53
    ethics, 234–43, 246, 251–53
        objectivity of, 236–41
    existence, 234–35

    evaluation of, 251–53
    feminism of, 234, 246–51
    freedom, 234, 237–43, 246–49, 251–53
    future, 241–45, 247, 250
    God, 235–36
    human condition, 234. *See also* ambiguity
    and Kierkegaard, 234–35
    liberation, 242–46
    oppression, 244–49
    as philosopher, 233–34
    social construction of gender, 246, 249
    transcendence and immanence, 247–48
    values, 235–36, 239–40, 242, 251, 257
    violence, 244–45, 252
deconstruction, 99, 101–102, 121n71, 269
    defined, 86
de Gaulle, Charles, 224
Deleuze, Gilles, 270
de Man, Paul, 269
Derrida, Jacques, 267, 269–71
de Sausurre, Ferdinand, 268
Descartes, René, 33, 38, 54, 108, 148, 273
determinism/determinists, 55, 204, 256–59
dialectical thinking. *See* thinkers/ thinking, dialectical thinking
Dilthey, Wilhelm, 268
Dirty Hands (Sartre), 191
Discourse on Thinking (Heidegger), 184–85n76
Don Giovanni (Mozart), 66–67
Dostoevsky, Fyodor, 37, 106, 238
doubt, 55. *See also* skepticism
Douglas, Kate, 166
dread. *See* angst/anguish/anxiety
Dreyfus, Hubert, 272
Dudjom Rinpoche, 160

Dumas, Alexandre, 66
dying. *See* death/dying

earth, 113, 155. *See also* world
Ecce Homo (Nietzsche), 84, 118n9
Economic and Philosophical Manuscripts of 1844 (Marx), 284
egoism/selfishness, 66–67, 112–13
Eighteen Upbuilding Discourses (Kierkegaard), 66
Either/Or (Kierkegaard), 52, 66–68
embodiment, 130–32, 211, 218–20
emotions. *See* feelings/affects/emotions; moods
End of Philosophy and the Task of Thinking, The (Heidegger), 184n75
Enlightenment, 16, 34
environment, 147, 245, 261–62
Epicurus, 159
epistemology. *See* certainty; doubt; knowing/knowledge; skepticism
epoché. See Husserl, *epoché*
equality/inequality, 101, 103–104, 248–50, 272, 291. *See also* de Beauvoir, equality of others
essence/essentialism, 17, 26–27, 31–32, 143, 194–97, 220, 222, 236, 246–47, 270, 272
    defined, 22
ethics, 13, 67–70, 73, 101–12, 190–91, 260–61
    of ambiguity. *See under* de Beauvoir: ambiguity, ethics, values
    objectivity of, 236–41, 252
    sentiment-based, 34
    subjectivism in, 237
    and universality, 27, 103, 226–27, 238–39, 251. *See also* Kant
    virtue-based, 26
Ethics of Ambiguity, The (de Beauvoir), 40, 234, 242, 247, 251–52, 266
exist/existence, 17, 19, 21–23, 51, 53–55, 115, 128, 141–42, 150–52, 164, 166, 172, 198–99, 234–35, 252, 257, 259–60, 265, 286–87, 290
    forgetting to exist, 158. *See also* Kierkegaard, existence/existing, forgetting to exist
existentialism/existentialists, 11–29. *See also* exist/existence; *individual existentialist philosophers*
    as affirmation, 19–22
    appeal/contributions/influence of, 11–12, 50, 263–72
    and atheism, 14, 201
    as attack on philosophy. *See* Heidegger, philosophy, end of; Heidegger, thinking; Kierkegaard, as critic of philosophy; Nietzsche, as culture critic
    criticisms of, 259–63
    defined, 13–16, 25, 187–92
    as diagnostic, 260
    and ethics. *See* ethics
    evaluation of, 256–59, 263–75
    and film, 12, 266
    historical origins of, 30–44
    and literature. *See* fiction
    and Marxism, 15. *See also* Marx/Marxism; Sartre, Marxism of
    and other movements of thought, 267–72
    as outdated, 30–31, 263–64
    and phenomenology, 153
    as "philosophical anthropology," 41
    and philosophical argument. *See* argument
    as philosophy, 15. *See also* argument
    and religion, 14, 18, 20. *See also* atheism; God; theism; *specific religions*
    as revolt, 16–18
    as social criticism, 22. *See also individual existentialist philosophers*
    as way of life, 273
Existentialism Is a Humanism (Sartre), 187–89, 201, 225, 251, 253n15

experience, 19, 60, 127, 129–30, 132,
141, 143–44, 159–60, 166, 196,
198–201, 203, 217, 223, 260,
281–84, 296

facticity, 23, 155–56, 196, 202–203,
205, 234, 240, 242, 245, 258
defined, 23. *See also* fatalism/fatal-
ists/fate; freedom; determinism
faith, 11, 21, 34, 39, 58, 263, 287. *See
also* fideism; Kierkegaard, faith
Fascism, 268
fatalism/fatalists/fate, 55, 115–16, 204
Fear and Trembling (Kierkegaard), 31,
61, 66, 70, 72
feelings/affects/emotions, 19, 34–36,
38, 99, 156–57, 205, 208, 286, 290.
See also moods
Feifl, Herman, 165
feminism, 124, 272. *See also* de Beauvoir, feminism of
Fichte, Johann Gottlieb, 35, 75
fiction, 21, 135, 142, 196, 199, 224–26,
263
fideism, 60. *See also* faith; Kierkegaard,
faith
Fingarette, Herbert, 296
finitude, 21, 23, 175. *See also* contingency; mortality
Flaubert, Gustav, 221
Fletcher, Iain, 208
Foucault, Michel, 101, 268, 270–71
Frankfurt School, 268
Frankl, Viktor, 166, 281–82
freedom, 11, 17, 20, 23, 34–35, 37,
136, 169, 187, 189–93, 198,
202–207, 212–16, 218, 220,
224–27, 233, 237–38, 250–53,
253n15, 256–59, 265, 271, 289. *See
also* de Beauvoir, freedom; de
Beauvoir, possibility; Sartre
as cooperative project, 261. *See also*
de Beauvoir, equality of others;
de Beauvoir, freedom

defined existentially, 20, 237
and determinism. *See* determinism
and responsibility. *See* responsibility
towards-death, 164–65
Freud, Sigmund, 36–38, 105, 209, 227,
295–96
Friedman, Maurice, 266
Fromm, Erich, 284

Gadamer, Hans-Georg, 268
Gelven, Michael, 148
gender, 272. *See also under* de Beauvoir:
feminism, social construction of
gender
Genealogy of Morals, On the (Nietzsche),
121n84
Genet, Jean, 221, 286
Gestalt, 137, 172
Glasser, William, 203–204
God, 11, 24–25, 31–32, 37, 39–40,
54–56, 61–62, 64, 69–70, 72, 75,
91–96, 109, 111, 116, 147, 151,
180, 188–89, 192, 202, 205–207,
213, 222, 235–36, 238, 260, 270,
284, 287. *See also* atheism; religion;
theism; theology; *individual
philosophers*
death of. *See* Nietzsche, God, death
of
Godwin, Mary Wollstonecraft, 34–35
Goethe, Johann Wolfgang von, 34
Greek philosophy, 31–32, 104, 168,
268–69, 291. *See also* Aristotle; Epicurus; Heraclitus; Plato; Socrates
Grene, Marjorie, 158
Guignon, Charles, 180, 264
Gyatso, Geshe Kelsang, 166

Habermas, Jürgen, 268
Hamrick, William S., 138–39
happiness. *See* pleasure/displeasure/
pain
Harper, Ralph, 141–42
Hartshorne, Charles, 54–55

hedonistic fallacy, 68
Hegel, Georg Wilhelm Friedrich, 36–37, 53, 151, 244, 268, 283–85
Heidegger, Martin, 12–14, 37–38, 123–24, 128, 130, 196, 200, 202, 204, 257, 261, 267–70, 272, 292
anxiety/dread, 156–58, 163–64, 173
art, 169–70
authenticity/inauthenticity, 153–54, 158–59, 161–65, 167, 175, 260
Being, 150–51, 171–74, 176, 178–81, 200–201
call of, 176–77, 201
care, 155–58
conscience, guilt, and resoluteness, 166–67
contrasted with Sartre, 200–201, 204, 264
Dasein, 151–61, 163–73, 200, 268
death/Being-towards-death, 37, 159–66
evaluation of, 178–81
everydayness, 153–55
existence, 150–51, 156. See also Dasein
existentiality/understanding, 156
fallenness, 155
idle talk, curiosity, and ambiguity, 154–55, 161
language, 156, 173–75
later writings of, 167–78, 180
metaphysical homesickness, 149–50, 153, 181–82n4
moods, 156–58
and Nazism, 179
and Nietzsche, 149, 155
nothing/nothingness, 171–73, 184n62
philosophy, 147–51, 168, 172–73, 175–78, 181, 184n75
end of, 178, 184n75
nature of, 147–49
poetry, 174–75, 181
religious view of, 14, 147, 149–50, 155, 200–201
technology, 170–71, 178
temporality/time, 158–59
the "they," 154, 161, 163–64, 167, 259
thinking, 163, 175–78, 184–85n76, 201
thrownness, 151, 156, 158
truth, 168–69
world, 152–53
Heraclitus, 151
hermeneutics, 268. See also interpretation
history, 19–20, 30–43, 53, 56–57, 94, 128, 150–51, 168, 177–78, 180, 225, 235, 260, 263–65, 267–68, 270, 272, 283, 287, 291–92
Hitler, Adolf, 83. See also Nazism/Nazis
Hölderlin, Friedrich, 175
honesty, 66, 166
Horkheimer, Max, 268
Human, All Too Human (Nietzsche), 100
human condition/human nature/humanity, 22–27, 151–58, 189, 228, 240–42, 252, 266, 277–79, 280–82, 284–85
humanism, 31–32, 201, 225, 261, 264. See also Existentialism Is a Humanism (Sartre); Letter on Humanism (Heidegger)
Hume, David, 33–34, 36, 38, 109
Husserl, Edmund, 38, 123–24, 126–28, 143, 166, 168, 171, 235
epoché, 126

I Heart Huckabees (film), 266
ideology, 93, 247, 249, 270
immoralism. See Nietzsche, immoralism
individual/individualism/individuality, 18–20, 32, 35, 46–47, 57, 70, 111, 192, 234, 261, 269, 272. See also person/personal identity; self/selfhood
Ingarden, Roman, 136–37

intentionality, 124–25, 128, 132–33, 172, 293–94. *See also* Brentano, Franz; Husserl, Edmund; phenomenology
interpretation, 94, 116–17, 143, 268, 271, 291. *See also* hermeneutics; perspectivism
Introduction to Existentialism, An (Olson), 289
intuition, 21, 34–35, 38, 142, 181, 190
Inwood, Michael, 268
Ionesco, Eugène, 286
Irigaray, Luce, 270
irrational, 19, 37, 84
Islam, 77

Jargon of Authenticity, The (Adorno), 268
Jaspers, Karl, 14–15
Jesus, 65, 73, 75, 95, 97, 260–61, 287
Job (Old Testament), 31
Judaism, 14, 31, 77, 93, 149

Kant, Immanuel, 34–37, 102–103, 129, 140, 151, 188, 240, 251
Kaufmann, Walter, 89, 106, 179–81
Keltner, Stacy, 260
Kierkegaard, Søren, 12, 14, 31–32, 36–37, 41–42, 84, 86, 93, 95, 128, 143, 152, 155–56, 189, 204, 214, 226, 234–35, 257–58, 261–63, 267, 271, 287
    appropriation, 58, 65
    approximation, 57
    argument types, 52–53
    "becoming subjective"/"becoming what one is," 74, 142, 236
    "Christendom," attack on, 45–46, 65
    Christianity, 45–46, 48–49, 53, 55, 57, 59–61, 64–66, 75–78
    as critic of philosophy, 53, 56, 62, 76–77, 270
    death of, 45–46
    despair, 68
    determinism and fatalism, 55
    as dialectical thinker, 48, 55, 59, 74
    direct and indirect communication, 50–51
    either/or choice, 53–54, 69
    ethical, the, 66–74
    ethics, first and second, 73
    evaluation of, 98–99
    existence/existing, 51, 53–55, 57, 271
        forgetting to exist, 53–54, 58, 155, 235
        spheres of existence, 66–74
    faith, 61–63, 70, 72–78
        knight of, 70–71, 151
        leap to, 72, 265
    God, 50, 55–56, 61–62, 64, 69–70, 72–73, 75, 77, 80n42
    God-relationship, 63–64
    honesty, 65–66
    "how should I live?," 56–57, 59
    individual/individuality, 46–48, 51, 55, 76
    inwardness, 58, 71, 74–77
        infinite passion of, 56
    irony, 48
    "Kierkegaardian Dialogue, A" (Fox), 61–63, 75
    and Nietzsche, 93, 95
    objective and subjective truth, 51, 56–63
        objective uncertainty, 58
        subjective truth defined, 58
    paradox, 48, 52, 58, 61, 75, 77–78
    person/personal identity, 46–47
    as philosopher, 51–53, 59–60
    pseudonyms of, 46–50, 65, 269
    reflection, 63
        double reflection, 51, 74
    religious, the, 66–74
    as social critic, 46, 63–66
    self/selfhood, 46, 55, 67–69, 72. *See also* individual/individuality; person/personal identity

loss of, 46. *See also* existence/
    existing, forgetting to exist
stages of existence, 66–74
subjectivity, 58, 71, 74–77
thinking existentially, 52
teleological suspension of the eth-
    ical, 72
"town criers of inwardness," 62,
    80n54
knowing/knowledge, 17–19, 21, 34,
    58, 61–63, 91, 116, 135, 148, 150,
    235, 271, 287, 291
Kockelmans, Joseph, 123, 180
Kohn, Alfie, 15, 265–66
Korsgaard, Christine, 272
Kristeva, Julia, 270
Kruks, Sonia, 272

Lacan, Jacques, 268, 270
language, 11, 90–92, 127, 154–56, 161–
    62, 168, 172–75, 246, 265, 271
Lawrence, D. H., 48
Leibniz, Gottfried von, 184n62
Letter on Humanism (Heidegger),
    181–82n4, 201
Levinas, Emmanuel, 138
Lévi-Strauss, Claude, 269–70
life, 64, 67, 69, 72, 74, 76–77, 88, 97,
    105, 108, 115, 140, 142, 153, 166,
    206, 221, 235, 265, 280–82,
    286–87
Liszt, Franz, 66
literature. *See* fiction
Locke, John, 109
love, 36, 57–58, 73, 141, 218–20. *See
    also* agape
divine, 77
Luther, Martin, 65
Lyotard, Jean-François, 271

Macquarrie, John, 39
Mallarmé, Stéphane, 221
Marcel, Gabriel, 14–15, 139–40, 272
Marcuse, Herbert, 268

Marx, Karl/Marxism, 15, 37, 231n80,
    244, 250, 268, 283–85
Matrix Trilogy, The (films), 266
McLuhan, Marshall, 60
McVeigh, Timothy, 162
meaning/meaninglessness, 25, 41, 91,
    115, 153, 164, 166, 174, 193, 197,
    207, 221, 235–36, 241, 252–53,
    257, 260, 265, 269–70, 272, 281,
    287, 289–91
meditation(s), 41, 167
Meditations on First Philosophy
    (Descartes), 33
meditative thinking. *See*
    thinkers/thinking, meditative
    thinking; Heidegger, thinking
Merleau-Ponty, Maurice, 38, 124,
    128–35, 270, 272
metaphysicians/metaphysics, 13, 36,
    53, 60, 62, 95, 149–50, 201. *See also*
    Kierkegaard, as critic of philos-
    ophy; ontology; philosophers/
    philosophy
mind-body problem, 131, 178, 195
modernity, 260
Molière (Jean-Baptiste Poquelin), 66
Montaigne, Michel de, 38
moods, 11, 36, 156–58. *See also* feel-
    ings/affects/emotions
mortality, 165. *See also* contingency;
    death/dying; finitude
Mozart, Wolfgang Amadeus, 66–67
music, 67, 124
mutuality. *See* relationship(s)
mystery, 21–22, 33, 51, 139, 169, 175,
    249, 261, 281
mysticism, 140, 181
Myth of Sisyphus, The (Camus), 40, 131

Nagel, Thomas, 272, 287
nature, 35, 170–71, 234, 261–62, 269,
    275, 284. *See also* earth; environ-
    ment
Nausea (Sartre), 196

Nazism/Nazis, 179, 281
necrophilia, 162. *See also* death/dying
Newton, John, 221
Nicomachean Ethics (Aristotle), 26
Nietzsche, Friedrich, 12, 14, 32, 36,
    128, 130, 132, 135, 174, 176, 181,
    188, 245, 257, 261–62, 267,
    269–71, 292
  "*amor fati,*" 115
  Antichrist, 83
  Apollonian and Dionysian energies,
    104–105
  appearance and reality, 109–10
  art, 90–92
  character as thinker, 83–84
  Christianity, 102, 106, 108–10, 112
  as convalescent, 84–86
  as culture critic, 86, 88–89, 102–104,
    107–108
  decadence, 86, 102
  eternal recurrence, 114–16
  evaluation of, 116–17
  freedom, 85, 99–100, 111
  and Freud, 105, 107
  gay science, 87
  genealogy of morals, 105–108, 116
  God, death of, 92–95, 111
  good and bad/good and evil, 33,
    98–99, 105–106, 111, 113
  "how one becomes what one is," 86,
    118n9, 142, 236
  how to read, 84–90
  immoralism, 102–104
  interpretation, 90–92, 94, 116–17
  and Kierkegaard, 93, 95
  language, 90–92, 271
  master and slave values/mastery,
    100, 106–108, 113
  nihilism, 95–97, 110
  overman, 112–16
  perspectivism, 90–92, 116–17,
    121n84, 271
  as physiologist, 88
  philosophy for the future, 112–16
  as psychologist, 86
  "remain faithful to the earth,"
    108–10, 113, 130, 149
  ressentiment, 84, 114
    defined, 107
  revaluation of values, 85, 101–12
  self-mastery, 100–101, 107, 111–13
  and Shakespeare, 37, 105
  as thinker against the grain, 88–89
  truth, 87–92, 272
  will to power, 97–101, 107–108
  as writer of aphorisms, 89–90
  Zarathustra, 101, 107–108, 110–12,
    114, 261
nihilism, 95–97, 149, 291–92
No Exit (Sartre), 223
Notebooks for an Ethics (Sartre), 225–27
nothing/nothingness, 23–24, 40, 94,
    157, 171–73, 184n62, 188, 193–
    200, 216, 237, 242, 277–79
Novalis (Friedrich von Hardenberg),
    149

objectification, 216, 220. *See also* de
    Beauvoir, oppression; Sartre,
    Look, the; self/selfhood, and
    Other
objectivity, 17, 21, 34, 59–60, 70–71,
    75, 92, 121n84, 234–38, 271
    defined, 17. *See also* subjec-
    tivism/subjectivity
Olafson, Frederick A., 19
Olson, Robert, 289
ontology, 132, 150–51, 153, 179, 196,
    218, 243, 246–47. *See also* meta-
    physicians/metaphysics
oppression/oppressor, 244–45, 265
Oration (Pico della Mirandola), 41
Other, the/otherness, 154, 161,
    214–20, 240, 242–43, 247
overman, 112–16

pain/suffering. *See* pleasure/
    displeasure/pain

paradox, 38, 63, 163, 177, 234–35, 260, 287
defined, 75
Pascal, Blaise, 33, 36, 38–41, 75, 287
"Pascal's wager," 39
peace, 107, 245
Pensées (Pascal), 33, 38–39
perception, 125, 134, 137, 143–44, 192, 234. *See also* experience
person/personal identity, 46–48, 220
defined existentially, 24. *See also* individual/individualism/individuality; self/selfhood
perspectivism, 135. *See also* interpretation; Nietzsche, perspectivism
phenomena, 132–33
phenomenology, 36, 38, 153, 164, 168, 172–73, 196, 200, 215, 252–53, 262–63, 268–71, 293
and appearances, 132
character of consciousness, 124–28
consciousness and world, 128–32
defined, 123–24
embodiment, 130–32
examples of, 133–42
as illumination, 133–42
phenomena, 132–33
and truth, 129, 142–44, 262–63
types of, 124
philosophers/philosophy, 11–15, 25–27, 31, 33, 35–36, 38, 40–41, 45, 49, 53–56, 60, 65, 75, 77–78, 87–88, 90, 95, 104, 108–10, 126, 128, 130, 132, 147–51, 168, 172–73, 175–78, 181, 184n75, 224, 233, 237, 257–59, 261–62, 264–65, 267, 286–87, 290–91
applied philosophy, 124
end of philosophy, 178, 184n75
Philosophical Fragments (Kierkegaard), 59
Pico della Mirandola, Giovanni, 41
Pinter, Harold, 286
Plato, 32, 108, 110

pleasure/displeasure/pain, 67, 98–99, 103
poetry/poets, 36, 153, 174–77, 181
politics, 75, 112, 224–25, 243–46, 249–53, 265, 270, 291
possibility, 20, 55, 67, 86, 156, 158, 163–64, 178, 189, 197, 206–207, 217, 234, 249, 252–53, 268. *See also* potentiality/actuality
"vertigo of," 194.
postmodernism, 60, 260, 270–71
post-structuralism, 270
potentiality/actuality, 27, 32, 67, 193, 197, 205
power, 55, 83, 86, 97–101, 138, 171, 180, 193, 215, 234, 243–45, 248–49, 258, 270, 284. *See also* Nietzsche, will to power; will/willing, will to power
presence, 21–22, 127–28, 136, 143, 172, 200, 215. *See also* absence
Present Age, The (Kierkegaard), 63
Preuss, Peter, 41
Prime of Life, The (de Beauvoir), 251
Principles of Nature and of Grace, Based on Reason (Leibniz), 184n62
problematic, the, defined, 148
Protestant Reformation, 65
psychiatry/psychoanalysis/psychology/psychotherapy, 37–38, 49, 52, 86, 99–100, 124–25, 165–66, 222, 258–59, 267, 281–82, 295–96. *See also names of individual practitioners*
Psychology from an Empirical Standpoint (Brentano), 125
Pyrrhus and Cineas (de Beauvoir), 242, 251

Quakers, 11
queer theory, 272
Quinton, Anthony, 27

racism, 220
rationality/reason, 16, 19, 33–35, 38,

41, 56, 58, 96–97, 262–63, 269–70, 286–87

reality, 36, 91, 108–10, 115, 138, 143, 247, 249, 270. *See also* appearance and reality

relationship(s), 19, 83, 107–108, 113, 138–41, 156, 214–20, 224, 226, 241–42, 246, 248–50, 252, 262–63, 284–85

religion, 18, 21, 34, 50, 64, 94, 114, 124, 181, 270, 284, 291. *See also discussions by individual philosophers; specific religions and religious movements*

Renaissance, 39, 150

Repetition (Kierkegaard), 66

repression, 107. *See also* Nietzsche, *ressentiment*

responsibility, 17, 20, 24, 165–67, 188, 195, 203–204, 212–14, 224–25, 252, 258–59, 296

ressentiment. See Nietzsche, *ressentiment*

Ricoeur, Paul, 268

Ring and the Book, The (Browning), 37

Roads to Freedom, The (Sartre), 226

Romanticism/Romantics, 34–35, 38, 149, 287

Rorty, Richard, 271–72

Rousseau, Jean-Jacques, 34, 212

Rubin, Edgar/"Rubin's vase," 137

Sartre, Jean-Paul, 11–12, 14–15, 27, 30–38, 123–24, 126, 128, 130, 135–36, 142–43, 233–35, 239–41, 243, 245, 251–52, 253n15, 257–58, 270–72, 295–96
  anguish, 189, 193–94, 204–207
  atheism of, 15, 200–201, 207
  bad faith, 207–14, 295–96
    defined 227–28. *See also* good faith (in this entry)
  being, and becoming, 194
    in-itself and for-itself, 196
    and nothingness, 196–98

choice/choosing, 189–92, 197–98, 205
  original choice, 220–22
consciousness, theory of, 192–98, 205, 210, 220
contrasted with de Beauvoir, 241–43, 251–52, 253n15
contrasted with Heidegger, 200–201, 204, 264
desire to be, 220–22, 235
determinism and fatalism, 204
ethics, 189–92, 195, 197, 225–27
evaluation of, 227–28
and "existentialism," 187–92
existential psychoanalysis, 220–22
explanation of behavior, 222–24
freedom, 188, 198, 202–204, 205–208, 211–22, 225, 227, 252
God, 188, 192, 202, 205–207, 213, 222
good faith, 214, 227–28. *See also* bad faith (in this entry)
hate, masochism, and sadism, 219–20
and Kierkegaard, 214
Look, the, 136, 216–18, 262
love and desire, 218–19
Marxism of, 15, 225, 231n80
negation, 193, 208, 230n47
négatités, 199, 229, 229n24
nothingness, 193, 196–200
obscene, the, 219
political engagement of, 224–25
pride, 230n53
self, 197–98, 206
  and Other, 214–20, 239–41, 247, 253n15
shame, 214–15, 217
sincerity, 209, 213, 227. *See also* bad faith (in this entry)
situatedness/situation, 203, 205
transcendence, 217, 230n62
values, 189–90, 193, 206–207, 251
Schelling, Friedrich von, 35–36
Schiller, Friedrich, 34

Schleiermacher, Friedrich, 268
Scholastics, 125
Schopenhauer, Arthur, 36–37, 97, 101
science, 18, 21, 56–57, 128, 142, 150, 168, 172, 178
Search for a Method (Sartre), 225
Second Sex, The (de Beauvoir), 234, 246, 248, 250
self/selfhood, 11, 19, 41, 46, 68–69, 101, 114, 134–35, 194–95, 197–98. *See also* individual/individualism/ individuality; person/personal identity
  alienation of, 283–85
  awareness of, reflexive, 125, 128, 139, 192–96, 207–18
  deception, 37, 208, 295–96. *See also* bad faith
  defined existentially, 24
  discovery of/self-knowledge, 20, 141, 166–67, 273
  loss of/regaining, 46, 166–67
  making of, 147, 164–65, 250, 253
  mastery of, 98–99, 100–101, 107, 111, 113, 147
  negation of, 208, 258. *See also* bad faith; Sartre, Look, the; *self-alienation* (in this entry)
  and Other, 68, 214–20, 239–44, 247, 249–53
  as process of choice/self-making, 20, 23, 35, 69, 259
  realization of, 24
semiotics, 269
sex/sexuality, 36, 66, 105, 112, 218–19
Shakespeare, William, 32–33, 209
shame, 214–15, 217
Shaw, George Bernard, 66
Sheehan, Thomas, 170
Sickness Unto Death, The (Kierkegaard), 55, 64, 66, 68
situatedness/situation, 20–25, 180, 203, 205–206, 213, 216–18, 223, 227, 235–36, 244, 248, 264, 282, 289

skepticism, 33, 132, 287, 291. *See also* doubt
Social Contract, The (Rousseau), 34
Socrates, 20, 31, 73, 163
Sokolowski, Robert, 143
Spinoza, Baruch, 258
Spivak, Gayatri, 269
Stages on Life's Way (Kierkegaard), 66–67
Stalin, Josef, 224, 268
St. Anselm, 78
St. Augustine, 32, 287
Steiner, George, 173–74
Stoics, 114
"Storm and Stress" movement. *See* Romanticism/Romantics
Strauss, Richard, 66
structuralism, 269
St. Thomas Aquinas, 78
subjectivism/subjectivity, 21, 34, 54, 56–63, 128, 188, 224, 237, 270–71, 284. *See also* Kierkegaard, objective and subjective truth; objectivity
sublimation, 105
Superman. *See* Nietzsche, overman

Taoism. *See* Daoism
Taylor, Charles, 272
technology, 170–71, 178
Tertullian (Quintus Septimius Florens Tertullianus), 41, 287
Theater of the Absurd, 271, 286. *See also* absurd/absurdity
theism, 15, 201. *See also* atheism; God; religion
theology, 12, 55
thinkers/thinking, 22, 40, 69, 80n42, 136, 148–49, 163, 172, 175–78, 184–85n76, 201, 233, 259–61, 269–70, 273, 286, 293–94
  dialectical thinking, 36, 48, 55, 59–60, 73–74, 283–85
  meditative thinking, 176–77
  thought experiments, 126

Thus Spoke Zarathustra (Nietzsche), 97, 100, 112
time, 38, 124, 127–28, 158–59, 197, 264
Toynbee, Polly, 162
transcendence, 86, 193, 195, 197–99, 214, 217, 219, 234, 244, 247–48. *See also* de Beauvoir, transcendence and immanence; freedom; Sartre, transcendence
Transcendence of the Ego (Sartre), 192
Truman Show, The (film), 266
truth, 33, 56–60, 87, 90–92, 108–109, 116–17, 121n84, 129, 142–44, 168, 178, 270, 291
  and illusion, 88, 91
Twilight of the Idols (Nietzsche), 84, 108–109

Übermensch. See Nietzsche, overman
Unamuno, Miguel de, 19
unconscious, the, 37, 100, 193, 195, 295
universe, 53, 87, 91, 97, 114, 286–87, 289, 291
utilitarianism, 103
utopianism, 18, 113, 245, 270

value(s), 25, 94, 96, 102–104, 116–17, 206–207, 237, 251, 265, 286, 291
  revaluation of. *See* Nietzsche, revaluation of values
Van Gogh, Vincent, 170
Venus of Milo, 136–37
Vietnam War, 224, 271
Vindication of the Rights of Women, A (Wollstonecraft Godwin), 34

violence, 220, 244–45, 252
virtue. *See* ethics, virtue-based
Voltaire (François-Marie Arouet), 224
voluntarism, 36. *See also* will/willing

Waiting for Godot (Beckett), 40, 180
Warnock, Mary, 262–63
Watkin, Julia, 76
West, Cornel, 272
What Is Metaphysics? (Heidegger), 171–72, 184n62
Whitmarsh, Anne, 263–64
will/willing, 33, 36, 75, 98–100, 248
  will to life/will to live, 36, 97
  will to meaning, 282
  will to power, 97–98
Will to Power, The (Nietzsche), 101, 114
wisdom, 163, 273, 281
Wittgenstein, Ludwig, 99, 177–78
Works of Love (Kierkegaard), 73
world, 17, 19, 71, 91, 113, 127–32, 135, 149, 152–53, 155–56, 169–71, 174–75, 189, 198–99, 205, 207, 218, 225, 236, 241, 245, 256–57, 262–63, 268, 271, 283. *See also* earth
World War II, 30, 179, 190, 224, 250

Yalom, Irvin, 165, 290

Zarathustra (Zoroaster), 101, 107–108, 110–12, 114, 261
Zen, 52, 71, 76–77, 180. *See also* Buddha/Buddhism
Zimbardo, Philip, 258